A MEDIEVAL OMNIBUS

SOURCES IN MEDIEVAL EUROPEAN HISTORY

Clifford R. Backman
BOSTON UNIVERSITY

NEW YORK   OXFORD
OXFORD UNIVERSITY PRESS

Oxford University Press is a department of the University of Oxford.
It furthers the University's objective of excellence in research, scholarship,
and education by publishing worldwide.

Oxford   New York
Auckland   Cape Town   Dar es Salaam   Hong Kong   Karachi
Kuala Lumpur   Madrid   Melbourne   Mexico City   Nairobi
New Delhi   Shanghai   Taipei   Toronto

With offices in
Argentina   Austria   Brazil   Chile   Czech Republic   France   Greece
Guatemala   Hungary   Italy   Japan   Poland   Portugal   Singapore
South Korea   Switzerland   Thailand   Turkey   Ukraine   Vietnam

For titles covered by Section 112 of the US Higher Education
Opportunity Act, please visit www.oup.com/us/he for the
latest information about pricing and alternate formats.

Published in the United States of America by
Oxford University Press
198 Madison Avenue, New York, NY 10016
http://www.oup.com

Library of Congress Cataloging-in-Publication Data
Backman, Clifford R.
   A medieval omnibus : sources in medieval European history / Clifford R. Backman,
Boston University. -- First edition.
      pages cm
   A sourcebook of medieval primary sources, all translated by the author, to accompany
The Worlds of Medieval Europe textbook published by Oxford University Press.
   ISBN 978-0-19-937231-7 (pbk. : acid-free paper)
 1. Europe--History--476-1492--Sources. 2. Civilization, Medieval--Sources.
3. Feudalism--Europe--Sources. 4. Monarchy--Europe--Sources. 5. Kings and rulers,
Medieval--Sources. 6. Mediterranean Region--Civilization--Sources. 7. Byzantine
Empire--Civilization--1081-1453--Sources. 8. Middle Ages--Sources. I. Backman,
Clifford R. Worlds of medieval Europe. II. Title.
   D131.B329 2014
   940.1--dc23
                                                          2014007045

Printing number: 9 8 7 6 5 4 3

Printed in Canada
on acid-free paper

CONTENTS

INTRODUCTION

Compiling *A Medieval Omnibus: Sources in Medieval European History* has been surprisingly enjoyable work, and I hope a sense of that pleasure comes through for the reader. History, after all, is the story of people—and to anyone who finds people interesting the study of history should hold an unfailing appeal. There really is no reason for a history book to be dull; if this one is, then I haven't done my work properly. I have included as wide a variety of sources as I could manage: prose histories, verse dramas, saints' lives, private letters, popular tales, legal extracts, sermons, memoirs, accounts of battles, mystical visions, poetry, travelogues. At some risk to dullness, I even include a few extracts from scholastic theology and science. A handful of charts, tables, and time-lines offer some relief from any textual tedium, although I have balked at including photographs. My book **A Medieval Omnibus: Sources in Medieval European History**, now in its third edition, is amply illustrated with explanatory captions, which vitiates the need, not to mention the expense, of providing more imagery here.

Reading primary sources is essential to historical understanding. The texts gathered here should not be regarded as entertainment (although many of them are extremely entertaining) or as examples that illustrate whatever is stated in a textbook or lecture. Rather, they are the evidence in the trial of the past. Historians are indeed akin to detectives—investigators trying to determine what happened, and how, and why. That is why students need to view the sources with a critical eye. Do not settle for simply noting what each record says; ask yourself who wrote it, and why. What kind of language does each text employ? To whom is it directed? Is there any indication that the author is biased or misinformed? What issues or ideas is the text not discussing?

An example may help. Here is a government record from the royal court in Messina, in Sicily, to the court in Barcelona, from the year 1308. The Sicilian king, Frederick III, writes to his brother, King James II of Aragon, about the behavior of an ambassador whom James had sent to conduct some important negotiations with the Sicilian court.

> To the most serene and renowned prince, Lord James, by God's grace the illustrious King of Aragon, Valencia, Corsica, and Sardinia, the Count of Barcelona, and the Standard-Bearer, Admiral, and Captain-General of the Holy Roman Church, and my most dear and reverend brother, King Frederick III, by that same grace, sends greetings and hope for your ever continued prosperity, with all brotherly affection.
>
> Just in this last month of June, sixth indiction, Mateu Oliverdar (a merchant from Barcelona, Your subject, and Our friend), sailing from Alexandria to Sicily while under our safe-passage with a cargo of goods destined for conducting business here, arrived at the port of Siracusa in a ship that carried his own goods as well as those of a number of other Catalan merchants. Hearing of this arrival, D. Bernat de Sarrià (Your Lord Admiral and subject,

and Our friend) immediately raced to Siracusa in the two galleys that You recently dispatched when You sent D. Bernat to Our court to serve as Your ambassador and nuncio. When he arrived at Siracusa he found the said merchant ship, but its cargo had already been unloaded and its captain and crew already ashore and hidden in the city, since they feared the admiral. D. Bernat thereupon seized the tradeship, in violation of Our peace and security, and demanded of the bailiff and judges of Siracusa that they should impound the missing cargo and hand it all over to him. The officials took possession of the goods in question but refused to give them to the admiral, offering any number of reasons for their refusal but especially the fact that they had received no order from Our court to do so.

But Mateu, the merchant, not wanting to be the cause of trouble, petitioned to have the goods restored to him, and then he himself handed them over to D. Bernat, who promptly brought the tradeship with him back to Messina, placing it and himself under Our protection, so that We might decree whatever We think should happen according to the agreement initially made between the contending parties and forwarded to Us by the aforesaid bailiff and judges. The said admiral, currently retaining possession of the ship and its goods on Our authority, but may not dispose of them to anyone, to the loss or detriment of the said Mateu and the other merchants. All of this matter We have patiently borne and put up with out of Our sense of honor and reverence for You—but there has indeed been grave harm done to Our entire realm by Your admiral, as indeed We have similarly suffered from a number of other pirates coming from Your kingdom—sufferings so great that We would regard them as unendurable if they came from any other foreigner.

Moreover, since We firmly believe and are confident that these matters will displease You, We forward this case to Your attention, beseeching You, in all fraternal love, that You, taking all matters into consideration, will order justice to be done for the aforesaid Mateu and the other merchants, that their goods and ship will be restored and accounted for. And if it please Your honor, You will kindly bestow Your gracious mercy in consideration of Our name and the urgency of Our prayers.

Given at Messina under Our privy seal on the 7th of July, 6th indiction.[1]

In brief, the royal admiral of Barcelona and official ambassador to Sicily interrupts his own diplomatic mission in order to pounce upon a richly laden merchant vessel, steal its goods, and hold its merchants for ransom—and then calmly returns to the royal court in order to continue his negotiations. King Frederick then asks his brother in Barcelona to see to it that justice is done to the victims of this ambassador-turned-pirate.

An interesting document, to be sure. (Perhaps I should have included it in the main body of *A Medieval Omnibus: Sources in Medieval European History*) It tells us much more than what a surface reading of it indicates, or at least it suggests much more. At the surface level it informs us of a variety of facts:

- Sicily engaged in lucrative trade with Egypt at this time.
- Merchants and government officials in the Mediterranean held various degrees of relationship with local courts ("Your subject" and "Our friend") that entitled them to different types of treatment.
- Bernat's reputation as a pirate was widespread, since the merchants in Siracusa rushed to unload their cargo when they learned, on arrival in Siracusa, that he was at the court in Messina.
- Bernat was also reputed to be a man of violence, since the merchants hid themselves throughout the city.
- No one saw the pirate raid as sufficient reason to halt the diplomatic mission.
- Bernat's raid was not a solitary incident.

But other notions can be inferred from the document, too. The calm bureaucratic tone is striking: Where is a sense of outrage? Today, if a foreign ambassador in Washington, D.C. interrupted his negotiations with the

---

1 The Latin text of this document appears in my *The Decline and Fall of Medieval Sicily: Politics, Religion, and Economy in the Reign of Frederick III, 1296–1337* (Cambridge, U.K.: Cambridge University Press, 1995), pp. 275–276.

president in order to rob a bank in New York and then returned to pick up where diplomatic talks had left off, no U.S. government official would complain by sending a form letter. Bernat had evidently gained renown as a pirate long before his diplomatic errand, and therefore piracy was no bar to holding high office. He also presumably held some sort of diplomatic immunity, but such immunity would not likely cover violent crime. The inference, then, is that piracy was not regarded as a crime in the sense we might expect; intimidation was acceptable (he attacked with two galleys, which meant he had at as many as 60 armed men with him), but unnecessary violence was not. Moreover, piracy did not necessarily consist of ships confronting one another on the high seas; in fact, it seldom involved such derring-do. Piracy was essentially amphibious: pirates attacked merchant vessels after they were tied up at port and their gods were either in transit or (as here) already under lock and key in the storehouses around the city. Piracy also customarily involved some form of kidnapping, usually holding the merchants themselves hostage in return for payments of ransom.

Medieval piracy was thus, to some extent, regarded as a business risk accepted by those who decided to engage in commerce. Since no government held jurisdiction over the sea itself, then what happened there was not technically illegal. As audacious as it was, Bernat's action was within the accepted standards of piratical behavior, and hence Frederick's letter requesting compensation for the merchant victims had this surprising matter-of-fact tone.

Readers of *A Medieval Omnibus: Sources in Medieval European History* will not find every text as intriguing as this one, but each selection has something in it that will reward a close, critical reading. I invite all readers to let me know which selections were the most, and which the least, worthwhile, and to suggest alternatives.

Clifford Backman

HOW TO READ A PRIMARY SOURCE

This sourcebook is composed of 67 primary sources. A primary source is any text, image, or other source of information that gives us a firsthand account of the past by someone who witnessed or participated in the historical events in question. While such sources can provide significant and fascinating insight into the past, they must also be read carefully to limit modern assumptions about historical modes of thought. Here are a few elements to keep in mind when approaching a primary source.

AUTHORSHIP

Who produced this source of information? A male or a female? A member of the elite or of the lower class? An outsider looking *in* at an event or an insider looking *out*? What profession or lifestyle does the author pursue, which might influence how he or she is recording his or her information?

GENRE

What type of source are you examining? Different genres—categories of material—have different goals and stylistic elements. For example, a personal letter meant exclusively for the eyes of a distant cousin might include unveiled opinions and relatively trivial pieces of information, like the writer's vacation plans. On the other hand, a political speech intended to convince a nation of a leader's point of view might subdue personal opinions beneath artful rhetoric and focus on large issues like national welfare or war. Identifying genre can be useful for deducing how the source may have been received by an audience.

AUDIENCE

Who is reading, listening to, or observing the source? Is it a public or private audience? National or international? Religious or nonreligious? The source may be geared toward the expectations of a particular group; it may be recorded in a language that is specific to a particular group. Identifying audience can help us understand why the author chose a certain tone or why he or she included certain types of information.

HISTORICAL CONTEXT

When and why was this source produced? On what date? For what purposes? What historical moment does the source address? It is paramount that we approach primary sources in context to avoid anachronism (attributing an idea or habit to a past era where it does not belong) and faulty judgment. For example, when considering a medieval history, we must take account of the fact that in the Middle Ages, the widespread understanding was that God created the world and could still interfere in the activity of humankind—such as sending a terrible storm when a community had sinned. Knowing the context (Christian, medieval, views of the world) helps us to avoid importing modern assumptions—like the fact that storms are caused by atmospheric pressure—into historical texts. In this way we can read the source more faithfully, carefully, and generously.

BIAS AND FRAMING

Is there an overt argument being made by the source? Did the author have a particular agenda? Did any political or social motives underlie the reasons for writing the document? Does the document exhibit any qualities that offer clues about the author's intentions?

STYLISTIC ELEMENTS

Stylistic features such as tone, vocabulary, word choice, and the manner in which the material is organized and presented should also be considered when examining a source. They can provide insight into the writer's perspective and offer additional context for considering a source in its entirety.

Clifford R. Backman
Christine Axen
Boston University

1. THE ROMAN WORLD AT ITS HEIGHT

1.1 Virgil, *The Aeneid*

Publius Vergilius Maro (70–19 BCE) is the author of three major Latin poems, the most famous of which was his commissioned epic, *The Aeneid*, which recounts the tribulations of the pious hero Aeneas, who fled the Trojan War and wandered the known world until he settled in Italy, symbolic of the founding of Roman civilization. Because Aeneas is the son of the goddess Venus, Virgil also thus creates a divine genealogy for Aeneas's purported descendent, the Roman Emperor Augustus (63–14 BCE). In this way, the enchanting poetry of the epic plays a political role as well. This opening scene begins *in medias res* and recounts the queen goddess Juno's destruction of the Trojan fleet, showcasing Aeneas's leadership qualities.

I sing of arms and a man—the man driven by fate, the man who
first came from the shoals of Troy to Italy, and to the Lavinian shore,
buffeted cruelly across land and sea by the will of the gods,
by fierce Juno's remorseless rage, and long enduring the wreck of war,
until he founded a city and brought his gods to Latium,
whence rose the Latin people, the lords of Alba Longa,
and the walls of noble Rome. Tell me, Muse, what caused it—
Juno's rage—how the queen of heaven was so galled
that she drove a man so renowned for virtue to endure
such dangers and face so many trials. Can such anger
exist in the minds of gods?
    There was an ancient city, Carthage, held by Tyrian settlers,
opposite Italy and the distant mouth of the Tiber, a city
rich in wealth and the savage arts of war. Juno, they say,
loved this one city above all others, more than even Samos.
Here she kept her weaponry and her chariot, and hoped and strove
that, Fate permitting, the city would gain supremacy
over all the world. But she had long ago heard
that descendants of Trojan blood would one day overthrow
her Tyrian stronghold, and that from them a nation would arise
that was wide-ruling and proud in war, and bring about
Libya's ruin. The Fates had decreed it. Fearing this, and
bearing in mind the long-ago war she had fought at Troy
for her dear Argos' sake—
    —and the seed of that anger and its bitter sorrow
still had not left the depths of her heart: the judgment of Paris,
the injury to her slighted beauty, the people she hated,
the honors given to abducted Ganymede—
Juno, the daughter of Saturn, driven farther into anger by this,

hurled into the sea those Trojans whom the
Greeks and pitiless
Achilles had spared, keeping them far from
Latium.

Driven by Fate from one sea to another, they
wandered for years:
So hard a task it was, to found the Roman
people.

1.2   Tacitus, *The Histories*

Gaius Cornelius Tacitus (56–after 117 CE) is perhaps the most renowned Latin historian. As an active statesman, in addition to holding the posts of consul and later governor of Asia, Tacitus had access to the inner workings of imperial Rome under Nero and his successors, which provides the cogent factual and analytical basis of this text. In his other major work, *The Annals*, Tacitus provides one of the earliest references (15.44) to the historical Jesus. The introduction to *Histories* describes Tacitus's view of the state of affairs in his day; his selection on Jewish practices, though he misunderstands them, nonetheless provides some insight into how the Romans viewed this ancient monotheistic religion and culture. Passages here are taken from Book 1, ch. 1–6, and Book 5, ch. 2–9.

[1] I begin these *Histories* with the year [69 CE] when Servius Galba held the consulship for the second time and Titus Vinius was his partner. Many authors have written of the preceding 820 years, reckoning from the founding of our city, and in describing all the doings of the Roman people they wrote with equal parts of eloquence and liberality. After the battle at Actium, when the only way to preserve peace was for all power to be held by a single man, those great writers passed away. The truthfulness of history took a blow, too, first through men's acquired ignorance of public matters (since they no longer played a role in them), and second through the passion to flatter their new masters even though they hated them. Between the people's servile nature, on the one hand, and their hatred, on the other, all regard for posterity disappeared. We instinctively recoil from any writer's use of an adulating tone, but we pay rapt attention when he makes snide and spiteful remarks, because a fawning tone implies a dishonorable servility but bitchiness comes across (though falsely) as bold honesty. . . .

[2] I am beginning the history of an era filled with disasters, frightful wars, and bitter civil strife. Even the period's peaceful times had their horrors. Four emperors died by the sword; there were three civil wars and even more foreign ones, and some of the conflicts had both qualities at once. Successes in the east were matched with losses in the west. There was trouble in Illyricum. Gaul's loyalty was never certain. Britain was crushed, but then abandoned. The Suevi and Sarmatiae joined forces to repel us. The Dacians scored a renowned victory over us, then suffered a renowned defeat. And the Parthians were spurred to action by the deceits committed by that fraud, Nero. Italy herself was struck by disasters, some entirely unexpected and others the result of a long build-up. The cities of rich Campania were swallowed whole and buried. Rome itself was beset with riots that consumed some of its most venerable temples; citizens set fire even to the Capitol itself. People profaned our sacred rites; our greatest nobles gave themselves to corruption; the sea was clogged with refugees, its rocks bloodied by violence. Even worse horrors took place in the capital city. Nobility and wealth became causes for political accusations, as did either accepting or declining public office. If one maintained a life of virtue, one was done for. The rewards gained by rumor-mongers were more disgusting than their crimes, for while some snatched up consulships and priestly offices as booty, others grabbed procuratorships and positions of a more personal

nature. But they all stole and pillaged in every direction, paying no heed to the hatred and terror they aroused in people. Slaves were bribed to betray their masters, and freedmen to inform on their patrons. Even those without any enemies were brought down—by their own friends.

[3] Bad as it was, the age wasn't so utterly bereft of good qualities that it did not exhibit a few examples of virtuous action. Mothers followed their sons into exile, as wives did for their husbands. Some kinsmen were brave, and some sons-in-law were loyal. Some slaves remained true to their masters even when subjected to torture. Some men of virtue were driven to the ultimate sacrifice [i.e., suicide] and faced it with courage, and their last moments resembled the most fabled deaths of antiquity. Despite the reckless chaos of men's actions, there were divine prodigies to be seen in the skies and on the earth: cautioning rumbles of thunder, for instance, and other signs of things to come, both auspicious and gloomy, doubtful and certain. In sum, at no other time did so many terrible disasters strike the Roman people, nor was there clearer proof that the gods care nothing for our happiness—only for our punishment.

[4] Before beginning, though, it is fitting that I review the conditions that existed in the capital, the mood of the soldiery, the atmosphere in the provinces, the various strengths and weaknesses to be found throughout the empire, for until we are acquainted with such matters, we cannot full comprehend the vicissitudes of the individual events we shall encounter—for events are not only matters of chance but are the result of the interplay of causes and effects. Now, news of the death of Nero had been welcomed with bursts of joy initially, but it eventually stirred any number of emotions among the senators, soldiers, and populace of Rome. In the provinces, too, it roused all the legions and their generals, for the simple reason that it had now been made evident throughout the empire that emperors could be appointed elsewhere than in Rome itself. The senators were the first to exercise fully this new-found freedom, for the new emperor [Galba] had just begun to rule and was in fact out of the capital city. The leaders of the equestrians shared the enthusiasm of the senators, and among the more respectable people in the city—that is, those connected with the most prominent families, were filled with hope. So too the clients and freedmen of convicted and banished political figures. Among the lower orders (those who frequent the arena and the theater), the most vile of the slaves, and those who, on account of being penniless, had depended entirely on handouts from Nero, though, every fresh rumor only made them more dejected.

[5] The soldiers of the capital, steadfast in their loyalty to their rulers, had not wanted to desert Nero but had been tricked and manipulated into doing so. They were now eager for change, especially after they learned that the bonuses awarded them in Galba's name [in return for their support for his elevation] were not forthcoming. They were learning that peace does not offer the same opportunities as war, for great deeds and great rewards, and that the good-favor of an emperor raised to power by the legions had to be nailed down early. . . .

[6] . . . Galba's rise to power had been slow and stained with blood. He had put to death both Cingonius Varro, the consul-elect, and Petronius Turpilianus, a former consul—Varro having been an accomplice of Nymphidius, and Turpilianus having been one of Nero's top generals. Both men disappeared without any sort of trial or hearing, even though they may have been innocent. Galba's entry into the city, coming as it did after the slaughter of so many thousands of unarmed soldiers, was ill-omened; even those who had carried out the executions were concerned. Rome was now crammed full of foreign troops—for Galba had brought in his Spanish legion even while the army levied by Nero from among the imperial fleet still remained there. Detachments from Germany, Britain, and Illyria (all selected by Nero) were there too. . . . The stage was set for a revolution. . . .

* * * * *

(5.2–9)

[2] Since I am about to describe the last days of a great and renowned city, it is fitting that I first describe its origins. According to some authorities, the Jews began as exiles from the island of Crete who settled on the northern coast of Africa about the time when Jupiter

overthrew Saturn from his throne. The evidence for this resides in their name, since the Idaei were the people who lived by the famous mountain on Crete called Mount Ida, and these Idaei became gradually known as the Judaei by the lengthening of their name in the vernacular. Others maintain the Jews originated in Egypt in the time of Isis, when excess population flowed into neighboring lands under the guidance of the figures Hierosolymus and Judas. Many others claim the Jews began as a race from Ethiopia who were driven out by the loathing of their neighbors to find a new homeland during the time of King Cepheus. A few insist they are Assyrians, a rabble who failed to find land to settle in Mesopotamia and so seized a part of Egypt, but not before establishing a number of cities in what is called Judaea, along the border with Syria. Lastly, some writers hold that the Jews sprang from quite a distinguished root, being none other than the Solymi people celebrated by Homer, who named their most famous city after themselves: Hierosolyma.

[3] Almost all writers, however, agree that at some point in the past a terrible disfiguring disease struck Egypt, for which King Bocchoris turned to the oracle of Hammon to discover the cure. Hammon instructed the king to purify his realm by driving out of the land this detestable race of Jews. Thee Jews were diligently rounded up and sent into the desert, where they remained, miserable, idle, and forsaken, until one of them, Moyses by name, convinced them to expect no rescue from God or man. They should rely only on themselves, and take for their leader whoever might guide them out of their present misery. . . .

[4] Wanting to secure his own position of authority, Moyses gave the Jews a unique form of worship, one that runs counter to everything practiced by all other nations. What is sacred to us is worthless to them, and they allow themselves what is forbidden to us. In their temple they have consecrated an image of the animal who guided them during their long, parched wandering. They slay rams, in derision of Hammon, and sacrifice oxen, to mock the Egyptian worship of Apis. They refuse to eat pork, which they associate in memory with leprosy. (Swine are liable to the disease.) They commemorate the long hunger of their wanderings by performing regular fasts, eating

only an unleavened bread in honor of what they had grabbed, in their haste, when entering exile. . . .

[5] Among themselves the Jews are unfailingly honest and compassionate, but they regard all other nations as their hated enemies. They sit apart from other peoples at meals and will not sleep under the roof of a non-Jew. As a race they are almost uniquely prone to lust, yet they will not couple with foreign women. . . . They practice circumcision as a way to distinguish themselves from others; anyone who joins their religion must submit to the custom. They despise all the gods of other nations. . . . The Jews have only a mental image of their God as a single essence, and regard representations of God in human form, made out of perishable materials, as profanations. They believe only the essence of things to be supreme and eternal . . . and do not allow any images to be put up in their cities—not even to flatter their own kings or to pay respect to our emperors. . . .

[6] Their country is bounded by Arabia to the east, Egypt to the south, Phoenicia and the Mediterranean to the west. To the north it commands a sweeping view of Syria. As a people the Jews are healthy and do not tire easily. Rain is uncommon in Judaea but the soil there is fertile. The crops produced by the land are similar to those we produce in Italy. They have balsam trees, though, and groves where tall and graceful palm trees grow. Balsam trees are shrubs, really, whose branches yield a sap that is used by physicians (but only if the branch is pierced by a fragment of stone or a pottery-shard—if one uses a metal blade, the veins wither). . . . The river Jordan does not empty into the sea but flows through two lakes before disappearing into a third. . . .

[7] Not far from this lake there lies a plain that [the Jews] claim was once very fertile and the site of splendid cities, before it was supposedly struck by lightning and consumed by flames. They insist that traces of this disaster can still be seen in the soil itself, which indeed has a scorched appearance and is now sterile. Any plant that appears there, whether wild or the result of planting . . . quickly grows black and rotten, before crumbling into ash. . . .

[8] Judaea consists largely of scattered villages but it does have some cities. Jerusalem is the capital where once stood a temple of immense grandeur. . . . Only a

Jew was allowed to approach its gates, and only their priests were permitted to cross the threshold. When Asia was under the control of the Assyrians, the Medes, and the Persians, they all regarded the Jews as the most contemptible of their subject peoples. When the Macedonians held sway, King Antiochus tried to annihilate the Jewish faith and introduce Greek ways, but his aims were thwarted by his war with the Parthians, which stopped him from his wish to improve the life of this most vile of nations. . . .

[9] Pompey was the first Roman to subdue the Jews, and availing himself of the right of conquest he entered their temple. That is how it became known that it was empty, with no image of their God inside and their shrine possessing no secret knowledge. The walls of Jerusalem were subsequently destroyed, but the temple was left standing. . . . Under the emperor Tiberius everything remained quiet. When Caligula, however, ordered his own statue to be set up in the temple, the Jews opted for war. . . .

1.3 Josephus, *The Jewish War*

Titus Flavius Josephus (37 ca.–100 CE) was a Roman citizen and Jewish historian. His contemporary work (written in Greek) chronicles the Jewish War (66–70 CE)—a bitter revolt against the Roman occupation of Judea, which resulted in the destruction of the Second Temple in 70 CE. This selection details the Roman invasion of Jerusalem and its gruesome aftermath. In writing about the Jewish religion in the first century, Josephus also provides a window into burgeoning Christianity—including references to the historical Jesus and John the Baptist.

CH. 1

The suffering in Jerusalem grew worse every day, and the leaders of the rebellion, who were themselves already in agony, were made even more miserable by the effects of the famine on the general populace. The number of corpses that lay in piles everywhere was indeed a horrible sight, and produced such a noxious stench that it hindered the movement of those who attempted to march forth from the city to fight the Romans. Even so, once the soldiers were suited up and in formation they marched without fear even though they sometimes had to step on the bodies. They did not consider this an offense to the dead or any sort of ill-omen for themselves, for they already bore the guilty stain of killing ten thousand of their own people, and as they moved against the Romans they acted as though they reproached God Himself—for being too slow in punishing them. They continued fighting, but without any hope of victory. . . .

When the Romans finished building their ramparts, the battlements struck fear in the Romans and the Jews alike. The Jews saw that their city would certainly fall if they could not destroy the ramparts by fire, and the Romans feared that they would not be able to replace them, if the Jews managed to burn them down, since the surrounding area was then so deforested and their men so exhausted by labor. . . . What discouraged the Romans the most was the fact that the Jews' courage was stronger than the sufferings they had had to endure. . . .

CH. 3–4

The rebels in the temple struggled every day to drive the Roman soldiers from their battlements. One day—it was the twenty-seventh day of Tamuz—they devised a plan. They stuffed the entire western portico with dry materials, bitumen, and pitch, all the way to the beams that supported the roof, and then made a show of sloughing off in a state of exhaustion. This inspired the most rash of the Romans to get excited and attempt to pursue them. They set the ladders against the portico and climbed atop it. That was when the more prudent Romans understood what was happening and stopped their climb. But by this time the roof was full of soldiers—and the Jews immediately set the whole trap on fire. Flames flew everywhere in an instant. The Romans who had halted their climb were anguished by the fate of their fellows, who cried out in distress. Seeing themselves surrounded by flames, they threw themselves headlong from the roof, some into the city streets and some into the temple courtyard itself, right in the midst of their enemies. . . . Among the Romans was a young man named Longus, who deserves to be remembered—so let him serve as a monument to all those who were slain. The Jews admired this Longus very much on account of his courage, and very much wanted him dead. They promised him no harm, if he would surrender himself to them. His brother Cornelius, however, told him not to hand himself over, since to do so would tarnish his honor and that of the whole Roman army. And so Longus lifted his sword and killed himself. . . .

The number of Jews who died of famine in the city was prodigious, their sufferings unspeakable. If so little as a morsel of any kind of food was found, violence broke out and even best friends would take arms against each other in order to get it. . . . People ran about in a daze, stumbling and staggering like mad dogs, reeling against doors like drunkards. . . . Their hunger was so great that they put anything at all into their mouths, even things that the vilest animals would not touch: belts and sandals, the leather that they stripped from their shields, husks of straw. . . . But why should I go on listing the shameful level that famine drove people to? Especially when I have a story to tell unlike any story in any book of history. . . .

There was a woman named Mary, the daughter of Eleazar, who came from the village of Bethezob (which means "house of hyssop" in Hebrew) beyond the Jordan river. Of good family and wealth, she had fled to Jerusalem like everyone else and was there when the Roman siege began. Everything she possessed that she had brought with her had been snatched away, including whatever food she had managed to save, by the rapacious guardsmen who burst into her house every day in search of something to eat. This drove her half-crazed and prompted her to hurl abuse and threats at the rebels, who, though they grew very angry at her, refrained from ending her misery by killing her. . . . When the famine grew so bad that it pierced her very bowels, she was driven to a point of madness . . . and snatching up her infant son, she said to him, "Poor child! How can I save you from this war, this famine, these rebels? As for the Romans, if we survive the war they will make us slaves. The famine will kill us, though, before our enslavement begins. And these rebels are a worse scourge than the other two. So come, dear child. Be my food, be a curse upon the rebels, and a warning to the whole world. Your death completes the sufferings of the Jews." Having said these words, she killed her son and roasted him. After she had eaten half of his body, she took the other half and put it away, and at this very moment the rebels returned to her home. Despite the horrible scent they warned her that they would cut her throat on the spot if she did not hand over whatever she had been cooking. Mary then replied that she had a nice portion for each of them and took the covering off what was left of her son. The men were filled with horror and revulsion as they look at the sight. "Come and eat!" she said. "This is my son. I did this myself. Eat, here's food for you; I've already had some. No? Don't pretend that you're more delicate than a woman, or that you have more compassion for him than I do. But if you're going to be so fussy, and reject my sacrificial offering, leave the second half for me too." Hearing this, the men withdrew with a shudder. Nothing had ever shaken them so, yet they found it difficult to leave the boy's remains with the mother. Soon the whole city had learned of this dreadful occurrence and everyone shuddered to picture the scene to themselves. Fearing that they too could be driven to such an extreme, many prayed for death and regarded those who had already perished as fortunate not to have survived to hear of such wretchedness. . . .

When two of the legions had finished building their ramparts, on the eighth day of the month of Ab, Titus ordered his battering rams to be brought forward and set against the western wall of the inner temple. Prior to this, a variety of smaller siege engines had blasted the wall non-stop for six days without making a crack in it. . . . But by this time some soldiers had already set fire to the gates, the silver-plating on which failed to stop the flames from reaching the wood underneath. The fire spread quickly then, and in no time reached the cloisters. When the Jews saw the flames engulfing more and more of the temple their spirits broke and they collapsed to the ground so horror-struck that hardly any of them ran to quench the fire or to flee; instead they watched in stunned silence. . . .

Titus sought his commanders' opinions about what should be done about the temple. Some of them advocated following the rules of warfare and demolishing it, since the Jews would never cease their rebellions against Rome so long as the temple stood. Others recommended that Titus save the building for the Jews on condition that they abandon it, remove all their weaponry from it, and surrender—but if the Jews refused, they urged, then Titus should let the flames consume it, since in that case the building could be regarded as more of a military base than a sacred dwelling. In such as case, they urged, the impiety of burning a sacred site would belong not with the Romans but with the rebels whose actions had led to this result. . . . [In the end] Titus ordered a company of volunteers to make their way through the ruins and put out the fire. . . . But when Titus retired for the night several Jews who had been laying in wait leapt out at the Romans once more, attacking those who were attempting to quench the fire in the inner temple. The Romans drove off their attackers and proceeded all the way to the innermost sanctum of the temple, whereupon one of the soldiers, unbidden and unconcerned for the consequences of his rash act, snatched a burning timber and set fire to a gilt-edged window, through which ran a passageway that extended to all the rooms on the north side of the temple. The flames quickly spread even further, and the Jews let out a great cry . . . for it was then certain that their entire holy house would perish. . . .

CH. 8–10

Then one of the temple priests—Jesus, the son of Thebuthus—came forward, having received Caesar's grant of safe-passage, bringing various treasures that had been deposited in the temple. He handed over to Caesar a treasure of candlesticks, tables, cisterns and vials, all made of solid gold and very heavy. He surrendered a number of veils and garments too, each studded with precious stones, and a great number of other precious vessels that they had used in their worship. Phineas, the temple's treasurer, also brought forth a wealth of purple and scarlet cloaks and priestly vestments, such as were worn in the Holy of Holies, along with vast quantities of cinnamon, cassia, and other sweet spices which they regularly used to mix together and offer as incense to God. . . .

Caesar, seeing so great a multitude of Jews in the city, but aware that his own men were exhausted from killing, ordered that no more Jews should be killed except those who had taken arms against Rome; all the rest were to be taken alive. . . . The number of captives was ninety-seven thousand, and the number of the dead was one million and one hundred thousand—the majority of whom were Jews who did not live in Jerusalem itself but had come up to the city for the feast of unleavened bread. . . . The number of those who perished exceeded those ever destroyed before by man or God, anywhere in the world. To consider only the publicly-known accounts, the Romans killed some, carried over others as captives, and even searched underground for more. Finding many of these latter ones, the Romans broke open the ground and killed everyone they found. They also found some two thousand Jews who had already killed themselves underground, and some who had died of famine. The stench of these corpses was so great that most of the Romans had to withdraw. Some others, though, were greedy, climbed over and picked through the heaps of dead bodies. The Jews had hidden much treasure in these caverns, enough to make many Romans think any way of acquiring it was unlawful. . . .

Thus was Jerusalem taken, in the second year of the reign of Vespasian, on the eighth day of the month of Elul. . . . From the time of King David, the first Jew to rule from there, to that of Titus' destruction of the temple were one thousand, one hundred, and seventy-nine years. But from the building of the city to its end were two thousand, one hundred, and seventy-seven years. Neither its antiquity, nor its riches, neither the spread of its people over all the earth, nor the extraordinary veneration given to it as a holy site, could save it from destruction. Thus ended the siege of Jerusalem.

1.4 Epictetus, *The Enchiridion*

The Greek philosopher Epictetus (55–135 CE) expounded on how Stoic philosophy must be more than an intellectual pursuit—it must direct one's way of life. One must stop struggling against inevitable Fate and accept events with discipline and emotional aloofness. In the early second century CE, his dictates were recorded by his disciple Arrian in *The Enchiridion* (*The Handbook*). These selections illustrate Epictetus's commitment to the daily application of Stoic values, such as self-control and acceptance of death, in order to achieve worth and find peace.

Some things we can control, others we cannot. We can control things like our opinions, our interests, our goals, our worries—in a word, our own actions. What we cannot control consists of things like our bodies, our properties, our reputation, our social position—in a word, whatever is not our own doing.... Strive to be able to say to any unfortunate occurrence, "You are just an image [of suffering], not the thing [Suffering] itself," and then think about it with the principles we have taught—and this one most of all: whether the [unfortunate occurrence] pertains to one of the things we can control or to one of the things we cannot control. If the latter, then you say that the whole matter means nothing to you....

Worry only about those things that you can control.... If you worry about sickness, death, or poverty you will always be miserable. Stop worrying about what you cannot control, and worry about what you can control. Try to suppress your desires, for if you desire what is not in your control, you will live in constant disappointment....

People do not fear specific things but the ideas and notions they associate with those thing. For example, death itself is not frightening, or else it would have appeared so to Socrates. The real terror of death is the frightful notions we have about it. So whenever we are scared, worried, or upset about something, let us not attribute it to the thing that scares, worries, or upsets us—but rather to our ideas about it. It is an ignorant person who blames his unhappiness on something outside of himself; a half-educated person will blame himself; but someone fully knowledgeable will blame neither any thing or himself....

Do not ask for things to happen as you want them to; instead, desire that things happen as they in fact do—that's the way to live....

You are a fool if you wish your wife, children, and friends to live forever, because that is wanting to control what you cannot control, or wanting to possess a power that belongs to another [i.e., God]. Similarly, you are a fool if you want your servant to be not so dishonest, for that is desiring his vice to be not vicious but good. But you can control your longing to have your desires fulfilled. Focus on what you are in fact able to do...

You should live your life as though you are a guest at a dinner party. Has someone passed a serving platter to you? Then reach out and take a modest portion. If the platter passes you by, don't reach out to stop it. Has the platter not yet come to you? Don't reach for it, but wait for it to come your way. This is how you should act in regard to your children, your wife, public honors, and wealth, and if you do, then you will have earned a place at the feast of the gods....

Remember always that you are an actor in a drama, in the role chosen for you by the Author. Maybe a short role, and maybe a long one. In whatever role He has cast you—a pauper or a cripple, a statesman, or a common person—play it naturally. Your duty is to play the role, not to assign it....

If you wish to be a philosopher, prepare to be laughed at. The crowd will sneer at you and cry out, "Oh, look who's a philosopher all of a sudden?" or "And where does that patronizing look come from, eh?" Be careful not to wear a patronizing look, and keep your mind focused on the matters that God (who made you for philosophy) intends. Remember: if you stay true to your calling, the people who laugh at you now will later admire you. But if you give in to their taunts, you will be doubly a failure. . . .

Keep silence, for the most part, and when you must speak use few words. To engage in a long conversation is certainly allowable, but only when the occasion is appropriate and the conversation has nothing to do with base topics like gladiators, horse races, sports heroes, or feasts. Neither should you talk about specific people, whether to blame, praise, or compare them to others. Whenever you can, steer a conversation away from such topics and toward worthy ones. Among strangers, it is best to keep silent. Do not laugh too easily, too frequently, or excessively. Avoid swearing altogether, if you can; if you can't, do it as little as possible. Avoid vulgar public entertainments. . . . Provide for your body's needs, but do not indulge it in the delights of meat, drink, clothing, housing, or even family. Get rid of everything showy and refined. Before you marry, abstain as much as you can from [sexual] contact with women. If you must give in to lust, do it lawfully. But do not sit in judgment and disapproval of those who give themselves sexual liberties—and do not boast of your own abstinence.

When someone tells you that another person has been gossiping about a mistake you have made, do not make excuses for your behavior but simply reply, "He must not know all my other faults, or else he would not have mentioned only that one." . . .

When engaging anyone in conversation, but especially someone of superior station, ask yourself first how Socrates or Zeno would behave in your situation. Then you cannot fail to behave properly. . . .

Men make mistresses of girls as young as fourteen, and these, perceiving that they are valued only for the pleasure they give to men, begin to give themselves over solely to adornment. Instead, we should strive to help them understand that their real value resides in their decency, modesty, and good behavior. . . .

Whatever moral principles you devise for yourself, obey them as though they were divine commands and that you would be guilty of the worst impiety by violating any of them. Pay no attention to what others say of you, for that is no concern of yours. . . . You are no longer a boy, but a grown man . . . so think yourself worthy of living a mature life. Let whatever is the best thing you can do in any situation be your guiding principle. . . .

Finally, keep these three maxims always in mind:

"Guide me, Oh Jupiter, and you, Oh Destiny,
to whichever place you have chosen for me."
   [Cleanthes]

"I follow gladly. If I were wicked and wretched
and did not wish to follow, I still would have to.
The man who accepts his fate is deemed wise
      among men,
and knows the laws of heaven." [Euripides]

"Crito, if my death pleases the gods, then let it come.
Anytus and Melitus can kill me, but they cannot
      hurt me." [Plato]

1.5   Marcus Aurelius, *Meditations*

Written while Marcus Aurelius (121–180 CE) was on campaign in lands that include modern-day Hungary, these compiled cogitations (written in Greek) reveal the Roman emperor's Stoic beliefs. Intended as a type of personal guide or reflective exercise, the *Meditations* touch upon mortality, morality, social cares, and self-control, among other themes. Consider the Roman emperor's elegant tone as well as his modest views of the transience of life, which contrast with his supreme political status.

Begin every morning by saying to yourself, "Today I will encounter meddling ingratitude, arrogance, deceit, envy, and selfishness, and all of these things will be due to the offenders' ignorance of the difference between Good and Evil. But I myself have long recognized the nature and magnificence of the Good, and the nature and meanness of Evil; the nature, too, of the one who does wrong, for he is my brother (not in the physical sense of blood and seed, but as a fellow-creature endowed with intellect and a share of the divine). Therefore none of those things can harm me, for no one can implicate me with what is base. Neither can I be angry with my brother, nor hate him, for we were created to work together, like a man's two feet or hands, two eyelids, or two rows of teeth, upper and lower. To oppose each other, therefore, is against Nature. Anger and aversion are obstructions.

* * * * *

Bear in mind always that as a Roman and a man you should perform your duties well and with dignity and in a spirit of kindness, liberality, and justice. In so doing you free yourself of the burden of all cares; and you will be successful in this so long as you approach every deed as if it were the last action of your life, setting aside inattentiveness and the desire to avoid the dictates of reason, hypocrisy, self-regard, and complaint about what life has doled out to you. You can see how little a man needs in order to lead a quiet life—which is a divine life. The gods themselves will require nothing more from a man who lives this way.

* * * * *

Even if he were to live for three thousand years or as many as ten thousand, every man has but one life to live and to lose—this one, and no other. Remember this, for all lives, the longest and the shortest, come to the same end. The present moment is the same to everyone, although that which perishes [at any moment] is not the same; that is why that which is lost appears to be only a mere moment. A man, after all, cannot lose either the past or the future, for how can anyone take from him what he does not possess? So remember these two things: first, that all eternal things are similar and come round in a circle, and it makes no difference at all whether one sees the same things for a hundred years or two hundred or for however so great a time; second, the man who lives the longest and the one who lives the briefest life both lose the same thing. The present moment is the only thing that one can lose, for it is all that one possesses—and you can only lose what you possess.

* * * * *

A man's soul does violence to itself when it turns into a canker or tumor upon the universe, to the extent that that is possible. To be irritated at anything that happens is to cut oneself off from Nature, since Nature consists of the natures of all things combined. The soul also does violence to itself when it turns away from any person or advances upon any with the intent to harm—such are the souls of the wrathful. The soul does a third kind of violence to itself when it surrenders itself to pleasure or pain, a fourth kind when it dissembles and does or says something insincerely or falsely. And a fifth kind of violence when it allows itself any act or movement that is without purpose or does anything thoughtlessly and without a care to its correctness. For it is right that even the smallest actions be done for a reason. The whole point of being a rational creature, after all, is to follow the dictates of reason and the law of the most ancient city and state.

The span of a human life is a mere point, its substance is in constant flux, its perception ever dim, the makeup of the body given to decay, its soul is a whirl, its destiny hard to determine, and its fame a matter without any meaning. In a word, everything that makes up a human body is a moving stream, what makes up the soul is a dream and vapor; life is a battle, a journey by a stranger, and what comes afterward is oblivion. What, then, is the one sure guide for a man in life? Philosophy. But Philosophy requires that a man keep his spirit free from violence and harm, above all pains and pleasures; that he does nothing without a purpose nor anything falsely and hypocritically; that he act without feeling that a duty should be left to another man's care; and that he accept everything that happens, everything that is fated—for everything comes from the place from which he himself comes. Finally, he accepts death with a calm mind, since death is nothing more than the dissolving of the particles of which every living being is made. If no harm comes to the elements themselves as they continually rearrange themselves in new being, why should a man fear the change the dissolving represents? For it is part of Nature, and nothing in Nature is evil.

1.6   The Third-Century Imperial-Succession Crisis

The massive and chaotic mess of Rome's civil war is made clear by this simple list of the individuals who held, however briefly, the imperial title in the third century. Almost all were generals. As you can see, only five died of natural causes.

Emperor	Reign	Manner of Death	Emperor	Reign	Manner of Death
Commodus	180–192	Murdered	Severus Alexander	222–235	Murdered
Pertinax	193	Murdered	Sallustius	225–227	Murdered
Didius Julianus	193	Murdered	Taurinus	225–227	Suicide
Pescennius Niger	193–194	Killed in battle	Maximinus Thrax	235–238	Murdered
Clodius Albinus	193–197	Killed in battle	Magnus	235–238	Killed in battle
Septimus Severus	193–211	Natural death (!)	Quartinus	235–238	Killed in battle
Caracalla	211–217	Murdered	Gordian I	238	Suicide
Geta	211	Murdered	Gordian II	238	Killed in battle
Macrinus	217–218	Murdered	Pupienus	238	Murdered
Diadumenianus	218	Murdered	Balbinus	238	Murdered
Elagabalus	218–222	Murdered	Gordian III	238–244	Killed in battle
Seleucus	218–222	Probably murdered	Sabinianus	240	Killed in battle
Uranius	218–222	Probably murdered	Philippus Arabus	244–249	Killed in battle
Gellius Maximus	218–222	Murdered	Pacatianus	248	Murdered
Verus	218–222	Murdered	Iotapianus	248	Murdered

(Continued)

(Continued)

Emperor	Reign	Manner of Death	Emperor	Reign	Manner of Death
Silbannacus	249	Killed in battle	Saturninus	267	Murdered
Sponsianus	249	Killed in battle	Claudius II	268–270	Plague
Philippus Iunior	249	Murdered	Censorinus	268–270	Murdered
Decius	249–251	Killed in battle	Laelianus	269	Murdered
Priscus	250	Murdered	Marius	269	Murdered
Licinianus	250	Murdered	Victorinus	269–270	Murdered
Henerrius	251	Killed in battle	Quintilius	270	Suicide
Hostilian	251	Plague	Aurelian	270–275	Murdered
Trebonianus Gallus	251–253	Murdered	Domitianus	271–272	Murdered
Volusianus	251–253	Murdered	Urbanus	271–272	Murdered
Aemilianus	253	Murdered	Septimius	271–272	Murdered
Valerian	253–260	Murdered	Tetricus I	271–274	Natural death (!)
Mareades	259	Murdered	Tetricus II	273–274	Natural death (!)
Gallienus	253–268	Murdered	Firmus	273	Killed in battle
Ingenuus	260	Suicide	Felicissimus	271	Killed in battle
Regalianus	260	Murdered	Faustinus	274	Probably murdered
Macrianus I	260–261	Natural death (!)			
Macrianus II	260–261	Murdered	Tacitus	275–276	Murdered
Quietus	260–261	Murdered	Florianus	276	Murdered
Postumus	260–269	Murdered	Probus	276–282	Murdered
Piso	261	Murdered	Bonosus	280	Suicide
Valens	261	Murdered	Proculus	280–281	Murdered
Ballista	261	Murdered	Saturninus	281	Murdered
Mussius Aemilianus	261	Murdered	Carus	282–283	Struck by lightning
Memor	261	Murdered	Numerian	283–284	Murdered
Aureolus	262	Murdered	Carinus	283–285	Murdered
Celsus	267	Murdered	Diocletian	288–305	Natural death (!)

2. THE RISE OF CHRISTIANITY

2.1 The Books of the New Testament in the Order of Their Composition

Dating the texts of the New Testament is extraordinarily difficult, but most scholars would agree on the basic outline provided here. As you can see, the earliest texts are the authentic letters of St. Paul, which were written at least 25 years after Jesus's death. (Paul, of course, was not an eyewitness to any of the actions or episodes of Jesus's life.) Hardly any of the later texts, written after the Jewish Revolt of the 60s, can be attributed with certainty to any author.

chronological order
↓

Year (CE)	Text	Author
50	1 Thessalonians	Paul
54–55	Galatians	Paul
55	Philemon	Paul
56	Philippians	Paul
56	1 Corinthians	Paul
57	2 Corinthians	Paul
57–58	Romans	Paul
(66–73 Jewish revolt and Rome's subsequent destruction of the Temple)		
68–73	Gospel of Mark	Mark[1]
70–90	1 Peter	?
80–85	Gospel of Luke	Luke[2]
80–85	Acts of the Apostles	Luke
80–90	Colossians [attr. Paul]	?
80–100	James [attr. James, brother of Jesus]	?
85–90	Gospel of Matthew	Matthew[3]
85–90	Hebrews [attr. Paul]	?
90–95	Gospel of John [attr. The Beloved Disciple]	?[4]
90–100	Ephesians [attr. Paul]	?
90–100	2 Thessalonians [attr. Paul]	?

Year (CE)	Text	Author
90–100	1 Timothy, 2 Timothy, Titus [attr. Paul]	?
90–100	Jude [attr. Jude, brother of Jesus]	?
92–96	Revelation	John[5]
95–100	1 John, 2 John	?
120–130	3 John	?
130–140	2 Peter	?

[1] Attributed by tradition. This is the "John Mark" mentioned in the Acts of the Apostles, who helped Paul on his first missionary tour. Textual evidence suggests that the author was a Greek speaker, not an eyewitness to Jesus's ministry, and is addressing an audience that has already experienced persecution.

[2] Luke was a physician and fellow-missionary with St. Paul. Textual evidence displays a Greek speaker who knew the Jewish Bible only in its Greek (Septuagint) version, and was also not an eyewitness to Jesus's career. He drew on Mark's Gospel. The author was not from Palestine and was almost certainly not born Jewish—hence possibly a Greek who converted to Judaism before subsequently converting to Christianity.

[3] Matthew, a tax collector, was one of the original 12 apostles. By textual evidence, the author was a Jewish Christian who spoke Greek, Hebrew, and Aramaic. He drew on Mark's Gospel, and was not an eyewitness to Jesus's life.

[4] Tradition attributes this gospel to John, the son of Zebedee and one of the original 12 apostles. Textual evidence suggests that the author was actually a redactor—a disciple of John who later gathered his teacher's sayings. It is possible that the redactor's work was itself later edited, ca. 100–110, by another disciple contemporaneous with the author of 3 John.

[5] Not the same John as the author of the gospel of that name.

2.2 New Testament Selections

Below are two passages from the New Testament. The first, from the Gospel of Matthew, sets the stage for, and relates, the "Sermon on the Mount" delivered by Jesus at the start of his three-year ministry, after he had taken over the preaching mission of John the Baptist. The second passage, from the First Letter to the Corinthians, presents St. Paul's teaching about the meaning of Jesus's resurrection from the dead.

MATTHEW, CH. 3–7 (ENTIRE)

[3] In those days John the Baptist appeared, preaching in the desert of Judea [and] saying, "Repent, for the kingdom of heaven is at hand!" It was of him that the prophet Isaiah had spoken when he said:

A voice of one crying out in the desert,
"Prepare the way of the Lord,
make straight his paths."

John wore clothing made of camel's hair and had a leather belt around his waist. His food was locusts and wild honey. At that time Jerusalem, all Judea, and the whole region around the Jordan were going out to him and were being baptized by him in the Jordan River as they acknowledged their sins. When he saw many of the Pharisees and Sadducees coming to his baptism, he said to them, "You brood of vipers! Who warned you to flee from the coming wrath? Produce good fruit as evidence of your repentance. And do not presume to say to yourselves, 'We have Abraham as our father.' For I tell you, God can raise up children to Abraham from these stones. Even now the ax lies at the root of the trees. Therefore every tree that does not bear good fruit will be cut down and thrown into the fire. I am baptizing you with water, for repentance, but the one who is coming after me is mightier than I. I am not worthy to carry his sandals. He will baptize you with the holy Spirit and fire. His winnowing fan is in his hand. He will clear his threshing floor and gather his wheat into his barn, but the chaff he will burn with unquenchable fire."

Then Jesus came from Galilee to John at the Jordan to be baptized by him. John tried to prevent him, saying, "I need to be baptized by you, and yet you are coming to me?" Jesus said to him in reply, "Allow it now, for thus it is fitting for us to fulfill all righteousness." Then he allowed him. After Jesus was baptized, he came up from the water and behold, the heavens were opened [for him], and he saw the Spirit of God descending like a dove [and] coming upon him. And a voice came from the heavens, saying, "This is my beloved Son, with whom I am well pleased."

[4] Then Jesus was led by the Spirit into the desert to be tempted by the devil. He fasted for forty days and forty nights, and afterwards he was hungry. The tempter approached and said to him, "If you are the Son of God, command that these stones become loaves of bread."

He said in reply, "It is written:

'One does not live by bread alone,
but by every word that comes forth from the
mouth of God.'"

Then the devil took him to the holy city, and made him stand on the parapet of the temple, and said to him, "If you are the Son of God, throw yourself down. For it is written:

'He will command his angels concerning you'
and 'with their hands they will support you,
lest you dash your foot against a stone.'"

Jesus answered him, "Again it is written, 'You shall not put the Lord, your God, to the test.'" Then the devil took him up to a very high mountain, and showed him all the kingdoms of the world in their magnificence, and he said to him, "All these I shall give to you, if you will prostrate yourself and worship me." At this, Jesus said to him, "Get away, Satan! It is written:

'The Lord, your God, shall you worship
and him alone shall you serve.'"

Then the devil left him and, behold, angels came and ministered to him.

When he heard that John had been arrested, he withdrew to Galilee. He left Nazareth and went to live in Capernaum by the sea, in the region of Zebulun and Naphtali, that what had been said through Isaiah the prophet might be fulfilled:

"Land of Zebulun and land of Naphtali,
the way to the sea, beyond the Jordan,
Galilee of the Gentiles,
the people who sit in darkness
have seen a great light,
on those dwelling in a land overshadowed by
    death
light has arisen."

From that time on, Jesus began to preach and say, "Repent, for the kingdom of heaven is at hand."

As he was walking by the Sea of Galilee, he saw two brothers, Simon who is called Peter, and his brother Andrew, casting a net into the sea; they were fishermen. He said to them, "Come after me, and I will make you fishers of men." At once they left their nets and followed him. He walked along from there and saw two other brothers, James, the son of Zebedee, and his brother John. They were in a boat, with their father Zebedee, mending their nets. He called them, and immediately they left their boat and their father and followed him.

He went around all of Galilee, teaching in their synagogues, proclaiming the gospel of the kingdom, and curing every disease and illness among the people. His fame spread to all of Syria, and they brought to him all who were sick with various diseases and racked with pain, those who were possessed, lunatics, and paralytics, and he cured them. And great crowds from Galilee, the Decapolis, Jerusalem, and Judea, and from beyond the Jordan followed him.

[5] When he saw the crowds, he went up the mountain, and after he had sat down, his disciples came to him. He began to teach them, saying:

"Blessed are the poor in spirit,
for theirs is the kingdom of heaven.

Blessed are they who mourn,
for they will be comforted.

Blessed are the meek,
for they will inherit the land.

Blessed are they who hunger and thirst for
    righteousness,
for they will be satisfied.

Blessed are the merciful,
for they will be shown mercy.

Blessed are the clean of heart,
for they will see God.

Blessed are the peacemakers,
for they will be called children of God.

Blessed are they who are persecuted for the sake
    of righteousness,
for theirs is the kingdom of heaven.

Blessed are you when they insult you and
    persecute you and utter every kind of evil
    against you [falsely] because of me.

Rejoice and be glad, for your reward will be great in heaven. Thus they persecuted the prophets who were before you. You are the salt of the earth. But if salt loses its taste, with what can it be seasoned? It is no longer good for anything but to be thrown out and trampled underfoot. You are the light of the world. A city set on a mountain cannot be hidden. Nor do they light a lamp and then put it under a bushel basket; it is set on a lampstand, where it gives light to all in the house.

Just so, your light must shine before others, that they may see your good deeds and glorify your heavenly Father.

Do not think that I have come to abolish the law or the prophets. I have come not to abolish but to fulfill.

Amen, I say to you, until heaven and earth pass away, not the smallest letter or the smallest part of a letter will pass from the law, until all things have taken place. Therefore, whoever breaks one of the least of these commandments and teaches others to do so will be called least in the kingdom of heaven. But whoever obeys and teaches these commandments will be called greatest in the kingdom of heaven.

I tell you, unless your righteousness surpasses that of the scribes and Pharisees, you will not enter into the kingdom of heaven.

You have heard that it was said to your ancestors, 'You shall not kill; and whoever kills will be liable to judgment.' But I say to you, whoever is angry with his brother will be liable to judgment, and whoever says to his brother, 'Raqa,' will be answerable to the Sanhedrin, and whoever says, 'You fool,' will be liable to fiery Gehenna. Therefore, if you bring your gift to the altar, and there recall that your brother has anything against you, leave your gift there at the altar, go first and be reconciled with your brother, and then come and offer your gift. Settle with your opponent quickly while on the way to court with him. Otherwise your opponent will hand you over to the judge, and the judge will hand you over to the guard, and you will be thrown into prison. Amen, I say to you, you will not be released until you have paid the last penny.

You have heard that it was said, 'You shall not commit adultery.' But I say to you, everyone who looks at a woman with lust has already committed adultery with her in his heart. If your right eye causes you to sin, tear it out and throw it away. It is better for you to lose one of your members than to have your whole body thrown into Gehenna. And if your right hand causes you to sin, cut it off and throw it away. It is better for you to lose one of your members than to have your whole body go into Gehenna.

It was also said, 'Whoever divorces his wife must give her a bill of divorce.' But I say to you, whoever divorces his wife (unless the marriage is unlawful) causes her to commit adultery, and whoever marries a divorced woman commits adultery.

Again you have heard that it was said to your ancestors, 'Do not take a false oath, but make good to the Lord all that you vow.' But I say to you, do not swear at all; not by heaven, for it is God's throne; nor by the earth, for it is his footstool; nor by Jerusalem, for it is the city of the great King. Do not swear by your head, for you cannot make a single hair white or black. Let your 'Yes' mean 'Yes,' and your 'No' mean 'No.' Anything more is from the evil one.

You have heard that it was said, 'An eye for an eye and a tooth for a tooth.' But I say to you, offer no resistance to one who is evil. When someone strikes you on (your) right cheek, turn the other one to him as well.

If anyone wants to go to law with you over your tunic, hand him your cloak as well.

Should anyone press you into service for one mile, go with him for two miles.

Give to the one who asks of you, and do not turn your back on one who wants to borrow.

You have heard that it was said, 'You shall love your neighbor and hate your enemy.' But I say to you, love your enemies, and pray for those who persecute you, that you may be children of your heavenly Father, for he makes his sun rise on the bad and the good, and causes rain to fall on the just and the unjust. For if you love those who love you, what recompense will you have? Do not the tax collectors* do the same? And if you greet your brothers only, what is unusual about that? Do not the pagans do the same?

So be perfect, just as your heavenly Father is perfect.

[6] [But] take care not to perform righteous deeds in order that people may see them; otherwise, you will have no recompense from your heavenly Father. When you give alms, do not blow a trumpet before you, as the hypocrites do in the synagogues and in the streets to win the praise of others. Amen, I say to you, they have received their reward. But when you give alms, do not let your left hand know what your right is doing, so that your almsgiving may be secret. And your Father who sees in secret will repay you.

When you pray, do not be like the hypocrites, who love to stand and pray in the synagogues and on street corners so that others may see them. Amen, I say to you, they have received their reward. But when you pray, go to your inner room, close the door, and pray to your Father in secret. And your Father who sees in secret will repay you.

In praying, do not babble like the pagans, who think that they will be heard because of their many words. Do not be like them. Your Father knows what you need before you ask him.

This is how you are to pray:

Our Father in heaven,
hallowed be your name,
your kingdom come,
your will be done,
on earth as in heaven.
Give us today our daily bread;
and forgive us our debts,
as we forgive our debtors;
and do not subject us to the final test,
but deliver us from the evil one.

If you forgive others their transgressions, your heavenly Father will forgive you. But if you do not forgive others, neither will your Father forgive your transgressions.

When you fast, do not look gloomy like the hypocrites. They neglect their appearance, so that they may appear to others to be fasting. Amen, I say to you, they have received their reward. But when you fast, anoint your head and wash your face, so that you may not appear to be fasting, except to your Father who is hidden. And your Father who sees what is hidden will repay you.

Do not store up for yourselves treasures on earth, where moth and decay destroy, and thieves break in and steal. But store up treasures in heaven, where neither moth nor decay destroys, nor thieves break in and steal. For where your treasure is, there also will your heart be.

The lamp of the body is the eye. If your eye is sound, your whole body will be filled with light; but if your eye is bad, your whole body will be in darkness. And if the light in you is darkness, how great will the darkness be.

No one can serve two masters. He will either hate one and love the other, or be devoted to one and despise the other. You cannot serve God and mammon. Therefore I tell you, do not worry about your life, what you will eat [or drink], or about your body, what you will wear. Is not life more than food and the body more than clothing?

Look at the birds in the sky; they do not sow or reap, they gather nothing into barns, yet your heavenly Father feeds them. Are not you more important than they? Can any of you by worrying add a single moment to your life-span? Why are you anxious about clothes? Learn from the way the wild flowers grow. They do not work or spin. But I tell you that not even Solomon in all his splendor was clothed like one of them. If God so clothes the grass of the field, which grows today and is thrown into the oven tomorrow, will he not much more provide for you, O you of little faith?

So do not worry and say, 'What are we to eat?' or 'What are we to drink?' or 'What are we to wear?' All these things the pagans seek. Your heavenly Father knows that you need them all. But seek first the kingdom (of God) and his righteousness, and all these things will be given you besides.

Do not worry about tomorrow; tomorrow will take care of itself. Sufficient for a day is its own evil.

[7] Stop judging, that you may not be judged. For as you judge, so will you be judged, and the measure with which you measure will be measured out to you. Why do you notice the splinter in your brother's eye, but do not perceive the wooden beam in your own eye? How can you say to your brother, 'Let me remove that splinter from your eye,' while the wooden beam is in your eye? You hypocrite, remove the wooden beam from your eye first; then you will see clearly to remove the splinter from your brother's eye.

Do not give what is holy to dogs, or throw your pearls before swine, lest they trample them underfoot, and turn and tear you to pieces.

Ask and it will be given to you; seek and you will find; knock and the door will be opened to you. For everyone who asks, receives; and the one who seeks, finds; and to the one who knocks, the door will be opened. Which one of you would hand his son a stone when he asks for a loaf of bread, or a snake when he asks for a fish? If you then, who are wicked, know how to give good gifts to your children, how much more will your heavenly Father give good things to those who ask him.

Do to others whatever you would have them do to you. This is the law and the prophets.

Enter through the narrow gate; for the gate is wide and the road broad that leads to destruction, and those who enter through it are many. How narrow the gate and constricted the road that leads to life. And those who find it are few.

Beware of false prophets, who come to you in sheep's clothing, but underneath are ravenous wolves. By their fruits you will know them. Do people pick grapes from thornbushes, or figs from thistles?

Just so, every good tree bears good fruit, and a rotten tree bears bad fruit. A good tree cannot bear bad fruit, nor can a rotten tree bear good fruit. Every tree that does not bear good fruit will be cut down and thrown into the fire. So by their fruits you will know them.

Not everyone who says to me, 'Lord, Lord,' will enter the kingdom of heaven, but only the one who does the will of my Father in heaven. Many will say to me on that day, 'Lord, Lord, did we not prophesy in your name? Did we not drive out demons in your name? Did we not do mighty deeds in your name?'

Then I will declare to them solemnly, 'I never knew you. Depart from me, you evildoers.'

Everyone who listens to these words of mine and acts on them will be like a wise man who built his house on rock. The rain fell, the floods came, and the winds blew and buffeted the house. But it did not collapse; it had been set solidly on rock. And everyone who listens to these words of mine but does not act on them will be like a fool who built his house on sand. The rain fell, the floods came, and the winds blew and buffeted the house. And it collapsed and was completely ruined."

When Jesus finished these words, the crowds were astonished at his teaching, for he taught them as one having authority, and not as their scribes.

* * * * *

I CORINTHIANS, CH. 15 (ENTIRE)

Now I am reminding you, brothers of the gospel I preached to you, which you indeed received and in which you also stand. Through it you are also being saved, if you hold fast to the word I preached to you, unless you believed in vain. For I handed on to you as of first importance what I also received: that Christ died for our sins in accordance with the scriptures; that he was buried; that he was raised on the third day in accordance with the scriptures, that he appeared to Cephas, then to the Twelve. After that, he appeared to more than five hundred brothers at once, most of whom are still living, though some have fallen asleep. After that he appeared to James, then to all the apostles. Last of all, as to one born abnormally, he appeared to me. For I am the least of the apostles, not fit to be called an apostle, because I persecuted the church of God. But by the grace of God I am what I am, and his grace to me has not been ineffective. Indeed, I have toiled harder than all of them; not I, however, but the grace of God [that is] with me. Therefore, whether it be I or they, so we preach and so you believed.

But if Christ is preached as raised from the dead, how can some among you say there is no resurrection of the dead? If there is no resurrection of the dead, then neither has Christ been raised. And if Christ has not been raised, then empty [too] is our preaching;

empty, too, your faith. Then we are also false witnesses to God, because we testified against God that he raised Christ, whom he did not raise if in fact the dead are not raised. For if the dead are not raised, neither has Christ been raised, and if Christ has not been raised, your faith is vain; you are still in your sins. Then those who have fallen asleep in Christ have perished. If for this life only we have hoped in Christ, we are the most pitiable people of all.

But now Christ has been raised from the dead, the first fruits of those who have fallen asleep. For since death came through a human being, the resurrection of the dead came also through a human being. For just as in Adam all die, so too in Christ shall all be brought to life, but each one in proper order: Christ, the firstfruits; then, at his coming, those who belong to Christ; then comes the end, when he hands over the kingdom to his God and Father, when he has destroyed every sovereignty and every authority and power. For he must reign until he has put all his enemies under his feet. The last enemy to be destroyed is death, for "he subjected everything under his feet." But when it says that everything has been subjected, it is clear that it excludes the one who subjected everything to him. When everything is subjected to him, then the Son himself will [also] be subjected to the one who subjected everything to him, so that God may be all in all.

Otherwise, what will people accomplish by having themselves baptized for the dead? If the dead are not raised at all, then why are they having themselves baptized for them?

Moreover, why are we endangering ourselves all the time? Every day I face death; I swear it by the pride in you [brothers] that I have in Christ Jesus our Lord. If at Ephesus I fought with beasts, so to speak, what benefit was it to me? If the dead are not raised:

Let us eat and drink,
    For tomorrow we die. [Isaiah 22.13]

Do not be led astray:

Bad company corrupts good morals.

Become sober as you ought and stop sinning. For some have no knowledge of God; I say this to your shame.

But someone may say, "How are the dead raised? With what kind of body will they come back?"

You fool! What you sow is not brought to life unless it dies. And what you sow is not the body that is to be but a bare kernel of wheat, perhaps, or of some other kind, but God gives it a body as he chooses, and to each of the seeds its own body. Not all flesh is the same, but there is one kind for human beings, another kind of flesh for animals, another kind of flesh for birds, and another for fish. There are both heavenly bodies and earthly bodies, but the brightness of the heavenly is one kind and that of the earthly another. The brightness of the sun is one kind, the brightness of the moon another, and the brightness of the stars another. For star differs from star in brightness.

So also is the resurrection of the dead. It is sown corruptible; it is raised incorruptible. It is sown dishonorable; it is raised glorious. It is sown weak; it is raised powerful. It is sown a natural body; it is raised a spiritual body. If there is a natural body, there is also a spiritual one.

So, too, it is written, "The first man, Adam, became a living being," the last Adam a life-giving spirit. But the spiritual was not first; rather the natural and then the spiritual. The first man was from the earth, earthly; the second man, from heaven. As was the earthly one, so also are the earthly; and as is the heavenly one, so also are the heavenly. Just as we have borne the image of the earthly one, we shall also bear the image of the heavenly one.

This I declare, brothers: flesh and blood cannot inherit the kingdom of God, nor does corruption inherit incorruption. Behold, I tell you a mystery. We shall not all fall asleep, but we will all be changed, in an instant, in the blink of an eye, at the last trumpet. For the trumpet will sound, the dead will be raised incorruptible, and that which is mortal must clothe itself with immortality. And when this which is corruptible and this which is mortal clothes itself with immortality, then the word that is written shall come about:

> Death is swallowed up in victory.
> Where, O death, is your victory?
> Where, O death, is your sting? [Hosea 13.14]

The sting of death is sin, and the power of sin is the law. But thanks be to God who gives us the victory through our Lord Jesus Christ.

Therefore, my beloved brothers, be firm, steadfast, always fully devoted to the work of the Lord, knowing that in the Lord your labor is not in vain.

2.3 Pliny the Younger, *Letters to Tacitus and to Trajan*

The nephew of the naturalist Pliny the Elder, Gaius Plinius Caecilius Secundus, called Pliny the Younger (61–112), passed through the *cursus honorum* under the emperors Domitian and Trajan. A friend of Tacitus (author of Document 1.2) and employer of Suetonius (author of *The 12 Caesars*), Pliny the Younger also wove his personal experiences of imperial Rome into his works. In his "Letter to Tacitus," Pliny poignantly describes his uncle's death in the eruption of Mount Vesuvius (79); in his "Letter to Trajan," he recounts his understanding of early Christianity in the Roman Empire.

TO TACITUS

You asked me to send you an account of my uncle's death, so that you may describe it accurately in your writings. I am honored by your request—for if this disaster is recorded by you, I am sure that it will live forever in memory. . . .

On the 24th of August, in early afternoon, my mother asked my uncle to take a look at a cloud of unusual size and shape. . . . He rose from his books and mounted a small hill nearby, from which he could get a better view of the uncommon sight. It was not clear at first which mountain the cloud was surrounding, but we later learned, of course, that it was Mount Vesuvius. The cloud, as it rose up from the mountain, was shaped rather like a pine tree and shot up to a tremendous height. . . . It appeared bright in some places, and dark and mottled in others, because of the dirt and ashes cast up in it. . . . My uncle ordered his small boat to be readied, and climbed on board. . . . He steered his course directly at the danger, the better to see what was happening and to dictate his observations of the whole dreadful scene [to his secretary]. . . . He got so close to the mountain that cinders, pumice-stones, and blackened bits of burning rock were falling into his boat, getting thicker and hotter the closer he drew. . . . Wide tongues of flame burst from the sides of Vesuvius, showing bright and clear. . . .

[After landing and advancing to the villages and towns under the mountain] he witnessed houses rocking from side to side as though shaken from their foundations by repeated blows. In the open fields burning rocks and cinders fell in profusion . . . forcing them to tie pillows to their heads with table napkins as their only defense against the storm of stones. . . . They thought it best to return to the shore and see if they could embark, but the waves were extremely high and roiling. My uncle lay down on a sail-cloth that his servants had spread out for him, and called twice for some water to drink. He drank, but as he did so a wall of sulphurous flames came so close that they had to rise and leave. Helped by two servants, my uncle stood—and instantly fell over, dead. I suppose he suffocated on the noxious fumes. . . .

TO TRAJAN

I always turn to you, my lord, when in doubt—for there is no one I trust better to guide me when I am uncertain and to teach me when I am ignorant of any matter. I have never had anything to do with a trial of Christians, and don't know what charges are made against them, or how they are investigated, and what degree of bother to go through in the effort. I am more than a little uncertain about whether to treat them all the same or to make concessions to the young and the aged among them. Are they to be pardoned if they express contrition? If a man used to be a Christian but has since ceased to be one, is he to be free of

punishment? If one is a Christian but has otherwise committed no offense, should he be charged [with a crime]? Or do we prosecute only those Christians who commit additional offenses?

In dealing with the Christians who have been brought before me, I have done as follows. First I questioned them as to whether or not they were Christians. Those who acknowledged it I then questioned a second and third time, threatening them with punishment. Those who persisted in their ways, I had executed. Whatever the nature of their beliefs, I decided, they deserved punishment simply for being so stubborn and obstinate. There were some among them who were Roman citizens, and I signed orders for them to be transferred to Rome.

Accusations against others then spread, as so often happens, and several things followed. An anonymous affidavit was published that listed the names of many people who were believed to be Christians. Those who denied that they were or had ever been Christians I put to the test; I had them invoke the Roman gods, offer prayer and incense and wine to your image (which I had ordered to be brought together for this specific purpose—along with statues of the gods), and curse Christ. It is said that no true Christian can be forced to do any one of these things—and so those who passed the test I ordered to be released. Others named by the anonymous tipster swore oaths that they were Christians—but then they denied it, saying that they used to be Christians but had long since ceased to be, anywhere from three to twenty-five years ago. These too all worshiped your image, sacrificed to the statues of the gods, and cursed Christ.

They testified, though, that the extent of their former error had been limited to meeting with other Christians on a fixed day, before dawn, and singing responsively a hymn to Christ as their god, and that they swore simply not to commit fraud, theft, or adultery, not to bear false witness, and not to refuse to return anything that had been entrusted to them. Having done this, they said, they usually separated but reassembled later [and somewhere else] in order to share a meal. A simple, regular meal, I should add. But they insisted that they has ceased even this limited participation after, in accordance with your instruction, I had released an edict forbidding political associations. Naturally, I thought it prudent to find out if this was really true by torturing two slave-women whom the Christians call "deaconesses." All that I learned from this, though, was disgusting and gross superstition.

That is when I stopped my investigation and hurried to consult you. The matter strikes me as warranting this appeal because of the number of people involved. There are many lives at stake—of every age and rank, and both sexes. This superstition is spreading like a contagion and is now to be found not only in the cities but also in villages and on farms; nevertheless, it is possible to stop it and cure it. It is abundantly clear that our temples, which for a time had been almost deserted, have once again begun to be frequented; that the established rites, so long neglected, are being resumed; and that sacrificial animals are coming in from everywhere—animals for which not too long ago hardly a single purchaser could be found. This is why I think it easy to imagine multitudes of people returning [to Roman ways] if an opportunity for amnesty is offered.

[TRAJAN RESPONDED TO PLINY WITH A BRIEF LETTER OF HIS OWN.]

You did well, Pliny, in sifting through the cases of the people charged with being Christians. It is not possible to lay down a single rule to serve as a fixed guide. Christians should not be sought out, but if any are accused and brought before you, and if you find them guilty, they should be punished. There is one exception to this rule. Anyone who denies being a Christian and proves it by worshipping our gods should be granted amnesty even if he was under suspicion in the past. Anonymous public accusations should have no place in our justice—for it would establish a dangerous precedent to accept such accusations, and it would be against the spirit of our age.

2.4   Minucius Felix, *Octavius*

Though little is known of Minucius Felix's (d. 250) personal information, his work *Octavius* provides many telling details about early understandings of the Christian faith. *Octavius* is staged as a discussion between a pagan, Caecilius Natalis, and a Christian, Octavius Januarius, in which Minucius Felix plays the peacekeeper. In this way, the author is able to correct misunderstandings and assumptions about Christian faith and practice.

I would like to meet the man who thinks or says that we engage in the blood-sacrifice of babies! Who can possibly believe anyone could injure an infant, so small, so tender, to draw blood from it and drain its life away before it even has a chance to live? The only person capable of doing such a thing is the one capable of thinking such a thing! Romans, I have seen you abandon your children to wild beasts and birds of prey! I have seen you crush them and strangle them! O, what miserable deaths. You have women who drink potent potions to end the lives that have begun in their wombs—murder before birth. And all these things you have learned from your gods. Saturn not only exposed his children—he devoured them. Parents in parts of Africa have been known to kiss and caress their bawling babies, soothing them so that Saturn not be given a sacrifice who was in tears. Both the Tauri of Pontus and the Busiri of Egypt immolate their own house-guests as a sacred rite. The Gauls inhumanely offer human sacrifices to Mercury. Roman priests have been known to bury Greek men and women alive—yes, and Gallic ones too! To this very day you worship Jupiter Latiaris with murder—a suitable sacrifice, actually, for a son of Saturn, gorged as he is with the blood of evil criminals. I believe it was Saturn himself taught Catiline how to swear a blood-oath to a political conspiracy; who taught Bellona to bathe her sacred rites in human gore; and who taught men to treat epilepsy by drinking human blood—a "cure" worse than the disease itself. Good followers of Saturn are those who eat the wild beasts in the arena, wet and dripping with the blood of their victims, and fattened with the flesh and entrails of men. No! To we Christians it is unlawful to see or permit murder. And not only do we shrink from human blood, we won't even use the blood of animals in our food.

Our devilish attackers have spread another lie about us too—namely, that we engage in incestuous orgies; our detractors' goal is to stoke popular loathing against us, staining the glory of our modesty with an outrageous charge, so that people hate us before they even have a chance to learn the truth. That is what your hatchet-man Fronto did. He levied a charge at us but offered no evidence, only some random rhetorical accusations. Other peoples, however, are the founders of this vile horror. Among the Persians son and mother are permitted promiscuous relations. Men marry their own sisters in Egypt as well as in Greece. Your legends and stage-tragedies—which you both read and hear with such pleasure—are filled with tales of incest. You worship incestuous gods who have intercourse with their own mothers, sisters, and daughters. Is it any

wonder that you permit and indulge in incest yourselves? Wretches! You probably even engage in it without knowing it, gratifying your lust, as you do, constantly, and fathering children everywhere. But in your wanderings you expose your children at home to the lusts of others. Is it any wonder, then, that all of you eventually return to your own seed? Thus you continue the stain of incest without knowing it.

We [Christians], however, preserve our modesty—not only in our appearance but in our hearts, living as we do, gladly, within the bonds of faithful marriage. We each approach our one and only wife, if we desire to procreate, or we approach no one at all. At our banquets the only thing we share is our food, and our banquets are modest and sober. We do not indulge in entertainments and long bouts of drinking. We temper our joy with gravity and chaste conversation. Our bodies too are chaste—and more than chaste, since many of us choose lives of sworn celibacy; we delight in our chastity but make no boast of it. So far are we, in fact, from incestuous indulgence that many of us cannot even hear of normal sexual relations between men and women without blushing.

2.5   *The Passion of Saints Perpetua and Felicity*

The Passion of Saints Perpetua and Felicity tells the story of the martyrdom of a Roman noblewoman and her servant, both Christians, who were imprisoned for refusing to venerate the emperor and were subsequently put to death in early 203 in Carthage. Their martyrdom was thus part of the general persecution that took place under Septimius Severus (r. 193–211). It is one of the earliest surviving works of hagiography and is certainly the earliest dedicated to martyred women. Of unique interest is the fact that roughly half of this text was written by Vibia Perpetua herself as she awaited death. The passage below contains all of the text that she herself wrote (ch. 3–10), framed by passages from the text's later editor.

Several young catechumens were then arrested: Revocatus and Felicitas, both slaves, Saturninus, Secundulus, and also Vibia Perpetua, noble-born, well educated, honorably married. She had both her father and mother then still living, as well as two brothers (one of whom was, like her, a catechumen), and an infant son whom she was still nursing. She was twenty-two

years old, and what follows next is told by Perpetua herself, since she left behind a written text, telling the tale of her martyrdom in her own words and in her own hand. Perpetua speaks:

[3] Some time after our arrest my father came to me, and out of his love he tried to persuade me to change my mind.

"Father," I said, "do you see this pot here—this water pot or whatever it is?"

"Yes, I do," he said.

"Well, could you call it by any other name than what it is?"

"No."

"And neither can I," I said. "I am what I am—a Christian."

That word—*Christian*—so angered my father that he started toward me as though he wanted to tear out my eyes, but he left it at that and departed quickly, defeated along with his devilish arguments. I thanked the Lord then for having a few days apart from my father and felt calmer in his absence. During those few days I was baptized, along with the rest, and I was inspired by the Holy Spirit to desire nothing after that saving water, other than the strength to endure. We were all transferred several days later into prison, and I was terrified since I never before have been in such a gloomy place. What a horror! The heat was stifling, since we were packed in so, and our guards were cruel. On top of everything else I was tormented with worry for my baby. But then Tertius and Pomponius, those blessed deacons who came to minister to us, bribed our guards to move us to a better part of the prison, which lifted our spirits. We all then left that dungeon and were able to take care of ourselves. I nursed my baby, who was by then nearly unconscious from hunger. Out of concern for him I spoke with my mother and my brother (whom I encouraged [to be steadfast in faith]) and entrusted my son to them. Seeing their pain was painful to me, and I was in agony for several days; but shortly thereafter I was able to have my baby brought back to me, which made me feel so much better and so lightened my cares and worries that my prison suddenly seemed like a palace and I felt that there was no place I would rather be.

[4] Then my brother said to me, "You've been blessed, sister. Perhaps, if you prayed for it, you could get a vision of your fate, whether you'll be freed or put to death." I promised him by my faith that I would do so, for I knew I could always talk to the Lord who had already given me so many blessings.

"Come again tomorrow, and I'll tell you [what I learn]," I said. Then I prayed, and this is what I saw in a vision.

I saw a tremendous ladder made of bronze that reached all the way to heaven but was so narrow that only one person could climb it at a time. Metal weapons—swords, spears, hooks, daggers, and spikes—were fixed to both sides of it, so that if one was careless and failed to pay attention while climbing he would be mangled, catching his flesh on the points and blades. At the foot of the ladder lay an enormous dragon who attacked anyone who tried to climb and scared off many from attempting it. Saturus was the first to go up, he who would later give himself up freely to death. (Although he was not present when we were arrested, our strong faith was of his building.) When he reached the top of the ladder he looked back and said to me, "I'll wait for you, Perpetua. But be careful! Don't let the dragon bite you."

"In the name of Christ Jesus," I answered, "he will not harm me."

The beast then stuck his head out from under the ladder—but slowly, as though he were afraid of me. I used its head as my first step and began to climb.

Suddenly I saw an enormous meadow, and in the middle of it there was a tall, gray-haired man, dressed like a shepherd and busy milking his sheep. Thousands and thousands of people stood around him, all clad in white. The man turned his face to me and said, "Welcome, my child." Then he called me over to him and gave me a portion of the milk he had drawn, which I took in my hands and swallowed. "Amen!" shouted the crowd.

At the sound of that word I awoke from my vision, but the taste of sweetness still lingered on my tongue. I then told all of this to my brother, and we both understood at once that we were destined for martyrdom, and that there was no longer anything to hope for in this life.

[5] A few days later word came that we were going to be given a hearing. My father returned from the city, worn out with worry, and tried again to persuade me [to change my mind]. "Have pity on my gray-haired head!" he cried. "As your father, don't I deserve your pity? Did I not raise you to adulthood? Did I not favor you over your brothers? Don't abandon me to the reproach of strangers. Think of your brothers, your mother, your aunt. Think of your baby! How will he live, if you are gone? Give up your pride, or you'll destroy us all. None of us will ever be able to speak openly again, if anything happens to you."

He said these things out of fatherly love, kissing my hands and collapsing at my feet. With tears in his eyes he addressed me not as a little girl but as a woman. I felt sorry for him, though, for alone of all my family he could not rejoice in my death. I tried to comfort him. "Whatever happens at the tribunal, it will be God's will," I said. "Know this for certain: our lives are not our own to control. We belong to God."

Nevertheless, he went away broken-hearted.

[6] One day, as we were eating, we were suddenly rushed off for our hearing. We arrived at the forum, and news of our arrival spread quickly through the neighborhood, for a large crowd gathered. We went up to the docket one at a time, and one by one they all confessed their guilt [i.e., the fact that they were Christians and would not participate in emperor-worship] when asked. Then it was my turn. But suddenly there stood my father, with my son in his arms; he pulled me from the step and cried, "Have pity on your baby! Perform the sacrifice!"

Seeing this, the procurator Hilarianus (who held his judicial authority as the successor of the late proconsul Minucius Timinianus) said to me, "Have pity on your old father and young son! Offer a sacrifice to the emperor's well-being."

"No."

Are you a Christian?

"I am," I said.

My father, meanwhile, kept crying out for me to change my mind, so Hilarianus ordered him to be knocked to the ground and beaten with a staff. I felt such pain for him, that it was as though I myself was being beaten. I was sorry for the sorrow that came with his old age.

Hilarianus then passed sentence on all of us, condemning us to the wild beasts. We were joyful as we returned to our cell. Since my baby was then used to being nursed and to staying with me in the prison, I sent our deacon Pomponius to my father's house to ask for the baby. But my father refused to hand him over. By God's will, though, the boy weaned himself from my breast and I suffered no inflammation. Thus I was spared any anxiety for the child and any pain in my breasts.

[7] A few days later we were all praying together when all of a sudden I said the name "Dinocrates" aloud. This was a surprise, for until that moment I had not thought of him at all. It hurt to think of what had happened to him, but I recognized that I was being blessed with an opportunity to pray for him. So I began

to pray for him, groaning to the Lord on his behalf—and that very night I had another vision. I saw Dinocrates emerging from a dark hole, where there were many others. He was hot and thirsty, pale and dirty, and on his face was the wound he had when he died.

Dinocrates, of course, had been my earthly brother, and he had died of a malignant growth on his face when he was only seven. A horrible death, one that made him a source of loathing to everyone. But I now offered my prayers for him. A great abyss lay between us [in my vision], and neither of us could go to the other, but on Dinocrates' side of the abyss stood a fountain filled with water. Its rim was above his head, so he had to stretch mightily in order to reach it. I felt sorry for him, because he wanted to drink but could not because of its height.

Then I awoke, realizing that my brother was suffering. I felt certain, though, that I could help him, and so I prayed for him every day until we were handed over to the garrison (since we were supposed to fight with the wild beasts at the soldiers' games held in honor of the emperor Geta's [r. 211] birthday). Day and night, with constant tears and moans, I kept praying on his behalf.

[8] Another vision came to me, one day while we were locked up. I saw the same place as before, but now Dinocrates was all clean, well dressed, and looking refreshed. Only a scar remained where his wound had once been, and the fountain I had seen before was there—only now its rim was at the level of his waist, and the water flowed without ceasing. Above the fountain appeared a golden bowl, which Dinocrates filled with the water and drank until he was satisfied. Then, as children do, he ran off and played.

Then I awoke and realized that he had been delivered from his agony.

[9] Several days after this, an adjutant named Pudens, who was in charge of the garrison's prison, began to pay us his respects, since he had come to understand that there was some great power in us. He even allowed many [fellow Christians] to visit us, so that we might all comfort each other.

When the day of the scheduled games arrived, my father once again came to me. Weary with sorrow, he began tearing at his beard and throwing the whiskers to the ground. He threw himself on the ground. He cursed his old age and spoke such words as would move all creation. Again I felt sorry for his unhappy old age.

[10] The day before our battle with the beasts, I had another vision. I saw Pomponius the deacon standing at the prison gates and knocking loudly. I went out and opened the gate for him. He was dressed in a white robe, without a belt, and wearing bizarre shoes.

"We're waiting for you, Perpetua. Come," he said.

Then he took my hand and led me through rugged, broken country until at last, breathing heavily, we came to an amphitheater. He placed me in the middle of it, and said, "Don't be afraid. I'm here, and I'll suffer with you." Then he left.

I looked out at an enormous crowd that stared back at me. I was surprised that there were no wild beasts released, for I knew that that is how I was to die. Instead, a vicious looking Egyptian came out, with his attendants, to fight me. A couple of handsome young men also came out to serve as my attendants. They stripped my clothes off me—and all of a sudden I was changed into a man. My attendants rubbed me down with oil (as is the custom in these contests). On the other side of the amphitheater, I could see the Egyptian rolling back and forth in the dust.

Next there emerged another man, extremely tall, so tall that his head stood above the height of the amphitheater. He wore a purple tunic that had no belt but did have two stripes running down his chest, one on the left and another on the right. He wore marvelous sandals made of gold and silver, and carried a rod like the kind used by gladiators' trainers. He also carried a green branch that had golden apples hanging from it.

He asked for silence, and then he said, "If this Egyptian defeats her, he will kill her by the sword; but if she defeats him, she will receive this bough." Then he withdrew.

The Egyptian and I drew close and began to fight with our fists. He tried to trip up my feet but I kicked him in the face with my heels. He lifted me off my feet, and I punched him over and over as best I could from mid-air. During a lull I put my hands together, interlocking the fingers, and grabbed hold of his head [to crush it]; he fell on his face and I stomped on his skull.

The crowd shouted and my attendants broke out in psalms. I walked up to the trainer and took the green bough from him. He kissed me and said, "Peace be with you, my daughter!" I walked away in triumph toward the Victor's Gate.

And then I awoke. I understood right away that my battle was not with wild beasts but with Satan himself—and that victory would be mine.

All of this I have written myself. The games are tomorrow. Whatever happens, let him tell it who will.

The next 10 chapters were supposedly written by Saturnus, the prisoner companion of Perpetua, after their deaths. He describes how Perpetua, after being killed by the beasts, was carried off to heaven by four angels, where they found all the other martyred members of their community. Saturnus also inserts the story of Perpetua's servant-girl Felicity, who was eight months pregnant when they were all arrested. Felicity gave birth in prison; the child was given to a friend to raise. Perpetua, Felicity, and Saturnus then were brought into the arena to face their deaths. A leopard, a bear, a boar, and "a mad heifer" were released on them all. Mauled and bloody, the martyrs were eventually dragged over to the executioner to be finished off.

---

[21] . . . And so the martyrs helped one another over to the place where their throats would be cut, as the crowd wanted. They sealed their martyrdoms by exchanging the kiss of peace, each with the other. Some of them submitted to the sword in silence, never moving a muscle, especially Saturnus, who was the first up the steps to the stage. He waited for Perpetua, but she was made to suffer more. She screamed aloud because the executioner's blade struck her on the breastbone, and she had to guide his trembling hand to her throat. So great a woman was she that the unclean spirit [of the executioner] feared her, and she could not be killed unless she willed it on herself.

O most valiant and blessed martyrs! You were truly called and chosen [to bear witness] to the glory of Our Lord Jesus Christ! Any person who magnifies, honors, and worships Christ's glory should read, for the edification of the Church, these examples of heroism which lose nothing in comparison with other tales of old. May these new proofs of virtue bear witness that the Holy Spirit is still at work among us, together with God Our Almighty Father, and His Son Jesus Christ, Our Lord, to whom be glory and endless power forever and ever. Amen.

2.6   The Edict of Toleration and the Edict of Milan

The Edict of Toleration was issued in 311 by the emperor Galerius (r. 293–311), reportedly as he lay on his deathbed. Galerius was not a Christian, but he thought it wise to end the Great Persecution initiated by Diocletian. The text of the edict is preserved in the historical memoir *On the Deaths of Our Persecutors* by Lactantius (d. 320), in the 34th chapter.

Along with all the other accords we have enacted for the lasting benefit of our society, we have ever endeavored to restore a universal harmony of our ancient Roman laws and public order. In particular, we have aimed to bring even the Christians—who have abandoned the religion of their fathers—back into good disposition. But the misguided Christians, in their foolishness, chose instead to disobey the ancient customs (some of which had probably even been established by their own ancestors), and in their willful self-regard elected instead to craft and observe their own laws, with which they now organize their fellows everywhere into congregations. After the promulgation of our edict commanding them to conform to ancient traditions, many of them were brought to heel by fear and many more by exposure to harm. Nevertheless, most of them persevered in their obstinacy; and now

that we see that they neither pay the reverence due to our gods nor make a show of worshipping their one god, we, with our usual clemency in extending mercy to all, have determined to grant our indulgence to them, so that henceforth the Christians may establish openly their places of worship, provided that they do nothing to disturb public order. We shall direct our magistrates how they are to accommodate the Christians in a separate edict. In return for this indulgence, let the Christians all pray to their god for our good health, for the well-being of the republic, and for their own benefit. May the Republic continue unharmed in every way, and may the Christians live securely in their own homes.

Published at Nicomedia on the first of the kalends of May, in the eighth year of our consulship, and in the second year of the consulship of Maximinus.

The Edict of Milan was promulgated in 311 by the emperor Constantine (who, as caesar or subemperor under Galerius, had affixed his name to the Edict of Toleration as well). Its text, too, survives in the memoir of Lactantius, in the 48th chapter; but another version was preserved in the *Ecclesiastical History* (Bk. 10, ch. 5) of Eusebius of Caesarea (260–340).

LACTANTIUS' VERSION

When we, the emperors Constantine and Licinius, met near Milan in order to confer about matters concerning public welfare and security, we decided that of all the things beneficial to mankind, the worship of God ought to be our first and principal concern, and that it is therefore fitting that Christians should have the same freedom as anyone else to follow whatever religion they desire. Thus may whatever God Who exists in heaven be propitious to us and to all who live under our rule. We therefore announce that all who choose to commit themselves to the Christian religion should be permitted to do so (all previous imperial decrees and instructions regarding them notwithstanding) without any hindrance, and are not to be troubled or molested in any way. And we have deemed it fit to bring this decree directly to all magistrates and officers of the state, so that you may know for certain that we have indeed granted Christians free and unrestricted freedom of religious worship. Understand that we also concede to all other religions the right of free and open observance of their rites—for it accords with the good order of the state and the peacefulness of our times that each man may freely worship as he pleases. In so doing, we do not detract from the honor due to any religion or its followers.

Specifically in regards to the Christians, we previously issued various directives about the places set apart for their worship—but now we are pleased to command that anyone who has purchased such sites from our treasury should restore them to the Christians without any demand for payment from them or any claim of recompense, fraud, or deceit. Anyone who has acquired such properties by gift are likewise directed to restore them to Christian ownership. Let all who restore such properties (whether they acquired them by purchase or gift) apply to their local *vicarii* for compensation, which they will receive by our imperial clemency. Let all affected properties be restored to their Christian communities with all speed and with our administrative assistance. Since the Christians are known to have possessed not only places of [open] assembly but also churches (which belonged to their entire community and not to individuals), we command that these too be restored with hesitation or contention, under the same law and with the same provision that all who freely restore the properties to Christian ownership may apply for compensation from our imperial clemency. We direct you to pursue these matters with the greatest diligence on behalf of the Christians, that our desires regarding them may be carried out promptly, for the fulfillment of our imperial largesse, public order may be restored. In this way may divine favor, which we have already enjoyed in

the most pressing public affairs, continue to grant us success and preserve the happiness of the state.

In order that this decree of our beneficence may be known by all, we direct that its text be proclaimed publicly throughout the state and brought to the common knowledge of all.

EUSEBIUS' VERSION

Since we long ago concluded that religious freedom should be denied to no one and that everyone should be allowed to hold true to whatever beliefs and practices they choose, we decreed that every person [in the state], Christians as well as non-Christians, should be free to observe the religion and mode of worship he desires. But since numerous conditions and exceptions have apparently been attached to that original decree, some groups have gradually demurred from the freedom of observance that the decree had granted to those very people.

When I, Constantine Augustus, and I, Licinius Augustus, came, under favorable auspices, to the city of Milan, we enquired into all the current issues pertaining to the public welfare and advantage, and we concluded that the issues surrounding [religious freedom] are of the first priority for the public good. We have resolved, therefore, to establish clear rules by which all due respect and reverence might be given to the [Christian] deity—that is, to give to Christians and everyone else the liberty to exercise whatever form of religious worship they desire, in order that whatever divine or heavenly powers might exist may look kindly upon us and all who live under our authority.

Therefore we have decided upon the following ordinances, which we have carefully and soundly reasoned:

No person whatsoever is to be denied the right to
    adhere to and practice the Christian form of worship;
and every person is to be granted the freedom to give
    his mind to whatever form of worship he feels is
    best suited to his needs;
in this way we hope that the [Christian] deity will be inclined to grant us all his usual favor and generosity.

It is our desire to promulgate this decree, making our pleasure known to all, in order to effect the complete nullification of all the conditions and exceptions attached to the earlier edict [that is, the Edict of Toleration] dispatched to all loyal state officials regarding the

Christians—for those measures were wholly unjustified and foreign to our imperial clemency. Now each and every Christian who wishes to do so may freely observe and pursue his form of worship without any interference. All of this we have decided to explain and communicate in full to your care and diligence, in order that you may know for certain that we have indeed granted the Christians full and absolute freedom to practice their own form of worship.

Once you have fully understood that this freedom has been granted by us absolutely, you in your loyalty will understand that such freedom is likewise granted to all others who wish to follow whatever religion or form of worship they desire—a privilege consistent with the tranquility of our times—so that all may be free to choose and practice whatever form of divine worship they wish. We have decided upon this in order to make clear that we are not undermining any religion or rite.

With regard to the Christians and the earlier Edict's specifications about the places where those Christians were accustomed to assemble, we further decree that if anyone shall have purchased those places from the imperial treasury or from anyone else, they must restore those lands to the Christians without any demand for payment or compensation and without any negotiation, delay, or fraud. Likewise, if anyone has received these lands as a gift, they must restore them without delay. Anyone who has either purchased those Christians' lands or has received them as a gift, may appeal to our imperial generosity and apply to the prefect or magistrate in charge of their district for recompense. All these transfers of property are to be carried out promptly, with determined zeal, and without delay.

Since the Christians possessed not only the properties where they used to assemble but also other sites belonging not to individual Christians but to their entire communities, we further decree, in accordance with the law stated above, that you restore without hesitation to the Christian communities themselves each and every property formerly owned by those communities. In accordance with this directive, every person who restores such properties may appeal to our imperial generosity, provided that they neither appeal to nor require of the Christian communities themselves for compensation.

In these matters it is up to you, our officials and magistrates, to exert yourselves fully on behalf of the aforesaid Christians, for we wish our orders may be carried out with all possible speed, in order that our imperial generosity may most effectively advance the common good and ensure public tranquility. As said before, by carrying out these acts of restoration we trust that divine mercy—which we have fortunately experienced many times in the past—may remain with us and keep us forever. In order that this program of our enactments and generosity may be made known to all, we desire that what we have here written should be published and proclaimed to all, for we wish the fact of our liberality to be known by every citizen.

2.7   Nicene Creeds

This creed was recorded at the Council of Nicaea (325 CE) to clarify early Christian beliefs as they were confronted with Arian heresy. The heretic Arius (ca. 250–336) held that although Jesus was the divine Son of God, he was also created, meaning that he was not eternal alongside God the Father. This posed problems for the orthodox Christian belief in a Trinity that was made of three distinct persons (Father, Son, and Holy Spirit) who were also one being—thus threatening the Son's eternal nature also threatened this unity. These versions of the Nicene Creed reveal how doctrine changed over time in order to accommodate and clarify changing Christian realities.

The First Version of the Nicene Creed

We believe in one God, the Father Almighty,
　　Makers of all things seen and unseen.

We believe in one Lord, Jesus Christ, the Son of God,
　　The only-begotten of the Father, God of
　　　　God, Light of Light,
　　true God of true God, begotten—not
　　　　made—
　　one in substance with the Father.
　　Through Him all things were made,
　　　　both those in heaven and those on earth.
　　For us men and for our salvation He
　　　　came down from Heaven, was
　　　　incarnate, and was made man.
　　He suffered [death] and rose again on
　　　　the third day. He ascended
　　　　into Heaven, and He shall
　　　　come again to judge the quick
　　　　and the dead.

We believe in the Holy Spirit.
And anyone who says that there was a time when
　　the Son of God was not, or that before
　　He was begotten He was not, or that He
　　was made of things that were not, or
　　that He is of a different substance or
　　essence [from the Father], or that He is
　　created, subject to change, or to
　　conversion—the Catholic and Apostolic
　　Church anathematizes him.

The Final Version of the Nicene Creed

We believe in one God, the Father Almighty,
　　maker of heaven and earth, and of all
　　that is, seen and unseen.

We believe in one Lord, Jesus Christ, the only Son
　　of God,
　　　　eternally begotten of the Father, God
　　　　　　from God, Light from Light,
　　　　　　true God from true God, begotten—not
　　　　　　made—
　　one in Being with the Father.
　　Through Him all things were made.
　　For us men and for our salvation He
　　came down from heaven; by
　　　　the power of the Holy Spirit he
　　　　was born of the Virgin Mary,
　　　　and became man.
　　For our sake He was crucified under
　　　　Pontius Pilate; He suffered,
　　　　died, and was buried. On the
　　　　third day He rose again in accordance
　　　　with the Scriptures;
　　　　He ascended into Heaven and
　　　　is seated at the right hand of
　　　　the Father. He will come again
　　　　in glory to judge the living and
　　　　the dead, and His kingdom will
　　　　have no end.

We believe in the Holy Spirit, the Lord, the giver
　　of life, who proceeds from the Father
　　and the Son. With the Father and the
　　Son he is worshipped and glorified. He
　　has spoken through the prophets.

We believe in one holy catholic and apostolic
　　Church. We acknowledge one baptism
　　for the forgiveness of sins. We look for
　　the resurrection of the dead and the life
　　of the world to come. Amen.

2.8　Celsus via *Origen*

The Greek philosopher Celsus (second century CE) wrote a treatise against early Christians entitled *On the True Doctrine*. While this work has not survived on its own, it was incorporated into the treatise *Against Celsus* by Origen (ca. 184–ca. 253), a theologian and Church Father who responded to Celsus's accusations, claim by claim. In this way, scholars could recreate Celsus's original text. The portions included here reveal Celsus's accusations of doctrine (such as the virgin birth), historical points (Jesus's affiliation with the lowest classes), and the relationship between Christians and their God.

It is by invoking the names of demons and reciting incantations that the Christians seem to possess [miraculous] power. That was how [Jesus] accomplished his marvels—by sorcery—and since he understood that others would eventually learn the same skills and do the same things as he, and that they would boast of doing them 'by the power of the Lord,' he therefore denied them admittance to his kingdom. But if he excludes sorcerers for doing the same things he had done, then he is wicked. And if he is not wicked for what he did, then neither are those who do the same. [1.6]

Celsus describes the case of the Jew who disputed with Jesus and defeated Him (or so he thought) on a variety of points. In the first place, he accuses Christ of having invented the story of His virgin birth, and reproaches Him for having been born in a Jewish village to a poor rustic who made her living by spinning and was denounced by her carpenter-husband because of her adultery. Rejected by her husband, she wandered aimlessly for a while until, in her shame, she gave birth to the bastard Jesus. This Jesus, being poor, eventually found work as a servant in Egypt—where he learned some of the magical powers that the Egyptians pride themselves on knowing. It was then that he returned to his homeland, full of himself because of his new knowledge, and by means of these powers proclaimed himself a God. [1.28]

I charge the Christians with nothing more than the truth, as you can see by the following. In other cults, anyone who wishes to invite [an outsider] to participate in its mysteries always says, "Anyone with clean hands and a pure tongue, [enter]," or "Whoever is without pollution, whose spirit knows no evil, and who has lived a just and upright life, [enter]." These are the invitations used by those who promise to purify people of sin. But who do these Christians invite? Every sinner! Everyone devoid of understanding! Whoever is a child! In a word, any miserable person at all! That's who they say will be received in the kingdom of God. But is a thief not a sinner? A cad? A burglar? A poisoner? One

guilty of sacrilege? A grave-robber? Who wouldn't a man invite [into a cult], if he would invite such criminals as these? [3.59]

The Christians say that it was specifically to sinners that God was sent. But why was he not sent to those who were without sin? What is wrong with not being sinful? It seems that God will welcome the unrighteous man who repents his wickedness but not the righteous man who approaches God with virtue from the very beginning! [3.62]

Isn't it ridiculous to think that the same God who, in his righteous fury, threatened the Jews, then killed them all (including their infants), and destroyed their city by fire, would send his own son among them, to endure the sufferings this Jesus endured? [4.73]

You may mock and scorn the statues of our divinities—but if you were to insult Bacchus or Hercules face-to-face you would feel the consequence of it. But those who crucified your God when He was living among you suffered nothing, neither then nor later. And what has happened since his death to make anyone believe that he wasn't a fake, this "Son of God"? So: the God who sent his own son to earth with teachings meant for all mankind let his son be treated abominably, and let his teachings vanish—and all without showing a single sign of concern? What father was ever so cruel? Now, you can say that he suffered so much because he wanted to, that it was his desire to endure all that came at him. But then you have to allow that the same could be true of those [pagan] gods you revile and reject—that they too want to be reviled, and that they are therefore now bearing it all patiently. You have to play fair on both sides. But [watch out]: our gods always punish those who scorn them. Get ready to run and hide, or be caught and perish! [8.41]

Do you not see the absurd contradiction in making so much of the human body as you do—to look expectantly for it to rise from the dead—as if it were the single most precious part of us, and yet, on the other hand, to treat it with such scorn that you willingly expose it to torture? Any person who values the body yet can think such things, is someone who doesn't deserve to be reasoned with. Instead, he exposes himself as a gross being, polluted, and determined to reject common sense for no reason at all. I wish to converse with people who hope to enjoy eternal life with God by means of their spirit or mind—whether they want to call it a "spiritual substance," or a "spirit of holy and blessed intelligence," or a "living soul," or a "heavenly and eternal offspring of a divine spiritual nature," or any other name they wish. For these are the people who are right—the ones who understand that those who live upright lives shall be blessed, and those who are unjust shall receive eternal torment—and who never waver from this truth. [8.49]

[The Christians] have to make a choice. If they want to refuse to render due service to the [pagan] gods and respect to those men who preside over their cults, then let them not grow to manhood, take wives, or have children; let them take no part in the business of life; and let them leave this world with all possible speed and leave no one behind them, so that their whole hateful race may disappear from the face of the earth. On the other hand, though, if they wish to marry and raise children, to taste the fruits of the earth and to partake of all of life's blessings and its appointed sorrows (for Nature has decreed a portion of sorrows to all men, since sorrows must exist—and earth is the only place for them), then they must accept the duties of life until they are released from its bonds, and they must pay the honor due to those gods who control the affairs of this life—unless, that is, they want to appear ungrateful. But it would be gross injustice, if they wish to receive the blessings that the gods bestow, but pay them nothing in return. [8.55]

2.9   The Gospel of Thomas

Discovered in 1945, the Gospel of Thomas numbers among the 52 writings preserved in a cave in Egypt. Written in Coptic, the Gospel of Thomas—the disciple of Jesus—is an extra-biblical text read by Gnostics. Though it was never accepted in the canonical Bible, the Gospel of Thomas was popular in certain geographical regions like Syria, where Thomas converted Christians after Jesus's death. The 114 sayings in this "Gospel" partly reflect the familiar sayings from the four synoptic Gospels and partly emerge from Gnostic understandings of early Christian tenets.

Jesus said, "If you do not abstain from the world, you will not find the kingdom of God. And if you do not keep the Sabbath, you will not see the Father." [1.4–11]

Jesus also said, "I stood amidst the world and appeared to the people in the flesh. I found everyone satiated, and no one thirsty. My heart worries about the children of man because they are blind in their hearts and they do not see." [1.11–21]

Jesus also said, "Wherever there are three, they are without God; but where there is only one, I say that I am with him. Lift the stone and there you will find me. Split the wood, and I am there." [1.23–30]

And Jesus said, "A prophet is not accepted in his own land, nor does a physician heal those who know him." [1.30–35]

Jesus also said, "A city set on the summit of a high mountain can neither fall nor be hidden." [1.36–41]

These are the hidden sayings that Jesus spoke when alive and that Judas, also called Thomas, wrote down. And he said, "Whoever understands how to interpret these sayings will not taste death." [654.1–5]

"Let the seeker not stop seeking until he finds [what he seeks]; and when he finds it, he will marvel.

When he marvels, he will have authority; and when he has authority, he will know peace." [654.5–9]

Jesus also said, "If those leading you say 'The kingdom [of God] is in the sky,' then the birds of the sky will guide you. If they say 'The kingdom is below ground,' then the fish of the sea will lead you. The kingdom of God is within you, and without you. Whoever knows himself will find this out. And when you know yourself, you will know that you are the children of the living Father. But if you do not know yourself, you live in poverty and you are poor." [654.9–21]

Jesus also said, "A person old in years will not hesitate to ask a child—even if he is only seven days old—about his place in life. . . . For many who are first will be last, and many who are last will be first. . . . [654.21–27]

Jesus also said, "Know what is in front of your face, and that which is hidden from you will be revealed. For there is nothing hidden that will not be made clear, and nothing buried that will not be raised again." [654.27–31]

His disciples said to Jesus, "When will we be visible? When will we be able to see you?" And Jesus answered, "When you are naked and not ashamed." [655i.17–23]

2.10   St. Augustine, *Two Sermons on the First Epistle of John*

Augustine's reputation as a theologian is so great (as it was in medieval times) that it can blind us to the fact that he was above all a powerfully charismatic and effective preacher. Hundreds of his sermons survive and provide the best evidence for why he was loved. Among the best of his sermons is the series of homilies he delivered on the First Epistle of John. The first sermon below emphasizes the importance of love as the defining characteristic of Christian faith. The second sermon, largely improvised, focuses on the same theme but has an ulterior motive: he delivered it to his parish on the day of a popular pagan festival that included singing, dancing, and a wild-beast circus, and he was determined not to be upstaged and to hold his audience from the temptation to join in the revelry.

No one has ever seen God. Yet, if we love one another, God remains in us, and his love is brought to perfection in us. This is how we know that we remain in him and he in us, that he has given us of his Spirit. Moreover, we have seen and testify that the Father sent his Son as savior of the world. Whoever acknowledges that Jesus is the Son of God, God remains in him and he in God. We have come to know and to believe in the love God has for us. God is love, and whoever remains in love remains in God and God in him. [1 John 4.12–16]

Love is a sweet word, but sweeter still is the deed. We cannot be always speaking of it, for we have so many things to do and our daily business pulls us in different directions. It's not that we don't have nothing better to talk about—we just don't have the time to sit around and talk about love. But although we cannot be always talking about it, we may always be loving. Just as with the "Alleluia" that we sing daily this time of year—are we in fact always singing it? Of course not. We don't sing "Alleluia" for an hour, by which I mean not only that we don't sing it for an entire hour but that we don't even sing it for a single minute out of every hour. We're too busy with other things.

"Alleluia," as you know, means "Praise the Lord." The person who praises God aloud cannot always be doing it, but the one who praises God by the way he lives his life, can do so always. Acts of mercy and love, the holiness of piety, chastity, and sobriety—all these are things we can practice all the time, in public or at home, with others or alone in our rooms, while conversing or keeping quiet, when busy or at leisure. And we should practice them always, because all of these are internal virtues. . . .

Dear brothers, you heard earlier in the Gospel reading (at least if you were listening not only with your ears but with your heart), "Take care not to perform righteous deeds in order that people may see them." [Matt 6.1] Now, did Jesus mean by this, that we should hide from the eyes of others the good things we do, out of fear of being seen? But if we fear spectators, then we will never have imitators—and so we ought to be seen doing good, but we should not do good in order to be seen doing it. . . . Do good not to win praise for yourself but for the God who has given you the ability to do good. . . . I tell you, my brothers, and in fact I would not let this go unsaid: Take up good works whenever you can, regardless of the season, the day, and the hour. . . . What you can, when you can. . . . Let your charity never cease or be interrupted. Love always, in every season. As it is written, "Let mutual love continue." [Heb 13.1]

Some of you have probably been wondering, while I've been talking about this epistle of St. John, why it is "brotherly" love he emphasizes so much. . . . He speaks over and over again of this love—and yet he seldom mentions the love we should have for God. (He does mention love for God, of course.) Similarly, he says hardly a word about loving our enemies. He extols and preaches charity with the greatest energy, but tells us only to love one another rather than to love our enemies. But we just heard, in our Gospel reading, "For if you love those who love you, what recompense will you have? Do not the tax collectors do the same?" [Matt 5.46] . . . Love is like fire: it touches first what is nearest before extending to what is further away. A beloved person is closer to you than a stranger, and a benign stranger is closer to you than a sworn enemy. So give your love to those who are closest to you . . . then extend it to strangers who have done you no ill, and then extend it again to your enemies. This is what the Lord requires of us—and it explains why John here says nothing about loving an enemy. . . .

All love—both common human love (for which we use the word *amor*) and spiritual love (the love we have for what we aspire to, and for which we use the word *dilectio*)—involves desiring the well-being of the one loved. Whether we mean *dilectio* or *amor* (the latter

being the word Christ used when He asked, "Peter, do you love me?" [John 21.17]), we do not mean that we love others in the way, say, that a glutton loves fowl—for he loves fowl in order to kill and eat them; his love desires the end of their existence. We love food in order to consume it and be strengthened by it—but that is not how we love people. That love is benevolent and springs from a desire to do good for others. If there is no good we can do for someone, the desire for it alone suffices to prove our love. We certainly don't wish someone to be wretched, so that we can extend mercy to him! Feed the hungry, certainly; but how much better it would be if no one knew hunger and we had no one to give bread to. Clothe the naked, but oh, that all were clothed and need did not exist! We bury the dead, but how we look forward to the time when life is eternal and no one dies! We reconcile those who are in disagreement, yet how much we hope for the eternal peace of Jerusalem, where everyone shall live in harmony! . . .

Dear brothers, I've spoken at some length here, because the importance of the love we give to others requires it. If there be no love in us, then my words are useless; but if we have that love, then my words will be like oil cast upon a flame. To one without a feeling of love, perhaps my words may kindle it; to one with flame already let, perhaps my words will fuel it. . . . "If we love one another, God remains in us, and his love is brought to perfection in us." [1 John 4.12] Begin to love, and be perfected—for God has thereby begun to dwell within you, and his in-dwelling will make you perfect. "This is how we know that we remain in him and he in us, that he has given us of his Spirit." [1 John 4.13] Thanks be to God! . . .

So much do I love to speak about love that I almost wish this epistle had no end. No other text is so impassioned in calling us to love; there is no message more sweet that can be preached to us, nor more healthful for us to imbibe—but only if we acknowledge God's gift by living in love. Let us not forget to be thankful for such a great and gracious gift. God had only one Son, but desires that He be not an only child. He wishes us to be His brothers, adopted by Him into eternal life.

* * * * *

I am so happy to see so many of you here today; such commitment on your part is more than I could have hoped for, and it's just the thing to cheer a preacher's heart when he feels overwhelmed with work and is struggling with the sheer difficulty of life sometimes. How sweet it is to see you all here, filled with love for God and the desire for a life of faith, constant hope, and devotion!

In today's Psalm we heard the poor and needy soul crying out to God, "Let the poor and needy praise your name." [Ps. 74.21] By now you know—for I have told you so many times before—that the voice we hear in the Psalms is not the voice of an individual person; but it is a single voice, one of an entire community of faith. They are as many as the grains of wheat lying among the chaff on a threshing room floor; they are scattered throughout the world, but they are still a single voice—for they are all members of the one Body of Christ, a poor and needy people who find no delight in the world's busy-ness outside. Their sorrows and joys are hidden away, known only to Him who hears their cries and fulfills their hopes.

What our world calls pleasure is empty; we long for it, but when it comes it does not last. Today's pleasure is gone tomorrow, for nothing ever stays the same in this life, neither with things nor with people. Everything changes, escapes, and vanishes like smoke. Miserable indeed are those who focus their love on such things, for the human soul adapts to, and becomes like, the things that it loves. . . . So be careful of what you love, if you hope for eternal life. You want to know how to find the abiding Word of God, so that you can love it? I'll tell you: "The Word was made flesh and dwelt among us."

Dear friends, we are "poor and needy," but it is this very poverty that makes us able to feel sorry for those people out there who think they have everything; their happiness is the giddiness of a madman (and we all know how happy lunatics can be). They laugh constantly and feel sorry for our unfortunate sanity. Once we were all like them, out of our minds. But we were cured by a heavenly medicine, so that we no longer love the things we used to. Let us pray in earnest for those outside who live in delusion. Christ can restore them to health too, if only they can see their lives for what they are and realize that the things of this world offer no real satisfaction. . . .

Christ Our Lord taught us: "Everyone who listens to these words of mine and acts on them will be like a wise man who builds his house on rock. The rain fell, the floods came, and the winds blew and buffeted the house. But it did not collapse; it had been set solidly on rock. And everyone who listens to these words of mine but does not act on them will be like the fool who built his house on sand. The rain fell, the floods came, and the winds blew and buffeted the house. And it collapsed and was completely ruined." [Matthew 7.24–27] . . . There is only one safe way to go. Let us build our house and build it on rock. . . . So listen, and act. This is the only way to salvation. How many people outside, today, have been swept away by the tide of this festival, and all as a result of hearing [the Word] but not acting upon it! Every year, when this festival comes round, it is like the rush of a river in flood, sweeping along in its course. But then it passes, and the land is arid once again. How can we not feel sorry for those who are carried away in the torrent? Please take it to heart, my dear friends: unless you both hear [the Word] and act upon it, you will not build upon rock nor live up to the great name that Our Lord set His seal upon. . . .

I've kept you a long time today, but I did so with a purpose—to wait until the danger was passed. I suppose those outside have finished their foolishness by now. In the meantime, my brothers, we have enjoyed the feast that really does make us whole. All that remains for us is to spend the rest of this Day of the Lord feeling the joy of God's love. O, how different this joy is from the cheap article on offer outside!

3. EARLY GERMANIC SOCIETY

3.1 Jordanes, *Getica*

Jordanes was a sixth-century *notarius* (secretary) who served in a frontier province along the imperial border with modern-day Romania and who turned to historical writing at the inspiration of Cassiodorus. His most important work is his *History of the Goths*, which is our principal source for the earliest period of Gothic history. Here he relates the movement of Attila the Hun into Europe.

[176] And what next? King Wallia [of the Visigoths] had little success against the Gauls, and after he died the throne passed to Theodoridus, a man who enjoyed somewhat better luck and success. By nature he was a man of great moderation and was noted for the extraordinary vigor of his mind and body. During the consulship of Theodosius and Festus [439], the Romans broke their truce with the Visigoths and took up arms against them, using Hunnish soldiers as auxiliaries, because a group of Goths banded together under the leadership of Count Gaina and had threatened Constantinople.

The patrician Aetius was in command of the army at that time. He came of stout Moesian stock and was the son of Gaudentius. He was born in the city of Durostorum [modern Silistra, in Bulgaria] and was in fact born to serve Rome, so to speak, since he was cut out for war. In his manhood he inflicted crushing defeats upon the Suevi and the barbarous Franks, and brought them under Rome's authority.

[177] It was with a battle-tested army, then, and allied with the Huns under their leader Litorius, that Aetius marched against the Goths. The two sides drew up lines against one another, but since they turned out to be equal in valor and strength, they bided their time and eventually decided to revive their old truce with one another. Concluding an honorable treaty, both sides withdrew.

[178] During the ensuing peace, a Hun named Attila became the ruler of his people—and indeed he very nearly became the monarch of all the tribes of Scythia and his fame grew so great he became known throughout the entire world. The historian Priscus, whom Theodosius II had sent as an ambassador to Attila's court, has this to say: "Having crossed the mighty Tisia [Tisza], Tibisia [Temes], and Drekon rivers, we reached the site where Widigoja, the bravest of all the Goths, long ago met his end, thanks to the treachery of the Sarmatians. Not far from there we soon arrived at Szeged, where Attila was staying. It was a village, to be sure, but it appeared rather like a great city, because the Huns had constructed around it wooden fortifications of exceedingly fine workmanship, whose joints were made so tightly that only by close scrutiny could one see that the wall was not built of a single, smooth piece of wood. Inside they had erected enormous dining halls and porticos, all of which were expertly laid out. A vast courtyard, surrounded by a covered colonnade, indicated by its grandeur that it was the royal palace."

This was the court of Attila, king of all the barbarian world, and he preferred living here more than in any city he captured. . . .

[180] Now Attila was the son of Mundzuk, and his brothers were called Oktar and Roas. The brothers actually held the throne before Attila did, although they never controlled as many Hunnish tribes as he did. Attila came to power after their deaths; originally he shared the kingship with another brother named Bleda, but wanting to make sure he was equal to the fight he was preparing for, he began by murdering his own brother and threatening any other relations he had.

[181] It was a detestable way to come to power, but Attila learned to off-set his cruelty with acts of justice. The result of this counterbalancing, though, was hideous. For after killing Bleda, who had ruled over a great number of Huns, Attila gathered the whole nation under his power. Soon he swept up a multitude of other peoples too, until he deemed himself ready to set his sights on the foremost nations of the world: the Romans and the Visigoths.

[182] According to reports, his army was five hundred thousand strong. He was a man seemingly put here on earth in order to terrify people, and he skillfully broadcast rumors of his ferocity. He strutted haughtily when he walked, casting his eyes left and right so that the arrogance of his power appeared in every movement he made. Although he loved war, he could exercise restraint; and while he spoke imperiously, he could be gracious and even kind to those who subjected themselves to him. He was short and had a broad chest, a large head, small eyes, a thin and grayish beard. His nose was flat and ugly, showing the sign of his origins.

[183] He was supremely confident in temperament, especially after he reportedly discovered the Sword of Mars, a sacred object among the Scythians. Priscus describes the discovery this way: "Once, when a shepherd saw one of his heifers limping, he went off in search of what had caused it. Following the trail of the heifer's blood, he found the point of a sword sticking out of the ground that she had stumbled upon while grazing. The shepherd dug up the sword and brought it straight to Attila, who was delighted with it, seeing it as a sign that he was destined to rule the entire world—for it was the Sword of Mars, which assured him of victory in every battle."

[184] When Gesalric, the king of the Vandals whom I mentioned earlier, learned that Attila was planning a world-conquest, he showered him with gifts and urged him to attack the Visigoths. Gesalric did this because he was afraid that Theodoridus, the Visigothic king, was plotting revenge on Gesalric for the harm done to his daughter. This daughter had been wedded to Gesalric's son, Huniric, and for a while the marriage was happy. But Hunirik grew cruel with time and beat their children. Moreover, he grew suspicious of his wife and believed she was planning to poison him, so he cut off her nose and ears and sent her back to her father in Gaul. The poor girl, all mutilated, looked like a battlefield-corpse, the victim of a cruelty that would rouse anyone to vengeance—and her father all the more so.

[185] Attila, therefore, plotting out the wars that Gesalric's bribes had urged, sent ambassadors to Italy in the hope of stirring up trouble between the western emperor Valentinian [III, r. 425–455] and the Goths; in this way he could let civil strife do the work of an offensive attack of his own. He insisted that his fight with Theodoridus the Visigoth did not violate in any way his friendly relations with Rome. He sweetened his message to the emperor with the usual flattering salutations, enough to cover up his lie.

[186] He then sent a similar letter to Theodoridus, urging him to break his truce with Rome by reminding him of various troubles the empire had recently caused him, for beneath his ferocity he was a cunning man who prepared for his battles with guile.

But Valentinian and Theodoricus saw through Attila's plot and joined forces against him. Aetius was appointed the commander of their armies and met Attila's forces [451] at the Catalaunian Plains, roughly 85 miles southeast of Paris.

---

[194] But before describing the battle we need to relate what events happened beforehand, for the conflict was as complicated and multifaceted as it was famous.

First, Sangibanus, the king of the Alans, was terrified. Not knowing what to expect, he had promised to surrender to Attila and hand over the city of Orleans (where he was living at the time).

[195] When Theodoricus and Aetius learned of this, they rushed to throw up large earthwork embankments around that city before Attila got there. In this

way they also kept an eye on Sangibanis and encircled him with their auxiliary forces.

This move caught Attila by surprise and he grew doubtful of what his troops might gain by attacking. While pausing to consider his next move, though, a disaster worse than death occurred—for he decided to consult an augur to read into the future.

[196] They did this according to custom, by examining the entrails and bones of sacrificed cattle, and the markings on the bones foretold a catastrophe for the Huns, with only the slight consolation that their enemies' commander in chief would fall in battle and cause his men to withdraw from an impending victory. Thus death would mar their triumph.

Attila considered Aetius' death as something to be desired even at the cost of his own life, so completely had he blocked the Hunnish king's maneuvers. The augur's prophecy had disturbed him, though, so when he drew up his battle plan he carefully held off beginning the fight until the ninth hour of the day, so that nightfall might come to his aid if things went badly.

[197] The armies met, as we said, in the Catalaunian Plains. Both armies tried to gain control of an incline that led to a strategic hilltop. The Huns seized the right side of the incline, while the Romans, Visigoths, and their allies took the left; then, leaving their positions, both sides raced to the top. Theodoridus and his Visigoths had the right wing of their combined forces, while Aetius and the Romans held the left. They positioned Sangiban, the commander of the Alans, in the center, thereby surrounding with their most loyal troops the man in whom they had the least confidence, knowing that the man who cannot escape is the man who resolves to fight to the end.

[198] But on the other side of the hill Attila had so arranged his men that his stoutest fighters were in the center of the line. Self-concern guided his thinking, for he thought he would be safest amid his most elite troops. The countless peoples of all the nations he had brought under his control held the wings. . . .

[207] The scene was dreadful to behold, but Attila's zeal gave courage to anyone whose courage was fading. The fighting was fierce, relentless, hand to hand, hopelessly confused. A fight like no other ever recorded, such that anyone who missed it could never have seen anything like it in a lifetime.

[208] In fact, if the reports of our ancestors can be trusted, a brook in the aforesaid plain overflowed its bank, so great was the amount of blood that flowed into it from the wounds of the fallen. . . . And those whose wounds parched their thirst and drove them to seek water, ended up drinking water mixed with gore, drinking the very blood that poured from their own wounds.

[209] King Theodoricus, riding wildly through his army and shouting encouragement to his men, was thrown from his horse and trampled by his own troops, ending his life at a ripe old age. Others, though, say he was killed by a spear-thrust from Andagis, an Ostrogoth. [The Ostrogoths were at the time part of Attila's empire.] Thus was fulfilled the augur's prophecy made to Attila, even though he misinterpreted it to refer to Aetius.

[210] At this point the Visigoths broke ranks with the Alans and attacked the center of the Hunnish army; they might very well have killed Attila himself, but he made a prudent retreat and shut himself and his officers back in their camp, which he had surrounded with wagons—a frail defense, indeed, for one who only a little while before could have broken through any fortification whatsoever. . . .

[212] Aetius became separated from his men in all the confusion and spent the night wandering among the enemy soldiers. Fearing the worst, he set off in search of his Visigoths and at last reached his allies' camps, where he spent the rest of the night under the protection of their shields. At dawn, the next day, the Romans saw the fields piled high with bodies, and believed themselves the victors since the Huns did not venture out [from their camp]. They knew, though, that Attila would not withdraw from the field unless he was overwhelmed by disaster. But he showed no sign of weakness or fear; rather, his men clashed their weapons, blew their horns, and threatened to attack. Attila was like a wounded lion, pacing back and forth before the mouth of his den, not daring to attack and yet terrifying all who saw him by his roaring. Even cornered like this, he still frightened those who had beaten him.

[213] So the Romans and Goths gathered in council and debated what to do with the defeated Attila. They decided to wear him out with a siege, since he had no supplies. Their archers were able easily to keep

him pinned down, unable to advance, with a shower of arrows they launched from safely within the Roman camp.

It is reported that Attila never lost his courage even in his plight, for he ordered his men to pile up their saddles and create a kind of pyre. If the Romans and Goths attacked, he intended to hurl himself into the flames in order to deprive his enemies of the pleasure of wounding or capturing the conqueror of so many nations. . . .

[217] . . . One hundred and sixty five thousand men are reported to have been killed in this battle, on both sides, not counting another fifteen thousand Gepids and Franks who had fought one another the night before (the Franks siding with the Romans, and the Gepids allied with the Huns). . . .

[219] The Visigoths' departure [after the death of King Theodoridus] was a happy sight for Attila, who grew confident as he watched his enemies disband and withdraw. He decided to take the offensive against the Romans, and [in 452] he besieged the city of Aquileia, the capital of Venetia—a site located on a point of land in the Adriatic Gulf. On its eastern side Aquileia is bordered by the river Natisone, which flows from Monte Picci.

[220] The siege was long and hard-fought, but in the end the brave Romans held out until Attila's own soldiers began to grumble and talk about withdrawing. One day Attila was walking around the walls trying to decide whether or not to break camp, when he saw some storks. These birds usually build their nests in the gables of houses, but when Attila saw them were flying with their young away from the city and into the countryside.

[221] Being a keen observer of auspices, he knew how to read the sign and announced to his men: "The flight of those birds is an omen. They are leaving because the city is certain to perish. . . ." What else can I say? He roused his men to renew their attack. They built battering rams and a host of other siege engines, and soon forced their way into the city. Once inside, they ransacked and pillaged Aquileia so savagely that hardly a trace of the city remains to be seen today.

[222] Growing bolder and thirsting for more Roman blood, the Huns rampaged through all the cities of Venetia, laying waste to Milan (the capital of Liguria and once home to the imperial court) and Pavia, then moving on to place after place until they had demolished almost all of Italy. Attila had set his mind on taking Rome itself, but, as Priscan relates, some of his officers tried to dissuade him—not out of love for the city, which they hated, but on account of the fate of Alaric, the Visigothic king who had sacked Rome before [in 410] but died soon thereafter.

[223] While Attila was trying to make up his mind, a peace embassy arrived. Pope Leo himself had come from Rome, and he met with Attila in the region of Ambuleia, in Venetia, at a bridge over the river Minucius.

After this meeting, Attila set aside his wrath, vowed peace, retraced his steps, and withdrew beyond the river Danube. He did make a threatening vow, though, to return to Italy and inflict even worse punishment on the land if the Romans did not send him Honoria, the sister of the emperor Valentinian, along with her share of the imperial wealth as a dowry.

[224] According to rumors, Honoria had been kept in confinement at her brother's command—he regarded her virginity as necessary to the dignity of his imperial court—and out of resentment had dispatched one of her eunuchs to entice Attila to come and take her from her brother's captivity. Shamefully, she had chosen to risk the public safety in order to gratify her lustful desire.

[225] So Attila returned to his own kingdom, angry at his campaign's end. Indeed he so hated peace that he sent an embassy to the eastern emperor Marcian [450–457] and threatened to wipe out his provinces because the tribute promised to him by Theodosius [II, r. 408–450] had not be paid in full—but really, he simply desired to appear more savage to his foes than ever. While thus engaged eastward with his threats, he craftily moved his army in another direction altogether, toward the Visigoths.

[226] But he was less successful against them than he had been against the Romans. Moving quickly and by an unexpected route he targeted the Alans who lived on the other side of the Loire river. His plan was to present a more terrible threat to the Visigoths by upsetting the balance of power among the nations of the west. Accordingly, he began with Dacia and Pannonia, where his Huns were then residing, and lashed out at the Alans.

[227] The Visigothic king Thorismund, however, was as cunning as Attila and saw through his tricks. Leading his men on forced marches, Thorismund reached the Alans before Attila did, and was in position to repulse the Huns' attack when they arrived. The battle scene was a repeat of the Catalaunian Plain, and the Visigoths smashed Attila's hope of a quick victory and drove him from the country. . . .

[254] Attila's death [in 453] was as sordid as his life was remarkable. As Priscan relates, in that year Attila married a beautiful girl named Ildiko. As was the Hunnish custom, she was one of many wives he had.

At the wedding celebration Attila over-indulged, and, filled with wine, fell into a heavy sleep. He began to bleed from his nose, but as he was lying on his back the blood could not flow out; instead it built up in his throat and choked him to death. A king famed throughout the world for warfare thus died in shame through drunkenness. The next day, his servants suspected something was amiss when Attila did not emerge by midday, and so with a shout they broke down the door to the king's bedroom and saw Attila lying there, unwounded but dead from a hemorrhage. Ildiko hid her face under the bedsheet and wept.

3.2 Sidonius Apollinaris, *Letters*

Sidonius Apollinaris (d. 489) was a Gallo-Roman aristocrat and bishop of Auvergne (today Clermont-Ferrand). His letters are among the most important evidence we have of life in Germanic Europe. Gregory of Tours cites two particular facts about Sidonius as exemplary of his piety: his ability to celebrate Mass from memory, without the use of a written liturgy, and his habit of "removing silver vessels from his home and giving them away to the poor without informing his wife—and on those occasions when she discovered what he was doing, and complained about it, he secretly purchased the vessels back from the poor and returned them to the pantry."

[AD 467] TO HIS NEPHEW SECUNDUS, GREETING

I bring you some terrible news: Yesterday some impudent men desecrated the grave where the body of my grandfather, your great-grandfather, lies. The hand of God intervened, however, and stopped them before they could finish their wicked act. The graveyard had long been overcrowded, so that no kind of interment—with or without a burning pyre—had been performed there in years. Cycles of snow and rain have caused all the burial mounds to settle and the topsoil to scatter, so the ground has resumed its flat surface of old, and this is what prompted a grave-digging crew to profane the land by churning up the soil with their tools just as though the land wasn't a burial site.

Shall I tell you what happened? The men had already started digging, so that black soil showed and was being heaped up on top of our ancestor's old grave. I just happened to be riding by, on my way to Clermont, and saw the offense from the top of a nearby hill. I spurred my horse and galloped over the intervening ground at full speed, not caring at all whether the way was flat or hilly. I stopped once or twice and shouted to them to stop their villainy. Caught in the act, the blackguards debated whether or not to flee, but I was upon them before they could run away. I was wrong to do so, probably, but I could not help myself: in an instant I gave them all such a thrashing that the bodies buried there will be safe from molestation, and their survivors will be able to pay their respects, for a long time to come. I ought to have taken the matter to our good bishop, but decided that my direct action was the better course. I knew that I was right—besides, the bishop has such a gentle nature that I feared he would have treated the rogues with excessive lenience and myself with too much harshness. He had a right to know what had happened, though, and so I informed him of the whole matter after I had resumed my journey. Such an upright and holy man! Not only did he freely absolve me, he even praised me for having been outraged! In his mind, he said, people who performed such outrageous acts deserved to get what our forefathers would have inflicted on them—namely, execution.

Because of this incident, no similar crime should happen in future, and I beg you to see to it that our ancestor's grave is restored to a proper burial mound, and to place a smooth flat slab placed over it—at my expense. I have already deposited enough money with the venerable Gaudentius to cover the cost of the stone and to pay the mason. Here are some verses I wrote on the night of the incident; I was busy preparing for my journey, so they are not as polished as they should be—but please have the mason carve them on the stone without delay. Be especially careful that he makes no mistakes or improvisations of his own. Anyone who reads them will assume I am the author. Thank you heartily for carrying out this task. . . .

> My father and paternal uncles having died,
> I, a grandson not unworthy of such renowned
>   ancestors,
> dedicate this gravestone, although belatedly, so that
> you, O Stranger, may not be unaware of the
>   reverence
> due to the one buried beneath this mound.
> Here lies Apollinaris, ruler of all of Gaul. Now
> residing in the hearts of a mourning nation, he
> was a scholar of law, a pillar of his community,
> He devoted his life to this land, and to the state,
> and championed eloquent speech. He set an
>   example
> for all by daring to live free even while tyrants
>   ruled.
> But his chief claim to renown was the fact that he
> was the first of his nation to anoint his brow with
>   the sign
> of the Cross and to cleanse his limbs with the
>   waters
> of baptism, abandoning forever the evil rites of
>   old.

> This was his supreme virtue, his greatest glory.
>   Indeed,
> when a man surpasses in eternal hope those
>   whom he equals
> in earthly honors, then it is fitting that he be
>   placed in a grave
> superior to those of his contemporaries with
>   similar titles.

The epitaph is not worthy of our accomplished ancestor, I know, and yet I suspect that the souls of men of sophistication are never averse to a poetic tribute. Neither of us needs to think we are too late in fulfilling our pious duty as heirs in the third and fourth degrees. After all, think how many years went by before Alexander celebrated the funeral rites for Achilles' shade, or before Julius Caesar honored the shade of Hector, whom he regarded as an ancestor! Farewell.

[AD 474] TO MY LORD BISHOP MAMERTUS, GREETING

According to rumors, the Visigoths are taking over our Roman land. Poor Auvergne is always the pathway the invaders follow. It seems that we are fated to be fuel for the fire of their hatred, since (with Christ's help) we are all that stands in the way of their goal of extending their border to the Rhone. That would make them masters of all the countryside from the Rhone to the Atlantic and the Loire. Their might has long been a burden to us, and they have swallowed up whole districts of ours, and threaten to swallow up even more.

We will resist, of course, although we understand our position and the risks we face. But we trust not in our meager walls (already weakened by fire), nor in our decayed walls, nor the defensive shields of our sentries (which they lean upon in continual watch). Our only help now is in the prayers you taught us. These prayers explain why the people of Clermont refuse to flee despite being surrounded by terrors. Having introduced and institutionalized your prayers, we have already gained new initiates to the faith—fewer converts, perhaps, than you yourself won, but no less fervent for it. We remember well the dire portents that desolated this city when you first introduced this form of prayer to us: first an earthquake that shook the palace walls until they shattered, then a fire that turned once proud houses into heaps of smoldering ash. But then, a miraculous sight! A herd of wild deer calmly taking refuge amid our ruins!

You saw our city gutted, all the people, both rich and poor, fleeing. But following the example of ancient Nineveh, you did not despair at the sight of divine vengeance but instead you trusted in God's providence, which gave proof of your great virtue. Your faith burned brighter than the flames of that great firestorm. For we all saw you stand before a fleeing, frightened crowd—and everyone marveled to see the flames themselves leap away from you and pull back like a beaten slave. It was an amazing miracle, unlike anything we had ever seen before. Fire, which fears nothing, fled from your presence!

You thereupon imposed a fast on all the members of our order and denounced our offenses; but in imposing our punishment you also promised us relief, clearly showing that where sin is punished so too is it forgiven. You taught us that prayer can save us from the threat of future harm; that the water of tears can better extinguish a raging fire than the waters of a river; and that firm faith can absorb and overcome the shock of any earthquake. The common people among us were the first to embrace your teaching, which inspired those of higher rank who had abandoned the town but were not ashamed to return to it. Their devotions pleased God, who sees into all hearts, and the prayers you taught them shall be counted toward your own salvation. You set an example for us all, and in so doing have protected us—for since those days we have suffered no similar dangers or disasters.

We in Clermont know full well that all our sufferings came before you and your company arrived from Vienne, before the introduction of your prayers; and that none of those ills have befallen us since. This is why we are so eager to follow you in holiness, and ask for the blessing of your own prayers on our behalf, in the words you have taught us. You are the only person in the west to have translated the relics of two saints—the body of St. Ferreolus and the head of the martyred St. Julian (which the executioner's bloody hand brought to his prosecutor in his court)—since the time of (St.) Ambrose the Confessor, who had discovered the remains of Sts. Gervasius and Protasius. It is only fair, therefore, that you bestow some part of your patronage upon us from Vienne, in return for the loss of our hallowed relic which now resides with you. We pray that you will keep us in your heart, dear Lord Bishop.

3.3 Gregory of Tours, *History of the Franks*

Gregory served as bishop of Tours from 573 until his death in 594. He wrote many hagiographies, which he collected into three volumes: the *Lives of the Fathers*, the *Glory of the Confessors*, and the *Glory of the Martyrs*. He is best remembered, though, for his lengthy and rambling *History of the Franks*, which covers the period from St. Martin of Tours (d. 397) to the year 591. Switching back and forth between the family of Clovis and the various bishops of northern France, he tries to present the Merovingian era as a chapter in God's plan for Christianizing western Europe. In the two passages below, he describes the last four years of Clovis's life (r. 481–511) (Bk. II, ch. 35–42) and Gregory's own encounter with a Jew in the court of King Chilperic (r. 561–584) (Bk. VI, ch. 5).

CLOVIS' LAST YEARS (BK. II, CH. 35–42)

[II, 35] King Alaric II of the Visigoths, seeing that Clovis was overrunning one nation after another, sent ambassadors to him, saying, "Dear brother, it would be wise for us to meet—if you are interested, and God willing." Clovis agreed and rode to meet Alaric. They convened just outside the village of Amboise, which is on an island in the Loire river, in the diocese of Tours. They negotiated and settled upon a treaty of eternal friendship, which they celebrated with a shared feast, after which they both rode home in peace. At that time there were countless people in Gaul eager for Frankish rule.

[36] One consequence of this treaty, however, was that Bishop Quintinianus of Rodez fell from favor and was driven out by the people of his own city, who had long criticized him, saying, "If it were up to you, the Franks would be our lords!" It did not take long for their resentment to burst into open quarrel with the bishop, for the Visigoths who lived in the city were suspicious of Quintinianus' loyalties, and the rest of the townsmen went so far as to accuse him publicly of wanting to hand the city over to the Franks. And so a plot was hatched to assassinate him. Quintinianus found out about it and fled one night, together with his most trusted attendants, to Clermont, where he was kindly received by St. Eufrasius, the bishop who had succeeded Aprunculus. Eufrasius was a native of Dijon. He gave Quintinianus fine lodgings amid fields and vineyards, insisting that "This diocese has ample resources to support us both—for the charity preached by the blessed Apostle [St. Martin] must be carried on by all of God's ministers." The bishop of Lyons also gave Quintinianus some property that he administered in Clermont. For more details regarding St. Quintinianus, the wrongs done to him, and the miracles performed by God through him, see the pertinent chapter in my *Lives of the Fathers*.

[37] "I cannot bear seeing Arians living in Gaul," Clovis announced one day to his ministers. "We're going to attack them, and with God's help we'll crush them and take over all their land." Everyone agreed with this idea, and so Clovis assembled his army and marched on Poitiers. Along the way, some of his troops passed through the diocese of Tours, so Clovis gave an order that, out of respect for St. Martin, none of his men should requisition anything in the region except fodder and water. It happened that one soldier came upon some hay belonging to a elderly, poor farmer, and the soldier said to him, "The king says we cannot take anything but fodder, right? Well, this hay is fodder; we won't be going against orders if we take it." Then he knocked the old man down and took his hay. When this was reported to Clovis, he pulled out his sword and executed the soldier on the spot. "We can give up

any hope of winning this campaign if we offend St. Martin!" he declared. Thus he made his point, and the rest of the army took nothing in the region after that. Then Clovis sent messengers loaded with gifts to the church of St. Martin, saying, "Go, and bring me back good tidings from God's house." And then he prayed, "O Lord, if you are on my side and wish to deliver into my hands the wretched [Arian] heretics who have shown themselves so hostile to you, then give us a sign as these messengers enter St. Martin's church, a sign that shows clearly your support for me, your servant Clovis."

The messengers set out, and as they had been commanded they soon arrived at Tours; they entered the church exactly when the choir's soloist was singing the antiphon:

> You girded me with valor for war,
> subjugated my opponents beneath me.
> You made my foes expose their necks to me;
> those who hated me I silenced. [Ps. 18.39–40]

When the messengers heard this, they gave thanks to God, made their vows to St. Martin, and returned gladly to report to the king.

When Clovis and his army reached Vienne, they could find no way to cross the river since it was swollen from heavy rains, and so he prayed that night that God would show him a way across. The next morning, as it happened, a large doe appeared and entered the river. Everyone recognized that this was a heavenly sign, and that they could follow the doe across the river. Once on the other side, Clovis marched toward Poitiers. They made camp one evening and saw a pillar of fire rise from the local church of St. Hilary and advance toward them. To everyone this appeared a clear sign that that blessed saint was adding his support to Clovis' campaign to rout the heretics, against whom St. Hilary had himself done battle in defense of the faith. Clovis instantly gave orders forbidding any looting by his men as they passed through the region—and indeed no one took from anyone.

On the outskirts of Poitiers at that time there lived a saintly and God-fearing man named Maxentius, who, although the abbot, lived in seclusion from the rest of his monastery. It would be pointless to mention the name of the monastery at that time, for it is now known only as the Cell of St. Maxentius. When the monks there saw the approach of some Frankish soldiers they hurried to their abbot and begged him to come out and bless them. He took such a long time in coming out of his cell that the monks grew frightened and forced his door open; then they pushed him out into the open. Maxentius walked fearlessly up to the troops, presumably to ask them not to harm the monastery, when all of a sudden a soldier drew his sword and swung it at Maxentius' head—but his arm froze in mid-air, right by the abbot's ear, and the sword clattered to the ground. The soldier instantly threw himself at the saint's feet and begged forgiveness. His companions, seeing all of this, raced back to the main army filled with dread that they would have to pay with their lives for such an offense. The saint, meanwhile, rubbed the soldier's arm with holy oil and made the sign of the Cross over him, and instantly the man recovered. Thus, thanks to Maxentius, the monastery escaped unharmed. Maxentius performed many more miracles in his lifetime, as any reader who is interested may find in my *Life of Maxentius*. But this particular event occurred in the fifteenth year of Clovis' reign.

Soon thereafter, Clovis met King Alaric [II] and his army of Visigoths on the battlefield at Vouillé, about ten miles from Poitiers. After several volleys of javelins, the soldiers fought hand to hand; in the end the Visigoths fled (as they so often did), giving the victory to Clovis, who had God on his side. (One of Clovis' allies in this fight was Chloderic, the son of Sigibert the Lame. Sigibert was been lame ever since being wounded in the knee in a battle against the Alamanni at their fortress at Zülpich.) Clovis killed Alaric. Just as the Goths were fleeing, however, two of them turned and rushed suddenly at Clovis, one on each side, and struck him with their spears. Fortunately, thanks to his stout leather corselet and his speedy horse, Clovis escaped—but he very nearly died.

A large contingent from Auvergne, under the jurisdiction of Apollinaris, took part in this battle but their commanders (all of senatorial rank) were all killed. Alaric's son, Amalaric, escaped and made it all the way to Spain, where he ruled wisely for many years. Clovis, meanwhile, sent his own son, Theuderic, to Clermont, passing through Albi and Rodez on the way. Theuderic brought every place he passed by under his father's rule, and thus all the lands between the Visigoths and the Burgundians came to belong to Clovis. Alaric II had been king for twelve years. Clovis spent the winter in Bordeaux, seized all of Alaric's treasure at Toulouse, and then advanced to Angoulême—where God showed him such favor that the city's walls collapsed of their own weight when Clovis merely looked at them. Clovis drove the Visigoths from the city and took command. This was the culmination of his victorious campaign, and afterward he returned to Tours where he bestowed countless gifts upon the church of St. Martin.

[38] One day some letters arrived for Clovis from the [Byzantine] emperor Anastasius I [r. 491–518], conferring the title of consul on him. There was a ceremony in St. Martin's, where Clovis stood and assumed a purple tunic and the military robes [of the empire], and crowned himself with a diadem. Then he mounted his horse and rode among the people, showering them with gold and silver coins, as he progressed from the doorway of St. Martin's to the cathedral at Tours. From that day forward he was addressed either as "consul" or "augustus." After Tours he went on to Paris, which he made the seat of his government. His son Theuderic accompanied him.

[39] After Bishop Eustochius of Tours died, Licinius was ordained his successor—the eighth bishop after St. Martin himself. The war I described just above took place during Licinius' episcopacy, and it was in his time too that Clovis came to Tours. Licinius is reported to have spent time in the east and even to have visited the Holy Land; some say he went all the way to Jerusalem and saw the very site of Our Lord's death and resurrection, about which we have read in the gospels.

[40] While living in Paris Clovis sent a secret message to Sigibert's son, Chloderic. He wrote, "Your father is old and lame in one leg. When he dies his kingdom will pass, rightfully, to you—and my alliance will come with it." Chloderic was thus tempted by a lust for power and began to plot his own father's death.

One day Sigibert exited the city of Cologne and crossed the Rhine river, since he wanted to walk in the forest at Buchau. In the middle of the day he took a nap in his tent, which is when Chloderic loosed assassins on him. Having murdered his father, Chloderic then took possession of the realm. But by God's judgment, Sigibert's killer fell into the very trap he had laid for his father. He dispatched messengers to Clovis to announce Sigibert's death—"My father is dead," he wrote, "and I have seized both his kingdom and his treasure. Send messengers of your own to me, and I will gladly bestow upon you anything you desire from this treasure." To this Clovis replied, "Thank you for your good will. Please do show your treasure to my messengers—but you may keep it all."

When the messengers arrived, they examined all the treasure that Chloderic was eager to show them. "This was the chest in which my father kept all his gold coins," boasted Chloderic.

Clovis' men replied, "Plunge your hand down to the bottom of the chest, so we can see how much is there." And as soon as Chloderic leaned forward to do so, one of the Frankish envoys raised his double-sided axe and split his skull with it. Thus did the wretch Chloderic shared his father's fate.

After Clovis heard that both Sigibert and Chloderic were dead he traveled to Cologne himself and ordered all the town's inhabitants to assemble. "While I was boating down the Scheldt river, Chloderic, the son of your king, conspired against his own father and spread a rumor that I was the one who wanted him dead. Sigibert fled through the forest at Buchau, but Chloderic's assassins caught up with him and killed him. Then when Chloderic was showing off his father's treasure, he too was murdered—by whom, I don't know. I am not responsible in any way. I have no interest to murder any of my fellow kings, for regicide is a terrible crime. But things have happened in this way, I advise you to make the best of the situation by turning to me and putting yourself freely under my authority."

The people, hearing him, pounded their shields and roared their approval, then they raised Clovis up on a shield and acclaimed him their king. This is how he acquired Sigibert's kingship, treasure, and people. With every passing day God inspired more and more people to submit themselves to Clovis, who consequently grew enormously in power—for he always walked before God with an upright heart and did whatever was pleasing in His sight.

[41] Clovis' next victim was Chararic. This fellow had been asked to help Clovis during his struggles with Syagrius, but he had remained neutral. He gave aid to neither side, preferring to wait to see who would win before declaring allegiance, and this is why Clovis now moved against him. He cleverly trapped Chararic and threw him in prison. He ordered both Chararic and his son to be tied up, then had their hair cut off, with the subsequent order that they be ordained as priest and deacon, accordingly. At this, Chararic burst into tears and cried out, "All you have done is cut leaves from a tree that is still green and thriving; they'll soon grow back, larger than ever! Death to the man who has done this to me!" Clovis heard about this, and so he had their heads cut off too, and after they were both dead he seized their kingdom, treasure, and people too.

[42] The king at Cambrai at that time was Ragnachar, a man so lost to lechery that he could not even leave the women of his own family alone. He had a counselor named Farro who defiled himself with the same filthy habit. It was said of this man that whenever Ragnachar had anything—whether food, gift, or anything else—placed before him, he would proclaim "It's good enough for me and Farro!" This put all the Franks in their retinue in a great rage. And so Clovis bribed Ragnachar's bodyguards with arm-bands and sword-belts that looked like gold but were really just cleverly gilded bronze, and with these he hoped to turn Ragnachar's men against him. Clovis then sent his army against Ragnachar; and when Ragnachar dispatched spies to bring back information on the invaders and asked them upon their return, how strong the attackers were, they replied: "They're good enough for you and Farro!" Clovis himself finally arrived and arranged his soldiers for battle. Ragnachar watched as his army was crushed and tried to sneak away, but his own soldiers captured him, tied his hands behind his back, and brought him—together with Ragnachar's brother, Ricchar—before Clovis.

"Why have you disgraced our Frankish people by allowing yourself to be tied up?" asked Clovis. "It would have been better for you if you had died in battle." And with that, he lifted his axe and split Ragnachar's skull. Then he turned to his brother Ricchar and said, "And as for you, if you had stood by your brother's side he would not have been bound in this way." And he struck Ricchar with another blow of his axe and killed him. When these two were dead, the bodyguards who had betrayed them discovered that the golden gifts they had received from Clovis were fake. It is said that when they complained of this to Clovis he answered, "That is all the gold a man should expect when he willingly lures his own ruler to death," adding that they should be grateful for escaping with their lives instead of being tortured to death for having betrayed their masters. Hearing this, the men begged for mercy, asking only for their lives.

Now both of these kings, Ragnachar and Ricchar, were relatives of Clovis; so was their brother Rignomer, whom Clovis had put to death at Le Mans. Then, having killed all three, Clovis took over their kingdoms and their treasuries. He carried out the killing of many other kings and blood-relations in the same way—of anyone, really, whom he suspected of plotting against his realm—and in so doing he gradually extended his control over the whole of Gaul. One day he summoned an assembly of all his subjects, at which he is reported to have remarked about all the relatives he had destroyed, "How sad it is for me to live as a stranger among strangers, without any of my family here to help me when disaster happens!" But he said this not out of any genuine grief for their deaths, but only because he hoped somehow to flush out another relative whom he could kill.

GREGORY AND THE JEW (BK. VI, CH. 5)

King Chilperic, who was then still at Nogent-sur-Marne, sent his baggage train ahead while he made the rest of his plans to travel to Paris. I had gone to pay my respects before he left, and while I was visiting him a Jew named Priscus came in. This fellow was on familiar terms with the king, having been an agent on his behalf in some commercial ventures. Chilperic placed his hand on the Jew's head, in a gentle manner, and said to me, "Come, bishop! You lay your hand on him too!" Instantly the Jew pulled away. "'O faithless and perverse generation!'" the king quoted [Matthew 17.17], "why can't you accept what was promised to you by your own prophets? Can't you see that the mysteries of the Church were foretold by the sacrifices of your own people?"

The Jew answered, "God has no need of a son! He never had a son, and He does not have any partner in His kingdom! Indeed, He Himself said, through Moses, 'See now that I, I alone, am he, and there is no god besides me. It is I who bring both death and life, I who inflict wounds and heal them'." [Deut. 32.39]

The king responded, "But God brought forth, by His Spirit, His own eternal Son from a womb—a Son no younger than Himself in time, and no lesser than Himself in power. For God said, 'From the womb of the morning-star have I begotten you' [Psalm 110.3]. This Son, born at the beginning of time, He later sent to heal the world. Your own prophet has declared, 'He sent His word and healed them.' And as for your other claim, that God never had a Son, listen to another of your prophets, who put these words in His mouth: 'Shall I bring a mother to the point of birth, and yet not let her child be born?' He said this in regard to the people born in Him by faith."

The Jew answered, "How is it possible that God should be made man, or be born of a woman, or submit to lashing, or be condemned to death?"

At this point the king grew silent, so I took up the debate myself. "God's becoming man, as the Son of God," I said, "was the result of our needs, not His—for if He had not become man, then He could not have saved us from the prison of sin and servitude to the Devil. And now, as in the story we've both read of David slaying Goliath, I'll run you through with your own sword, pulling my proof not from the Gospels or the writings of any apostle (none of which you would accept) but from your own Scriptures. Listen to this, one of your own prophets prophesying:

He is both God and man, and who has known him?

"And also by the same:

Such is our God;
    and no other is to be compared to him
He has uncovered the whole way of understanding,
    and has given her to Jacob, his servant,
    to Israel, His beloved.

Afterwards did He show Himself upon earth,
    And conversed with mortals. [Baruch 3.37–38]

"And here is proof that He was born of a Virgin, from another of your prophets:

Behold, a virgin shall conceive and bear a son,
    And shall call him Emmanuel, "God is with us." [Isaiah 7.14]

"Still another prophet showed beyond doubt that He would submit to being lashed:

They pierced my hands and feet, and divided my garments among them. [Psalms 22.17]

"In another place this same prophet says:

They gave me poison for my food;
    And for my thirst they gave me vinegar to drink. [Psalms 69.22]

"And finally, to show that it would be through the Cross that He would restore the world (long lost to Satan) to His Kingdom, the same prophet David says:

The Lord reigns from a tree. [Psalms 96.10]

"But this doesn't mean that He did not reign before [the Crucifixion], together with the Father. Instead it means that He accepted a new and unprecedented dominion over the people whom He delivered from slavery to Satan."

The Jew then replied, "But why would God need to suffer these things?"

"I have already answered you," I said. "Mankind was innocent at Creation, but was tricked by the Serpent's guile and led to break God's commandment. Thus he was cast out of Paradise and condemned to suffer on the earth. It was only by the death of Christ, God's True and Only Son, that man was reconciled to God."

The Jew asked, "But couldn't God have sent more prophets or messengers to call mankind back to the path of salvation? Why did He Himself have to be humbled in the flesh?"

I retorted, "Mankind was inclined to sin from the very beginning of time. The Great Flood, the destruction of Sodom, the plagues on Egypt, the miracle of the parting of the sea and the river Jordan—none of these were enough to frighten mankind into obedience. He kept on resisting God's word and refusing to believe the prophets. More than that, he even killed the prophets who were preaching repentance! No, if God Himself had not come down from heaven, man's salvation would never have happened. We were reborn by Christ's baptism, cured by His wounds, raised up by His Resurrection, and glorified by His Ascension. Your own prophet declares the necessity of God's coming to heal us:

He bore the punishment that makes us whole,
    and by his wounds we were healed.
        [Isaiah 54.5]

"and he continues:

He bore the sins of many and interceded for the transgressors. [Isaiah 53.12]

"and:

Like a lamb led to slaughter,
    Or a sheep silent before shearers
    He did not open his mouth.
Seized and condemned, he was taken away.
    Who would have thought any more of his destiny?

"and:

The Lord of Hosts is his name. [Isaiah 54.5]

"This is the One of Whom Jacob speaks—the very Jacob whom you proudly claim as your ancestor—when he blesses his son, Judah; for in addressing Judah it is as though he is addressing Christ, the Son of God, in person:

You, Judah, shall your brothers praise
    —your hand on the neck of your enemies;
    the sons of your father shall bow down to you.
Judah is a lion's cub,
    You have grown up on prey, my son.
He crouches, lies down like a lion,
    Like a lioness—who would dare rouse him? . . .
His eyes are darker than wine,
    And his teeth are whiter than milk.
        [Genesis 49.8–9, 12]

"And even though Christ Himself said, 'No one takes [My life] from me, but I lay it down on my own,' the apostle Paul wrote, 'If you confess with your mouth that Jesus is Lord and believe in your heart that God raised him from the dead, you will be saved.'"

In spite of all my proofs, this wretched Jew was unyielding and showed no sign at all of believing me; instead, he just stood there in silence. King Chilperic recognized that he would never be made to feel remorse, no matter what we said, and so he turned to me and said that he had to leave but wanted my blessing first. "Bishop," he said, "I will say to you the words

Jacob said to the angel: 'I will not let you go unless you bless me'." [Genesis 32.26] And as he said this he ordered water to be brought to him. We both washed our hands, and I said a prayer. Then I took some bread, gave thanks to God for it, and received it along with the king. We drank some wine, and wished each other Farewell as we departed. Chilperic mounted his horse and set off for Paris, together with his wife, children, and all the members of his household.[1]

---

[1] Compare the biblical passages as translated by the Jewish Publication Society, noting first that the book of Baruch is not accepted in the Jewish canon.

    Isaiah 7.14: "Assuredly, my Lord will give you a sign of His own accord! Look, the young woman is with child and about to give birth to a son. Let her name him 'Immanuel'."

    Psalm 22.17: "Dogs surround me; a pack of evil ones closes in on me, like lions [they maul] my hands and feet."

    Psalm 69.22: "They give me gall for food, vinegar to quench my thirst."

    Psalm 96.10: "Declare among the nations, 'The Lord is king!' The world stands firm; it cannot be shaken; He judges the people with equity."

    Isaiah 54.5: "For He who made you will espouse you—His name is 'Lord of Hosts.' The Holy One of Israel will redeem you—He is called 'God of all the Earth'."

    Isaiah 53.12: "Whereas he bore the guilt of many and made intercession for sinners."

    Genesis 49.8–9, 12: "You, O Judah, your brothers shall praise; Your hand shall be on the nape of your foes; Your father's sons shall bow low to you. Judah is a lion's whelp; On prey, my son, have you grown. He crouches, lies down like a lion, Like the king of beasts—who dare rouse him? . . . His eyes are darker than wine; His teeth are whiter than milk."

3.4   Ethelbert of Kent, *Laws Regarding Women*

Ethelbert was king of Kent from roughly 590 to 616 and, inspired by St. Augustine of Canterbury, was the first English king to have converted to Christianity. He is also the author of the earliest surviving Germanic law code. Its text, written in Anglo-Saxon, survives in a single manuscript (a twelfth-century copy). The code consists of 90 distinct statutes that deal, in order, with offenses against the Church, the king, and his household (nos. 1–12); offenses against nobles (nos. 13–14); offenses against free commoners (nos. 15–32); *wergeld* compensation for personal injuries (nos. 33–72); offenses against women (nos. 73–84); offenses against servants (nos. 85–88); and offenses against slaves (nos. 89–90). Statutes regarding women are scattered among the various sections. Regarding the coinage: there were 20 *sceattas* in a shilling, and a shilling was roughly the amount of money it took to purchase an ox.

---

10. If any man has sex with a maiden belonging to the king, he shall pay 50 shillings in compensation.
11. If the maiden is a domestic slave, the compensation is 25 shillings; if she is a menial slave, 12 shillings.

14. If a man has sex with a nobleman's servant-girl, he is to pay 20 shillings in compensation.
16. If a man has sex with a commoner's servant-girl, he is to pay 6 shillings in compensation; if he has

sex with a commoner's domestic slave, then he is to pay 50 *sceattas*; if he has sex with a commoner's menial slave, he is to pay 30 *sceattas*.

31. If a commoner has sex with the wife of another commoner, he must pay the *wergeld*; he must also obtain another wife for the wronged commoner and deliver her to him.

64. If a man wounds another man's penis such that it is destroyed, he shall pay 3 times the *wergeld*; but if he [merely] damages it on the outside or inside, then he shall pay 6 shillings.

73. If a freewoman, one with long hair, commits any sort of misconduct, she is to pay 30 shillings in compensation.

74. The compensation owed for injury to a free-woman is to be the same as for a freeman.

75. Failure in guardianship over a noble-born widow of the highest rank is to be compensated by 50 shillings; a noble-born widow of the second class, 20 shillings; one of the third class, 12 shillings; one of the fourth class, 6 shillings.

76. If a man takes a widow who does not belong to him, the penalty shall be doubled.

77. If a man purchases a woman [for marriage], she is to be purchased for [a full bride payment of] cattle, and let there be no fraud. But if there is fraud, she is to be brought back to her home, and the man's property will be restored to him.

78. If she bears a child who lives, she is to receive half the property if the husband dies first.

79. If she wishes to leave [her husband], taking the children with her, she is to have half the property.

80. If the husband wishes to keep the children, the wife is have a child's portion.

81. If a wife does not bear a child, her kinsmen are to receive her goods and her morning-gift.

82. If a man carries off a maiden by force, he is to pay 50 shillings to her owner, and afterwards buy from the owner his consent [to the marriage].

83. If the maiden is already betrothed to another at a bride-price, he is to pay 20 shillings in compensation.

84. But if the woman is returned, the man who took her shall pay 35 shillings to her owner and another 15 shillings to the king.

85. If anyone has sex with a servant's wife while her husband is still alive, he shall pay a two-fold compensation.

4. CLOISTER AND CULTURE

4.1 Sulpicius Severus, *Life of St. Martin*

Just as Martin, Bishop of Tours (316–397), was among the most popular of saints in the Middle Ages, so too was the *Life* written of him by Sulpicius Severus (363–425) among the most widely read of medieval hagiographies. In fact, it served as a model for most subsequent efforts to narrate the miraculous deeds of the saints. Sulpicius came from a wealthy aristocratic family and spent most of his life near Toulouse, in southwest France. He received a solid classical education and worked for a time as a lawyer. An early marriage ended with his wife's death, and it was shortly afterwards that Sulpicius met Martin, who converted him to Christianity and persuaded him (much against his father's wishes) to sell all he owned and give the money away to the poor. From that time on, Sulpicius was a dedicated follower of Martin.

[2] Martin was born at Savaria in the province of Pannonia [today Szombathely, in Hungary], but grew up at Pavia, in Italy. His parents were of some social status, as the world reckons such things—his father, in fact, served as a military tribune (though he had begun as a rank-and-file soldier). But they were both pagans. In his early years Martin was enthusiastic for the military life and he enlisted in the imperial guard, serving first the emperor Constantine [r. 306–337] and afterwards Julian [r. 360–363]. But his heart was never fully in military matters, for from his youth he harbored a desire to serve [the Christian] God instead. . . . But when an imperial edict was issued declaring that the sons of military veterans were required to undertake military service themselves, his father (who had long looked askance on his son's Christian aspirations) enrolled him in the army. Martin subsequently was captured and chained by some officials and was dragged away to take the oath of service. He was only fifteen at the time. . . .

[3] Once, in the middle of a winter that was much more severe than usual, so much that the bitter cold was killing many people, Martin happened upon a poor old beggar, dressed in rags, at the gate to the city of Amiens. Martin was wearing nothing but his plain military garb, and began to beg passers-by to take pity on the old man, but they simply moved on without notice . . . what should he do? He himself had nothing but a cloak, having already given away the rest of his clothes to the needy. So he pulled out his sword and cut his cloak in half, giving one part to the old beggar and keeping the other half for himself. . . .

[5] After resigning from military service Martin set off in search of Hilary, the bishop of Poitiers [d. 368]. Hilary was renowned for his faith and was held in universal esteem; Martin lived with him for some time, and Hilary ordained him into the office of deacon. Wanting to bind Martin even more closely to him, Hilary tried to persuade Martin to take priestly orders so they could celebrate the Holy Mass together, but Martin always refused, asserting that he was unworthy. That was when Hilary, a perceptive man, saw that the only way he could persuade Martin to accept a higher station would be to appoint him to a position that could actually be harmful to him—and so he appointed Martin to be an exorcist. Martin did not refuse this mission, for he feared that, if he refused, people might suspect him looking down on it as beneath him. Not long afterward, he was warned in a dream that he should hasten to visit his parents [in Pannonia], who were still deeply attached to their pagan ways, and bring them to the right path. He set out at once, with

Hilary's blessing, although his patron (amid many tears and prayers) made him promise to return as soon as he could. It is reported that Martin began his journey in a melancholy mood, having told his friends that he felt sure that many sufferings lay ahead of him.

His prediction came true. First, while following some winding paths through the Alps, he was attacked by robbers. One of them raised his axe high and aimed it at Martin's head, but another robber blocked the blow with his right hand. Martin was then handed over, hands bound behind his back, to a third robber, who was to strip him and stand guard over him; but this robber pulled Martin away so they could talk privately and asked him who he was. Martin replied that he was a Christian, nothing more. When asked if he was afraid, Martin answered confidently that he had never before felt so safe, for he knew that God in His mercy would be especially close to him in his trials, then added that he felt sorry for the robber because by living a life of crime he was showing himself unworthy of the mercy of Christ. This led to a long discussion, during which Martin preached the gospel truth to the robber. Why waste time in saying it—the robber came to the Lord. Stopping only to express his gratitude, he sent Martin on his way, entreating him to keep him in his prayers. This robber later entered the religious life, and in fact the account I have given here is based on his own testimony.

[6] Martin left that place, and after he had passed the city of Milan Satan himself confronted him on the road, having taken the form of a man. "Where are you going?" asked the devil.

"Wherever the Lord leads me," answered Martin.

"No matter where you go or what you do," said Satan, "the Evil One will oppose you."

Martin replied in a prophetic voice, "The Lord is my helper; I will not fear what any man can do to me." Instantly, the Enemy vanished out of sight. Martin continued on his way, and fulfilled his heart's wish by freeing his mother from the error of her paganism. (His father continued to cling to its evil ways, however.) Nevertheless, Martin saved many people by his ministry.

In the meantime the Arian heresy spread throughout the world and took deep root in Illyria. There, Martin struggled against it mightily and almost singlehanded since many of the local priests plotted against him and he was frequently attacked. Once he was even publicly flogged, after which he had to leave the city he was in. Martin then traveled to Italy, where he learned that the churches in Gaul were in a sorry state after the departure of the blessed Hilary—who had been driven into exile by a group of violent heretics—and so he stayed in Milan and established a monastery of his own. But even there he was not safe, for Auxentius [d. 374], the founder and leader of the Arians there, persecuted him bitterly, attacking him numerous times until he finally forced him from the city. Seeing no alternative, Martin withdrew to the island of Gallinaria [today, Isola d'Albenga] where he lived with a certain priest (a most excellent man) as his only companion. In time he was reduced to eating the roots of plants, and thus he unwittingly ate hellebore, which is, as many know, poisonous. Sensing the poison course through him and feeling close to death, Martin fought back by means of prayer—and in an instant all his pain subsided. Shortly thereafter he heard the news that the emperor [Constantius II, r. 350–361] had repented of his rashness and had invited blessed Hilary [whom he had sent into exile in 356, on account of his campaign against Arianism] to return to Gaul. Martin hoped to meet Hilary at Rome, and set out for there at once.

[7] Hilary had left, though, by the time Martin got there, so Martin hurried after him into Gaul. They finally reunited at Poitiers and celebrated. Martin then established a monastery for himself not far from the town [at Ligugé], where he was soon joined by a catechumen who was eager to learn all that Martin could teach him about the ways of holiness. After only a few days, however, the catechumen took ill and was confined to his bed with a violent fever. Martin happened to be away from the monastery for a few days, and when he returned he found the catechumen had died. He had not been baptized. His body was laid out by the other monks, who were performing their mournful offices over it, when Martin approached, full of tears and lamentation. Calling up the Holy Spirit by fervent prayer, Martin asked the other monks to leave the cell where the body lay, then bolted the door behind them and stretched out his own body full-length on top of the departed brother. He spent a long time in earnest prayer. And then, feeling the power of the Holy Spirit to be present, Martin lifted his head a little and looked his

dead brother in the face, waiting for the Spirit of the Lord to show His mercy—and only two hours later he clearly saw the dead catechumen stir back to life and his eyes flicker open. Martin shouted out to the Lord in thanksgiving, which prompted the monks who were standing outside the door to come rushing inside, where they beheld the miracle of the dead monk brought back to life. This fellow, restored to life, immediately received baptism and lived for many years afterward. He was, in fact, the first witness who offered his testimony to me of Martin's miraculous power. . . .

[8] Not long afterwards, another miracle. Martin happened to be passing by the estate of a man named Lupicinus, a man well respected in the region; a crowd of people came out to Martin, shouting and wailing. When Martin, concerned, asked them the reason for their sorrow, they told him that one of the family's slaves had killed himself by hanging. Martin immediately ran to the room where the corpse was laid out, and again he asked the crowd to leave them alone, then stretched his own body out on top of the dead man, and began to pray. It was not long before the slave returned to life, his face beaming and his eyes fixed on Martin's. In a tentative effort to rise, the slave took the right hand of the saintly man, and with his help rose to his feet. Then he emerged with Martin and walked to the porch of the house while the whole crowd watched and marveled.

Hilary died at Poitiers in 368. Three years later Martin was appointed the bishop of Tours.

---

[10] It is beyond my power to describe adequately how Martin distinguished himself in the performance of his episcopal duties. Let me simply state that he remained perfectly true to all the virtues he had shown before—the same humble heart, the same simplicity of dress, the same combination of dignity and courtesy. He fulfilled his duties as a bishop should, but never lost sight of the discipline and virtue of a monk. For some time, in fact, he continued to use the cell attached to the church. Eventually, however, the sheer number of people who visited him there made life intolerable, so he built a retreat for himself about two miles outside the city in a secret location, where he could occasionally retire and enjoy the solitude of a hermit. On one side it had an enormous boulder that had tumbled down from the mountain above, while the rest of its perimeter consisted of a kind of bay that stretched out from the river Loire; thus the retreat could only be approached by a single, narrow, pathway. He, then, built his simple wooden retreat. Many other monks also established little sanctuaries for themselves in the region, but most of these consisted of caves and hollows in the side of the overhanging mountain. There were about eighty such hermits in all, all of whom patterned themselves after the saintly example set by Martin. No one owned anything, all possessions were shared; buying and selling were strictly forbidden. The only art practiced by them was scribal copying, but even this was done only by the younger monks; the older ones spent all of their time in prayer. Except for when they assembled for group prayer or meals (which they shared after completing their ritual fasts), none of them ever emerged from their places of refuge. No wine was ever drunk, except when medically necessary. Most of the brethren wore rough hair-shirts; anything soft they avoided as though to wear it were a crime—a fact all the more remarkable when one considers how many of them had come from noble families. For despite their upbringing, they now accepted an exceptional degree of humility and longsuffering. Many of them later became bishops themselves. After all, what city or church would not want to have priests drawn from the monastic discipline of blessed Martin? . . .

[15] I must tell you what happened in the village of Aedui. Martin had gone there to destroy a pagan temple, and as he was doing so a large number of pagan farmers rushed at him in fury. One of them was bold enough to pull out a sword—but Martin calmly pulled back his cloak and stretched out his bare neck for the man to attack. The fellow did not hesitate an instant and began to swing. Suddenly he crashed to the

ground, struck down by the fear of Almighty God and begging Martin to forgive him.

On another occasion, Martin was destroying a number of pagan idols somewhere when another fellow advanced on him with a knife. Even as he lunged to stab Martin, though, the knife simply disappeared.

It sometimes happened, too, that Martin confronted angry crowds of pagans determined to protect their temples, and simply by the power of his words he so won over the people that they embraced the light of Truth he revealed to them and willingly demolished their own pagan altars. . . .

[26–27] Now it is time to bring this book to an end; I have had my say. I finish now not because I have run out of things to praise about Martin, but because just as exhausted poets often grow less careful toward the end of a long work, I am aware that I am worn out by the sheer vastness of his virtue. For while I could describe adequately his outward deeds, no words I possess could ever do justice to the inner life and discipline

of his spirit. His mind was constantly on heaven, such that no one could ever adequately describe his perseverance and self-control in fasting and in chastity, his diligence in performing prayer-vigils. . . . If Homer himself were to rise from the shades below, he could not do justice to this man. . . .

No one ever saw him angry or giddy, or lost in despair or levity. He was steady and sure, always displaying a kind of heavenly happiness; he seemed at times to have surpassed the limits of human nature. There never was a word on his lips except "Christ," just as there was never anything in his heart except piety, peace, and tender mercy. . . . I conclude with the simple observation that anyone who can read this narrative and still not believe [in Martin's holiness], is certain to be lost to sin. I am aware that I have been led to write these things out of persuasion by the facts, as well as by love of Christ . . . and I am confident that God has prepared a special reward for anyone who not only reads what I have written but believes it all.

4.2   St. Gregory the Great, *The Life of Saint Benedict* and *Letter to Empress Constantina*

Pope Gregory I (r. 590–604) was the first Roman pontiff to wield anything like universally recognized authority in Christendom, although his prestige may have owed more to his person than his office. Certainly he is the first pope to leave behind enough writings to permit a full view of his complex and multi-faceted personality. In the first reading below, his *Life of St. Benedict* (which forms one part of a much larger work called the Dialogues), Gregory reveals as much of his own character as of Benedict's. The second selection presents a letter he sent to the Byzantine empress Constantina, tactfully explaining why he could not grant her demand to have the head of St. Paul sent to her by courier.

LIFE OF ST. BENEDICT [CH. 1–2, 11, 38]

[1] There once was a man who led a most venerable life, blessed by grace and in name, for he was called Benedict. Even as a youth he possessed the mind of a mature man. He was always younger in years than he was in virtue, and although he lived in the world and had opportunity to enjoy all the delights it has to offer,

he always despised vain pleasure. The world's vanities he regarded as worthless nothings. Born to noble parents in the district of Nursia, Benedict was raised in Rome where he had the opportunity to study the human arts, but since he saw so many people, similarly situated, fall into dissolute and base ways, he stepped back from the world he knew. He feared becoming too well acquainted with lewdness, which would end only in a headlong fall into a dangerous and godless existence. Therefore he gave up his studies and renounced his claim to his father's house and wealth, and wanting nothing more than to serve God, he went out in search of a place where he could pursue his longing for a holy purpose in life. He went forth, armed with a simple wisdom that took the place of his learned but ignorant scholarship.

I was unable to unearth all the marvelous things he did in his life, but I did manage to learn any number of things about him (which I now record) from four of his disciples: Constantinus, an exceptional and pious man who succeeded Benedict as abbot; Valentinianus, who was in charge of the Lateran Abbey for many years; Simplicius, the third minister-general of Benedict's order; and Honoratus, who is currently the abbot of the monastery where Benedict began his sanctified life.

[2] One day when Benedict was alone, temptation came to him in the form of a blackbird that flew so closely about his face that, if he could, the holy man might have grabbed it with his hand. Instead, he simply blessed himself by making the sign of the cross—and the bird flew away. He was beset, however, by a terrible bout of temptation of the flesh such as he had never experienced before.

He had once happened to see a particular woman, and the spirit of temptation burned her memory into his mind, and the image of her now inflamed him with lust so powerfully that for a moment the servant of God nearly was overcome with it. The thought of abandoning his wilderness life came upon him, but with God's grace he came to his senses. Seeing a thick patch of briar- and nettle-bushes growing nearby, Benedict threw off his clothing and leapt headlong into them, rolling back and forth so long that by the time he stood up his flesh was covered with the most pitiful lacerations. The wounds to his body cured the wounds to his soul by turning its pleasure into pain, and by the searing hurt to his outer form, he quenched the raging fire of lustful thought within his soul. One fire replaced another, and he overcame his sin.

He would often tell his disciples in later years that this episode so reduced any temptation of the flesh in him that he scarcely ever felt it anymore. Many people soon began to abandon the world too, in the hope of becoming one of his disciples—for having freed himself from temptation he turned himself into a man of masterful virtue. In the book of Exodus, recall, Moses commands the Levites that while men may serve as priests from the age twenty-five, only those aged fifty and above may be ordained as keepers of the holy vessels. [Num 8.24–26]. . . .

[11] Another time a group of monks were working on an extension to a certain wall when the Old Enemy [Satan] appeared to Benedict, that man of God, as he was praying in his cell, and jeered at him, saying that he was going to cause trouble with the monks. Benedict's spirit then rushed to the monks' aid, telling them to be careful for the devil was at hand. No sooner had Benedict's voice spoken than the Evil Spirit knocked down the wall on which the monks had been working, and killed a young monk—a boy, really, the son of a certain nobleman. This pitiful occurrence drove everyone into a profound grief, not for the wall but for the death of their little brother. The monks wasted no time in bringing the sad news to Benedict, who quickly ordered them to bring him the lad's body. Being so mangled and maimed, the body had to be delivered in a sack since the stones of the wall had not only broken the boy's limbs but had crushed his very bones.

Benedict had the monks lay the boy on the floor in his cell, on the precise spot where he always knelt when in prayer. Then he sent the monks away, closed his cell door, and immediately began to pray. What a marvel then occurred! Within the space of an hour Benedict's prayers had healed the boy, who stood up as lively as ever and returned to his work, helping the monks repair the wall. The Old Serpent had thought he could insult Benedict, but Benedict emerged triumphant. . . .

[38] The cave [at Subiaco] where Benedict first took up his solitary vigil even to this day continues to work miracles, if those who pray there are in need of them. What I am about to tell you happened only recently. A certain woman had so lost the use of reason that she became insane and spent days and nights on end walking up and down and back and forth, in mountains, in valleys, through woods and fields, and rested only when she collapsed from exhaustion, wherever that happened to occur. It happened one day that, wandering again at random, she chanced to arrive at Blessed Benedict's cave. Not knowing anything about the site,

she entered the cave and spent the night. The following morning she awoke fully healed, her mind and wits as sound as they had ever been, and to the day she died she lived a healthy existence, as though her madness had never happened. . . .

There can be no doubt that the saints perform countless miracles at the spots where they lie buried. . . . Since simple-minded people might doubt whether or not a particular saint is actually present to hear their prayers, he or she works an even greater miracle at the site [than elsewhere] to compensate for the weakness of the visitors' souls. But he whose mind is firmly fixed on God has a stronger faith, and he knows that the saint is there in spirit to hear his prayer even though he may not be there in body. For as Our Savior himself said, "If I do not go, the Advocate will not come to you." [John 16.7]

* * * * *

LETTER 30

Gregory to Constantina.

Most Serene and Pious Lady, inspired by the great zeal for religion and the love of holiness that have made you so famous, you have seen fit to charge me with the order of sending you the head of St. Paul, or perhaps some other part of his body, so that it may be placed in the church you are building in his honor in your palace. Looking forward as I do to receiving any command from you—so that by my prompt obedience I might ever encourage your good favor toward me—it grieves me to report that I neither can nor even dare to carry out what you ask of me. The bodies of those great apostles, Sts. Peter and Paul, glow with such miraculous and terrifying power that one cannot even enter their church to pray without great fear. To offer a simple example: when my predecessor of blessed memory [Pelagius II (r. 579–590)] wanted to re-cast the silver that overlays the tomb of the Blessed Peter, a pall of dread halted him in his steps when he was still fifteen feet from the tomb. I myself likewise had it in mind once to repair some items not far from St. Paul's tomb, and for this it was necessary to dig fairly deeply at a spot near his resting place. The project foreman subsequently found some bones while digging, and even though they were certainly not Paul's own, the simple facts that they were near Paul's tomb and that their

disinterment disturbed the site were enough to cause terrible portents. The foreman died on the spot. . . .

Apart from these particulars, Most Serene Lady, you should know that it is a Roman custom, when transferring holy relics, never to touch the actual body of the saint in any way. Our relics remain enclosed at all times. Whenever a relic transfer is performed, we place a fine cloth inside a reliquary and set it near the actual tomb of the saint; this reliquary is afterward lifted with all due reverence and deposited in the [new] church dedicated to the saint. By this rite alone such miraculous power is transferred to the cloth that it is indeed as though the saint's very bones were introduced into the newly dedicated church. It happened in the pontificate of Leo of blessed memory [Leo I (r. 440–461)], I once heard, that when a number of Greeks expressed their doubts to him about this practice, he pulled out a pair a scissors and cut one such cloth *from which blood began immediately to flow.* Thus here in Rome and throughout all of western Europe it is an unthinkable sacrilege to want to touch directly the body of a saint. The temerity even to think of such a thing, we believe, will not go unpunished. This is why we can scarcely believe it when you Greeks say that you often take up the bones of saints. A little more than two years ago a number of Greek monks came here and dug up, in the silence of the night, the bodies of some men in a field not far from St. Paul's tomb. They then packaged up the bones and prepared to take them back to Greece—and when we stopped them and inquired into their actions, they replied that they intended simply to bring the bones to Greece and pass them off as holy relics. . . .

I trust in Almighty God that I will not lose your kind good will toward me [by this refusal]. I pray that the power of the holy apostles, whom I know you love with all your heart and soul, will always protect you—even if their actual bodies are not there with you in Constantinople. As for the wrapping cloth [around St. Paul's bones] that you also requested, I am afraid that it cannot be touched or even approached. However, My Serene Lady, since I would not have desires as pious as yours go entirely unsatisfied, I will gladly send you some links from the chains that bound St. Peter, by his neck and hands, when he was held in prison. Countless miracles have been attributed to these chains by our people. I have now only to manage to remove a few links by filing. . . .

4.3 St. Benedict, *The Rule of St. Benedict*

St. Benedict of Nursia (480–547) turned to an ascetic life after he became disgusted with the lax morals of early medieval Rome. Initially a solitary hermit, he gradually came to favor communal monastic living and wrote the *Rule* that bears his name. His *Rule* was based on an earlier monastic constitution (its author is unknown) called the *Rule of the Master*—an echo of which can be heard in the prologue that follows. By the time of Charlemagne, if not earlier, Benedict's model of monastic life had become the default position of Latin monasticism. After the prologue, I include the text of the fourth chapter of the *Rule*, which delineates the "good works" required of monks.

PROLOGUE

My son, listen to your master's words and open your heart to them. Your loving father offers you advice that you should receive gladly and carry out with determination, in order that through the virtue of obedience you may return to the Lord, from Whom you strayed on account of the sloth of your disobedience. I address these words of mine to you—whoever you might be—who is preparing to renounce your own will in order to do battle under the Lord Christ, our True King, by taking up the strong and gleaming weapons of obedience.

First of all, whenever you begin good works of any sort, beg the Lord with most earnest prayer to perfect them, so that He Who has mercifully counted us among His children may not ever be grieved by our sinful behavior—for we must always serve the Lord with the good things He has blessed us with, in order that He will never, as an angry Father, disinherit His children, nor ever, as a fearsome Lord, be so provoked by our sins that He hand us over to everlasting punishment, like wicked servants who stubbornly refuse to follow Him in His glory.

So let us arise, then, for as the Scriptures say, "Now is the hour for us to rise from sleep." Let us open our eyes to the divine light and our ears to the warning that the divine voice cries out to us every day, "Today, if you hear His voice, do not harden your hearts." And again, "He who has ears to hear, let him hear what the Spirit says to the churches." And what does He say? "Come, My children, and listen to Me; I will teach you the fear of the Lord. Run while you have the light of life, lest the darkness of death overtake you."

The Lord, seeking His [loyal] worker in the crowd to which He calls out, says, "Who is the man who will have life, and desires to see good days?" If you hear Him and answer, "I am," then God will respond in turn, "If you will have everlasting life, keep your tongue from evil and your lips that they speak no guile. Turn away from evil and do good; seek peace and pursue it. When you have done these things, My eyes will be upon you, and My ears will be open to your prayers—such that even before you call upon Me, I will say to you, 'Behold, here I am'."

My brothers, what can be sweeter than this—the voice of the Lord inviting us? For in His loving kindness the Lord shows us the way of life.

Therefore gird up your loins with faith and good works, and let us walk in His ways, guided by the Gospels, that we may deserve to behold Him Who has called us to His kingdom. For if we wish to dwell in the tent of that kingdom, we must rush to it by good works, or else we will never reach it. But, like the prophet, let us ask the Lord, "Who shall dwell in Your tent, O Lord, and who shall rest on Your holy mountain?" And having asked this, my brothers, let us listen to His answer as He shows us the way to His tent. He answers, "He who walks without stain and practices justice; he who speaks truth from his heart; he who does not use his tongue for deceit; he who does no evil to his neighbor; he who has done no slander to another."

It is also the one who, despite the evil temptations of the devil, stands firm and casts those temptations and the devil himself aside, far from his heart; the one who is quick to grab hold of the devil's thoughts and dash them against the rock of Christ.

It is they, the many, who fear the Lord and do not pride themselves on their good observance; they who, convinced that all that is good in them cannot come from themselves but from God, glorify the Lord's work in them, in the words of the prophet, "Not to us, O Lord, not to us, but to Your Name be the glory." The apostle Paul similarly attributed the success of his preaching not to himself, saying, "By the grace of God I am what I am," and also, "He who glories, let him glory in the Lord."

The Lord Himself says in the Gospel, "Whoever listens to these words of Mine and acts upon them, I will liken him to the wise man who built his house upon rock: the floods came, the winds blew and beat against the house, but it did not fall because it was built upon rock." Having given us this assurance, the Lord waits every day for us to respond to His admonition by our good deeds. The days of this life are lengthened and a truce is granted for this very reason, that we may amend our sinful ways. As the apostle says, "Do you not know that God's patience is inviting you to repent?" The Lord in His mercy tells us, "I desire not the death of the sinner, but that he should be converted and live."

And so, my brothers, now that we have asked the Lord who is to dwell in His tent, and now that we have heard His response to all who would dwell there, it remains for us to do what we are supposed to do. Therefore let us prepare our hearts and bodies to do battle, in the spirit of holy obedience to His commands, and let us beseech God that it may please Him to grant us the blessing of His grace when confronting anything which is too challenging for us. If we wish to escape the pains of hell and attain life everlasting, then now, while there is still time and we have health and strength to do what we should, let us undertake those actions that will help us to gain eternity.

For this reason we are resolved to build a school that will serve the Lord. In establishing it we intend not to introduce any discipline that is too harsh or burdensome; however, if a certain strictness should arise from our desire to pursue what is right for the amendment of vice and the preservation of charity, we hope you will not be dismayed and flee from this path to salvation—a path whose entrance cannot be other than narrow. As we grow in faith and in the religious life, our hearts grow too—and soon enough we happily run the way of God's commandments with an indescribable sweetness of love. And thus, by resolving never to leave His school but to remain dedicated to it according to His teaching until death, we may patiently share in the sufferings of Christ and earn a share in His kingdom.

CHAPTER FOUR: THE INSTRUMENTS OF GOOD WORKS

1. First, to love the Lord God with the whole heart, the whole soul, and the whole strength.
2. Next, to love one's neighbor as oneself.
3. Next, not to murder.
4. Then, not to commit adultery.
5. Not to steal.
6. Not to covet.
7. Not to bear false witness.
8. To respect all.
9. Not to do to another what one would not want done to oneself.
10. To deny oneself in order to follow Christ.
11. To chastise the body.
12. Not to become attached to pleasures.
13. To love fasting.
14. To relieve the poor.
15. To clothe the naked.
16. To visit the sick.
17. To bury the dead.
18. To help those in trouble.
19. To comfort the sorrowful.
20. To become a stranger to the ways of the world.
21. To prefer nothing to the love of Christ.
22. Not to give way to anger.
23. Not to hold a grudge.
24. Not to entertain deceit in one's heart.
25. Not to give a false peace.
26. Not to forsake charity.
27. Not to swear, out of fear of perjury.
28. To speak the truth from the heart and the lips.
29. Not to return evil for evil.
30. To do no wrong to anyone, and to bear in patience the wrongs done to oneself.
31. To love one's enemies.
32. Not to curse those who curse us, but to bless them.
33. To endure persecution for the sake of justice.
34. Not to be proud.

35. Not to be addicted to wine.
36. Not to be a glutton.
37. Not to be half-awake.
38. Not to be lazy.
39. Not to complain.
40. Not to detract from others.
41. To put one's hope in God.
42. To credit God, not oneself, for what is good in oneself.
43. To recognize always that one's evil actions are one's own doing, and admit it.
44. To fear the Day of Judgment.
45. To fear Hell.
46. To desire eternal life with all the passion of the spirit.
47. To keep death constantly before one's eyes.
48. To be ever vigilant over one's actions.
49. To know for certain that God sees one everywhere.
50. When evil thoughts enter one's heart, to break them instantly against the rock of Christ.
51. To make them known to one's spiritual guide.
52. To guard one's tongue against evil and depraved speech.
53. Not to love talking too much.
54. Not to speak silly words that move one to laughter.
55. Not to love boisterous laughter.
56. To listen readily to the sacred readings.
57. To devote oneself to frequent prayer.
58. To confess one's sins to God every day, with tears and sighs, and to amend them in the future.
59. Not to fulfill the desires of the flesh, and to hate one's will.
60. To obey at all times the commands of the abbot, even if (God forbid) he should act improperly, mindful of the Lord's command, "Do what they say, not what they do."
61. Not to wish to be called holy before one is holy; rather, be holy in order to be called holy.
62. To fulfill God's commandments every day.
63. To love chastity.
64. To hate no one.
65. Not to be jealous or envious.
66. Not to love contention.
67. To beware of pride.
68. To respect one's elders.
69. To love one's minors.
70. To pray for one's enemies, in the love of Christ.
71. To make peace with one's adversary before sunset.
72. Never to despair of God's mercy.

4.4 Caesarius of Arles, *Rule for Nuns*

Bishop Caesarius of Arles (470–542) was one of the leading ecclesiastical figures of the sixth century, noted especially for his efforts to help the poor rustics caught in the crossfire of the ongoing wars between Burgundians, Franks, Ostrogoths, and Visigoths. As bishop he distributed food to the starving peasants of his diocese regardless of their ethnicity or religion, ransomed captives of war, and consistently championed the inclusion of the laity in church worship services. Over 250 of his sermons survive, but he is best remembered for the *Regula ad virgines*, or the *Rule for Nuns*—the first monastic rule written specifically for women.

To his holy and venerable sisters in Christ, residing in the monastery we established with God's help and inspiration, Bishop Caesarius sends greeting.

[1] Since Our Merciful Lord saw fit to inspire me to establish a monastery for you, I have taken it upon myself to establish for you in addition some spiritual and religious precepts on how you ought to live in that monastery, basing these on the statutes laid down by the ancient fathers. In order that, with God's help, you may adhere to these precepts, you must constantly invoke in prayer the assistance of the Son of God while living in your monastic cells. Only thus may you later

say with confidence, "I found him whom my soul loves." [Cant. 3.4] . . .

[2] Monasteries of women being different from those of men, I have chosen selectively from older statutes, looking for precepts suitable to both younger and older women, so that they may fulfill their spiritual calling in ways suitable to their sex.

These are the things I deem best suited to your blessed souls. If any maiden, leaving her parents, wishes to renounce the world and enter the holy flock and thereby seek to escape (with God's help) the jaws of spiritual wolves, then let her not leave this monastery until she dies—not even to enter a church, where she may be seen.

[3] She should strive, too, to avoid making any oaths or curses, shunning them as though they are the venom of the devil himself.

[4] Having been converted [to monastic life] by God's holy inspiration, she ought not to put on the clothing of the religious right away, unless her determination has already been proven by surviving many challenges. Instead, let her retain her own clothing for an entire year while living under the care of one of the senior nuns. The questions of whether or when she may exchange her clothing [for a religious habit] and take a bed in the regular community should be under the jurisdiction of the prior. When he judges her ready in body and spirit, whether earlier or later, the decision is his.

[5] Women who come to the monastery as widows, or who have left their husbands, even if they have already changed their clothing, are not exempted from this precept: they must first relinquish all that they own, by deed, gift, or sale, and dispossess themselves of everything they possess or control. This is according to God's own command: "If you wish to be complete, go and sell your possessions" [Matthew 19.21], and "So then, none of you can be my disciple who does not give up all his possessions" [Luke 14.33]. That is why I say, dear daughters, that a nun who has [private] possessions cannot achieve perfection. Even those of you who enter religious life as chaste virgins, if you do not fulfill this command, you neither will be received nor allowed to put on religious garb until you have freed yourself entirely from the possessions and cares of the world. . . .

[7] None of you—not even your abbess—is to have a nun as a servant. If one of you is in need, then ask assistance from one of the younger sisters. Moreover you must do all that you can to avoid taking into the monastery any girl until she is at least six or seven years old, can read and write, and is capable of obeying this Rule. No matter if they are the daughters of nobles or of commoners, no girl is to be received simply for the purpose of raising her or teaching her.

[8] No nun is to choose for herself what works or daily tasks she shall perform; it is the business of the mother superior to decide such duties.

[9] No nun shall be allowed to choose private accommodations, nor to have a bedroom of her own; neither should she have a chest that can be locked up privately. All nuns should stay in a single room, though in separate beds. In order to give proper care to nuns who are sick or worn out with age, they should not be placed in single cells but instead all be housed in a single ward, where they shall remain.

Let no nun ever speak with a loud voice, following the word of the Apostle, "Let all clamor be put away from you." [Ephesians 4.31] Loud speaking is never useful or suitable.

[10] In a similar vein, no talking or activity is permitted during hymns.

[11] Let no nun presume to serve as godmother to any girl, rich or poor, for one who has relinquished her own liberty out of love for God ought not to seek or have the love of others. Only thus can she devote herself wholly to God, without impediment. . . .

[19] All sisters are to learn to read and shall dedicate two full hours to reading daily, from sunrise until the second hour of the day. For the rest of the day after that, let them go about their duties, losing no time in idle conversation. . . .

[23] Resist every effort by Satan to desire the gaze of men. You cannot say you have a chaste soul if you have unchaste eyes, for an unchaste eye is the telltale sign of an unchaste heart. If one of you does look lustfully on a man, do not think you have not been seen, for you most certainly will be seen even if you think you have not—for even if not witnessed by another person, what about God Who sees all? Nothing is hidden from God. . . .

[24] If any of you sees another sister behaving more freely than is proper, admonish her in private as your sister—and only if she does not heed you, should you bring it to the attention of the mother superior. . . .

[25] And if one of you (God forbid!) should succumb to such evil temptation as to receive letters, advice, or gifts from someone, let her be forgiven and prayers be said for her, if she confesses this voluntarily. But if she is accused or proven wrong while trying to keep such behavior secret, let her be treated more severely, according to the statutes of the monastery. . . .

[36] In order to protect your reputations, above all, let no man enter the private domain of the monastery or into the oratory. The only exceptions to this rule are bishops or the monastery's patron (who may enter if accompanied by a priest, deacon, sub-deacon and one or two lectors, if of suitable age and reputation), who must celebrate masses on occasion. If your building needs repair or remodeling, if new doors or windows need to be built, or if any other such repair is required, then whatever craftsmen and workers as are necessary may enter, but only if they are accompanied by the monastery's patron, and only if this is

done with the full knowledge and permission of the mother superior. . . .

[40] If any woman from another city comes to the monastery to inquire after her daughter or simply to visit the monastery, let her do so if she is a religious; and if the abbess deems it permissible, she should be invited to a banquet. But apart from these cases, no others should be allowed in—for holy virgins dedicated to God ought to pray for all people everywhere, as part of their devotion to Christ, rather than keep busy preparing worldly feasts. If a female visitor wishes to see her sister or daughter, or any other kinswoman, she should be allowed to converse with her, if in the presence of the hospital matron or some other senior nun. . . .

[47] I admonish and urge you, most blessed and venerable mother superior, and you, prioress of the holy congregation, before God and His angels, never to succumb to any arguments or pressures to weaken your will such that you relax any part of the institution of this holy and spiritual Rule. If you remain steadfast, I am confident that by God's mercy you will not be found wanting, and your holy obedience will prove so pleasing to God that you will happily gain eternal bliss in paradise.

5. THE EMERGENCE OF THE MEDIEVAL WORLDS

5.1 Gildas, *On the Ruin of Britain*

Gildas (500–570) was a British cleric living when the last of Roman culture in Britain was snuffed out by Germanic invaders (the era that gave birth to the Arthurian legends). As the primary contemporary account of British events in the sixth century, Gildas's three-part sermon offers his explanation of why the situation had become so dire: because of the sins and corruption of the British kings, people, and clergy. The work is modeled on the biblical prophets who decry the state of the world and warn civilization that it must change, before it is too late.

[1.3–4] The island of Britain sits almost at the edge of the world, off to the west and northwest, where it plays its part in what is called the divine balance that sustains the entire world. From its southwestern tip it stretches some eight hundred miles to the north and another two hundred across, not counting several promontories that reach out from curved bays. It is protected by broad, impassable seas on all sides except for the straits on the southern coast, where ships cross to Belgian Gaul. It benefits from the estuaries of two great rivers—the Thames and the Severn—along which valuable goods from other lands come via ships. There are also many smaller streams, twenty-eight cities, numerous strongholds, and some other major, if unremarkable, monuments—walls, fortified towers, gates, and houses whose roofs are firmly built even though they appear dangerously high. Britain is rich with widespread plains, well-situated hills that are amenable to cultivation, and mountains that provide convenient pasturage for cattle. Colorful flowers line the paths along these highlands, giving them a beautiful appearance like that of a bride adorned with bright jewels. The land is fed by many clear springs, whose flowing waters bring a cascade of snow-white gravel; by many bright rivers that move with a gentle murmur, offering to those relaxing on their banks a promise of sweet sleep; and by many lakes that overflow with cool streams of living water.

The history of this island, so proud and resilient from its origins, is one of ungrateful rebellion—rebellion against God, against its fellow men, and sometimes against distant kings and their peoples. Of all that reckless men are capable of doing, what vileness and unrighteousness can be worse than to deny God the fear that is owed Him, to deny charity to one's fellow man, and to deny honor to those in positions of authority over them? What can do greater harm to our faith than to violate heavenly and human desires, or, having already violated these, to give oneself over to lusts and selfishness?

I pass over in silence the ancient sins by which the whole human race was held in bondage before the coming of Christ; neither will I bother to narrate the most hellish horrors (surpassing in number even those of the Egyptians) of my native land. True, some of these exist even today, to disfigure our land everywhere according to their savage custom. . . . The only evils I wish to publicize are those our island has suffered, and has at times inflicted on others, since the time of the Roman emperors. I will do this to the best of my ability. No native writings or records can assist me, since these (if they even existed!) have been destroyed by fires or carted off in ships carrying our exiled leaders. Instead, I have to rely on foreign writers whose accounts are far from clear, since they contain so many gaps. . . .

[1.23–26] In stout ships of war under full sail came the cries of a brood of fierce cubs born of a savage lioness—the Saxons—whose cries came to us as omens and auguries. A prophecy had foretold that they would occupy for three hundred years the country toward which they directed their prows, half of that time (that is, 150 years) spent in ravaging the land. They sailed under the command of their brutish leader and sank their deadly talons in the eastern shore of our island, and their homeland, seeing the success of this first contingent, sent out another ship, and another, to join their bastard companions. Thus were the seed of iniquity and the root of bitterness planted in our soil, until the poisonous plant grew and developed strong branches and full foliage. Having gained a foothold, the Saxons negotiated to have us supply them with provisions, as though they were our defenders preparing to endure great hardship on our account. For a time our provisions closed the dog's maw, to use an expression; but soon enough they complained that our monthly offerings were insufficient and declared that if we did not increase their volume they would break our treaty with them and lay waste the whole island. They did not wait long to turn their threats into deeds.

Because of our earlier sins, the fire of divine vengeance blazed across our land from coast to coast, stoked continually by the wretches from the east. This fire devoured all the scattered settlements and lands, and did not stop until it had consumed nearly the entire island, licking the western ocean with its red and savage tongue. The catastrophe bears comparison with that of the Assyrians upon Judaea, for there was fulfilled among us, as among the Jews, the prophet's lament, "They have set your sanctuary on fire, profaned your name's abode by razing it to the ground," [Ps 74.7] and again, "O God, the nations have invaded your inheritance; they have defiled your holy temple." [Ps 79.1] All our settlements were brought low with the repeated blows of battering rams. Our people were cut down everywhere by gleaming swords and raging fires, including the priests and bishops. Sadly, the streets of our villages are filled with the ruins of once-high towers that have been pulled to the ground, with stones pried from fences or left over from the smashing of sacred altars, with dismembered pieces of human bodies that are so covered with lurid clots of blood that they look as though the people had been run through a wine-press, and whose only chance for any kind of burial is to rot in the ruins of collapsed homes; all the rest will simply fill the stomachs of ravenous beasts and birds. . . .

Some surviving wretches were apprehended in the mountains and killed in heaps; others were so overcome by hunger that they surrendered themselves to their enemies, to be enslaved forever. . . . Eventually the barbaric raiders returned to their homeland, and what was left of our people came together from all around, as bees rush to their hive when a storm is brewing, and prayed as one to God with their whole hearts. As the phrase goes, "burdening the air with unnumbered prayers" they begged not to be destroyed. Rather, they took up arms and elected to challenge their conquerors in battle under the leadership of Ambrosius Aurelianus, a man of modest character. Alone of all the Romans, he had managed to survive the tumultuous times (his parents, being clothed in imperial purple, had been killed), and his descendants in my own time are fallen far from his ancient nobility. Nevertheless, these people gained a victory, with God's help.

Since that time, our people won some more victories and so did our enemy. Indeed, the Lord is testing our nation—the Israel of today—and the depth of its love for Him. The struggle continued up to the time of the battle of Badon Hill, the last great slaughter inflicted upon us. This was in the year of my birth, one month less than forty-four years ago, and to this very day not one of our villages is what it used to be. Instead, all lie desolate, routed, and ruined. . . .

Britain has kings, but they are nothing but tyrants. Britain has judges, but they are wicked men who engage in non-stop plunder and pillage of helpless commoners, to the delight and benefit of criminals and thieves everywhere. [Our rulers] have innumerable wives—harlots and adulteresses all. They swear oaths only to perjure themselves and to lie every time they make a vow. They fight wars, but evil ones against their own subjects. And while they pursue simple thieves relentlessly throughout the entire country, the robbers who sit with them at their noble tables are not only esteemed but rewarded. . . .

[108] But why mince words? . . . I will say what I mean. . . . You are not priests of God but enemies to Him, not bishops but practiced sinners! Not ministers of Christ, but traitors to the holy apostles whom you supposedly succeed! You may have heard the words of the apostle Paul but you have not absorbed them and you do not feel their weight. Like stone idols which can

neither see nor hear, you stood at the altar while his words came pouring down like thunder at you! "Brethren," he said, "this saying is trustworthy and deserves full acceptance." [1 Tim 1.15] He spoke of trustworthiness and deserving. "Whoever aspires to the office of bishop desires a noble task." [1 Tim 3.1] But you seek the bishops' offices out of covetousness, without even pretending it involves spiritual worthiness; you certainly put no store in good works. "Therefore a bishop must be irreproachable, married only once, temperate, self-controlled, decent, hospitable, able to teach, not a drunkard, not aggressive, but gentle, not contentious, not a lover of money." [1 Tim 3.2–3] This calls for tears, not more words. . . . How horribly things have changed,

to see the commands of heaven crushed under foot. The lot of you arm yourselves with deeds and words in order to attack these teachings, to destroy them. Teachings that one ought to suffer for and lay down one's life for! . . .

[110] Priests! Not a single one of you should flatter yourself on the purity of your body. The souls of your flocks . . . will be asked on the Day of Judgment, and they will denounce you as murderers of souls! . . .

May Almighty God, the God of all consolation and mercy, preserve His very few good priests from all evil and make them citizens of His city the Heavenly Jerusalem, where is the assembly of all saints. In the name of the Father, Son, and Holy Spirit, to whom be honor and glory for ever and ever. Amen.

5.2   Bede, *The Ecclesiastical History of the English People*

The Venerable Bede (ca. 673–735), as he is known, is also called the Father of English History not only because of the wide scope of his account, but also because he applied historical inquiry to his work—interviewing living witnesses to events, interpreting, and moving beyond the hagiographies used by his fellow writers. As the title indicates, Bede is a source for the particular development of the "insular" church—that is, of the British Isles—in contrast with the church of continental Europe. The first portion of this selection recounts the arrival of St. Augustine of Canterbury, who was sent by Pope Gregory the Great to establish an English church and convert the pagan locals; the second portion memorializes Pope Gregory.

[1.25] Encouraged by the kind words of the blessed father Gregory, Augustine and his fellow-servants of Christ resumed their work in God's name and soon arrived in Britain. The most powerful of the kings at that time was Ethelbert of Kent, whose realm extended northward to the river Humber, which marks the boundary of the northern and southern Angles. To the east lay the island of Thanet, which the English reckon as six hundred hides from end to end. A waterway of roughly three furlongs, called the Wantsum, separates Thanet from the mainland and can be crossed at only two places. This is where Augustine and his companions—reported to have numbered forty—landed. Following Pope Gregory's instructions, the

missionaries had brought Frankish interpreters with them, and they sent them to Ethelbert to deliver the news that they had come from Rome and that anyone who heard their message would undoubtedly receive the joy of eternal life in the kingdom of heaven with the one, true and living God. Ethelbert listened to what the interpreters had to say, and sent back the message that Augustine and his companions were to stay on the island; the king would provide for them all until he had decided what course of action to take. He was already familiar with Christianity, since his wife Bertha—a member of the Frankish royal house—was a Christian. Indeed, her family had consented to the marriage only on the condition that she should remain free to hold and practice her faith without any hindrance, and to this end they had assigned a bishop, Liuthard, to accompany her as a spiritual guide.

Several days later King Ethelbert came to Thanet and summoned Augustine and his companions to an open-air audience. He was careful not to meet them inside any house, for he maintained the ancient English superstition about practicers of magic, that they work their spells of deception and control best when indoors. The monks, though, were empowered by God, not the Devil, and they duly approached Ethelbert while carrying a silver cross as a standard and a wooden placard on which they had painted a likeness of Our Lord and Savior. They began by singing a litany for their own eternal salvation and for those on whose account they had come this far. The king then commanded them to sit and bade them to preach the "Word of Life" to him and his court. When they had done so, Ethelbert replied, "Fair words and fair promises. But their content is new to us, and seems doubtful. I cannot accept them, if that means abandoning the ancient beliefs by which I and the whole English nation have lived. But you have travelled far, and I can see the honest sincerity of your desire to share with us what you find to be true and worthy. We will not harm you, but instead extend our hospitality to you. We do not forbid you to preach to our people and to convert however many you can; in fact, we will provide you with all the supplies you need."

The king awarded them a residence in the city of Canterbury, which was his capital, and remained true to his word, granting the missionaries full provisions and not restricting their freedom to preach. According to tradition, the monks approached the city while carrying aloft the holy cross and the painted likeness of Our Lord and King Jesus Christ, and, as was their custom, singing aloud, "We pray to you, O Lord, in all your mercy, that although we are all sinners, you turn your wrath away from this city and from your holy house. Amen."

[1.26] As soon as they had settled into the house given them by the king, the missionaries started to emulate the life of the apostles and the early Church: constant prayer; fasting and keeping vigils; and preaching the Word of Life to any who would listen. Material things meant little to them, and they would accept gifts of food

and other necessities only from those to whom they preached. They gladly endured any hardship, even death, for the sake of the truth they proclaimed, and as a consequence, after a brief time, a number of the heathens, who admired the simplicity of their holy lives and the promise of their heavenly message, converted and were baptized. On the eastern side of the city there stood an old church consecrated to Saint Martin that had been built during Roman times; this was where the Christian queen mentioned above came to pray. The missionaries and their converts congregated there to sing psalms, pray, celebrate Mass, preach, and baptize, until King Ethelbert's own conversion gave them even more freedom to preach and to build or restore churches throughout the realm.

Eventually the king and others [in his court], guided by the holy example of the missionaries' lives and moved by their promises of salvation (the truth of which was confirmed by many miracles that they performed), also converted and were baptized. From that point on, large crowds gathered daily to hear God's Holy Word, and they too abandoned their pagan rites and entered the unity of Christ's Holy Church as full-fledged believers. Ethelbert was pleased by their conversions and faithfulness, but he still refused to compel anyone to accept Christianity, for he had learned well from his teachers and spiritual guides that service to Christ must be freely undertaken and never the result of force. Before long he gave his teachers at Canterbury another residence, one appropriate to their station, and a variety of landholdings to provide for their needs.

[2.1] Gregory was born a Roman, the son of Gordian and a descendant of many noble and devout ancestors, among whom was Felix, the former bishop of that see [of Rome] and a man of great distinction in Christ's Church, and Gregory dutifully maintained the family tradition by the nobility and devotion of his own religious life. With God's help he took his natural gifts for worldly success and dedicated them entirely to attaining heavenly glory—for he withdrew from secular life and sought admission to monastic life. There he lived a life of such perfection in grace that in later years he would weep at the memory of how firmly his mind was then set on high things, soaring above everything transient, and how completely he dedicated himself to thoughts of heaven. It was as though, while rooted in his body, he could transcend its bounds in contemplation. He even looked forward to death—something most men regard as a punishment—as the entry to a new life and the reward for all his labors. Whenever he mentioned this, he did so not to call attention to his superior virtue then, but to lament what he regarded as the decline in his virtue as a result of his pastoral work. Once, conversing intimately with his deacon Peter about his earlier life in the spirit, Gregory said sadly, "Pastoral work requires me to deal with worldly men. And compared to the cloudless beauty of my former life, my spirit now feels polluted with the muck and mire of worldly affairs. After being wasted in attending to the mundane matters of countless people, my soul tries to meditate on purely spiritual matters, but can't help but do so with diminished energy. Comparing what I have to put up with now, with what I have lost, I can't help feeling that the burden is great—greater than ever. . . ."

From the day he was called from his monastic life, was ordained to priestly life, and was sent to Constantinople as the representative of the Holy See, Gregory never gave up his spiritual exercises, even amid the maelstrom of earthly politics. Some of his fellow monks had accompanied him to the imperial city, out of devotion to him, and he always maintained a regular religious observance with them. This served as an anchor for him, holding him fast to the peaceful shore of prayer-life even while his daily life tossed on the endless waves of worldly affairs; studying with them always refreshed his mind after it was worn down by mundane things. . . .

Here I must stop to tell a story handed down by our forebears that explains the origins of Gregory's deep desire for the salvation of our [English] nation. The story goes, that one day some merchants, recently arrived in Rome, put their goods on display in the marketsquare when Gregory happened to be among the crowd who gathered around. His eye fell upon some boy-slaves who were for sale—fair-skinned, fine-cut features, and with beautiful hair. Intrigued by them, he asked where in the world they had come from.

"They are from Britain," he was told; "everyone there looks like this."

He asked next if the Britons were Christians or still ignorant heathens.

"They are pagans," came the answer.

"Oh, how sad!" Gregory sighed, "How sad that such bright-faced people are still in the clutches of the Author of Darkness, and that such graceful features conceal minds ignorant of God's grace! Tell me, what is the name of these people?"

"They're called 'Angles'," someone said.

"The name suits them," Gregory replied, "for their faces are angelic. It would be a good thing if they shared in the inheritance of the angels in heaven. Tell me, what is the name of the province they come from?"

"Deira," came the answer.

"That's good," said Gregory. "They will one day be rescued from the wrath [*de ira*] of God and called to the mercy of Christ. And what is the name of their king?"

"Aelle," he was told.

To which Gregory replied one last time, making a play on the king's name, "Then it is fitting that their land shall one day echo with the praise of God, our Creator, with the 'Alleluia'."

BEDE, *ECCLESIASTICAL HISTORY OF THE ENGLISH PEOPLE*

This excerpt from Book 5 describes the years 725–731, which close his *History*. Bede then appends a brief autobiography and lists his other works.

---

[23] ON THE PRESENT STATE OF THE LAND OF ENGLAND, AND OF ALL OF BRITAIN

In the year of the Incarnation of Our Lord 725 (which was the seventh year of the reign of Osric over the Northumbrians—Osric being the successor of Coenred)

King Wictred of Kent, the son of Egbert, died on 23 April, after thirty-four and a half years on the throne, and left as heirs to the kingdom his three sons Ethelbert, Eadbert, and Alric.

The following year Bishop Tobias of the church of Rochester died. As described before, he was a man of great learning, the pupil of such revered teachers as Archbishop Theodore and Abbot Hadrian, from whom he not only acquired erudition in ecclesiastical and other matters but mastered Greek and Latin to such a degree that he knew them as well as he knew his own native language. He was buried in the porch dedicated to St. Paul the Apostle, which he had established within the church of St. Andrew specifically for his own burial. Aldwulf took up the episcopate after him, and was consecrated by Archbishop Bertwald.

In the 729th year of Our Lord's Incarnation a great terror occurred: two comets near the sun. One of them flew by the rising sun in the morning, and the other followed the setting sun in the evening. People took this for a sign of coming destruction, from east to west, since the first comet hailed the coming of the day while the second proclaimed the coming of the night—a sure sign of calamities to come at both times. The comets' flaming tails pointed north, as though they intended to set the world on fire. They both appeared in January of that year and lasted a fortnight, which was precisely when a great plague of Saracens attacked France, spreading slaughter everywhere. Their wickedness did not have to wait long, however, to receive due punishment.[1]

In that same year the holy man of God, Egbert, went to God, as stated above, on Easter Day. On the following 9 May, after Easter, King Osric of Northumbrian departed this life after a reign of eleven years; he had appointed as his successor Ceolwulf, the brother of Coenred (who had reigned just before him). Ceolwulf's reign, right down to today, has been filled with so much upheaval that it is impossible to know what to say about it, or about what will become of it.

In the year of the Lord's Incarnation 731 Archbishop Bertwald died of old age, on 9 January, after thirty-seven years, six months, and fourteen days of service to his diocese. His successor, appointed the same year, was Tatwine, who hailed from the land of the Mercians, where he had been a priest in the monastery known as Briuden. He was consecrated as archbishop in Canterbury on Sunday, 10 June, by the venerable Daniel, bishop of Winchester; Ingwald, archbishop of London; Aldwin, bishop of Lichfield; and Aldwul, bishop of Rochester. Tatwine was renowned for his piety and wisdom, a notable scholar of the Scriptures.

At present, therefore, Bishops Tatwine and Aldwuld preside over the churches in Kent; Bishop Ingwald watches over the province of the East Saxons; in East Anglia the bishops are Aldbert and Hadulac; in the land of the West Saxons, Bishops Daniel and Forthere preside; Aldwin is bishop to the Mercians. On the western side of the river Severn, Walstod is bishop. Wilfrid is bishop to the Wiccians, while Bishop Cynebert presides over Lindisfarne province. Diocesan authority over the Isle of Wight belongs to Bishop Daniel of Winchester. The province of the South Saxons has lacked a bishop for some years now, but a prelate from the West Saxons ministers to them in that capacity.

All of these provinces, plus all those to the south as far as the river Humber, together with their kings, are subject to King Ethelbald.

In Northumbria, where King Ceolwulf now reigns, four bishops preside: Wilfrid in York, Ethelwald in Lindisfarne, Acca in Hagulstad, and Pechthelm in the church known as the "White House" and which has lately been elevated to episcopal status on account of the increase in the number of the faithful there, with Pechthelm as its first bishop.

The Picts now are at peace with England and rejoice in being joined in peace and truth with the Catholic Church. The Scots, contented with the lands they hold in northern Britain, have no violent deigns on the English. The Britons, though, on account of their innate hatred for us, oppose the English through their incorrect and wicked rejection of the Catholic Church's calculation of the time of Easter. Considering the Divine and human powers confronting them, they will never prevail in this matter. They are masters of themselves only to a degree, and will be brought (at least on this issue) under subjection to the English.

In general, ours are peaceful and tranquil times. Many Northumbrians—nobles as well as commoners—have laid aside their weapons and are more likely to dedicate themselves and their children to tonsured life as avowed monks than martial life. How things will end, only time will tell.

---

[1] A reference to Charles Martel's victory at the Battle of Tours-Poitiers (732).

Such is the state of Britain in this the 285th year since the arrival of the Anglo-Saxons, in the 731st year of the Incarnation of Our Lord, in Whose reign may the earth forever rejoice, may Britain exult in the profession of His faith, and may these many island be ever glad and sing praises to the honor of His Holiness.

[24] RECAPITULATION OF THE ENTIRE WORK, AND ABOUT THE AUTHOR HIMSELF

I have decided it is wise to summarize, in chronological order, the deeds that I have discussed at length, the better to assist in preserving the memory of them.

In the 60th year before Our Lord's Incarnation, the Roman leader Caius Julius Caesar invaded Britain, and though he won several victories he failed to gain the entire realm.

In the 46th year after Our Lord's Incarnation, Claudius was the second of the Romans to invade Britain. A large part of the island surrendered to him, which he added, together with the Orkney Islands, to the Roman Empire.

In the year of the Incarnation of the Lord 167, Eleutherius became bishop of Rome and governed the Church with distinction for fifteen years. King Lucius wrote to him from Britain, asking to be made a Christian; his request was granted and fulfilled.

In the 189th year from the Incarnation, [Septimius] Severus became emperor and ruled Rome for seventeen years. He marked the limit of Britain with a trench from the Irish to the North Seas.

In 381 Maximus became emperor while he was in Britain. He sailed to Gaul and slew [his rival] Gratian.

In 409 Rome itself was sacked by the Visigoths. From this time onward no Roman emperor had control over Britain.

In the year 430 Pope Celestine dispatched Palladius to be the first bishop of the Christian Scots.

In 449 Martianus became emperor along with Valentinian and ruled for seven years. It was during his reign that the Anglo-Saxons were drawn into Britain by the Celts.

In 538 there was a solar eclipse on 16 February, from the first to the third hours of the day.

In 540 there was another eclipse on 20 June, during which the stars were visible for almost half an hour after the third hour of the day.

In the year 547 King Ida began his reign. He inaugurated the royal line of the Northumbrians, and ruled for twelve years.

In the year 565 the priest Columba, a Scot, came to Britain to convert the Picts. He built a monastery on the island of Hii.

In 596 Pope Gregory sent Augustine to Britain, along with a company of monks, to preach the Word of God to the Anglo-Saxons.

In 597 they arrived in Britain—this was roughly the 150th year since the coming of the Anglo-Saxons to Britain.

In 601 Pope Gregory sent the pallium to Britain for Augustine, who had already been made bishop. He sent several other missionaries too, including Paulinus.

In the year 603 occurred the Battle of Degsastane.

In the year 604 the East Saxons embraced the Christian faith under their king, Sabert, and their bishop, Mellitus.

In the year of the Incarnation of Our Lord 605, Pope Gregory died.

In the year 606 King Ethelbert of Kent died.

In the year 625, Archbishop Justus ordained the venerable Paulinus as bishop of the Northumbrians.

In the year 626, the daughter of King Edwin, Eanfleda, was baptized on Whit-Saturday, along with twelve others.

In the year 627, King Edwin himself was baptized, at Easter, along with all his people.

In 633 Paulinus returned to Kent after the death of King Edwin.

In 640 King Eadbald of Kent died.

In 642 King Oswald was killed.

In the year 644 Paulinus, first the bishop of York and then of Rochester, went to God.

In 651 King Oswin was killed, and Bishop Aidan died.

In 653 the Angles of the Midlands, under their ruler Penda, received the mystery of our faith.

In 655 Penda was slain, and the Mercians became Christian.

In 644 a solar eclipse occurred, King Earconbert of Kent died, Colman returned to the Scots, a plague swept through, and Ceadda and Wilfrid were consecrated as bishop to the Northumbrians.

In 669 Theodore was consecrated bishop.

In 670 King Oswy of the Northumbrians died.

In 673 King Egbert of Kent died, and a synod was held at Hertford (Archbishop Theodore presiding) in the presence of King Egfrid. The synod accomplished many good things, and its canons are written in ten chapters.

In 675 King Wulfhere of the Mercians died after a reign of seventeen years. He left his crown to his brother Ethelred.

In 676 Ethelred ravaged Kent.

In 678 a comet appeared, Bishop Wilfrid was driven from office by King Egfrid, and Bosa, Eata, and Eadhed were consecrated as bishops to replace him.

In 679 Elfwine was slain.

In the year 680 a synod was held at Hethfield, regarding matters of the faith. Archbishop Theodore presided, but John, the Roman abbot, was also present. In this same year Abbess Hilda died at Streaneshalch.

In the year 685 King Egfrid of the Northumbrians was killed. In this same year King Lothere of Kent died.

In 688 King Caedwalla of the West Saxons journeyed from Britain to Rome.

In 690 Archbishop Theodore died.

In the year 697 Queen Ostritha was killed by her own people, the Mercian nobles.

In 698 King Berthred of the Northumbrians was killed by the Picts.

In the year 704 Ethelred abdicated after thirty years as King of the Mercians and became a monk. His realm passed to Coenred.

In 705 King Alfrid of the Northumbrians died.

In 709 King Coenred of the Mercians, six years into his reign, traveled to Rome.

In 711 Earl Bertfrid fought with the Picts.

In the year 716 King Osred of the Northumbrians was killed, King Coenred of the Mercians died, and Egbert, man of God, brought the monks of Hii to observe the Catholic Easter and monastic tonsure.

In 725 King Withred of Kent died.

In the year 729 comets appeared, holy Egbert died, and Osric too.

In the year 731 Archbishop Bertwald died. In that same year Tatwine was consecrated as the ninth archbishop of Canterbury, in the fifteenth year of the reign of King Ethelbald of Kent.

This is as much of the Ecclesiastical History of Britain, and more especially of England, as I have been able to learn or glean from the writings of the ancients, the oral tradition of our ancestors, or from my own experience and knowledge. With God's help, this has been accomplished by me, Bede, the servant of God and priest of the monastery of the Blessed Apostles Peter and Paul, at Wearmouth and Jarrow. I was born in this very district, and at age seven was handed over to be educated by the most reverend Abbot Benedict,

and afterwards by Ceolfrid. I spent the whole of my subsequent life in this monastery, applying myself assiduously to the study of the Sacred Scriptures. Observing the discipline of our Rule and singing daily in the church, I have always delighted in studying, teaching, and writing. I was ordained a deacon at age nineteen and was brought into the priesthood at thirty, both at the hands of the most reverend Bishop John, at the direction of Abbot Ceolfrid. From then until now, at age fifty-nine, I have put myself to the useful work of studying, interpreting, and explicating the works of the venerable Fathers. Thus far I have written:

On the Beginning of Genesis (to the birth of Isaac and the Condemnation of Ismail, three books.

On the Tabernacle and Its Vessels, and Of the Priestly Garments, three books.

On I Samuel (to the Death of Saul), four books.

On the Building of the Temple, an allegorical interpretation in two books.

Thirty Questions on the Book of Kings.

On the Proverbs of Solomon, three books.

On the Canticles, seven books.

On Isaiah, Daniel, the Twelve Prophets, and Part of Jeremiah, discussion of various chapters taken out of St. Jerome's Treatise.

On Esdras and Nehemiah, three books.

On the Song of Habakkuk, one book.

On the Book of the Blessed Father Tobias, an allegorical exposition concerning Christ and the Church, one book.

Various Chapters in the Pentateuch of Moses, Joshua, and Judges.

On the Books of Kings and Chronicles.

On the Book of the Blessed Father Job.

On the Parables, Ecclesiastes, and Canticles.

On the Prophets Isaiah, Esdras, and Nehemiah.

On the Gospel of Mark, four books.

On the Gospel of Luke, six books.

On Homilies on the Gospels, two books.

On the Apostle [Paul], a careful transcription of everything I could find in the works of St. Augustine.

On the Acts of the Apostles, two books.

On the Seven Catholic Epistles, one book on each.

On the Revelation of St. John, three books.

Various Chapters on the Readings from the New Testament, not counting the Gospels.

A book of Epistles to various people: one on the Six Ages of the World, one on the Mansions of the Children of Israel, one on the Words of Isaiah

("And they shall be shut up in prison, and after many years they shall be visited"), one on the Reason of the Bissextile (or Leap Year) and the Equinox, according to Anatolius.

As for the histories of the saints, I have translated into prose the Life and Passion of St. Felix the Confessor, from Paulinus' work in verse. I also corrected the poor translation, from Greek, of the Life and Passion of St. Anastasius, by some unknown writer.

I have also produced, as author:

The Life of the Holy Father Cuthbert, who was both a monk and a prelate, in verse and prose.
The History of the Abbots of this Monastery (Benedict, Ceolfrid, and Huetbert), two books.
The Ecclesiastical History of Our Island and Nation, five books.
The Martyrology of the Birthday of the Holy Martyrs (in which I struggled to set down all I could learn about their martyr-days, persecutions, and persecutors).
A Book of Hymns, in various meters and rhymes.
A Book of Epigrams in heroic, or elegiac, meter.
A Book on the Nature of Things, and Another on the Reckoning of Time.
Another, larger Book on the Reckoning of Time.
A Book on Orthography, another on the Art of Poetry, and another still on Tropes and Figures (that is, the rhetoric and diction of the Holy Scriptures).

And now I beg you, Lord Jesus, to vouchsafe to me—one to whom You have so graciously granted the ability to partake of the sweet words of Your wisdom and knowledge—that I may one day come to You, the Fountain of All Wisdom, and behold Your face, Who lives and reigns, world without end. Amen.

5.3   Martin of Braga, *On the Correction of Peasants*

Martin (d. 580) was archbishop of Braga, which today is part of Portugal. Like the British Isles, the Iberian peninsula was Christianized twice, but whereas Celtic Christianity had reigned supreme in Britain until the arrival of the Anglo-Saxons in the sixth and seventh centuries, Iberia had been initially converted to Arian Christianity under the Visigoths. The shift of allegiance to the Roman rite happened more or less contemporaneously with the English transition. In the following sermon, which he wrote in the form of a letter to a fellow bishop, Martin warns of the extent to which pagan traditions, not only Arian ones, persist in the rural population.

BISHOP MARTIN TO HIS FELLOW BISHOP AND PIOUS BROTHER IN CHRIST, POLEMIUS, SORELY MISSED. . . .

[In a few opening paragraphs, Martin summarizes the origins of Satan and his demons; these demons, he suggests, appeared to humans in the form of the pagan deities—Jupiter, Juno, Mars, Venus, Apollo, etc.—in order to trick people away from the worship of God and involve them in rituals that keep them in a kind of spiritual slavery.]

[8] Such the wretchedness of these lost souls, whom the ignorant many were duped into honoring! They took on names for themselves, so that people would worship them as gods and make sacrifices to them and imitate their deeds. They even persuaded the people to build temples to them and set up idols (statues of evildoers, really) and altars on which they sacrificed not only the blood of animals but even that of humans. Moreover, these spirits—all of them exiles from heaven—claimed to have authority over the seas,

rivers, and forests, and men began worshipping them as gods and offering sacrifices to them instead of the One True God. The demon in the sea they call Neptune, those in rivers and streams they call Lamias and Nymphs; spirits in forests become Dianas. All of them are wicked and evil, causing injury and harm to faithless men who are ignorant of the protection offered to them by the sign of the Cross.

It is not without God's own permission, though, that the demons do their harm, for humans have angered God by still rejecting faith in Christ. Humans have so rejected Christ that they even name the days of the week after demons—one each for Mars, Mercury, Jupiter, Venus, and Saturn. But these did not create the days; they were merely evil men and criminals who lived among the Greeks.

[9] . . . What idiocy it is for people baptized into the faith of Christ not to observe the Lord's day, when Christ rose [from the dead], but should honor days dedicated to adulterers, magicians, and evil frauds who died ignoble deaths in faraway lands! By continuing use of these names, stupid people give worship and honor to demons!

[10] Consider too the falsehood maintained by so many ignorant rustics—namely the error that January 1st marks the beginning of the calendar. What idiocy! The Holy Scriptures clearly state that the beginning of the year comes on March 25th, the time of the equinox. For it is written [in Genesis 1.4]: "God divided the light from the darkness." For to divide something means to split it equally, and on March 25th the light of day and the darkness of night share the same number of hours. That is why it is false to say that January 1st marks the beginning of the calendar year. . . .

[14] Mark this point well: When the end of the world arrives, all nations and all human beings from the time of Adam and Eve on, shall rise, both the good and the evil, and all shall come before the judgment seat of Christ. Those who, in their lifetimes, were faithful and good will be separated from the evil and shall enter the kingdom of God with all the holy angels. Their souls will be rejoined with their bodies and dwell in eternal rest, never again to die; and they will know no labor or pain, no sorrow, no hunger or thirst, no heat or cold, no darkness, no night. They will be like the angels of God, forever happy and blessed, living in splendor and glory, for they will have deserved to enter the kingdom from which Satan and his evil-minded demons fell. And in that kingdom all the faithful will live forever.

But those who have not been faithful or were not baptized (or, if they were baptized but returned to idol-worship and the sins of murder, adultery, perjury and died without repentance) will be damned along with Satan and his demons, whom they worshipped and whose works they carried out. These will be rejoined with their bodies and be cast into eternal hell-fire, where an unquenchable flame burns forever and their flesh will live in everlasting torment. They will long to die again, so that they may cease to suffer their punishment; but they will not be allowed to die, and will suffer everlasting torment. This is what the Law proclaims—and the prophets, and the gospel of Christ, and the apostles, and all of Holy Scripture! (I say this for you in few words, to summarize the entire witness of the Scriptures.) Beloved sons, you may trust in the eternal rest of the Kingdom of God—as I have described it here—if you live correctly from here on. But if you continue in your wickedness (may God forbid it!), you may expect nothing but the eternal fires of Hell. It is up to each man to choose between eternal life and eternal death—and as he so chooses, so shall he receive what he deserves. . . .

[16] Bear in mind your commitment to God and how you are bound by it! How can it be, therefore, that so many of you, who renounced [at your baptism] Satan and his demons, his worship and evil works, have now returned to the worship of the devil? To place lit candles before stones, trees, and streams, or at crossroads—is this anything else but devil-worship? To consult diviners and augurs, and to maintain a calendar of idols—is this anything else but devil-worship? When you observe things like the Vulcanalia or the kalends,[2] or

---

2   The Vulcanalia was an old Roman rite in honor of the god Vulcan held every August 25, when it was feared that the high heat of late summer might scorch the crops before harvest. The rite consisted of chanting around large bonfires into which were thrown gifts of food to placate the god. The kalends were a feast held at the start of every lunar month in honor of the pagan gods.

when you decorate tables, set up wreaths, and carefully set fruit and poured wine onto a log burning in your hearth, or when you set bread floating upon a river—is this anything else but devil-worship? When women sit at their looms and invoke the protection of Minerva; when people schedule their weddings on the feast-day of Venus; when people consult soothsayers for the most auspicious day to set out on a journey; when someone tries to place a curse on someone else by chanting words or calling upon the names of demons over some herbs—is this anything else but devil-worship? Nor is this all you do! There are too many evil practices to mention! And remember: you do these things after having renounced Satan in your baptism. . . . Why do your soothsayers not harm me or any other righteous Christian? Because the sign of the Cross exists, the sign of the Devil is as nothing. Why do they harm you? Because you dismiss the sign of the Cross and fear the thing you have taken on for yourselves. . . .

[17] My dear beloved sons, if you recognize yourselves in what I have described; if you know that you have done such things after having received baptism and thereby been faithless to Christ; do not despair! Do not say in your heart, "Because I've done these evils even after baptism, God will not forgive me." Never doubt the mercy of God. Only promise the Lord in your heart that you will no longer worship demons nor adore anything other than the God of heaven, that you will no longer sin by murder, adultery, fornication, robbery, or perjury; and once you have made this promise with your whole heart, and give up such sinning, then you may indeed hope for God's forgiveness, for God Himself says in prophetic scripture: "But if the wicked man turns from all his sins which he has committed and observes all My statutes and practices justice and righteousness, he shall surely live; he shall not die. All his transgressions which he has committed will not be remembered against him; because of his righteousness which he has practiced, he will live." [Ezechiel 18.21–22] . . .

[18] And so I beseech you, dearest sons and brothers, to remember these lessons that God has seen fit to pass on to you through me, as low and unimportant as I am, and keep in mind how you can save your own souls. Do not simply take care of this present life or focus on the affairs of this transitory world! Rather, bear in mind the Creed in which you promised to believe—that is, in the resurrection of the flesh and in life eternal. . . .

[19] Behold! In saying these things, as heard and witnessed by God and all His angels, I have repaid my debt to you for your charity, and all the wealth of the Lord I pay over to you, as I have been commanded. It is up to each and every one of you to reckon how, on the Day of Judgment, you will repay to God, with interest, what you have received. I pray for God's mercy, that He will protect you from all evil and make you worthy companions of His angels in His Kingdom. In the name of He Who lives and reigns now and forever, amen.

5.4 Procopius, *A View of the Emperor Justinian*

Procopius (d. 565), as the emperor Justinian's official biographer, worked close to the emperor and accompanied his general, Belisarius, on his campaigns to restore imperial authority over Italy and North Africa. His two authorized works—*The Wars of Justinian* and *The Buildings of Justinian*—are seldom read by anyone but specialists. His unauthorized and anonymous *Secret History*, however, has become famous. In it, Procopius unleashes a stream of pent-up hostility against Justinian, his wife Theodora, the general Belisarius, and his wife Antonina. His claims about Theodora's sexual adventures are exaggerated and perhaps entirely fictional. The whole tenor of the *Secret History* is one of a perverse fantasia.

FROM *THE SECRET HISTORY* (CH. 8–10)

Such is how things stood in Constantinople and everywhere else, for as is the case with any disease, the evil that started there in the capital quickly spread throughout the entire empire. But the emperor [Justinian] hardly noticed anything wrong at all, for he was incapable of seeing even what was happening in front of his own eyes in the Hippodrome. He was, in fact, a cretin, with no more sense than an ass that follows, with a twitch of its ears, anyone who pulls on its reins.

Behaving this way, he made a mess of everything. No sooner had he taken over the government from his uncle than he began to squander the public's money wildly, once he got his hands on it. He wasted a lot of it on the Huns, time and again, for supposedly serving the empire, which resulted, predictably, in our provinces being constantly attacked—for once the savages had tasted imperial wealth, they were forever on the road to the capital. He was as quick to throw money into the sea, by erecting at vast expense a series of breakwaters to hold back the surging waves. These stretched far out into the sea, as though he believed he could rival the roaring strength of the ocean by the power of cash.

He confiscated for himself private estates of Roman citizens throughout the land, either by accusing them of some crime they had never committed or by flattering them into thinking they were giving him a gift. Others, who actually had committed murders and other felonies, made over their estates to him and thus escaped prosecution; while still others, who were engaged in fraudulent suits to gain control of their neighbors' lands, when they realized they couldn't win in the courts, simply transferred their claim to Justinian and left the whole matter. In this way, by means of empty gestures, they won the emperor's favor and gained access to him by handing over property they had no legal claim to—all at their victims' expense.

This seems a fitting time to describe Justinian's personal appearance. In body he was neither tall nor short, just average; not thin (in fact, slightly fat). He had a round and not-unpleasant face. Even after a two-day fast he had good color. To sum up his appearance quickly, he bore a strong resemblance to [the emperor] Domitian, the son of Vespasian, whose behavior so outraged the Romans that they were not satisfied even with hacking him to pieces, but appeased their wrath by a Senate decree that his name should be obliterated from all inscriptions, and that no statue or portrait of him should be allowed to survive. Thus his name was chiseled out of every inscription in the empire and everywhere else it appeared, leaving the rest intact; that is why no likeness of him exists anywhere, except for a single bronze statue, which survived in the following way.

Domitian's wife was a respectable woman of good birth who had never done the slightest wrong to anyone and never assented to any of her husband's evil doing. Being held in such affectionate regard, she was sent for by the Senate, who invited her to ask any favor of it at all—to which she replied only that she would like to bury his body and put up a bronze statue of him somewhere. The Senate agreed, and the widow, whose secret desire was to create a memorial of the savagery of those who had butchered her husband, devised a plan. Collecting the pieces of Domitian's corpse, she fitted them together and stitched the body up, then took it to the sculptors and ordered them to reproduce in bronze the form of the wretch. The artists quickly produced the statue, which she subsequently took and set up in the street that leads to the Capitol, on the right-hand side as you approach from the Forum. It stands there to this day, a reminder to all both of Domitian himself and his tragic death.

One can see clearly in this statue the very likeness of Justinian—his build, expression, and general appearance.

So much for his outward appearance, but it is beyond my ability to describe his inner character, for he was both a villain and a dupe. In plain language, an asshole. He was deceitful, never speaking a word of truth to anyone, but fell for any lie that anyone wanted to tell him. His character was an unnatural mixture of stupidity and wickedness—an example of a saying by one of the ancient Peripatetic philosophers, that sometimes opposite qualities can combine in a man's character, like the blending of colors. But I will try to describe him as accurately and truly as I can, based on the facts.

Well, then. He was a fraud and a cheat. Hypocritical, cruelly two-faced, secretive; a practiced con artist who never showed any genuine emotion but could shed tears either of joy or sorrow, depending on the situation, whenever he perceived the need. A liar in every word—and not just in a haphazard way, but with real determination, affirming his schemes in writing and with the most solemn oaths, even in dealings with the public. But he regularly broke every agreement and pledge he ever made, like a contemptible slave who stands by his lies until only the threat of torture can drive him to confess the truth. A faithless friend and a treacherous enemy, with a crazed lust for murder and plunder; quarrelsome, extremely unruly, easily led to anything evil but stubbornly refusing any suggestion to do good. Quick to plot mischief and carry it out, but averse even to hearing a word of any noble action.

How could anyone describe his character in words? He had all the vices described above, and more, to an inhuman degree, as though Nature herself had withheld every inclination to evil from the rest of mankind, solely for the purpose of implanting them in the soul of this one man. On top of everything else, he was overeager to hear accusations against anyone, and over-eager to inflict punishment, for he never bothered to listen to the facts of any case and simply issued his verdict as soon as he had heard the accuser's side of any story. He gave orders to seize towns, pillage cities, and enslave entire countries without a moment's hesitation, without any provocation at all. If one wanted to tally up all the calamities that have befallen Rome from the very beginning of history, and compare them with this man's crimes, I am confident that Justinian would be reckoned to have murdered more people than anyone, ever.

As for other people's money, he had no scruples at all and never even bothered to offer an excuse, justifiable or not, for confiscating what was not his. But once money was in his hands he was more than ready to squander it in wasteful expenditure or by throwing unnecessary bribes at the barbarians. In short, he saved none and allowed no one else to save any either, apparently driven not by avarice but simple envy of anyone who had money. Thus he drove all wealth from the Roman realm and became the cause of near-universal poverty.

Such, then, was the outline of Justinian's character, so far as I am able to describe it.

He married a woman who nearly destroyed Roman society from top to bottom, and whose character and upbringing I must now try to explain.

There was a fellow here in Constantinople named Acacius; he was a member of the Green faction and worked as a keeper of the Circus animals, specifically he was the bear-warden. He became ill and died during

Anastasius' reign, leaving behind three daughters named Comito, Theodora, and Anastasia. (Comito was the eldest, being just shy of seven years old.) His widow remarried and hoped her new husband would share in the job of managing her family and the Circus animals—but an official in the Green party, a dance-instructor named Asterius, was bribed to remove the newlyweds from their positon. He was able to do so because the dancing-masters had authority over such offices; and he used his power to install his own chief accountant in the job. One day, when the Circus was packed with people, the wife placed wreaths on her daughters' heads and bands on their arms, and made a show of them in public as beggars. The Greens would not lift a finger for them, but the Blues, whose own bear-warden had recently died, awarded their open position to the family.

As soon as each girl had grown to a suitable age and seemed mature enough, their mother put her on the stage, since they were all attractive girls. In no time at all Comito, the eldest, was one of the most popular whores in the city. Theodora, the second-born, went about dressed like a slave-girl, in a short tunic with long sleeves, and acted as her sister's servant, following her everywhere and carrying a small bench on which she sat whenever appearing in public. Theodora was at that time not quite ready to give anyone a true woman's fuck, and so she offered instead the vile service rendered by male prostitutes. She was not choosy and made herself available to the lowest sort of customer, even to slaves, who, after accompanying their masters to the theater, rushed to her in order to divert themselves in this revolting way. She worked in a brothel for quite some time and specialized in this unnatural type of sex. Once she had grown and developed a woman's body, however, she joined the other whores on stage and quickly became known as the type of slut our ancestors used to call "soldiers' slop." She had no musical talent for either the flute or the harp, and was not even skilled enough to join a company of dancers; her only attraction was her body, every part of which she placed at any customer's disposal. . . . Being a tease, Theodora loved to keep her customers waiting, but by constantly finding new ways to fuck she always kept horny men coming to her. She also never waited to be solicited, and used lewd talk and gestures to entice men, especially teens, to come to her, and so it seemed that she was more wholeheartedly devoted to lust than anyone yet born. Sometimes she would attend "pot-luck dinner parties" with no fewer than ten young studs in tow, all at the peak of their powers and with no other thought than fucking in mind, and would spend the entire night screwing every single one of them; and even after she had exhausted every one of them, she would then turn her attention to the servants—as many as thirty of them!—and screw them all. But even then she was not satisfied. . . .

Justinian was mad with passion for her. At first he kept her merely as a mistress, although he promoted her to patrician status, which opened the door to her acquiring influence and a large fortune. Now as it often happens to men who are sexually enslaved to a particular woman, Justinian had no greater delight than in showering Theodora with every favor and treasure at his disposal—and he had the entire Empire at his disposal. With Theodora's help, he impoverished the people more than ever before, not only in the capital bur throughout the realm. . . .

And that is how Theodora, reared and "educated" as she was, against all the odds ascended to the imperial throne. It never even occurred to Justinian that his choice was a shocking one. Given his position, he had the pick of every high-born noble woman in the world, of the most impeccable character and the most unimpeachable reputation for modesty. . . . But no, he had to select the lowest woman in the world! Ignoring everything known about her, as recorded here, he preferred to marry a diseased whore who was guilty, through abortion, of countless child-murders!

5.5   Islam: The Qur'an

The Holy Qur'an was revealed to Prophet Muhammad over the course of 22 years, from 610 to 632. The *surat* ("chapter") that follows came early, while Muhammad was still living in Mecca. It describes the ranks of the good and the evil, from the angels in heaven to the earthly prophets (and those who rejected them). It is interesting to compare these verses with the corresponding passages in the Hebrew Bible. Note, for instance, that here Abraham offers his son Ismail (born of his servant-woman Hagar), rather than Isaac (born of his wife Sarah), as a sacrifice to God. Words and phrases in square brackets are added to complete the sense of the sentence and do not appear in the Arabic.

SURAT 37. AS-SAFFAT: THOSE RANGED IN RANKS

In the name of Allah, Most Gracious, Most Merciful.

[VV. 1—21]

By those who range themselves in ranks,
those who so are strong in repelling [evil],
those who thus proclaim the Message [of Allah]!
Verily, verily, your God is One!
Lord of the heavens and of the earth,
and all between them, and Lord of every point at
    the rising of the sun!
We have indeed decked the lower heaven with beauty
[in] the stars,—
[for beauty] and for guard against all obstinate
    rebellious Satans.
[So] they should not listen their ears in the direction
of the Exalted Assembly and they are cast away
    from every side,
repulsed. And for them is a perpetual chastisement,
except such as snatch away something by stealth,
    and they
are pursued by a flaming fire, of piercing
    brightness.
Just ask their opinion: Are they the more difficult
To create, or the [other] beings We have created?
Them have We created out of a sticky clay!

Truly dost thou marvel while they ridicule,
And when they are admonished, pay no heed,—
And, when they see a Sign, turn it to mockery,
And say, "This is nothing but evident sorcery!
What! When we die, and become dust and bones,
Shall we [then] be raised up [again]?
And also our fathers of old?"
Say thou: "Yea, and ye shall then be humiliated
[on account of your evil],
then it will be a single [compelling] cry;
and behold, they will begin to see!
They will say, 'Ah! Woe to us! This is the Day of
Judgment!'
[A voice will say,] 'This is the Day
of sorting out, whose truth ye [once] denied!'"

[VV. 22–74]

"Bring ye up," it shall be said, "the wrong-doers
and their wives, and the things they worshipped—
besides Allah, and lead them to the Way, to the
[Fierce] Fire!
But stop them, for they must be asked:
'What is the matter with you, that ye help not
each other?'"
Nay, but that day they shall submit [to Judgment],
And they will turn to one another,
And question one another.
They will say: "It was ye who used to come to us
From the right hand."
They will reply: "Nay, ye yourselves had no faith!
Nor had we any authority over you. Nay, it was
ye who were a people in obstinate rebellion!"
"So now has been proved true, against us, the
Word
of our Lord that we shall indeed [have to] taste
[the punishment for our sins]:
We led you astray: for truly we were ourselves astray."
Truly, that Day, they will [all] share in the
Chastisement.
Verily, that is how We shall deal with Sinners.
For they. when they were told that there is
no god except Allah, would puff themselves up
with Pride,
and say: "What! Shall we give up our gods
For the sake of a Poet possessed?"

Nay! He has come with the [very] Truth,
And he confirms [the Message of] the messengers
[before him].
Ye shall indeed taste of the Grievous
Chastisement;—
And you are requited naught save what ye did.
But the chosen servants of Allah,—
For them is a Sustenance determined,
Fruits; and they [shall enjoy] honour and dignity,
In Gardens of delight.
Facing each other on raised couches,
Round will be passed to them a Cup
From a clear-flowing fountain,
Crystal-white, of a taste
Delicious to those who drink [thereof],
Free from headiness;
Nor will they suffer intoxication therefrom.
And besides them will be chaste women;
restraining
Their glances, with big eyes [of wonder
and beauty].
As if they were [delicate] eggs closely guarded.
Then they will turn to one another and question
one another.
One of them will say:
"I had an intimate companion [on the earth],
who used to say, 'Do you really believe?
When we die and become dust and bones, shall we
Indeed receive rewards and punishments?'"
He said: "Would you like to look down?"
He looked down and saw him in the midst of the
Fire.
He said: "By Allah! Thou wast little short
Of bringing me to perdition!
Had it not been for the Grace of my Lord,
I should certainly have been among those
brought [there]!
Is it [the case] that we shall not die,
Except our first death, and that we shall not be
punished?"
Verily this is the supreme triumph,
For the like of this let all strive, who wish to strive.
Is that the better entertainment or the Tree of
Zaqqum?
For We have truly made it [as] a trial
For the wrong-doers.

For it is a tree that springs out of the bottom of
  Hell-fire:
The shoots of its fruit-stalks
Are like the heads of devils:
Truly they will eat thereof and fill their bellies
  therewith.
Then on top of that they will be given
A mixture made of boiling water.
Then shall their return be to the [Blazing] Fire.
Truly they found their fathers on the wrong Path;
So they [too] were rushed down on their
  footsteps!
And truly before them, many of the ancients went
  astray;—
But We sent aforetime among them, warners.
Then see what was the End of those who were
  warned
Except the chosen servants of Allah.

[VV. 75–113]

[In the days of old] Noah cried to Us,
and We are the Best to hear prayer.
And We delivered him and his people from the
  great Calamity,
and made his progeny to endure [on this earth];
and we left [this blessing] for him among
  generations
to come in later times:
"Peace and salutation to Noah among the nations!"
Thus indeed do We reward those who do right.
For he was one of Our believing Servants.
Then the rest We overwhelmed in the Flood.
Verily from his party was Abraham.
Behold, he approached his Lord with a sound
  heart.
Behold, he said to his father and to his
  people, "What
is that which ye worship?
Is it a Falsehood—gods other than Allah that ye
  desire?
Then what is your idea about the Lord of the
  Worlds?"
Then did he cast a glance at the Stars,
and he said: "I am indeed sick [at heart]!"
So they turned away from him, and departed.

Then did he turn to their gods and said,
"Will ye not eat [of the offerings before you]?
What is the matter with you that ye speak not?"
Then did he turn upon them, striking [them] with
  the right hand.
Then came [the worshippers] with hurried steps
  to him.
He said: "Worship ye that which ye have
  [yourselves] carved?
But Allah has created you and your handiwork!"
They said: "Build him a furnace, and throw him
  into the blazing fire!"
[This failing], they then plotted against him,
but We made them the ones most humiliated!
He said: "I will go to my Lord! He will surely
  guide me!
O my Lord! Grant me a righteous [son]!"
So We gave him the good news of a forbearing son.
Then, when [the son] reached [the age of
serious] work with him, he said: "O my son!
I have seen in a dream that I offer thee in sacrifice.
Now I see what is thy view!" The son said:
"O my father! Do as thou art commanded:
Thou will find me, if Allah so wills one of the
  steadfast."
So when they had both submitted [to Allah],
and he had laid him prostrate on his forehead
  [for sacrifice],
We called out to him, "O Abraham!
Thou hast already fulfilled the dream!"—thus
  indeed
do We reward those who do right.
For this was a clear trial—
and We ransomed him with a monstrous
  sacrifice:
And We left for him among generations [to come]
  in later times:
"Peace and salutation to Abraham!"
This indeed do We reward those who do right
for he was one of Our believing Servants.
And We gave him the good news
of Isaac—a prophet—one of the Righteous.
We blessed him and Isaac: but of their progeny
are [some] that do right, and [some]
  that obviously
do wrong, to themselves.

[VV. 114–138]

Again, [of old] We bestowed Our favour on Moses
  and Aaron,
and We delivered them and their people from
  [their] Great distress,
and We helped them, so they were victorious;
and We gave them the Book which helps to make
  things clear;
and We guided them to the Straight Way.
And We left for them among generations [to
  come] in later times:
"Peace and salutation to Moses and Aaron!"
Thus indeed do We reward those who do right.
For they were two of Our believing Servants.
So also was Elias among those sent [by Us].
Behold, he said to his people,
"Will ye not fear [Allah]? Will ye call upon Baal
and forsake the Best of Creators,—
Allah, your Lord and Cherisher,
and the Lord and Cherisher of your fathers of old?"
But they rejected him, and they will certainly
be called up [for punishment],
except the chosen Servants of Allah [among them].
And We left for him among generations
[to come] in later times:
"Peace and salutation to such as Elias!"
Thus indeed do We reward those who do right.
For he was one of Our believing Servants.
So also was Lüt among those sent [by Us].
Behold, We delivered him and his adherents, all
except an old woman who was among those who
  lagged behind:
Then We destroyed the rest.
Verily, ye pass by their [sites] by day—
and by night: Will ye not understand?

[VV. 139–182]

So also was Jonah among those sent [by Us].
When he ran away [like a slave from captivity]
to the ship [fully] laden,
he [agreed to] cast lots, and he was of the rebutted:
Then the big Fish did swallow him,
and when he had done acts worthy of blame.
Had it not been that he [repented and] glorified
  Allah,

he would certainly have remained inside the Fish
till the Day of Resurrection.
But We cast him forth on the naked shore in a
  state of sickness,
and We caused to grow, over him, a spreading plant
of the Gourd kind.
And We sent him [on a mission]
to a hundred thousand [men] or more.
And they believed; so We permitted them
to enjoy [their life] for a while.
Now ask them their opinion: Is it that thy Lord
has [only] daughters, and they have sons?—
Or that We created the angels female, and they
are witnesses [thereto]?
Behold, they say, out of their own invention,
"Allah has begotten children"? But they are liars!
Did He [then] choose daughters rather than sons?
What is the matter with you? How judge ye?
Will ye not then receive admonition?
Or have ye an authority manifest?
Then bring ye your Book [of authority] if ye be
  Truthful!
And they have invented a kinship
between Him and the Jinns: But the Jinns know
[quite well] that they will be brought before Him.
Glory to Allah! [He is free] from the things they
  ascribe [to Him]!
Not [so do] the Servants of Allah, the chosen ones.
For, verily, neither ye nor those ye worship
can lead [any] into temptation concerning Allah,
except such as are [themselves] going to the
  blazing Fire!
[The angels] "Not one of us but has a place
  appointed;
And we are verily ranged in ranks [for service],
and we are verily those who declare [Allah's] glory!"
And there were those who said,
"If only we had had before us a Message
from those of old,
we should certainly have been Servants of Allah,
sincere [and devoted]!"
But [now that the Qur'an has come], they reject it:
But soon will they know!
Already has Our Word been passed before [this]
to Our Servants sent [by Us],
that they would certainly be assisted,
and that Our forces,—they surely must conquer.

So turn thou away from them for a little while,
and watch them [how they fare], and they soon
shall see [how thou farest]!
Do they wish [indeed] to hurry on our
    Punishment?
But when it descends upon their courtyards
before them, Evil will be the morning for those who
were warned [and heeded not]!
So turn thou away from them for a little while,

and watch [how they fare] and they shall
    soon see
[how thou farest]!
Glory to thy Lord, the Lord of Honour
and Power! [He is free] from what they ascribe
[to Him]!
And Peace on the messengers!
And Praise to Allah, the Lord and Cherisher
of the Worlds.

Ibn Ishaq, *The Life of Muhammad*

Ibn Ishaq (704–770) is one of the earliest of the Prophet's biographers. The original text of his biography does not survive; it was edited, separately, by two of his pupils, and only one of those recensions (made by Ibn Hisham) survives. Below are two passages—one depicting the famous "night journey" of the Prophet's spirit to Jerusalem and its vision of paradise, the other a narrative of the fate of the Jewish community at Medina, the Banu Qurayza. Some scholars reject this (long) section of Ibn Ishaq's work, arguing that it cannot be trusted since it derives only from the recollections of Jewish converts to Islam.

THE NIGHT JOURNEY

I have heard the traditions that were passed on by Abdullah b. Mas'ud, Abu Sa'id al-Khudri, the Prophet's wife Aisha, Mu'awiya b. Abu Sufyan, al-Hasan b. Abu'l-Hasan al-Basri, Ibn Shihab al-Zuhri, Qatada, and Umm Hani d. Abu Talib. Each person passed on what he or she was told about what happened when the Prophet went on his Night Journey, and I have placed their information together in what follows. The question of the *masra* of the Journey, and the details surrounding it, is so complicated that only the power and authority of Allah Himself can understand it—a lesson for us all who would learn, and a blessing and mercy for all who believe.[3] But surely it was by the will of Allah that He took the Prophet by night and showed him all that He wished him to see, proving to the

Prophet the mighty authority and power by which Allah accomplishes whatever He wants.

The traditions I have heard assert that Abdullah b. Mas'd reported that al-Buraq—the winged animal whose stride reached as far as a man can see, and on whom all earlier prophets rode—was brought to Muhammad, who mounted it. The Prophet's Companion [Gabriel] flew with him, and together they saw all the wonders of heaven and earth before landing, at last, at the temple in Jerusalem. There they saw the friends of God—Abraham, Moses, and Jesus—standing with a group of prophets. The Apostle prayed with them, after which someone brought him three jars, one of milk, one of wine, one of water. The Apostle [later] said, "When these jars were brought forward I heard a voice, saying 'If he chooses the water, he and

---

3   The word *masra* in this context can mean either the time or the place of the journey. Muslim tradition teaches that the Prophet went to Jerusalem on this mystical trip (as Ibn Ishaq himself accepts); some scholars, though, question this. The Qur'an (17.1) states only that the Prophet traveled to "the farthest mosque" (*al-masjid ul-aqsa*) from Mecca.

his people will drown; if he chooses the wine, he and his people will lose their way; but if he chooses the milk, he and his people will be rightly guided.' I chose the one with milk, and drank it, and then Gabriel said to me, 'You and your people will be rightly guided, O Muhammad'."

* * * * *

A member of Abu Bakr's family told me that the Prophet's wife Aisha used to say, "The Apostle remained with me, but Allah took his spirit, that night."

Ya'qub b. Utba b. al-Mughira b. al-Akhnas reported to me what Mu'awiya b. Abu Sufyan replied, when someone asked him about the Night Journey of the Prophet: "It was truly a vision from Allah." This report does not disagree with the report of al-Hasan, since it was Allah Himself who said, "I have shown you this vision as a test for mankind." Neither does it disagree with Allah's word in the story of Abraham and his son, when Abraham said, "O son! I have seen in a dream that I am to make a sacrifice of you," and then acted upon it. In my opinion, Allah's revelation comes to His prophets whether they are awake or asleep.

I have heard, too, that the Apostle used to say, "My eyes may sleep, but my heart stays awake." Allah alone knows the truth of revelation, and how it was that Muhammad saw his vision. Asleep or awake, it all truly happened.

Now al-Zuhri claimed to have heard from Sa'id b. al-Musayyab that the Prophet once described Abraham, Moses, and Jesus to some of his companions, in talking about that night, and supposedly said, "I never saw a man who resembled me as much as Abraham did. Moses had a red face, was tall and thin, had curly hair and a hooked nose, like a member of the Shanu'a tribe. Jesus, the son of Mary, was of medium height, and he also had ruddy skin, but he had many freckles on his face and had long straight hair, like one who has just emerged from a bath. It is possible that his hair was dripping with water, but there was no water visible on it. The one among you who looks most like Jesus is Urwa b. Mas'ud al-Thaqafi."

* * * * *

One in whom I trust reported to me, on the authority of Abu Sa'id al-Khudri: "I once heard Allah's Apostle say, 'When I was finished in Jerusalem, a ladder appeared before me—the finest I have ever seen. It was the ladder that all men see, when Death approaches them. My companion [Gabriel] climbed it with me. When we reached the Gate of the Watchers we beheld an angel, Isma'il, who was its guard. He had twelve thousand angels under his authority, each one of whom had another twelve thousand under its command.' Whenever the Apostle told this story, he always added, *No one but Allah knows the strength of His army.* [Sura 74.31] When Gabriel brought me forward, Isma'il asked me who I was, and when I told him that I was Muhammad he asked me if I had been entrusted with a mission. When I replied that I had, he wished me well."

Another witness, one who heard it from someone who had heard it directly from Allah's Apostle, reported that Muhammad said: "When I entered the lowest heaven, all the angels smiled and welcomed me, and they all wished me well—except for one. This one spoke along with the others but he did not smile or show any joy. I asked Gabriel the reason for that one's behavior, and he answered that [that angel] has never smiled and never will—but if by chance he ever were to smile, he would smile at me; and the reason he never smiles is because he is Malik, the Keeper of Hell. I said to Gabriel. . . . 'Would you tell him to show me Hell?' 'Certainly,' answered Gabriel, adding, 'O Malik, show Muhammad Hell.' Then Malik raised the lid that covers Hell. Flames shot so high into the sky that I feared they would devour everything, and so I begged Gabriel to order Malik to send the flames back to where they had come from—which he did. The feeling of [the flames'] return to Hell was like the descent of a shadow. Once the flames were back in place, Malik replaced the lid."

Abu Sa'id al-Khudri relates that the Apostle said: "When I entered the lowest heaven I saw a man sitting in judgment of the spirits who passed before him. To some he would say, 'A good soul in a good body!' while to others he would frown and say, 'An evil spirit in an evil body!' I asked Gabriel who this was, and he replied that it was our ancestor Adam, reviewing all the souls of his descendants. The souls of all believers gave him great delight, but the souls of unbelievers filled him with disgust, as I described.

'Then I saw some men with distended lips, like those of a camel; they held in their hands flaming coals. They would thrust these down their throats, and the burning coals would then emerge from their anus. Gabriel told me these were the damned who [in life] had stolen and consumed the wealth belonging to orphans.

"Then I saw some other men, suffering like the family of Pharaoh. They had enormous bellies, so large that they trampled over their own stomachs like a herd of camels maddened by thirst. Having been cast into Hell, they constantly tramped themselves ever deeper, unable to get out of their own way. These were those guilty of usury.

"Then I saw sitting men sitting at a table, with piles of good fat meat in from of them, but also piles of stringy, stinking meat. They were eating only the rancid meat. These were the damned who forsook the women whom Allah had permitted to them [i.e., their wives] and pursued only the women denied them [i.e., mistresses].

"Then I saw women hanging from their breasts. These were the women who had given their husbands bastard children."

I heard from Ja'far b. 'Amr, who heard it from al-Qasim b. Muhammad, that the Apostle said: "Allah's wrath is great against any woman who brings a bastard into her family. Bastards deprive legitimate sons of their inheritance-portion, and learn private things they have no right to know."

As related by Sa'id al-Khudri, "the Messenger of God said: 'Next I was lifted up to the second heaven, where I encountered the cousins Jesus, the son of Mary, and John, the son of Zakariah. In the third heaven there was a man with a face like a full moon—Joseph, the son of Jacob. In the fourth heaven I saw a man named Idris—and We raised him to a lofty station [Sura 19.57]. In the fifth heaven I saw a man with long white hair and beard, more handsome than any man I have ever met. This was Aaron, son of Imran, beloved by his people. In the sixth heaven I saw a man with dark skin and a hooked nose, like those of the Shanu'a tribe. This was my brother Moses, son of Imran. Then in the seventh heaven I saw a man sitting on a throne, beside the gate that led to the immortal abode [i.e., Paradise]. Every day seventy thousand angels went in, never to emerge until the Day of Resurrection. I have never seen a man more like me—this was Abraham, my father. Abraham himself took me, then, into Paradise, where I saw a woman with ruby-red lips. I asked her whose woman she was, for she was very pleasing to me. She answered, "Zayd b. Haritha". Later, the Apostle of Allah told this story to Zayd, and made him very happy."

THE MASSACRE OF THE BANU QURAYZA

Muhammad issued an order that no one was to perform the afternoon prayer until after he had reached Banu Qurayza, and he sent Ali ahead of him, bearing the Apostle's banner. The soldiers rallied when they saw it, and Ali advanced as far as the town's fortifications. While camped outside the town, Ali heard some Jews say insulting things about Muhammad, which prompted him to turn quickly and rush to meet the Apostle on the road. He told him that he did not need to come any closer or deal with the miserable Jews.

"Why not?" Muhammad asked. "Did you hear them slandering me?" And after Ali replied that he had done exactly that, the Prophet went on, "Once they see me they will stop."

Then the Apostle approached the Jews' fortifications and cried out, "Listen, you animals! God has rejected you and brings His vengeance upon you!" . . .

The Prophet stopped by one of the Jews' wells near Banu Qurayza, at a place called the Well of Ana. His men joined him. Some of them arrived after the evening prayer, but they had skipped the afternoon prayer because of what the Prophet had said about not praying the afternoon prayer until he had arrived at Banu Qurayza. These men had kept busy instead with a multitude of preparations for battle, in the time for afternoon prayer, and they prayed the afternoon prayer after the evening prayer, as the Prophet had instructed them. Allah did not blame them in His Book, and neither did the Prophet reproach them. . . .

[The Muslim army besieged Banu Qurayza for 25 days. Finally the Jews asked the Prophet to send an emissary with whom they could discuss the terms of surrender.]

Then the Jews sent a message to the Apostle, saying, "Send us Abu Lubaba . . . so that we may negotiate." Muhammad agreed and sent him. The Jews rose to meet him, and suddenly the [Jewish] women and children raced up to him with tears in their eyes, crying "O, Abu Lubaba! What should we do? Should we surrender to Muhammad?"

"Yes," replied Abu Lubaba, and as he spoke he drew his finger across his throat, indicating that otherwise they would be slaughtered. He felt sorry for them; nevertheless, he afterwards reported, "I knew before I had taken a single step that I had been disloyal to Allah and His Messenger [in warning the Jews of their fate]." He left Banu Qurayza—only he did not return to Muhammad. Instead he shackled himself to a column in the [nearby] mosque and vowed, "I will not leave this place until Allah forgives me for what I have done!" He further swore that he would not return to Banu Qurayza nor allow himself to be seen anywhere in the town where he had been disloyal to Allah and His Apostle.

Muhammad, meanwhile, waited a long time for Abu Lubaba to return, and when he heard what his emissary had done, he said, "If Abu Lubaba had come to me, I would have asked Allah to forgive him. But since he has sworn his oath I will not let him leave the mosque until Allah forgives him."

(I later heard from Yazid b. Abdullah b. Qusayt how the Apostle of God learned of Allah's forgiveness of Abu Lubaba. It happened one morning while the Prophet was at home with Umm Salama. She said to me, "One morning at sunrise I heard the Apostle laugh. 'Why are you laughing?' I asked him. He answered, 'Because Abu Lubaba has been forgiven.' 'May I tell him?' I asked. When the Messenger agreed, Yazid hurried to the mosque and stood in the doorway of the women's quarter—this was before the wearing of veils was required of women—and announced, 'Rejoice, Abu Lubaba! Allah has forgiven you!' Several men then rushed forward to release him from his shackles, but he said, 'No! Not until the Prophet himself frees me by his own hand!' Soon the Apostle himself came by as he was going to morning prayer, and he set Abu Lubaba free.")

[After the Jews surrendered, Muhammad decided their fate.]

And so the Jews surrendered. Muhammad confined them in Medina in the vicinity of d. al-Harith, a woman of al-Najjar, and walked to the marketplace (which is the site of today's market, still, in Medina) and had several trenches dug. Afterwards he gave orders for the Jews to be brought to him in small groups, and he cut off their heads. Two whom he singled out were Huyayy b. Akhtab (that enemy of Allah!) and the Jewish leader, Ka'b b. Asad. Altogether he killed between six hundred and seven hundred of them, although some sources claim a number as high as eight hundred or even nine hundred. All of them, as they were brought forward to Muhammad, asked Ka'b what was going to happen to them. He replied, "Death, by God! What do you expect? Can't you see that he [Muhammad] never stops summoning, and that no one ever returns?"

It went on like this until the Apostle had put an end to all of them. At the last, Huyayy b. Akhtab himself was brought forward. He wore an elaborate robe in which he had torn countless holes, by sticking his fingers through the fabric, in order to ruin its value as booty. His hands were tied with a rope that hung his neck. When he saw the Apostle of Allah he declared, "I swear by our God that I do not regret opposing you! Anyone who forsakes God will be forsaken!" And then he turned to his men and said, "God's command is just—for He has called in His Book for a massacre of the sons of Israel." Then he sat down and his head was cut off. . . .

(I learned from Muhammad b. Ja'far b. al-Zubayr (who had heard it from Urwa b. al-Zubayr) that the Prophet's wife Aisha once said, "Only one Jewish woman was killed. She had been standing with me and talking. All of a sudden she started to laugh loudly; this is when the Apostle of Allah was beheading her [peoples'] men in the marketplace. A voice came out of nowhere and called her name. 'By heaven, what is happening?' I asked. 'I am to be killed,' was her reply. 'But why?' I asked. 'Because something I once did,' she answered. Then she was taken away and beheaded." Afterwards Aisha used to say sometimes, "I will always marvel at her good spirit and her laughter when she knew she was going to die.")

... Then the Apostle divided the spoils of Banu Qurayza—the property, the women, and the children—among the Muslims after taking out a one-fifth portion. He decreed the amount of shares to each person: each horseman received three shares (two for the horse, one for its rider); each foot-soldier received one share. On the day of the battle against Banu Qurayza, there were thirty-six horsemen. It was the first time that booty was distributed, after taking out a one-fifth portion, and it was the precedent used by the Prophet for dividing the spoils from all future raids.

After this the Messenger of Allah sent Sa'id b. Zayd al-Ansari (the brother of b. Abdul-Ashhal) with a number of the Jewish women of Banu Qurayza to Najd, where he sold them for weapons and horses.

The Apostle had chosen one of the Jewish women for himself. She was Rayhana d. Amr b. Khunafa, a woman of the Banu Amr b. Qurayza. She remained with him until she died. The Apostle proposed to marry her and place the veil on her, but she said, "No. Keep me for yourself, if you will, but do not marry me. That will be better for both of us." So the Apostle left her and put her away in anger at the fact that she had shown disdain for Islam, once she was captured, and clung to her Judaism. But one day the Prophet was sitting with his companions when he heard the approach of sandaled feet behind him. He announced, "I hear Tha'laba b. Sa'ya coming! She is bringing good news: Rayhana has accepted Islam!" This gave him great pleasure.

5.6 Periods of Islamic History

In terms of political developments, Islamic history can be easily divided into discrete eras. The early centuries were characterized by Arab dominance of the Muslim world, after which came the era of Persian ascendancy, after which came the long expanse of Turkish hegemony.

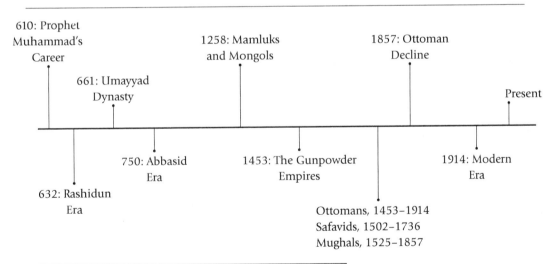

Emergence of the Holy Qur'an

610	Prophet Muhammad begins to receive Qur'an
632	Muhammad's death
632–644	First regional codices of Qur'an prepared (Ibn Mas'ud; Abu Musa al-Ash'ari; Miqdad ibn 'Amir)
644–656	Full text of Qur'an prepared under caliph 'Uthman
656–850	Final perfections brought to Qur'anic text

5.7 Genealogies of Islam

THE GENEALOGY OF ISLAM, I

Sunni Islam does have separate denominations, as the Shi'i tradition does, but it developed distinct legal traditions. This chart shows the origins of the major legal schools as well as the branches of the Sufi mystical tradition.

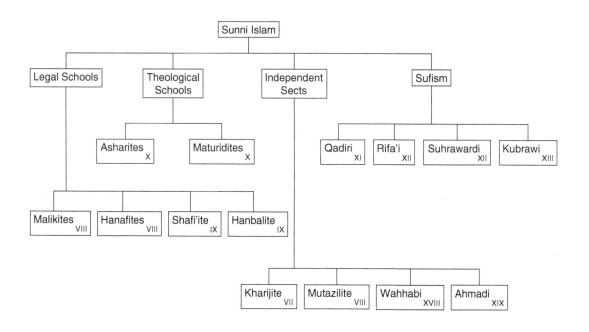

THE GENEALOGY OF ISLAM, II

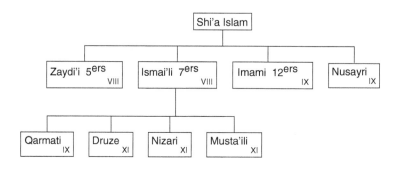

5.8 The Umayyad Caliphs

The Umayyads governed the empire from their capital in Damascus, from which they oversaw the completion of the Islamic conquests from Spain to the borders of India. The stalling out of the conquests in the early eighth century provided the pretext for their overthrow, in 750, by the Abbasids.

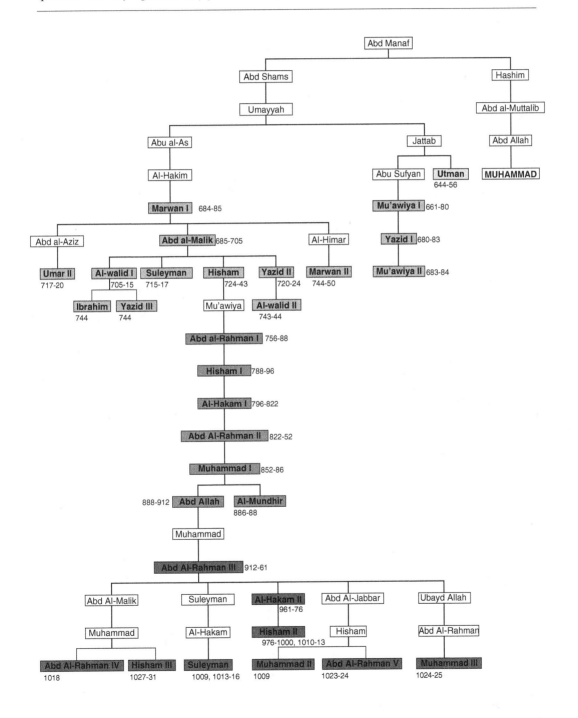

5.9 The Shi'ite Imams

The three main currents within Shi'ite Islam are defined by the number of authentically inspired imams they recognize. In each case, believers maintain that the last imam in their tradition did not truly die but went into an otherworldly hiding (or "Occultation"), from which he will return and lead the final reformation of the world before the arrival of the Day of Judgment. This messianic figure is known as the Mahdi.

Imami (Twelvers)	Isma'ili (Seveners)	Zaydi (Fivers)	Dates of Imamate	Notes
I. Ali ibn Abu Talib [Abu al-Hassan]	I. [same]	I. [same]	632–661	Poisoned by a Kharijite rebel. Buried in Najaf (Iraq).
II. Hasan ibn Ali al-Mujtaba [Abu Muhammad]	II. [same]	II. [same]	661–669	Poisoned by his wife, on order from the caliph Muawiyya. Buried in Jannat al-Baqi (Saudi Arabia).
III. Husayn ibn Ali al-Shahid [Abu Abdullah]	III. [same]	III. [same]	669–680	Killed in battle against the caliph Yazid I. Buried in Karbala (Iraq).
IV. Ali ibn al-Husayn [Abu Muhammad]	IV. [same]	IV. [same]	680–713	Poisoned on order of caliph Al-Walid I. Buried in Jannat al-Baqi.
V. Muhammad ibn Ali al-Baqir [Abu Ja'far]	V. [same]	V. Zayd ibn Ali al-Shahid	Muhammad, 713–733 Zayd, 713–740	Zayd was Muhammad's half-brother. Sources differ as to whether Zayd claimed the imamate for himself, but a group of his supporters certainly claimed it for him after he led a rebellion against the unpopular Umayyad dynasty. Muhammad was murdered on order of caliph Hisham Ibn Abd al-Malik; buried at Jannat al-Baqi. Zayd was killed in battle against the Umayyads and beheaded; his corpse was then desecrated by his enemies and its ashes were scattered in the Syrian desert.
VI. Ja'far ibn Muhammad al-Sadiq [Abu Abdullah]	VI. [same]		733–765	Poisoned on order of caliph al-Mansur. Buried in Jannat al-Baqi.
VII. Musa ibn Ja'far al-Kadhim [Abu al-Hassan]	VII. Muhammad ibn Isma'il ibn Ja'far		Musa, 765–799 Muhammad, 765–809	There was a disputed succession to Ja'far ibn Muhammad, who died in 765. Ja'far's eldest son and presumptive heir was Isma'il; but Isma'il had died in 755, leaving a young son named Muhammad. In 765 most Shi'a (Twelvers) accepted Ja'far's younger son, Musa, as imam; others accepted Muhammad, the son of Isma'il, thus starting the sect of the Seveners. Musa was murdered on order of caliph Harun al-Rashid; buried in Baghdad (Iraq). Isma'ilis believe Muhammad to be in Occultation, awaiting return.
VIII. Ali ibn Musa al-Ridha [Abu al-Hassan II]			799–811	Poisoned on order of caliph al-Ma'mun. Buried in Mashhad (Iran).

IX. Muhammad ibn Ali al-Taqi [Abu Ja'far]	811–835	Poisoned by his wife on order of caliph al-Mu'tasim. Buried in Baghdad.
X. Ali ibn Muhammad al-Hadi [Abu al-Hassan III]	835–865	Poisoned on order of caliph al-Mu'tazz. Buried in Samarra (Iraq).
XI. Hasan ibn Ali al-Askari [Abu Muhammad]	865–874	Poisoned on order of caliph al-Mu'tamid. Buried in Samarra.
XII. Muhammad ibn Hasan al-Mahdi [Abu al-Qasim]	874–?	Living in Occultation, will return as the Mahdi.

6. THE CAROLINGIAN ERA

6.1   The Donation of Constantine

This document is perhaps the most famous forgery in Western history. Most, but not all, of the text was published by Gratian in his Decretum (Pt. I, D. 96, ch. 13–14).

In the name of the holy and undivided Trinity—Father, Son, and Holy Spirit—I, the emperor Caesar Flavius Constantinus, ever faithful in Christ Jesus (who is truly one of the same Holy Trinity, our Savior, and our Lord and God), ever merciful and beneficent, Alamannicus, Gothicus, Sarmaticus, Germanicus, Brittanicus, Hunicus, ever pious, ever fortunate, ever victorious, ever triumphant, ever August, to the most holy and blessed Sylvester, father of fathers, bishop of the city of Rome, and Pope; also to all his successors as pontiff who shall hold the see of Peter until the end of time; and also all the most reverend and blessed Catholic bishops, present and future, who by this imperial constitution of mine are subjected throughout the entire world to the Church in Rome, send greetings. May grace, peace, love, joy, long-suffering, and mercy from God the Father Almighty, from Jesus Christ His Son, and from the Holy Spirit be with you all.

In the grace of serenity I wish to proclaim, in clear language and in the form of an imperial decree, to all the people in the entire world what wonderful things Our Savior and Redeemer, Jesus Christ Our Lord, the Son of Our Father on High, has seen fit to accomplish through His holy apostles Peter and Paul and by the intervention of our dear father Sylvester, pontifex maximus and universal pope. . . .

Indeed, I wish to repeat for you all to know, what I have already proclaimed in an earlier imperial decree, that having renounced the worship of idols (those deaf and mute man-made objects) and having fled the devilish tricks and temptations of Satan, I have come to the true light and everlasting life of the pure Christian faith. I now believe just as Pope Sylvester, my revered supreme father and teacher, has taught me: in God the Father, the Almighty, Maker of heaven and earth, and of all things visible and invisible; in Jesus Christ, His only Son, our Lord God, through whom all things were made; and in the Holy Spirit, the Lord and the Giver of life. I do confess these—the Father, Son, and Holy Spirit—in a perfect Trinity in which there is fullness of divinity and unity of power. The Father is God, the Son is God, and the Holy Spirit is God; and these three are united in Jesus Christ. . . .

[Editor's Note: I omit a long paragraph that reviews the major Christological controversies and asserts Constantine's total agreement with the papal position on them all.]

After the horrifying filth of leprosy had beset my flesh, I was treated by many court physicians but none could restore me to health. There then came to me several [pagan] priests from the Capitol, who directed me to construct a font on the Capitoline Hill and fill it with the blood of undefiled children, assuring me that by bathing in the children's blood while it was still warm I might thereby be healed. On their orders a great number of children were selected for sacrifice, but when the pagan priests were about to slaughter them and fill the font with their blood, my serenity was broken by the sobs of the children's mothers, and I cancelled the whole abhorrent project. Out of pity for the mothers I ordered the children to be restored to them and enriched them with carts filled with gifts of various sorts; rejoicing, they all returned to their homes.

At the end of that day, when silent night descended and it was time to sleep, the blessed apostles Peter and Paul appeared to me in a vision and said: "Since you saw fit to end your sinfulness and withdraw from shedding innocent blood, we have been sent to you by Our Lord God, Christ Himself, to lead you to health, so hear our words and obey. Sylvester, the bishop of Rome, flees your persecutions and is even now in hiding with a company of priests in the caverns on Mount Serapte. Call him into your presence, and when you do so he will show you a different pool, one of true piety, and after he has dipped you into it three times, all the strength of your leprosy will be washed away. Once this has been done, promise to your Savior that you will order all the churches in the world to be restored. So purify yourself! Abandon your idols! Worship and adore the true and living God, who alone is true, and dedicate your life to performing His will."

[Constantine then summons Sylvester, tells him of his vision, and asks to see images of Peter and Paul so that he might verify the identities of the men who appeared in his vision. Sylvester provides the images, and Constantine submits to a period of penance for his persecutions of the Church, after which he is baptized by the pope. As promised, the baptism heals his leprosy. Constantine then pledges his loyalty to the Church and its undoubted leader, the pope.]

I therefore, together with my satraps, the entire Senate, my loyal magnates, and all the people of the Roman empire who are subject to the glory of my rule, have concluded that just as Peter is known to have been the vicar of God's Son on earth so too are all the pontiffs, as the successors of that chief of the apostles, deserve to receive from me and my realm a supreme power greater than the authority the clemency of my own imperial serenity has hitherto conceded to them. In so doing I call upon the same prince of the apostles, and all of his successors, to be my constant witnesses before God. By the full authority of my earthly imperial power I therefore decree that the holy Roman Church shall be honorably venerated and that the sacred see of St. Peter shall be gloriously exalted even more than my empire and earthly throne, by bestowing upon it the power, the dignity of glory, strength, and honor of the empire. I furthermore ordain and decree that the bishop of Rome shall also exercise supremacy over the four principal sees of Alexandria, Antioch, Constantinople, and Jerusalem in addition to all of God's churches throughout the entire world. I ordain and decree likewise that the pontiff, who for now presides over the holy church of Rome, shall be raised above and made superior to all the priests of the whole world, such that all issues of service owed to God and of the health and well-being and Christian faith shall be determined according to his judgment. For it is fitting that the sacred laws [by which we live] should have the center of their power rooted in the place where Our Savior, the font of all sacred law, directed St. Peter to see up the seat of his apostolate, and where, enduring the agony of crucifixion, he accepted the cup of a blessed death and thereby showed himself a true follower of Our Lord and Master. . . .

I have conferred many of my imperial estates on the church of Sts. Peter and Paul and have enriched it with diverse treasures, so that it may continue to provide true light to all the faithful, and by imperial mandate I have also granted it numerous properties in the east as well as the west, in the north as well as the south—namely in Judea, Greece, Asia, Thrace, Africa, and Italy, as well as various islands—all on the condition that they remain in the domain of our most blessed father, Sylvester the supreme pontiff, and all of his successors.

I also confer upon Blessed Sylvester and his successors for all eternity . . . my imperial Lateran palace, which surpasses all the palaces in this world, and the imperial diadem, which is the crown of my own head, and my mitre and the stole which has of custom surrounded my neck; likewise the purple cloak and scarlet tunic and my other imperial robes. . . .

And I decree that the various clergy who serve the same holy Roman church, regardless of the order to which they belong, shall enjoy the same eminence, distinction, power, and precedence that now gloriously adorns my illustrious Senate; namely, they shall be made patricians and consuls, and be accorded other imperial dignities. . . .

By the edict I further grant permission to Father Sylvester and all his successors to appoint priests as he deems fit, according to his own counsel and pleasure—and let no man ever presume to control or influence [the Roman pontiff] in this matter. . . .

Wherefore in order that the authority of the pontifical crown shall never weaken, but rather that the dignity and power of an office greater than any earthly rule be further adorned, we relinquish and hand over to the aforesaid Blessed Sylvester, universal pope, in addition to our aforesaid palace, sovereignty over the city of Rome and Italy and all the provinces of the West. In bequeathing these places to him and his successors, and in placing them his and their authority, I hereby resolve and decree, by full imperial sanction and by means of a fixed, divine, sacred, and authoritative pronouncement, that these places hereby be placed at his (and their) disposal, and grant them as a permanent possession of the holy Roman church.

On account of all the above, I have deemed it fitting to transfer my empire and the power of my government to the east, and have so ordered a city to be built in the region of Byzantium, at the most suitable site and to be named after me, where I might re-establish my government—for it can never be right that an earthly emperor wield authority in a place where the supremacy of priests and the head of the Christian religion have been established by the Emperor of Heaven.

Lastly, I decree that all the things declared above in this sacred imperial charter and enacted in other sacred decrees shall remain inviolate and unmolested until the end of the world. Therefore, by the Living God Who commanded me to reign, and in the face of His terrible judgment, I entreat all my successors in imperial office, all my satraps, magnates, glorious Senators, and all my subjects, now and forever, never to let anyone violate or undermine these decrees. But if someone (God forbid!) show himself an enemy or challenger to these donations, let him be held and bound over to eternal damnation; let him feel the wrath of God's saint Peter and Paul, chief among the apostles, forever, and may he burn in deepest hell and perish with Satan and all the damned.

In confirmation of all this, I do place this imperial decree with my own hands upon the tomb of St. Peter, chief of apostles.

Given at Rome on the third of the kalends of April, when my lord Flavius Constantinus Augustus and Galliganus, both illustrious men, held the consulship for the fourth time.

6.2   Einhard, *The Life of Charlemagne*

Einhard (ca. 775–840) was a longtime scholar and companion in the Carolingian court during the rules of Charlemagne and his son Louis the Pious. In a short, charming work perhaps modeled on Suetonius's *Lives of the Twelve Caesars* (a medieval favorite), Einhard provides a glimpse into the daily life of Charlemagne—his likes and dislikes, his accomplishments and shortcomings. Though history remembers Charlemagne as a man of insatiable ambition and tireless political work, Einhard tempers this proto-divine view with the reminder that Charlemagne, for all his imperial titles, also loved the company of his family and friends.

[6] After his struggle with the Lombards [in Italy] ended, Charles renewed his war with the Saxons, which he had laid aside temporarily. The Franks never waged any war with such persistence and bitterness, or with so much effort, as this one, because the Saxons were as ferocious a tribe as any among the German peoples. They worshiped demons, hated Christianity, and thought nothing of breaking any law either human or divine. . . . The border between us and the Saxons passed almost entirely through open country, which meant there was no end of murder, theft, and arson on both sides, until the Franks became so swollen with bitterness that, giving up on revenge raids, they resolved on full and open war. This war with the Saxons lasted for thirty-three consecutive years and was fought with great fury—with the Saxons getting the worst of it. The war might have ended sooner, but for the dishonesty of the Saxons, since many times they were defeated and submitted themselves to King Charles with many promises to obey his commands, exchange hostages, and recognize the officials sent by him to govern them; and several times there were so crushed that they promised to renounce their pagan ways and adopt Christianity. But they proved to be as quick to break their vows as to make them, until one could hardly tell which came more easily to them. Hardly a single year passed without them committing such treason. . . . King Charles never let their faithlessness go unpunished, and his army (sometimes led by him personally, sometimes commanded by his counts) always wreaked vengeance on them until it received satisfaction. At last, after he had conquered and subdued everyone who resisted him, Charles went to the banks of the river Elbe and seized ten thousand Saxons who lived there, along with their wives and children, and resettled them across Gaul and Germany. Thus ended this lengthy war, with the Saxons finally accepting the king's terms, renouncing their pagan ways and the worship of demons, accepting Christianity, and joining with the Franks to form a single nation. . . .

[9] In the midst of this tenacious and nearly non-stop war with the Saxons, King Charles erected a number of garrisons at strategic places along the front, then marched southward over the Pyrenees, into Spain, with as large a force as he could muster. Every town and castle he attacked surrendered, and his forces suffered no losses whatsoever until the time of their march homeward. Passing [northward] through the Pyrenees, however, he suffered the treachery of the Gascons. The mountain passes there are well suited to ambushes because of the thick forests that cover the land. As Charles' army was moving through, marching in a long narrow line as required by the path, the Gascons, who waiting for them on the top of the high surrounding hillsides, suddenly attacked the baggage train and the rear-guard that was protecting it, tossing them to the bottom of the ravine. In the fight, they slew every single Frankish soldier, then plundered the baggage-train, and disappeared into the night, running in every direction. . . . Eckhardt the king's steward, Anselm the Count Palatine, and Roland the lord of the March of Brittany fell with the rest. For the time being, Charles could not avenge their deaths since the enemy had scattered so far and fast that he had no idea where to find them. . . .

[15] So much for the brilliant and successful wars waged by this mighty king through the forty-seven years of his reign. He increased the Frankish kingdom, which was already large and strong when he inherited it, to such an extent that his additional territories measured more than twice the original kingdom. Frankish rule had originally governed only the area between the Rhine and Loire rivers, the Atlantic Ocean and the Baltic Sea, and also that part of Germany inhabited by the so-called East Franks and bounded by Saxony and the Danube, Rhine, and Saale rivers. . . . By the wars described earlier King Charles subjected Aquitaine, Gascony, and the entire Pyrenees region as far as the river Ebro. . . . He next brought all of Italy to heel, from Aosta to southern Calabria . . . then Saxony (which makes up a considerable part of Germany and is by itself nearly twice the size of the Franks' original realm), both Upper and Lower Pannonia, Dacia beyond the river Danube, Istra, Liburnia, and Dalmatia (except for its coastal cities, which he left untouched out of friendship for the Byzantine emperor and the treaty he had made with him). . . .

[17] Charles showed his greatness not only in extending his kingdom and subjecting foreign nations to his rule but in planning and carrying out so many projects to the benefit and beautification of his kingdom, and bringing several of them to completion in his lifetime. Among the most deserving of mention

are the basilica of Holy Mary at Aix-la-Chapelle . . . a half-mile long bridge over the Rhine river at Mayence . . . two magnificent palaces, one near his manor at Ingelheim, not far from Mayence, and the other at Nimeguen on the river Waal. . . . Above all, he cared for the churches throughout his entire realm. When he came across any that were collapsing from age, he ordered the local priests and officials to repair them, and he appointed commissioners to watch out over the work and report on it when it was completed. He fitted out a fleet to wage war with the Norsemen and stationed the ships on the rivers that flow from Gaul and Germany into the North Sea. . . . In the south, in the regions of Narbonne and Septimania, and along the entire Italian coast as far south as Rome he established outposts as a precaution against the Moors, who were then just starting their campaigns of piracy. . . .

[19] Charles' approach to his children's education was to have both his sons and his daughters learn the liberal arts, which he himself was studying. Once they were old enough, his sons were taught horsemanship, fighting, and hunting, while his daughters learned to spin and weave, lest they allowed idleness to become a habit of laziness. Indeed, he fostered in them every virtue. Only three of his children died before he himself did, two sons (Charles, the eldest, and Pepin, whom he had appointed king of Italy) and one daughter (Hruodrud, the eldest, whom he had betrothed to Constantine [VI], the Byzantine emperor). Pepin left a son (Bernard) and five daughters (Adelaide, Atula, Guntrada, Berthaid, and Theoderada); at the time of Pepin's death, King Charles gave a powerful illustration of his fatherly love by appointing his grandson (Bernard) to succeed Pepin, and by having his granddaughters brought up as his own daughters. When Charles, Pepin, and Hruodrud died, Charles was less stoic than one might have expected from a man of his makeup. His emotions, though, were as strong as his resolve, and he was moved to tears. And when he learned of the death of Pope Hadrian in Rome, whom he had loved most among all his friends, Charles wept as though he had lost a brother or another son. He had a gift for forming friendships, in fact; he made friends easily and kept them devotedly, cherishing the connections he had with each one. He took great care in the raising and training of his children, and never took his meals without them, when he was at home, and never travelled without them, when he could avoid it. His sons always rode at his side; his daughters rode behind, with a bodyguard assigned to protect them. It was curious that he never allowed them to marry, either to any Frank or foreigner. They were all handsome girls, and he loved them all so dearly that he insisted on keeping them all at home until he died, saying that he could not bear living without them. Though outwardly happy, he thereby brought on his own misfortune regarding them. For the while, though, he hid his knowledge of the rumors that circulated about them and the suspicions whispered about the girls' honor. . . .

[26] Christianity had been instilled in him since birth, and he cherished its teachings with profound passion and dedication. That is why he built the lovely basilica at Aix-la-Chapelle and decorated it with gold and silver lamps, and with railings and doors of polished brass. He ordered the marble columns to be shipped from Rome and Ravenna since he could find nothing suitable anywhere else. He worshipped regularly here as long as his health permitted, praying morning and evening, and often after night had fallen, in addition to attending Mass [on Sundays]. He insisted that all the services performed there were conducted scrupulously, often even warning the sextons to check that nothing improper or unclean was present anywhere in the building. He presented the church with innumerable gifts of sacred vessels made of gold and silver, and with so many fine clerical robes that not even the doorkeepers (the lowest office in the church) wore their everyday clothes when performing their duties. Lastly, he took great pains to insure that the liturgical readings and the singing of the psalms were performed well. Charles himself was highly skilled in both arts, but he never read or sang in public. He preferred to follow along, in low tones, with the rest of the worshippers.

[27] Charles was an energetic helper of the poor, in the unasked-for generosity called "alms" in Greek; indeed, his generosity was so great that he not only provided for the poor in his own kingdom, but when he learned that many Christians lived in poverty in Syria, Egypt, and Africa, and in the cities of Jerusalem, Alexandria, and Carthage, he showed his compassion

by sending them money across the sea. He also worked to keep the friendship of the [Muslim] rulers in these places so that he could more easily deliver aid and relief to the Christians living under their rule.

He loved the church of St. Peter, the Apostle, at Rome more than any other and filled its treasury with vast quantities of gold, silver, and precious stones. The gifts he sent to the popes during his lifetime were numberless, and he always insisted that his dearest wish was to re-establish the ancient honor of the city of Rome—under his personal care and control—and to defend, enrich, and beautify the church of St. Peter so that it stood far above all other churches. But while he held Rome in such high esteem, he went there only four times during his forty-seven year reign, to pay his respects and offer prayers.

[28] On his last visit, he had an additional plan in mind. Crowds in Rome had grievously injured Pope Leo, plucking out his eyes and cutting out his tongue, which forced the pontiff to send for Charles for assistance. Charles came at once, quickly restored order to the Church, and spent the entire winter there. That was when he received the titles of "emperor" and "augustus"—titles he initially resented so much that he swore that had he

known what the pope was planning to do, he would not have set foot in the church that day even though it was a feast day. The [Byzantine] emperor took this coronation very ill, and Charles bore their resentment with great patience. By means of a parade of embassies and letters (in which he addressed the Greek as his brother), Charles tamed the Byzantines' arrogance with his own magnanimity—a quality he held in vastly greater quantity than they did.

[29] After receiving the imperial title, Charles wanted to harmonize the laws of his many peoples. Those laws were highly problematic: the Franks alone had two very different complete sets of laws. He resolved to fill in gaps, to correct discrepancies, and fix what was defective or erroneous in the laws. He only got as far as supplementing the laws with a number of capitularies (and even some of these were imperfect), but he did achieve this: he had all the unwritten laws of all the peoples under his rule compiled and put into writing. He also had their ancient songs of the deeds and battles of their ancient kings written down, for posterity's sake. He began work on a grammar of his native Frankish language, and renamed the months in his own tongue, to replace the Latin and non-Frankish names used by so many. . . .

6.3   Dhuoda, *Handbook for William*

A strikingly rare example of a well-versed female author in the Carolingian period, the noblewoman Dhuoda (ca. 803–ca. 843) recorded a list of courtly guidelines for her son William, who was retained as a hostage by King Charles the Bald to ensure the loyalty of Dhuoda's husband. In a world of belligerent conflict between the heirs of Charlemagne, Dhuoda, right before her death, instructs William in how to become a loyal vassal, a useful member of court, and, above all, a good Christian. In the genre of a "mirror" or "handbook," this work expresses a mother's sense of loss blended with pride and hope for her distant son.

In the name of the Holy Trinity, here begins the handbook which Dhuoda, his mother, sent to her son William.

I know very well how most women rejoice to be with their children in this world, but I, Dhuoda, live far away from you, William, am anxious and want to

do something special for you—so I am sending you with little book of mine, written down [by a scribe] in my name. Read it and learn from it, keeping it as a mirror, so to speak. I rejoice in the hope that it may remind you, when you are reading it, of how you should behave—for my sake.

[Pr 1.1] For we humans, attaining perfection requires great and persistent effort. We combat evil things by applying the medicines that counteract them. We must struggle not only against worldly people who burn in the maw of Envy but also, as the Apostle [Paul] says, we must combat "the evil spirits in the heavens." [Eph 6.12] Why? Because there are people who, despite their worldly success and material wealth and out of some secret malice, still are jealous of others and plot against them as much as they can, even while feigning friendship. . . .

[Pr 1.4] You have many books at hand—and you will receive more—in which to read and excite your curiosity, to ponder and scrutinize, and to contemplate; you also have (and will receive more) learned men who can teach you and by whose example you can most easily learn how to behave in both aspects of your life. Consider how it is with doves—who keep watch for herons and falcons, their predators, even when drinking clear-flowing waters, lest they be captured—they fly away, laughing, and escape to wherever their pleasure takes them. You will do likewise if you, in your reading, look to the words of the orthodox saints and those Fathers who went before us, and if you observe how the greatest magnates and court figures faithfully obey the commands of God and their earthly lords. Follow their examples, if you can, and you will not only avoid the hidden snares set by those of evil spirit, but you will also elude the clutches of those who are your open enemies. Then you will increase in spiritual and physical strength and, with Christ's help, succeed. Read and consider closely what is written in Solomon's book, "I will now praise the godly, our ancestors, in their own time." [Sira 44.1]

[Pr 1.5] Although we are merely unimportant exiles who do not number among the great magnates, yet we bear within ourselves the faults of this world and are thus always pulled downward rather than lifted up toward heaven. But according to the warning given in the Old Testament, we ought to bear the names of the twelve patriarchs on our foreheads, just as the Holy Scripture commands us, according to the vision granted to Ezechiel, to take as our examples the creatures with six wings and eyes in both the front and the back of their heads. And so I offer this to you as a guiding principle: detest the wicked, flee from the immoral, the

sluggish, and the proud; and in all that you do, avoid those who are sick in their souls. Why? Because they lay snares, like mousetraps, to deceive people. They never give up paving the way to scandal and wickedness—even if they themselves tumble in order to bring others down with them. This has happened in the past; I exhort you to avoid it in the present and future. May God permit that your fate be in no way joined to theirs.

[Pr 1.6] Inquire into, hold close, and observe faithfully the examples of those men of great worth in the past, present, and future who have proven their faithfulness to God and have persevered in this world. That is the meaning of the Scripture verse that commands us to hold the written names of the twelve patriarchs in our hands and to wear them on our foreheads, and to keep our eyes looking both forward and behind. These are virtues! When these twelve men were in this world they were constantly aiming toward heaven, growing and flourishing toward God. Wise in faith and soul, theirs was a happy path as they set themselves to worthy ends in thought and deed, and they left behind for us an example, so that in seeking that same path, we may do as they did. . . .

[Pr 6.1]If by chance your heart suffers harm, perhaps at the instigation of the devil, by the temptation to fornicate, or any other goading of the flesh, resist it with chastity, and keep in mind the purity of the blessed patriarch Joseph, and of Daniel, and of those others who maintained the purity of their bodies and souls by faith as regarded their masters and neighbors. They deserved to be saved and given high honor, and to be gathered up by the Lord among the number of His saints. For as the Apostle says, "God will judge the immoral and adulterers;" [Heb 13.4] and the Psalmist relates that those who fornicate will perish far from you. And the Apostle likewise says, among other things, "Every other sin a person commits is outside the body, but the immoral person sins against his own body." [1 Cor 6.18]

[Pr 6.2] Therefore, son, avoid fornication and keep your mind turned away from prostitutes. It is written, "Do not let your passions be your guide, but keep your desires in check." [Sira 18.30] Do not let your soul fly away in pursuit of evil desires. For if you do risk giving in to one of these ills, then certainly they will make you fall upon your sword or into the hands of your enemies. They will say with the prophet [Isaiah], "Bow down, that we may walk over you." [Isa 51.23] May this never happen to you! . . . By seeking God's help, you may escape the thrill of such embraces and such tempestuous turmoil. It is indeed the eyes in your head that ignite the flesh to carnal desire, yet the struggle against these evils is an interior one. . . . "Death has come up through our windows," [Jer 9.20] and "Everyone who looks at a woman with lust has already committed adultery with her in his heart." [Matt 5.28]

[Pr 6.3] But for those who maintain continence and suppress all carnal desires, you will find it written, "The lamp of the body is the eye. If your eye is sound, your whole body will be filled with light." [Matt 6.22] . . . Learned teachers do not deny sanctified marriage to the union of flesh, but they do strive to root out filthy and wrongful fornication. Enoch was chaste, along with Noah, Abraham, Isaac, Jacob, Joseph, and Moses, and all those others who struggled to keep their hearts pure in Christ through the institution of marriage. What more can I say?

[Pr 6.4] And so, my son, whether you keep your body in the splendid gift of virginity, or in the chastity of the marriage-union, you will be free from starting this great sin. Your mind will rest secure and be in that peace that comes through the eight beatitudes. And there will be fulfilled in you, along with other worthies, as it is written, the worthy praise offered by many: "Blessed are the clean of heart, for they will see God." [Matt 5.8]

7. THE TIME OF TROUBLES

7.1 Asser, *Life of King Alfred*

Alfred the Great's reign (871–899) is uniquely well documented for the early Middle Ages. Many of Alfred's laws and letters survive, along with several translations from Latin into Anglo-Saxon attributed to him (most significantly, a translation of Boethius's *Consolation of Philosophy*). Two major narrative sources also survive: the multi-authored *Anglo-Saxon Chronicle* and the *Life of King Alfred*, written by his tutor, advisor, and friend Asser, a Welsh cleric.

To my venerable and most pious lord, Alfred, ruler of all the Christians of the island of Britain and king of the Anglo-Saxons, Asser, the lowest of all the servants of God, wishes thousand-fold prosperity in the present life and in the life yet to come, by his prayers and desires.

[1] In the year of Our Lord's Incarnation 849, Alfred, the king of the Anglo-Saxons, was born at the royal estate called Wantage in the district known as Berkshire (on account of Berroc Wood, where the box-trees grow abundantly). This is his geneaology: Alfred was the son of King Ethelwulf, the son of Egbert, the son of Ahlmund, the son of Eafa, the son of Eoppa, the son of Ingild. Ingild's brother was Ine, the renowned king of the West Saxons who journeyed all the way to Rome, where he died an honorable death and entered the Kingdom of Heaven to reign forever with Christ. . . .

[2] His mother, a most pious woman, was Osburh; she was noble in her character as well as in her birth. She was the daughter of Oslac, the well-known butler of King Ethelwulf. Oslac was a Goth, by blood, for he was descended from the Goths and the Jutes—specifically from the line of Stuf and Wihtgar, two brothers (indeed, ealdormen) who had acquired authority over the Isle of Wight from their uncle Cerdic and his son Cynric, their cousin, and promptly killed the few remaining British inhabitants they could find on it, at the place called Wihtgarabyrig. All the other inhabitants of the island had either been killed before or else had fled as exiles. . . .

[8] In 853 King Ethelwulf sent his son Alfred to Rome with great pomp, accompanied by a great multitude made up both of nobles and commoners. Pope Leo was lord of the apostolic see at that time, and he not only anointed the boy as king, ordaining him properly, but he also took him in as an adopted son and confirmed him. . . .

[11] In the year 855 the venerable King Ethelwulf relinquished one tenth of the customary royal tributes and service paid to him throughout his entire kingdom, and gave it over instead (swearing by the Cross of Christ) as an everlasting inheritance to the Holy Trinity for the redemption of his soul and those of his predecessors. He traveled to Rome that year in great state, taking Alfred with him—the boy's second journey there—because he loved Alfred more than his other sons. They remained in Rome for a full year, after which they returned to Britain. They brought back with them Judith, the daughter of Charles [the Bald], the king of the Franks. . . .

[13] When they returned from Rome, the entire kingdom was so overjoyed, and fittingly so, for his son Ethelbald [who had administered the realm in Ethelwulf's absence] had been so greedy that, if Ethelwulf had allowed it, the people would gladly have driven Ethelbald and his cronies out of the entire kingdom. But Ethelwulf, showing his great forebearance and wisdom, forbade it since doing so would only bring harm to the kingdom. Instead, and without any resistance from the nobles, he ordered that Judith, Charles' daughter, whom he had duly received from her father, should sit next to him on

the royal throne for the rest of his life, even though this ran contrary to the established custom of the country. For the West Saxons never allowed their queens to sit beside the kings; in fact, they never even called any of them "queen," preferring instead the simpler title of "king's wife." According to the ancients in that land, this somewhat disputed custom and infamous custom arose long ago, when a particularly grasping and evil-minded queen of theirs did all that she could to bring down her lord and the entire kingdom. In the process, she earned herself the people's everlasting hatred, which culminated in her banishment from the realm and in the lasting foul stigma on every queen of theirs who followed. Thus on account of this one woman's wickedness, the whole West Saxon people swore that they would never again accept the rule of a king who allowed his wife to sit beside him on the royal throne. . . . I myself learned the truth of this custom from my own Lord Alfred, king of the Anglo-Saxons, who still enjoys telling the tale of it to this day, having himself learned it from a number of reliable sources, including especially from certain elders who remembered the events in every detail. . . .

[22] Now Alfred was loved by both his father and mother (indeed, by everybody) with a united and profound love, more than any of his brothers, and he was raised entirely at the royal court and nowhere else. Passing through infancy and boyhood, he became more finely formed than all his brothers, more pleasing in his looks, his words, and his manners. From the cradle onwards, amid all the pressing pursuits of life, he was possessed of a greater desire for wisdom than for anything else, and this fact, combined with the nobility of his birth, marked the noble temperament of his mind. Because of the shameful negligence of some of his elders and tutors, however, he remained ignorant of reading and writing until he was twelve if not older. But he listened attentively to the Anglo-Saxon poetry that was read to him every day and night, until by such frequent recitations he was able to commit them all to memory. He was a keen huntsman who excelled in every type of hunting—and not in vain, either, for there was no one who equaled him in that art, just as in all other gifts from God, as I myself have seen so many times. . . .

[25] He said many times, complaining and sighing repeatedly from the depth of his heart, that of all the troubles and burdens of life the greatest for him was the sorrowful knowledge that in his youth, when he had the leisure and aptitude for learning, he lacked the teachers; but when he was older he had the teachers and scribes to some extent, but was unable to learn from them properly on account of being harassed day and night by his various illnesses (which none of the physicians on this island knew how to treat), the cares of royal office at home and abroad, and all the pagan invasions of the kingdom by land and sea. Still, amid all these earthly troubles he has never lost, from infancy right down to today, his insatiable longing for an education. He yearns for it even now. . . .

[29] In the year 868 of Our Lord's Incarnation, the 20th year from Alfred's birth, that same highly-honored Alfred (who was then holding the position of heir-apparent) courted and married a woman from Mercia—the nobly-born daughter of Ethelred, the ealdorman also known as Mucil. Her mother was named Eadburh, a descendant of the royal line of the Mercians. I myself saw his wife with my own eyes many times before she died; she was indeed a venerable woman who lived the chaste life of a widow in the years after her husband's death.

Alfred became king in 871. Chapters 30–55 relate a series of campaigns, mostly unsuccessful, against the Vikings for the next six years. His first major victory came in the spring of 878.

---

[56] The next morning at dawn Alfred moved his forces to a place called Edington, where he drew his men together in a tight formation, making a wall of their shields, and fought a ferocious battle against the Vikings. A long fight ensued, but by God's will Alfred gained the victory. He routed the Vikings with great slaughter and pursued those who fled all the way to their stronghold, where he hacked them all down. He seized everything he found outside their encampment—men (all quickly killed), horses, and cattle—and he

boldly set up his own camp for his army right outside the very gates of the Viking stronghold. After a siege of fourteen days the Vikings were so worn out with hunger, cold, and fear that they fell into despair and sued for peace. Peace was agreed upon on this condition: that Alfred could take as many Vikings hostage as he wanted, while offering none himself to the invaders. Never before had anyone ever reduced the Vikings to such terms.

After meeting with the Viking leaders, Alfred was moved by his usual compassion and took all the hostages he wanted. The Vikings, after the hand-over was completed, swore that they would abandon the kingdom altogether, and their king, Guthram, promised to accept Christianity and receive baptism at Alfred's own hand. All of this was duly done. Only three weeks later King Guthram and thirty of his leading men met with King Alfred at Aller, near Athelney, where Alfred brought them all to the holy font of baptism. Alfred received Guthram as his adoptive son. The unbinding of Guthram's baptismal robe took place eight days later at Alfred's estate at Wedmore, where the two kings remained for another twelve nights and Alfred bestowed many wonderful gifts on all the men. . . .

[76] Despite all the daily demands of his life and constant interruptions, not to mention the wars, Viking invasions, and the infirmities of his constant illness, Alfred never ignored his responsibility to govern the realm. He continued his dedication to every type of hunting. He gave lessons to his goldsmiths and other craftsmen of his court; he taught his falconers, hawk-keepers, and dog-trainers; he created wonderful jewelry of his own design that was far superior to anything ever done by his predecessors. He read aloud from books written in English and learned much English poetry by heart. He directed the activities of his whole retinue. And everything he did, he did to the best of his ability. He never missed his daily offices or Mass, and often participated in psalm-readings and in morning- and evening prayer services. Sometimes, at night, he would slip out from his chambers and visit local churches and shrines without anyone noticing, to offer more prayers. He was steadfast in charity and constantly distributed alms to everyone in need, regardless of their nationality; his kindness and generosity to all people was truly incomparable. He was

equally interested in the pursuit of knowledge, and as a consequence many Franks, Frisians, Gauls, pagan Vikings, Welsh, Scots, and Bretons, nobles and commoners alike, willingly put themselves under his authority. As befitted his royal status, he governed, loved, honored, and enriched them all, just as much as he did his own people. He regularly listened, eagerly and attentively, to public readings of the Holy Scriptures by his countrymen, and sometimes also when read by, and in the company of, foreigners. His affection for his bishops and clergy, ealdormen and nobles, officials and courtiers, was most affecting. And even in the face of so many duties and obligations, he was always willing to devote hours, day or night, to the instruction of the children of the whole royal court, guiding them in morals as in letters, and he loved them all as much as he did his own sons. . . .

[87] In the year 887, King Alfred learned to read and translate Latin all in one day, thanks to divine inspiration. In order for this to be understood by the ignorant, I shall explain at some length how this happened, despite his late start. [88] One day I was sitting with Alfred in the royal chambers, discussing all sorts of matters as we so often did, when I happened to read aloud a passage from a certain book. Listening intently with both ears and turning over in his mind all that I was reading, he suddenly pulled out a small book that he always carried in his tunic, even from his youth, in which were written all the daily collects, psalms, and prayers, and he asked me to copy out what I was reading into it. . . . [89] Once the passage was written, Alfred straightaway was impatient to translate it into English so that he could pass it on to others. . . . Prompted by heaven, Alfred thus undertook to master at least the rudiments of the Holy Scriptures [in Latin]. It was the Feast of St. Martin [11 November] when he thus began to study the truths that flower there. . . .

[91] Despite his royal position, King Alfred has suffered the piercing nails of tribulation, for from his twenty-fifth to the present day, his forty-fifth year, he has been afflicted continually by the attack of an unknown malady, such that he has not known a single hour's peace. He continually suffers either from the painful infirmity itself or from the expectation of its attack. It drives him nearly to despair. . . .

7.2 Hrotsvitha, *Dulcitius*

Hrotsvitha von Gandersheim (935–1002) is among the earliest female authors in European literature and is certainly the first woman playwright. She wrote poetry also, including a verse history of the reign of Otto the Great (the founder of her monastery at Bad Gandersheim, in lower Saxony) and several legendary tales. *Dulcitius*—translated here in its entirety—is her best known play, probably for the broad humor of its kitchen scene.

DULCITIUS (A PLAY IN 14 SCENES)

CHARACTERS

Diocletian (Roman emperor)
Agape ⎫
Chionia ⎬ Three Christian virgins
Irene ⎭
Dulcitius (the governor of Thessalonika)
Soldiers, and Palace Guards
Sisinnius
Wife of Dulcitius

SCENE 1

DIOCLETIAN: The great nobility of your lineage and your extraordinary beauty are such that you deserve to be married to the most prominent figures in our court—and so I decree it. Provided, of course, that you first deny your Christ and make sacrifice to our pagan gods.

AGAPE: We beg you to forget about us; it's futile to plan any marriage for us, for nothing will ever make us deny that Name or surrender our virginity.

DIOCLETIAN: What did you say? What sort of craziness is this?

AGAPE: Do you detect any craziness in us?

DIOCLETIAN: Seems clear enough to me!

AGAPE: How so?

DIOCLETIAN: It's simple: You toss away an ancient religion and chase after this ridiculous new Christian superstition.

AGAPE: Don't be so daring. It is dangerous to slander the majesty of Almighty God.

DIOCLETIAN: Dangerous—to whom?

AGAPE: To you and the state you govern.

DIOCLETIAN: The woman is insane. Take her away!

CHIONIA: My sister is not insane! She's right to point out your folly.

DIOCLETIAN: This one's even nuttier than the first. Take them both away, and bring me the third!

IRENE: That's me. You'll find me every bit as stubborn as the others.

DIOCLETIAN: Irene, you're the youngest in age; show yourself the most mature in behavior.

IRENE: How do I do that? Tell me.

DIOCLETIAN: Bow your head to our gods, and set a good example to your sisters. It may result in their freedom.

IRENE: The only people who bow before idols are those who want to incur the wrath of the Most High! This head of mine has been anointed with heavenly oil; I will not dishonor it by lowering it at the feet of phony idols.

DIOCLETIAN: The worship of the gods brings no dishonor to its practitioners. Quite the opposite.

IRENE: What lie could be worse—what baseness any greater—than to venerate a slave as though it were a lord?

DIOCLETIAN: I'm not asking you to worship any slaves, but the gods of princes and lords!

IRENE: Any god that can be bought cheap in the market—what is it other than a slave?

DIOCLETIAN: Enough of this. A bit of suffering will soon change your minds.

IRENE: That is what we hope for! We desire nothing more than to suffer tortures for the love of Christ.

DIOCLETIAN: Place these stubborn women in chains and throw them into the dungeon. Defy my decrees, will you? Let Governor Dulcitius deal with them.

SCENE 2

DULCITIUS: Soldiers, bring the prisoners forward.

SOLDIERS: Here they are.

DULCITIUS: O gods! How beautiful they are! What grace, what charm!

SOLDIERS: They're perfect, aren't they?

DULCITIUS: They're stunning. I can't take my eyes off them.

SOLDIERS: No wonder!

DULCITIUS: I wonder if they would ever make love with me?

SOLDIERS: We doubt you'll have any success.

DULCITIUS: Why?

SOLDIERS: Their faith is strong.

DULCITIUS: What if I try a few "sweet words"?

SOLDIERS: They despise flattery.

DULCITIUS: What if I threaten them with torture?

SOLDIERS: They wouldn't care.

DULCITIUS: What will work, then?

SOLDIERS: That's for you to figure out.

DULCITIUS: Lock them in the closet—the one in the storage room, where the pots and pans are kept.

SOLDIERS: Why there?

DULCITIUS: "Easier access".

SOLDIERS: As you command.

SCENE 3

DULCITIUS: What are the prisoners doing this time of night?

SOLDIERS: They're singing hymns.

DULCITIUS: Let's get closer.

SOLDIERS: Even at this distance we can hear how sweet their voices are.

DULCITIUS: Grab your torches and guard the doors. I'm going in to have my way with them.

SOLDIERS: Go on in. We'll stand guard.

SCENE 4

AGAPE: Outside the door—what's that sound?

IRENE: It's Dulcitius, that wretch. He's coming in!

CHIONIA: God help us!

AGAPE: Amen.

CHIONIA: What's he doing? Hear that clashing of pots and pans and fire-irons?

IRENE: I'll take a look. O, come quick! Take a peep through the crack in the door!

AGAPE: What is it?

IRENE: Look! The poor fool, he must be out of his mind! He thinks he's having his way with us!

AGAPE: What's he doing?

IRENE: He's clutching the saucepans to his chest, and now he's making love to the kettles and frying pans! He's kissing them passionately!

CHIONIA: How ridiculous.

IRENE: Look at his face, his hands, his clothes! They're all filthy—as black as soot! He looks like an Ethiopian!

AGAPE: Serves him right. A body to match his soul, both possessed by the Devil.

IRENE: Look now, he's getting ready to leave. Let's see what the soldiers do once he's out the door.

SCENE 5

SOLDIERS: What's that thing coming out the door? It's either a demon or the Devil himself. Run away!

DULCITIUS: Men, why are you running? Stay, wait! Guide me back to my chamber with your torches!

SOLDIERS: That's our commander's voice, all right, but the face is a devil's. Don't waste any time, let's get out of here. That demon means to do us in!

DULCITIUS: I must get back to the palace and tell the whole court how I've been insulted.

SCENE 6

DULCITIUS: Guards, let me into the palace. I have important information for the emperor.

GUARDS: What vile, horrible monster is this? Dressed in filthy tattered rags. Let's beat it and throw it down the stairs. Then it won't be so quick to come try us again.

DULCITIUS: Ow! Oh! What's going on? Aren't I dressed in the finest of robes, my body all clean and glowing? But everyone who sees me acts like I'm some kind of foul monster! I will go see my wife. She'll tell me the truth of it all. Here she comes! But . . . her hair is wild, and all her attendants are in tears!

SCENE 7

WIFE: My lord, Dulcitius, what has happened to you? You've lost your mind—did the Christ worshippers put some kind of spell on you?

DULCITIUS: Now I get it! Those women played a trick on me!

WIFE: What troubled me the most, what was most painful, was that you didn't seem to know there was anything wrong with you.

DULCITIUS: I hereby command—those no-good wenches will be stripped naked and paraded in public. Let them have a taste of the mockery I've endured!

SCENE 8

SOLDIERS: All this effort—and nothing happens! No matter how hard we try, these women's clothes cling to their bodies like a second skin. And our commander, who ordered us to strip them naked, sits there snoring in his chair—and there's no way of waking him. Let's go to the emperor and tell him what's going on here.

SCENE 9

DIOCLETIAN: It grieves me to hear how Lord Dulcitius has been insulted. A wretched trick! I'll not allow those contemptible women get away with mocking our gods and our rites. I'll hand them over to Count Sisinnius: he'll see to it they're punished, all right.

SCENE 10

SISINNIUS: Men, where are the sluts who are supposed to be tortured?

SOLDIERS: There, in the cell.

SISINNIUS: Keep Irene back, and bring out the others.

SOLDIERS: Why hold one back?

SISINNIUS: She's still a child, and may prove more malleable when she's not influenced by her sisters.

SOLDIERS: Yes, sir!

SCENE 11

SOLDIERS: Here are the two you asked for, sir.

SISINNIUS: Agape and Chionia, I advise you to do as I say.

AGAPE: If we do, what then?

SISINNIUS: Then you sacrifice to our gods.

AGAPE: The only sacrifice we offer is a perpetual sacrifice of praise to the One True God, the eternal Father, Son, and Holy Spirit.

SISINNIUS: That's not what I advise. That's what I'll prohibit—by torture if need be.

AGAPE: You cannot stop us. And we will never sacrifice to demons.

SISINNIUS: Don't be so stubborn. Perform our sacrifice, or by order of the emperor Diocletian I will kill you.

CHIONIA: Do what you must. Your emperor has ordered our death, so go ahead and kill us, since we scorn his decree. If you spare us out of pity, he'll order you killed too.

SISINNIUS: What are you waiting for, soldiers? Seize these blasphemers and throw them into the fire!

SOLDIERS: We'll built a pyre at once. The raging flames will soon put an end to their insolence.

AGAPE: O Lord, we know that it is not beyond Your power to make the fire forget its true nature and obey You instead, but we are weary of the ways of this world. We beg You to break the bonds that hold our souls, so that, with our bodies dead, our souls may rejoice with You in heaven!

SOLDIERS: It's a miracle! Astonishing! Their souls have left their bodies, but there are no signs of any hurt! The flames have done nothing! Their hair, their garments, their bodies—all untouched!

SISINNIUS: Bring Irene here!

SCENE 12

SOLDIERS: Here she is.

SISINNIUS: Irene, be warned: If you follow your sisters' example, you will perish like them.

IRENE: I want to follow their example, and die. Then I can share in their eternal joy.

SISINNIUS: Listen to me: Give in!

IRENE: I will never "give in" to someone urging me to sin!

SISINNIUS: If you won't, I'll deny you a quick death. I'll draw it out as long as I can, a new torment every day.

IRENE: The more I shall suffer, the greater my glory!

SISINNIUS: Torture doesn't frighten you? Then I shall try another method—one guaranteed to make you shudder.

IRENE: With Christ's help I can survive anything you devise.

SISINNIUS: I'll send you to a whorehouse, where your body will be defiled and abused.

IRENE: Far better that my body should be defiled than my soul be polluted with idols!

SISINNIUS: But if you become a whore, your pollution will make it impossible for you to be numbered among the virgins.

IRENE: It's lust that is a sin, not the being forced into it. If the soul doesn't consent, there is no guilt.

SISINNIUS: It's no good; I've tried to spare her and show some pity on her youth!

SOLDIERS: As we expected. No threat can break her. She will never worship our gods.

SISINNIUS: Then I can show no more mercy.

SOLDIERS: That's right.

SISINNIUS: Then take her! And show no kindness! Rough her up and throw her in the dirtiest brothel in town.

IRENE: They'll never get me in there!

SISINNIUS: And what's going to stop them?

IRENE: The power that rules the world.

SISINNIUS: We'll see about that.

IRENE: Yes, you will. And soon!

SISINNIUS: Men, have no fear of this blasphemer's silly predictions.

SOLDIERS: We're not afraid. We'll carry out your orders at once.

SCENE 13

SISINNIUS: Who are these men approaching? They can't be the same soldiers who took Irene away. But it is them! Why have you come back so quickly, and why are you panting for breath?

SOLDIERS: We rushed back to find you.

SISINNIUS: And where's the girl?

SOLDIERS: On top of the mountain.

SISINNIUS: Mountain? What mountain?

SOLDIERS: One of the nearby ones.

SISINNIUS: Idiots! Have you lost your senses?

SOLDIERS: Why are you so angry? Why the threatening face and tone?

SISINNIUS: May the gods destroy you all!

SOLDIERS: Why are we in trouble? What did we do to wrong you? All we did was to obey orders.

SISINNIUS: Didn't I tell you to throw the wretched girl into a brothel?

SOLDIERS: Yes, you did. But as we were heading there, two young strangers came up to us and said that they had been sent by you to lead Irene to the summit of that mountain.

SISINNIUS: I know nothing of these youths!

SOLDIERS: We can see that.

SISINNIUS: These strange youths, what did they look like?

SOLDIERS: Wonderfully dressed. They looked like noblemen.

SISINNIUS: Did you follow them?

SOLDIERS: We did.

SISINNIUS: Well . . . and what did they do?

SOLDIERS: They stood on either side of Irene, and told us not to waste time but to rush and tell you what we had seen.

SISINNIUS: It seems all I can do now is mount my horse and find out for myself who these men are who have played such a trick on us.

SOLDIERS: We'll come too.

SCENE 14

SISINNIUS: What's going on? I don't know what I'm doing. Those Christ-lovers have put some kind of wretched spell on me—I walk round and round this mountain, and no matter what path I take I can neither climb higher nor return to where I started!

SOLDIERS: We're all under the same spell, and we're terribly exhausted. If this insanity lasts any longer, it will be the death of us all.

SISINNIUS: Quick, any one of you, take a bow and pull it back as far as you can, and shoot an arrow through this miserable witch!

SOLDIERS: Right away!

IRENE: Shame on you, Sisinnius, shame! You poor man—what a shameful defeat. You couldn't get the better of a delicate little virgin girl without resorting to weapons.

SISINNIUS: Whatever scorn you want to heap on me, I accept it gladly, for at least now I am assured of your death.

IRENE: My death is a cause of joy to me, but it will only bring you sorrow, for on account of your great cruelty you will be damned in Hell. But I will receive the martyr's palm and the crown of virginity, and I shall enter the heavenly palace of the Eternal King—to Whom be glory and honor, now and forever!

7.3   Ibn Fadlan, *Risala*

We know little about Ibn Fadlan; even his ethnicity is uncertain. He was an expert in Islamic religious law (a faqih), and in 921 the Abbasid caliph al-Muqtadir (r. 908–932) dispatched him as a member of an embassy to the Muslim client-state of Bulgars who lived near the confluence of the Volga and Kama rivers. His travelogue (*Risala*, or "Journeys") provides the first detailed description of the Vikings who settled in Russia and established what would become the kingdom of Kievan Rus. In this passage he describes the Viking custom of burying the dead.

I saw some Rus people when they were camped along the river Volga while on one of their trade journeys. They were the best representatives of their people I ever saw: as tall as date-palms, with yellow hair and reddish skin. The Rus wear neither tunics nor robes; their men wear a cloak that covers one side of their bodies while leaving their opposite hand free. Each man carries an axe, a sword, and a knife—and is never without them all. Their swords are broad-bladed and grooved, like those of the Franks. All the men are tattooed from the tips of their fingers to their necks with images of green trees and other such things.

Their women wear boxes on their breasts, one on each. Some boxes are made of iron, others of copper, silver, or gold; the costliness of the boxes indicates the wealth of each woman's husband. Wives also wear gold and silver necklaces; each necklace represents ten thousand *dirhams* of her husband's wealth, and some of the women have many. Their most valued ornaments, though, are beads made of green glass. These resemble, in manufacture, some of the ceramic items I saw on their ships. The women trade these beads with one another, or else buy them from one another—sometimes at the exorbitant price of a dirham for a single bead! The beads are then strung as necklaces.

The Rus are the dirtiest creatures God ever made. They defecate and urinate anywhere, without shame. Like beasts, they do not wash their privates after sex and do not wash their hands after eating. After their travels they drop anchor (or, as with the ones I saw, tie up their ships along the shore of a river like the great Volga) and build large wooden huts for themselves on the shore. Each hut can hold between ten and twenty people. Inside, each man rests of a couch. They have

lovely slave girls with them, whom they will sell to slave-merchants eventually, and each man has sexual intercourse with a slave girl whenever he wishes, even in front of his companions. Sometimes the whole company gets involved, each with his own girl, all in each other's presence. If a merchant happens along who wants to buy a girl, he simply looks on and waits for the man to be finished.

They wash their faces and heads every day, but they do it in the foulest and most disgusting way imaginable. Every morning a servant-girl carries in a tub of water, which she presents to her master. He washes his hands, face, and hair in it, then combs out his hair, blows his nose, and spits—all right into the tub. The servant then brings the tub to the next person, who does the same, and to the next, until everyone in the entire household has washed their face and hair, blown their nose, and spat into the water.

* * * * *

Once I had heard a bit of the various actions they perform when one of their great leaders dies, including cremation, I was eager to learn more. One day, finally, I learned all about the death of one of their great men. First, they placed him in a grave—which had a kind of roof on it—for a period of ten days, during which time they had several garments cut and sewn for him. (Now, if a poor man dies they simply make a little boat, lay him in it, and set it alight. But when a rich man dies they gather all his goods and divide them into thirds—one third for his family, another to pay for his funeral garb, and the last portion to provide the liquor that everyone will drink until the day when the dead man's slave-girl will offer herself to be killed and cremated with her master. Indeed, they drink non-stop, night and day, until they stupefy themselves. Some of them even die with their drinking cups still in their hands.

Now, when the man I first mentioned died, his slave-girls were asked, "Which one of you wants to die with him?" one of them answered, "I will." She was then handed over to two young women whose job it was to watch over her. They accompanied her everywhere and even washed her feet with their own hands. Meanwhile, the dead man's funeral garments were prepared and everything was made ready for the funeral. The slave-girl busied herself throughout this time with drinking, singing, and indulging in every pleasure.

When the day of the cremation finally arrived, I went to the river to see the burial ship. It had been drawn up onto the shore [. . .] and was being guarded. A kind of dome or pavilion had been constructed in the middle of the ship and was covered with cloth; then they brought a couch with a mattress, decorated in the Greek style, and set them on the boat. An old woman, whom they called the Angel of Death, then came forward and made up the couch, mattress, and furnishings. She is the person in charge of preparing all the clothes, arranging all the funeral settings, and actually killing the slave-girl. She was a large woman, fat and grim.

The men then moved to the grave, removed the earth from the wooden roof over the dead man, pulled off the roof itself, then lifted out the dead body that was still wrapped in its funeral garb. The corpse had turned black, because of how cold that country is. They removed the liquor, fruits, and musical instruments that had been buried with him. The corpse did not yet reek, because of the cold, but had only changed color. The people then dressed him in new trousers, stockings, boots, tunic, a fine cloak with gold buttons, and a fur-trimmed hat. They carried him onto the ship and into the pavilion, and set him on the mattress, propped up with pillows, before bringing gifts of liquor, fruits, and flowers, followed by bread, meat, and onions. Everything was set before the dead man. At this point they carried in a dog, which they promptly cut in half and set inside the ship, along with the man's weapons, which were placed at his side. They then took two horses and made them gallop until they were sweating;

they then cut the horses into pieces with their swords and placed the pieces in the boat too. They likewise killed a rooster and a hen and threw those in also. At this point the slave-girl who had asked to be killed went throughout the entire camp, into every hut, and the master of each hut had sexual intercourse with her. "Tell your master that I did this out of love for him," each said to the girl afterwards.

On Friday afternoon the men led the slave-girl to a construction that resembled the frame of a door and lifted her high by the feet so that she stood overlooking this object. She spoke some words, after which they lowered her; then they lifted her up a second time and she said something more, then was lowered again. This was all repeated a third time. The crowd then brought the girl a young hen. She cut off its head, which she tossed aside, and threw the hen's body into the burial ship. When I asked my interpreter to explain, he said that the first time the men had lifted her she had called out, "I can see my mother and my father!" The second time she had said, "I see all my relatives who have died, all seated together!" The third time, she had called out, "I see my master in paradise—how beautiful and green it is! He is surrounded by servants, young and old! He is calling me—quick, take me to him!" So then the men led her to the burial-ship. She removed two bracelets she was wearing and handed them to the old woman whose job it was to kill her, the one called the Angel of Death. Next she took off two rings that she had on her fingers and handed these to the Angel of Death's two daughters, who were in attendance. The crowd then raised her onto the burial-ship, but she halted before entering the pavilion.

The men approached her, carrying shields and staves. Given a cup of liquor, she sang briefly and drank; my guide explained that she was bidding farewell to her slave-girl companions. Given another cup of it, she sang a longer song while the Angel of Death urged her to drink and enter the pavilion where her master lay. It was clear to me that the girl was hesitant. She tried to enter but could only poke her head inside. The Angel of Death, however, quickly seized her by the nape of her neck and guided her in. Instantly the men began to beat their shields with their staves so the girl's cries could not be heard, lest the other slave-girls grew too afraid ever to perform the same task for their masters. Six men then entered the pavilion and one by one they all had sexual relations with the girl, after which they left her laying at her master's side. Two men then held her feet and two others gripped her hands. The Angel of Death then re-entered the pavilion, wound a rope around the girl's neck and placed the ends of the rope in the hands of the last two men. She then drew out a large dagger, which she repeatedly plunged into the girl's chest while the men strangled her with the rope until she was dead.

After the girl was dead and had been laid out next to her master, one of the dead man's family members took a lit piece of wood from a fire and walked naked toward the boat, so that he might set it aflame. He walked backwards, however, keeping his face turned toward the crowd. One hand held the burning torch, while the other covered his exposed backside. The crowd then came forward, each carrying a piece of tinder or larger firewood, which the kinsman lit with his torch before it was added to the boat. The flames quickly engulfed the piled-up wood, then the boat, the pavilion, the man and the slave-girl, and everything that was on the ship. A strong wind blew and whipped up the flames so they became more fierce and hot.

One of the Rus men stood beside me, and I overheard him say something to my interpreter. When I asked what he had said, my guide answered, "He says that you Arabs are fools, because you take your most dear and beloved fellows and bury them in the ground where they are eaten by insects and worms, whereas when we burn our beloved ones, they enter paradise immediately." Then he started to laugh loudly. When I asked him to explain, he answered, "Our companion's god loved him so much he sent the wind to carry him away in only an hour." In truth, only an hour had indeed passed before the ship, the wood, the slave-girl and her master were nothing but ashes and cinders.

Then they piled up a mound in the place where the ship had lain after they had pulled it from the river, and in the middle of this mound they erected a tall wooden post on which they carved the man's name and the name of the Rus king at that time. Then they all departed.

7.4   Al-Kindi, *On First Philosophy*

Abu Yusuf Yaqub al-Kindi (801–873) was the first great Muslim philosopher. An Iraqi Arab, he was born into a prominent family at Kufa, about 100 miles south of Baghdad. As a young man he earned a position in the caliph's court and as a scholar at the "House of Wisdom" (*Bayt al-hikhma*), the translation center established in the capital. Al-Kindi was the first figure to urge Muslims to adopt the teaching of the Greek philosophical and scientific tradition, seeing in them nothing that undermined or challenged Islamic orthodoxy. He was more of a popularizer than a scholar. In some ways, parallels can be drawn between him and Boethius, the sixth-century scholar who attempted to harmonize Christianity and the Platonic and Aristotelian schools.

Philosophy, that is, the understanding of the true nature of things, to the extent it is humanly possible, is the most noble and honorable of the human arts. The goals of a philosopher are two: in knowledge, to attain true understanding; in deed, to act truthfully. But the work of philosophy is not infinite, since once we have attained the truth, we stop and go no further.

We do not find any truth without finding a cause. The cause of all existence, and the thing that makes everything continue to exist is Truth itself—for everything that exists contains some truth. The Truth exists of necessity; it is the reason why anything exists at all.

The most noble and honored part of all philosophy is called "First Philosophy." It consists of the knowledge of the First Truth, which is the cause of all truths. Therefore the best and most noble philosopher will be he who grasps this noble knowledge. Knowledge of causes is superior to knowledge of effects, for we only have perfect understanding of everything we know when we have fully understood everything's cause. . . .

It is fitting that we show sincere gratitude to those who contributed even a small portion of the truth, and how much more so to those who contributed much truth. Truly these people have shared the fruits of their labor with us, and have assisted us on our inquiries into further truth, however hidden it may be, by making clear the principles that facilitate our search for truth. If not for these people, the principles we have learned that guide us in our search for truth would not be known, no matter how intense our efforts. . . . Aristotle, the greatest of the Greek philosophers, wrote that "we should be grateful to the fathers of those who have contributed anything of truth, since they were the cause of the philosophers' existence." . . . How beautiful is his statement. We need feel no shame in appreciating the truth or in acquiring it from wherever it comes from—even if the truth comes from peoples and races far distant from us and far different from us. To the man who seeks truth, nothing is more important than the truth. Truth cannot be disparaged, and neither should be the one who speaks it or conveys it. Truth, indeed, diminishes no one and exalts all.

Because we desire the perfection of mankind (since truth will be found in this), we do well, in this book, to continue the practice we used in all our other writings—which is to present all the teachings of the ancient philosophers on our subject, and to do so in the most straightforward and effective ways known to philosophers. We shall bring to fruition what they were unable to complete, as far as we can, given the limitations of language. We face the disadvantage of not being able to pursue extended discussions of complicated and ambiguous issues. We are also careful to avoid the misinterpretations offered by many who are today praised for their conjectures; but these people are strangers to truth, even though they wear undeserved crowns of truth. They have indeed the narrowest understanding of philosophical methods, and paltry knowledge of what true scholars think; no, their knowledge is only opinion and common prejudice. An unbecoming envy controls their base souls, and draws a dark veil that obscures their perception of the light of truth. They label as bold and dangerous enemies people who possess in full all the virtues in which they are lacking. The thrones of wisdom they inhabit—undeservedly!—they use only to retain positions of leadership in our civic and religious life, but they themselves are without religion. For trade involves selling, and what one sells one no longer has. That is why I say that those who trade in religion do not have religion, and it is right that they, since they resist the gaining of true knowledge and call it unbelief, should be stripped of their religious offices.

Understanding the true nature of things includes: knowledge of divinity, unity, and virtue; knowledge of what is helpful to humans and how to attain it; and knowledge of how to avoid what is harmful to humans and why. This is the understanding held by the prophets of God (great be His praise). But the true prophets (may the blessings of God be upon them) gave us [only] a pronouncement of God's divinity, an exhortation to the virtues that are pleasing to Him, and a warning to avoid the vices that oppose virtue both in themselves and in their effects. That is why dedication to the pursuit of this most precious thing is obligatory for all who would possess truth. We must strive with all our strength in this pursuit. . . .

In the task of proving His divinity and explaining His unity, and in defending Him against all the unbelievers by arguments that destroy their unbelief and pull the veils from their shameful acts (thus exposing the faults in their terrible creeds), we ask Him who knows our innermost thoughts and motives to admit us into the fortress of His eternal might, to clothe us in the armor of His protection, and to aid us by the sharp edge of His sword and the invincible might of His strength. May He bring us to our goal of helping and advancing the cause of truth. May He treat us the same as those whose intentions He supports, whose works He accepts, and to whom He grants victory over His enemies (who deny His mercy and veer from the truth which is pleasing to Him).

We now bring to an end this chapter, with the help of the Patron of All Virtues and the Receiver of All Good Works.

8. REVOLUTIONS ON LAND AND SEA

8.1 Burchard of Worms, *The Corrector*

Burchard's handbook on dealing with popular religious practice forms one part (Bk. 19) of his large compilation of canon law. Book 19 is called *The Corrector, or the Physician* and is in the form of a penitential—that is, it consists of a series of 194 questions regarding a sinner's behavior, followed by the appropriate penance for the priest to assign. Burchard was the bishop of the southern German town of Worms from 1000 to 1025. Roughly one-third of the questions listed by Burchard deal with some aspect of pagan beliefs and/or rituals.

[61] Have you followed these pagan customs that have lasted even to this day—fathers passing them on to each generation like a Satanic inheritance: Have you worshipped the elements [of Nature], the moon or sun, the moving stars, the new moon? Have you chanted and shouted to restore the light to a moon in eclipse? Have you prayed for the forces of Nature to bring you aid? Have you prayed to have power over them? Have you waited for a new moon before starting construction of a new house, or for celebrating a wedding?

—If so, you shall do penance for two years on the appointed fasting days, for it is written, "All, whatsoever you do in word and in work, do all in the name of Our Lord Jesus Christ." . . .

[63] Have you ever tied knots, performed incantations, or cast spells the way that certain wicked men, swineherds, oxherds, and huntsmen do? They do this while intoning Satanic chants over scraps of bread and some herbs, all tied together with foul strips of cloth—and then they hide these talismans in trees, or throw them into crossroads, all as a means of supposedly curing their swine and cattle, or their dogs, of illness, or else as a way to cause illness in the herds of others.

—If so, you are to do penance for two years on all the appointed fasting days.

[64] Have you ever observed or participated in the worthless efforts of women, who, when starting to weave, offer magical chants over the ends of the threads in the loom, believing that if they cease the Devil will make the whole warp and woof disappear?

—If so, you are to do penance for thirty days on bread and water.

[65] Have you gathered medicinal herbs while reciting evil incantations and not, as you should do, chanting the Creed (the "Credo in unum Deum") or the Lord's Prayer (the "Pater noster")?

—If so, you shall do penance for ten days on bread and water.

[66] Have you ventured to any special place of prayer other than a church or s specified site shown you by your priest or bishop? That is, to a spring or stone, to a tree or an orchard? And have you reverently lit a candle or torch in such a site? Have you made an offering of bread or any other food? Have you sought healing of body or mind from the site?

—If so, you shall do penance for three years on the appointed fasting days.

[67] Have you looked for prophecies in any books or tablets, the way that many presume to do when reading the psalter, the Gospels, or any other holy books?

—If so, you shall do penance for ten days on bread and water.

[68] Have you ever participated in, or believed in, the grave sin of thinking certain spellcasters can control the weather by invoking demons with their chants? Or can control the minds of others?

—If so, you shall do penance for one year on the appointed fasting days.

[69] Have you ever participated in, or believed in, the falsehood that certain women, by means of spells and chants, can turn a man's hatred to love, or his love to hatred? Or that they can so bewitch a man that they can steal away all he possesses?

—If so, you shall do penance for one year on the appointed fasting days. . . .

[79] Have you ever attended a wake for the dead in which the bodies of Christians were surrounded by pagan rituals? Have you there sung demonic songs or danced dances while inspired by Satan? While there did you ever drink and laugh as though, devoid of piety or love, you rejoiced at your brother's death?

—If so, you shall do penance for thirty days on bread and water. . . .

[82] Have you ever joined others in eating the food-offerings left at pagan ritual spaces, or at gravesides, or by springs, trees, stones, or crossroads? Have you raised burial mounds? Have you ever placed amulets on the crosses that stand at crossroads?

—If so, you shall do penance for thirty days on bread and water. . . .

[150] Have you ever shared the common belief that, when setting out on a journey, one dare not depart before cock-crow because the evil spirits of the night lose their power when the cock crows? Do you believe a rooster has more power to banish evil than the Divine Mind that exists in man through his faith and the sign of the Cross?

—If so, you shall do penance for ten days on bread and water.

[151] Have you ever shared the common belief that "the Fates" exist, and can do what people attribute to them? For many people believe that the Fates can control a person's whole life the moment he is born: No matter what the person may want, they can transform him into a werewolf or some other shape.

—If you have ever believed this, that a man, made in the image of God, can be changed into something else by anything other than God Almighty, you should do penance for ten days on bread and water.

[152] Have you ever shared the common belief in those female spirits called "forest nymphs"? Some say that they can take womanly form, when they wish to,

and approach their lovers; and when they have finished with their pleasure, they disappear.

—If so, you shall do penance for ten days on bread and water.

[153] Have you ever done as some women do—that is, in preparing the table at home they set out three knives for the three "Fates" (those sisters who, according to old superstitions, sometimes come to homes for refreshment)? In so doing, have you diminished the Divine Piety and given encouragement to Satan, by believing the "sisters" have it in their power to help you?

—If so, you shall do penance for one year on the appointed fasting days. . . .

[170] Have you ever believed as some women do, tempted by Satan—that is, believing that as you lie with your husband in the silence of the night you can even yet in bodily form exit your home and fly through the skies, around the whole world? Or that you can, in such a way and without any visible weapons, kill baptized persons, redeemed by the blood of Christ? And that you can cook and eat their flesh? Or that you can remove their hearts and fill the empty spaces with straw or wood or anything else? Or that when these people have been eaten you can bring them back to life again?

—If so, you shall do penance for forty days (known as a "carina") on bread and water, for seven consecutive years. . . .

[180] Have you done what some devil-inspired women do—that is, when a child of theirs dies without baptism, they take the corpse of the child and hide it, securing it on the ground with a stake driven through it? For they say that if they do not do so, the little child would rise from the dead and bring harm to countless others.

—If so, you shall do penance for two years on the appointed fasting days.

[181] Have you ever done as many women do when prompted by the devil—that is, when a woman is in labor and cannot deliver, or if she delivers and dies in the process, they fix the mother and child in a grave with a stake driven through them and into the earth?

—If so, you shall do penance for two years on the appointed days.

[83] Have you ever placed your child, whether male or female, on the roof of your house or on top of

your oven, in order to cure him or her of some illness? Have you ever burned grain on the spot where a corpse has lain, or tied knots in a dead man's belt in order to place a hex on someone? Have you ever taken the combs that women use to prepare wool for spinning and clapped them together over a corpse [as a means of scaring off the dead man's spirit]?

—If so, you shall do penance for twenty days on bread and water.

[161] Have you done what many women do—that is, to turn away from your husband and expose your buttocks, then have him knead bread-dough on your buttocks, then feed that bread to him, as a means of increasing his desire for you?

—If so, you shall do penance for two years on the appointed fasting days.

[164] Have you ever done what so many women do—that is, to take your menstrual blood and mix it into the food and wine that you give to your husband, for many believe that this will keep him in love with you?

—If so, you shall do penance for five years on the appointed fasting days.

[179] Have you ever done what many women so often do—that is, they strip off all their clothes and smear honey over their naked bodies; then they roll their honeyed bodies back and forth over grains of wheat heaped up on a sheet that they have spread out on the ground? Then they gather up all the grains of wheat that stick to their moist bodies and take them to a mill, where they turn the mill slowly in the direction opposite the sun and grind the wheat into flour. Then they bake bread from this flour and feed it to their husbands—who immediately fall sick and die.

—If so, you shall do penance for forty days on bread and water.

8.2   Adso of Montier-en-Der, *The Antichrist Letter*

Adso (d. 992) was the abbot of a Cluniac monastery and a close friend of Gerbert d'Aurillac, who later became Pope Sylvester II (r. 999–1003). A prolific writer and advocate for reform, Adso is best remembered for an eschatological treatise he wrote for the benefit of Gerberga of Saxony, the wife of King Louis IV of France (r. 936–954). After her husband's death, Gerberga relinquished the throne and became a nun. Adso's *Letter to Gerberga on the Origin and Time of Antichrist* illustrates many of the "end of the world" concerns that were felt across western Europe at the end of the tenth century.

To his most excellent Queen, strong in royal dignity, beloved by God and all His saints, mother of all monks and preeminent among all holy women, to his lady Queen Gerberga, Brother Adso, the least of all her servants, wishes glory and eternal peace.

From the moment I first merited the grace of your pity, Lady Mother, I have always been faithful to you in everything, as though I were your own slave. That is why, however unworthy my poor prayers might be in the eyes of God, I nevertheless beg His mercy for you and your elder lord the King and for the safety of your children, that He may deign to preserve you as the Pillar of Governance in this life and to have you reign blissfully with Him in the life to come in Heaven. For we know without a doubt and do firmly believe that if God grants prosperity to you and long life to your children, God's Church will be exalted and our religious order will grow and grow. I, your faithful servant, do pray for this and desire it greatly; if it were in my power to increase your royal authority, I would gladly do so. But since it is not, I shall pray to the Lord for your salvation and that of your children, so that His grace will always go before you in your deeds and His glory will follow you in piety and mercy, and so that, being ever intent on divine commands, you may accomplish all the good deeds which you long for, whereby the crown of the Heavenly Kingdom might be granted to you. And therefore, since you always listen with pious zeal to the Scriptures and frequently speak about Our Redeemer, and since you long to know about the impiety and persecution of Antichrist, as well as his power and origin, just as you have seen fit to teach me [in these matters], I have wanted to write something for you about Antichrist, to tell you a bit about him, even though you hardly need to be instructed by me, since you have with you a most prudent pastor, Lord Roricus, the brightest mirror of all wisdom, eloquence, and morals in this age of ours.

Since you wish to learn about Antichrist, you should therefore first find out why he is so named. The answer is that because he is the opposite of Christ in all things and will always act in a way contrary to Him. Christ came as a humble man; Antichrist will come as a proud man. Christ came to raise up the lowly and pass judgment on sinners; Antichrist will cast down the lowly, glorify sinners, exalt the impious, teach vices rather than virtues, destroy the Gospel law, bring demon-worship back into the world, seek his own glory, and call himself God Almighty. Furthermore, Antichrist's wickedness has many agents, many of whom have already come before him into this world—men like Antiochus, Nero, and Domitian. In our own time, we know there are even now many Antichrists. For anyone—layman, cleric, or monk—who lives contrary to justice, opposes the rule of his station in life, and blasphemes against the good is an Antichrist and a servant of Satan.

Let us now consider the origins of Antichrist. What I have to say is not the product of my own imagination or invention, but the result of my diligent researches in all the books I have read. My authors say that Antichrist will be born of the Jews, specifically of the tribe of Dan according to the prophet who said, "Dan is like a snake in the road, an adder on the path." For he will sit like a serpent in the road and strike, like an adder, those who walk on the paths of righteousness, and he will kill them with the poison of his malice. He will be born of the coupling of a man and a woman, just like other men, and not, as some say, of a virgin alone. Nevertheless, he will be entirely conceived in sin, developed in sin, and born in sin. From the very moment of his conception, the Devil will enter with him into his mother's womb, and by the Devil's strength he will be nurtured and protected in his mother's womb, and the strength of the Devil will be in him always. Just as the Holy Spirit entered the mother of Our Lord Jesus Christ, covered her with His strength, and filled her with divinity, so that she conceived of the Holy Spirit and what was born of her was divine and holy, so also the Devil shall go down into the mother of Antichrist, fill her completely, surround her completely, hold her completely, and possess her completely, inside and out, so that, with the Devil's help, she will conceive by man, and the child born of them will be utterly foul, evil, and doomed. Hence this man will be called the Son of Perdition, because he will do all that he can to destroy the human race, just as he himself will ultimately be destroyed [at the Last Judgment]. And now you know how he will be born.

So hear, now, where he will be born. Just as Our Lord and Redeemer had preordained Bethlehem as the place where He would deign to be born and assume human form for our sake, so does the Devil know an apt place for the Man of Perdition, called Antichrist, which will serve as the root for all spreading evil— namely, the city of Babylon. In that city, which was formerly renowned as a glorious center of civilized men and the capital of the Persian Empire, Antichrist will be born. My texts say that he will be raised and brought up in the cities of Bethsaida and Corozaim, cities that the Lord condemned in the Gospels, saying "Woe to you, Bethsaida; and woe to you, Corozaim." Antichrist will have magicians, criminals, wizards, and soothsayers, who, inspired by the Devil, will raise him and teach him every type of iniquity, falsehood, and nefarious art. Evil spirits will be his constant guides, associates, and closest comrades. Then he will venture to Jerusalem, and all the Christians whom he cannot convert to join him he will kill by various tortures, and place his own throne in the Holy Temple.

The Temple built for God by Solomon is destroyed, but Antichrist will restore it to its former glory; then he will circumcise himself and announce the lie that he is the son of God Almighty. Kings and princes will be the first to join him, and through their efforts the common people will follow. The places where Christ the Lord once walked and glorified with His Presence, he will then visit and destroy. Then he will send his agents and preachers throughout the entire world. His teaching and his power will prevail from sea to sea, from the east to the west, and from north to south. He will produce many signs [of his power], marvelous and unheard of miracles. He will cause terrifying fire to fall from the sky; trees to suddenly bloom and dry up; seas to stir wildly and instantly subside; things in nature to change their forms; the course of rivers to alter; the skies to shake with winds and storms; and countless other stupendous things. He will even raise the dead in the sight of the living, causing even the elect to fall into error (if such a thing is possible). When people see so many and such wondrous signs, many of them, even the righteous and elect of God, will start to question whether or not he is the Christ Who, according to the Scriptures, will come again at the end of time. He will incite persecution of the Christians and all the elect throughout the world. He will raise himself up against the faithful in three ways—but means of fear, gifts, and miracles. He will lavish gifts of gold and silver on all those who believe in him, and those whom he cannot corrupt by bribes he will conquer by fear. Those whom he cannot win by fear, he will seduce by means of signs and wonders; and those whom cannot convince by miracles, he will simply put to a most miserable, cruel death in the sight of all. Then there will be such tribulation as has not existed on earth from the time when people began to walk the earth, right down to the present. Those who live in the fields will flee to the mountains, and those who live on rooftops will not climb down into their houses in order to take anything out of them. Every faithful Christian they find will either deny God or will perish by the sword, furnace-fire, serpents, wild beasts, or some other kind of torment, if he should remain faithful.

This horrible, terrifying tribulation will last throughout the whole world for three and a half years, but then the days will be cut short, on account of the elect, because if the Lord does not cut the days short, no one will be saved. The Apostle Paul has said as much in his Letter to the Thessalonians, in revealing the time when Antichrist will come and when the Day of Judgment will begin ("I desire you similarly to make manifest the coming of Our Lord Jesus Christ"), when he says that: "Dissension must come first; the man of sin and the son of perdition must [first] be revealed." We know that after the Greek or Persian Empires, each one of which

thrived in glory and flourished in extraordinary power, finally, like all other empires, there came the Roman Empire, which was stronger than all earlier kingdoms and had every one of those kingdoms under its power; all people everywhere either lived under the Romans or paid tribute to them. This is why the Apostle Paul says that Antichrist will not enter the world until after dissension arises—that is, not until all the lands that were once subject to the Roman Empire, break away from it.

This time has not yet arrived, though, for even though we can see that the Roman Empire is, for the most part, in ruins, nevertheless, as long as the Frankish kings (who possess the Roman title) survive, the dignity of the Roman state will not perish altogether, since it will live on in those kings. In fact, some of our learned writers say one of the Frankish kings, who will come very soon, will control of the whole Roman Empire in its entirety, and will be the greatest and last of all its kings. After governing his realms well, he will ultimately move on to Jerusalem, where he will lay his crown and scepter atop Mount Olivet. This will be the end and consummation of the empire of the Romans and Christians; and immediately afterwards, these writers say, that Antichrist will arrive, in accordance with the aforesaid statement of the Apostle Paul. That is when the man of sin will be revealed—Antichrist, who, although a man, will be the font of all sins, the son of perdition, the child of Satan (not in a natural sense, by in terms of imitation), because he will carry out the Devil's will in all things. The fullness of diabolical power and evil nature will dwell bodily within him; in him will be hidden all the treasures of wickedness and sin. "This is the enemy," that is, the one who opposes Christ and all His members, "who lifts his head," that is, rises up in pride, "above all that is called God," that is, above all the pagan deities—Hercules, Apollo, Jupiter, Mercury, whom the pagans believe to be gods. Antichrist will be extolled above all of these, because he will make himself greater and mightier than all of them—and not only above these, but above "all that is held in reverence," that is, the Holy Trinity, which alone is to be worshipped and adored by every person alive. He will exalt himself so much that he will "enthrone himself in God's temple and proclaim himself God." For as we have said above, after his birth in Babylon he will enter Jerusalem and circumcise himself, saying to the Jews,

"I am the Christ Who has been promised to you, and I have come for your salvation, to gather together and protect you, who have been dispersed." Then all the Jews will flock to him, thinking that they are accepting God when they will really be accepting the Devil. Antichrist will also "enthrone himself in God's temple," that is, the Holy Church, and he will exalt and glorify himself by turning all Christians into martyrs, because in him will be the summit of all evils, the Devil, who is the king of all the sons of pride. But lest Antichrist should come suddenly and unexpectedly and deceive and destroy the whole human race by his falsehood, two great prophets will be sent into the world before his arrival—namely, Enoch and Elijah—to strengthen God's faithful with divine arms, teach them and comfort them, preparing the elect for war. They will teach and preach for three and a half years. These two great prophets and teachers will convert to the grace of faith all the sons of Israel whom they can find in that time, and under the pressure of so great a tumult they will render their new faith invincible among the elect. Then will the saying of Scripture be fulfilled, "But though the number of the sons of Israel be like the sands of the sea, a remnant will be saved." After three and a half years of [the prophets'] preaching, Antichrist's persecution of them will blaze up suddenly and he will take arms against them and kill them, as is said in the Apocalypse: "And then they have finished bearing witness, the beast that rises from the Abyss will make war upon them, defeat them, and kill them." Once these two prophets are killed, he will then persecute the rest of the faithful, either turning them into glorious martyrs or returning them to his side as apostates. And whoever believes in him will receive the mark of his letter on his forehead.

Now that we have discussed his beginnings, let us now consider his end. This Antichrist, the son of the Devil and the foul author of all evils, after he has vexed the whole world with a great persecution and has tortured all God's people with various torments for three and a half years, as we already have said, and after he has killed Elijah and Enoch and has crowned the remnant who have stayed true in the faith with martyrdom, will finally come before the ultimate judgment of God, as the blessed Paul writes, "The Lord Jesus will destroy him with the breath of his mouth." Whether Lord Jesus kills him by the power of His virtue, or if the archangel Michael kills him, [Antichrist] will perish through the virtue of Our Lord Jesus Christ and not through the virtues of [Michael] or any other angel or archangel. Our learned men state, moreover, that Antichrist will die on Mount Olivet, in his tent and upon his throne, across from the spot from which the Lord ascended into Heaven.

And you ought to know that the Day of Judgment will not follow immediately upon the death of Antichrist. The Lord will not come to judge right away. Rather, as we understand from the book of Daniel, the Lord will grant the elect forty days to do penance for the fact that they were seduced by Antichrist. But no one knows how long an expanse of time will be, after they have completed their penance, before the Lord comes in judgment. This remains up to God, Who will judge the world at the time He fixed for the judgment of the world, even before He created it.

Now, Lady Queen, I your faithful servant have fulfilled what you asked of me. And I remain ready to obey you in any other thing you should deign to command.

8.3   The Abbasid Caliphs

The period of the Abbasid dynasty (750–1258) is commonly regarded as the Islamic Golden Age—the era of the greatest attainments in intellectual, literary, and artistic life. It is also the period marked by the breakup of the empire into a loose network of rump kingdoms, principalities, and emirates.

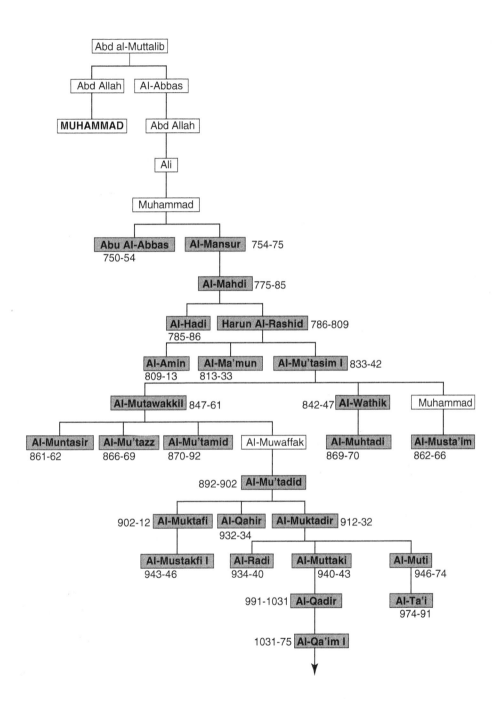

Abd al-Muttalib

Abd Allah — Al-Abbas

MUHAMMAD — Abd Allah

Ali

Muhammad

Abu Al-Abbas 750-54 — **Al-Mansur** 754-75

Al-Mahdi 775-85

Al-Hadi 785-86 — **Harun Al-Rashid** 786-809

Al-Amin 809-13 — **Al-Ma'mun** 813-33 — **Al-Mu'tasim I** 833-42

Al-Mutawakkil 847-61 — 842-47 **Al-Wathik** — Muhammad

Al-Muntasir 861-62 — **Al-Mu'tazz** 866-69 — **Al-Mu'tamid** 870-92 — Al-Muwaffak — **Al-Muhtadi** 869-70 — **Al-Musta'im** 862-66

892-902 **Al-Mu'tadid**

902-12 **Al-Muktafi** — **Al-Qahir** 932-34 — **Al-Muktadir** 912-32

Al-Mustakfi I 943-46 — **Al-Radi** 934-40 — **Al-Muttaki** 940-43 — **Al-Muti** 946-74

991-1031 **Al-Qadir** — **Al-Ta'i** 974-91

1031-75 **Al-Qa'im I**

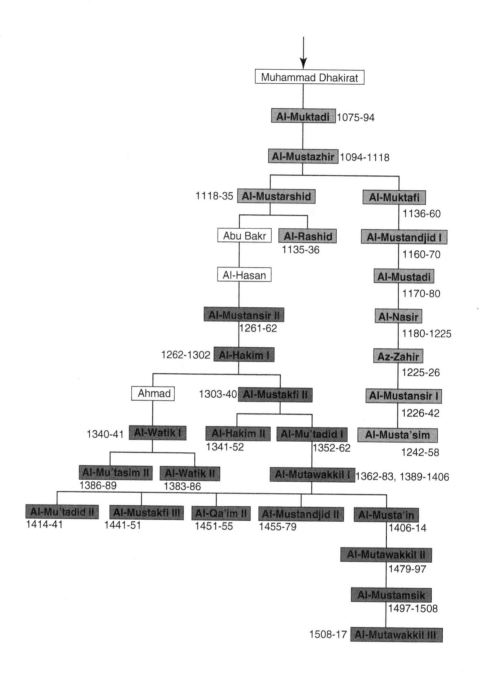

Muhammad Dhakirat

Al-Muktadi 1075-94

Al-Mustazhir 1094-1118

1118-35 Al-Mustarshid

Abu Bakr

Al-Rashid
1135-36

Al-Hasan

Al-Mustansir II
1261-62

1262-1302 Al-Hakim I

Ahmad

1303-40 Al-Mustakfi II

1340-41 Al-Watik I

Al-Hakim II
1341-52

Al-Mu'tadid I
1352-62

Al-Mu'tasim II
1386-89

Al-Watik II
1383-86

Al-Mutawakkil I 1362-83, 1389-1406

Al-Mu'tadid II
1414-41

Al-Mustakfi III
1441-51

Al-Qa'im II
1451-55

Al-Mustandjid II
1455-79

Al-Musta'in
1406-14

Al-Muktafi
1136-60

Al-Mustandjid I
1160-70

Al-Mustadi
1170-80

Al-Nasir
1180-1225

Az-Zahir
1225-26

Al-Mustansir I
1226-42

Al-Musta'sim
1242-58

Al-Mutawakkil II
1479-97

Al-Mustamsik
1497-1508

1508-17 Al-Mutawakkil III

9. A NEW EUROPE EMERGES: NORTH AND SOUTH

9.1 *The Song of Roland*

This *chanson de geste* was passed down orally for several generations and recorded between 1140 and 1170. The oldest existing work of vernacular French literature, it recounts the story of the brave count Roland, a kinsman of the emperor Charlemagne, who led the rear guard of the Frankish army into Spain on a mission to liberate Christian cities from Saracen, or Muslim, rule. Historically, the devastating battle described in this story occurs in 778 in a mountain pass in the Pyrenees, called Roncevaux—but between the Frankish forces and local Basque tribes, not Muslims as depicted in this story. A troubadour would have sung this tale; allegedly, it was performed for the army of William the Conqueror while waiting on the Norman beach to cross the English Channel. Consider how this tale might have appealed to aristocratic, warrior audiences.

91

Roland has made it to the mountain pass
astride his fine, swift horse Veillantif.
Well armored, he makes a fine sight
and brandishes his spear, pointing its tip
to the bright sky. A snow-white pennant streamed
down its length, and its golden fringe played
about his hands. His body is nobly-formed,
his face fair and smiling. His Frankish companions
hail him as their leader and close around him.
Humbly, he addressed noble words to them all:
"Ride gently, dear barons, and not too fast.
The Saracens are rushing to their own slaughter,
and today we will gain such glorious spoils
as no king of France has ever yet achieved!"
And with these words, the two armies strike.

111

The battle was wild and fierce: Oliver and Roland
stood in the thick of it, striking powerful blows,
while the archbishop [Turpin] dished out more than
a thousand. None of the knights held back, and all
the Franks fought as one. Hundreds of the
    enemy fell,
then thousands more. Certain death awaited all
    who did not flee;
wishing it or not, they witnessed the end of
    their lives.
But the Franks started to lose some of their best
    knights;
nevermore would they see their fathers or
    kinsmen,
or King Charles who awaited them beyond the pass.
Then a terrible storm passed over France, a tempest
filled with thunder and raging wind. Rain and hail
beyond measure started to fall, and lightning
    struck
again and again. The whole earth from Besançon
to the port of Wissant, and from Mont Saint
    Michel to Seinz,
started to quake. No house escaped losing its walls.
At noon a great darkness gathered and there was
    no light
save from a few cracks in the sky's gloom.
Fear fell on everyone who saw it. Many cried that
the end of the world was approaching. They were
    wrong,
but without knowing it they thereby began
The great dirge for the loss of Roland.

115

The archbishop rode to the head of the battle
astride the swift and lively war-horse he won
    in Denmark,
when he slew the king, Grossaille. Its hooves
were finely cut and its legs trim, short-haunched
and broad-chested, long-flanked and
high along the back. It had a white tail and
yellow mane, with small ears and a tawny head.
No horse could match it for speed. The
    archbishop boldly
spurred him forward, eager to confront Abisme,
    whom
he dealt a massive blow on his shield studded with
precious stones—amethyst and topaz, fiery
    gemstones all.
It had once belonged to the emir Galafres, whom
    a demon
inspired to give it to Abisme in Val Metas.
Turpin hammered at it without giving it a thought,
until it was hardly worth a penny, then he cut
    right through
Abisme and flung his dead body to the bare
    ground.
The Franks shouted, "Turpin's bravery is worthy
    of him!
The crozier is safe in that archbishop's hands!"

134

In deadly agony, filled with pain and woe,
Count Roland mightily sounded his horn.
Bright blood burbled from his mouth and
the temples in his skull burst from the effort.
The blast of the horn carried far on the air
and King Charles heard it as he went through
    the pass.
Duke Naimes heard it too, along with all the
    Franks.
"That is Roland's horn!" cried the king. "He would
never blow it unless battle was upon him."
"Battle?" said Ganelon, "there is no battle.
You're an old man, white-haired and hoary.
Such talk makes you sound like a child. Have you
Forgotten Roland's great pride? I'm surprised
God Himself has put up with it so long."

171

Roland was aware of his eyesight failing
and rose to his feet, using all his remaining strength.
All the color had left his bloodless face.
In front of him stood a dark brown stone,
    and on it
he smote Durendal, his sword, ten strong blows.
In bitter sorrow he saw the steel grate on the rock;
but it would not break or chip. "Holy Mary!"
    he cried,
"help me! O Durendal, trusty sword, what an
    ill fate!
I am dying and have no further need of you—
you, with whom I won so many battles in the field
and conquered so many vast realms that now
are under King Charles' dominion. May you never
be possessed by one who runs from an enemy.
A brave and true vassal held you for so long—one
    whose
like will never be seen again in France!"

172

Roland swung again at the hard stone. The
    steel again
grated but did not shatter or crack; when
    Roland saw
that he could not break it, he called out in lament.
"O Durendal! How fair and bright, how
    gleaming, you are!
You shimmer and glint in the sun! It was when
    Charles rode
in the Vale of Maurienne that God sent an angel,
    commanding
him to award you to a brave captain—and the
    noble king promptly
strapped you upon me. With you I conquered
    Anjou and
Brittany, Poitou and Maine; with you I conquered
    untamed
Normandy, Provence, and Aquitaine, and Lombardy
and all of Romagna. Burgundy and Apulia too.
Also Constantinople, who gave Charles the
    homage he deserved.
And Saxony also now obeys his commands.
    With you,

Durendal, I conquered Scotland, Ireland, and
England, which now

also serve our king. How many lands have I won
with you,

to the honor of white-bearded Charles. For you
I grieve.

I would rather die than leave you to fall into
pagan hands.

O God, our Father! Spare France from this
disgrace!"

173

Roland swung yet again at the dark stone and
broke off

more of it than I can tell—but still the sword
only grated,

refusing to shatter or crack, and then bounced
back toward the sky.

When the brave count saw that he would never
break it

he murmured a soft lament: "O Durendal, how
fair and holy

you are! In your hilt are sacred relics—a tooth of
Saint Peter's

and some blood of Saint Basil! Hair from the
head of

Saint Martin, and a piece of Holy Mary's robe!

It would be shameful for pagans to possess you.

No! You must lie in the hand of a Christian knight,

one who never shrinks from battle! With you I have

conquered lands unnumbered, which
white-bearded

Charles now holds, making him rich and mighty
on earth."

176

Count Roland laid down beneath a pine tree and

turned his face toward Spain. A rush of memories
filled

his mind: of all the lands he conquered, of the
fair realm

of France, of the men in his bloodline, of King
Charles,

his lord, who raised him. He could not help
weeping, nor

control his sobs, but he remembered to mind
his soul

and so called our his confession and prayed
for grace:

"O Father, ever True and unstained by a lie,

You Who raised Lazarus from the dead and
rescued Daniel

in the lions' den, protect my soul from the perils
I deserve

on account of all the sins I have committed in life!"

He removed his right-hand glove and held it aloft.

Saint Gabriel appeared and took it from
Roland's hand.

Then Roland laid his head to one side and with
hands clasped

he went to his rest. God sent His angel Cherubin
and Saint Michael

of the Peril, along with Saint Gabriel, and
together they

lifted Roland's soul to paradise.

177

Roland was dead but his soul was with God.

When King Charles arrived at Ronceveaux he found

no road or path, no clearing, not even a square yard

that did not lay covered with Frankish and
pagan dead.

Charles cried out, "Roland, dear nephew! Where
are you?

Where is the archbishop and Count Oliver?

Where is Lord Gerin and his comrade-in-arms
Gerier?

Where is Lord Otto and Count Berenguer?

Yvon and Yvor, so dear to me? Engelier of
Gascony,

Duke Samson, and brave Anseis? Where is old
Gerard

of Roussillon? Where are my twelve peers, the
ones I left behind?"

But it was all in vain: no answer came.

"O God!" cried the king, pulling at his beard in
his grief,

"what a sorrow that I was not here for this battle!"

His brave knights wept, and full twenty thousand
of them

fell instantly to the ground in a faint.

9.2   *The Song of the Cid*

The Song of the Cid provides a sharp contrast to its roughly contemporary *Song of Roland*.

1

Tears streamed plentifully from his eyes
as the Cid turned his head toward the crowd,
standing there he saw opened doors and
    unlocked gates
empty pegs without tunics or cloaks and
    perches
without falcons or moulted hawks. He sighed
for he was heavy with great cares. But then
the Cid spoke, nobly and with measured
    speech
"I give thanks to You, O God, Our Father in
    heaven.
My enemies have done this evil to me!"

2

Prepared for their journey and letting go
    the reins,
they left Vivar. A crow flew on their right, which
they saw again, on their left, when entering
    Burgos.
With a shrug of his shoulders the Cid nodded
    his head:
"Cheer up, Alvar Fañez! We are banished from
    this land!"

3

The Cid, Ruy Díaz, entered Burgos
with his company of sixty knights.
Men and women everywhere came to see him,
while the burghers and their wives stood at their
    windows
weeping sorrowfully, so great was their pain.
With one accord they all spoke aloud:
"O God, such a good vassal! If only he had a
    good lord!"

4

They would have received him gladly, but no
    one dared
out of fear of the king's wrath. His declaration
had arrived the night before, severe and heavily
    sealed:
No one was to give shelter to the Cid, and any
    one who did
would certainly forfeit all he possessed; his
    eyes would be
plucked out, and he would lose both body and soul.
All Christians were overcome with sorrow,
    therefore,
and hid from the Cid, nor dared to speak to him. . . .

The Cid built a small army with funds he borrowed (under shady circumstances) from some Jewish friends, and the Cid and his men then set out for the frontier, fighting and raiding, sometimes for themselves and sometimes as mercenaries. They fought against, and for, Christians and Muslims alike. As they grew wealthier, the Cid attracted more and more recruits, until he was ready to launch an assault on the Moorish-held city of Valencia.

72

He taught the people of Valencia a valuable
    lesson

such that they dared not come out of the town to
    do battle.

He cut down their crop fields and did tremendous
        damage.
For several years in a row the Cid cut off their
        food supply.
The Valencians cried out, for they were at their
        wits' end
with no food to be found anywhere. Fathers could
        do nothing
for their sons, nor sons for their fathers; neither
        could anyone
console a friend. A cruel fate it is, my lords, for
        men to watch
their wives and children die, for want of food.
        They faced disaster
and there was nothing they could do about it.
        They appealed
for aid to the king of Morocco, but he was mired
        in war already
with the [Muslim] ruler of the Atlas Mountains,
        and could send
neither supplies nor assistance. News of this
        pleased the Cid,
who set out from Murviedro, marching all night
        until he arrived
in the land of Monreal. He sent messenger to
        proclaim
throughout Navarre, Aragon, and Castile that
        anyone who wanted
to exchange poverty for prosperity should rush
        to join the Cid,
who was planning to ride on to the siege of
        Valencia and restore
it to the Christians.

73

"Whoever wishes to join me in the attempt on
        Valencia,
let him come, freely and of his own accord. I will
        force no one.
I shall wait for three days at Canal de Cella!"

74

So spoke the Cid, the one born in a fortunate
        hour.
He returned to Murviedro, which he had already
        conquered.

His words were heard everywhere, and all with
        a taste
for plunder rushed to join him. Countless good
        Christians
entered his service, and the Cid of Vivar grew in
        wealth.
When he saw the multitude he was filled with joy,
and not wanting to delay he hurried on to
        Valencia
and began the siege. He encircled the city—
No one in, and no one out. News of his exploits
spread throughout the land, and far more people
        joined him
than left. He decided on a deadline for Valencia
        to surrender:
Nine months he besieged them, and in the tenth
        they gave in.
Great was the joy throughout the region when
        the Cid
won Valencia and entered the city. His
        foot-soldiers
were rewarded with horses, and there was so
        much gold and silver
to distribute (who could possibly count it all?)
        that everyone
became rich. The Cid, Don Rodrigo, commanded
        that
his one-fifth share be set apart—and this alone
amounted to thirty thousand marks, while the
        remainder
was beyond reckoning. Happy was the Champion
and all his men when they saw his banner flying
above the citadel.

75

The Cid and his company could rest at last.
When the [Muslim] king of Seville learned of
        Valencia's fall,
he came with thirty thousand men at arms and
        joined
battle with [the Cid] on the surrounding plain.
Don Rodrigo, his long beard flowing, routed
        them all
and chased them to Játiva. When the Moors tried
        to cross

the Jucár river, they struggled in the current and
nearly drowned.
The king of Morocco escaped with three wounds,
while
the Cid returned laden with booty. As profitable
as the seizure

of Valencia had been, this victory brought even
greater wealth,
since every Muslim soldier received one hundred
silver marks.
The Cid's wealth grew as great as his fame.

The Cid then brought his wife and two daughters, who had been housed with friends for safekeeping
during his campaign, to Valencia.

87

Then the Cid led them up to the citadel and even
to the
highest tower, from where they could cast their
fair eyes
over the whole scene. They marveled at the city
that lay
before them, with the sea on one side and the
broad, fertile
plain on the other. They raised their hands in prayer
to thank God for the good fortune that had
befallen them.
The Cid and his company were well-pleased.
The winter was ending, and March was coming in.
And now I must bring you news from across
the sea—
news of King Yusuf of Morocco.

88

The Moroccan king raged against Don Rodrigo:
"He attacks my land—and credits his success to
Jesus Christ!"
And so he mustered his forces, fifty thousand strong,
and set to sea in ships, bound for Valencia, to seek
the Cid.
When the ships landed, they all disembarked.

89

Having reached Valencia, which the Cid had
captured,
they pitched their tents and set up their camps.
Receiving this news, the Cid cried aloud:

90

"Thanks to Our Creator, Our Father in Heaven!
All that is dear to me is here in Valencia, which
I won
with hard fighting. It is now my inheritance, and
only death
can make me give it up. Thanks to Our Creator and
His Blessed Mother, Mary, I have my wife and
daughters here.
And now a treat comes from across the sea! I will
take up arms (how can I resist?), and now my
family
will be able to see me fight, and with their own eyes
they will see how we earn our bread and make
our homes
in this strange land." He placed his wife and
daughters
in the high citadel, and when they saw all the
tents and camps
his wife cried out: "What is all this, my Cid?
Heaven, save us!"
"Noble wife," he replied, "have no fear. A great
and wonderful
treasure awaits us! No sooner have you arrived,
than these
people here wish to give you a present! Your
daughters are
of marriageable age; these people are offering you
a dowry!"
"Thanks to you, my Cid," she answered, "and to
Our Heavenly Father."
"Stay here in the castle, dear wife," said the Cid,
"and do not fear

when you see me in battle. For by the grace of
God and
His Holy Mother, Mary, I feel stronger of heart
because
you are here. With God's help, I will be
victorious."

91

Dawn broke over the Moors' encampments, and
they started
beating their drums. This pleased the Cid, who
cried out:
"What a great day this will be!" His wife was
frightened and
clutched at her heart; their daughters and their
ladies-in-waiting
were fearful too; they had never been so scared
a day in their lives.
Stroking his beard, the Cid, the Champion,
called out:
Do not be afraid! All will be well! I will capture
those war-drums
within fifteen days, please God, and lay them
before your eyes
for you to inspect. After that, however, they'll
belong to
our bishop, Jerome, who will hang them up in
the Church of Our Lady,
the Mother of God." Such was the Champion's
vow. His ladies
grew less fearful and were heartened. Meanwhile
the Muslims
from Morocco advanced boldly into the plain,
showing no fear.

92

A guard saw them approach and rang the
alarm bell.
Quickly the Christian soldiers were on the alert,
and donning
their armor they boldly marched out of the town.
They fell upon the Moors and attacked them
at once,
driving them forcefully from the plain and killing
some five hundred of them before the day
was done.

93

They pressed hard on the Moors, accomplishing
much
and pursuing them all the way to their camps. But
Alvar Salvadórez was taken prisoner by them.
The company
returned to the Cid and told him what they had
accomplished,
which he had seen from a distance, and the Cid
was pleased.
"Hear me, brave knights!" he called. "It is not yet
finished!
Today has been a good day, and tomorrow will
be better.
Be armed and ready for battle at daybreak.
Bishop Jerome
will celebrate Mass for us and grant us
absolution; then
we will ride out and attack in the name of Our
Creator and
His Apostle Saint James. It is better that we
defeat them
than to let them endanger our food supply.
Everyone replied: "We will, freely and out of our
love for you!"
Then Minaya quickly added: "If you are willing,
my lord,
grant me one hundred and thirty knights, ready
for battle,
and when you attack from the front I will lead
an attack
from the flank. With God's help, at least one of
us will succeed."
The Cid replied: "I grant it willingly."

94

The day had ended and night had arrived
when the Christians began to arm themselves
again.
At three hours before sunrise Bishop Jerome
celebrated Mass
and absolved them all with these words:
"I absolve the sins
of each man among you who dies confronting
the enemy.

God will receive your souls. And now to you,
    Don Rodrigo,
born in a fortunate hour, I direct some words:
    I have sung

the Mass for you this morning; do now grant me
    the favor
of letting me strike the first blows."
"It is granted!" said the Champion.

After another great victory, the Cid returns to Valencia. King Alfonso reconciles with him and as a sign of their renewed friendship arranges for the Cid's daughters to marry two royal princes.

111

They set to work preparing the palace: they hung
fine silks, satins, and other priceless cloths on
    the walls
and spread them on the floors. What a pleasure,
    to be among
those who were part of the feast! All the knights
    crowded in.
The princes of Carrión, being summoned, rode to
    the castle
beautifully clothed and in full armor. They
    entered,
marching in a stately way. How dignified they were!
The Cid and his vassals received them. The
    princes
bowed low to him and his wife, then sat on a
    beautiful bench.
The Cid's trusty men paid close attention to the one
born in a fortunate hour. He rose to speak:
"Since we are here for a purpose, let us not delay!
Come here, my dearly loved Alvar Fañez. I place
in your hands my beloved daughters, as I had
    promised
the king. I do not want to fail in any detail.
    Take them
by the hand and deliver them to the princes of
    Carrión;
Let them all receive the marriage blessing, and so
    fulfill
our promise." Minayo answered: "With pleasure,
    my lord!"
The daughters rose and the Cid handed them to
    Minaya,
who then addressed the princes of Carrión:
    "Behold!

I, Minaya, stand before you two brothers. By order of
King Alfonso I present you with these two noble
    ladies,
the beloved daughters of this place, to be your
    lawful wives."
The princes received them with affection and joy,
    and kissed
the hands of the Cid and his wife. When the
    ceremony
had ended, they all left the palace and hastened
    to the Church
of Holy Mary, where Bishop Jerome, who had
    already
donned his vestments, awaited them at the door.
He blessed them and sang the Mass. Once they
    had left
the church, the men rode alone to the seashore of
    Valencia.
Heavens, what a show of arms the Cid put on!
    Three times
he changed horses, making a fine display, and he
    was pleased
to see the fine horsemanship of the princes of
    Carrión too.
Afterwards the men rejoined the women in the
    city, where
the rest of the wedding festivities were celebrated
    in the castle.
The next day the Cid set up seven planks, which
    were lowered
into place for the company to enjoy a banquet.
    For fifteen days
they celebrated, and when these days drew to a close
the nobles left for home. Don Rodrigo, born in a
    fortunate hour,

presented gifts to them first: palfreys, mules, and
chargers,
a hundred in all, along with mantles and furs and
other
fine garments; neither did he forget [to bestow]
vast sums
of money. The Cid's vassals also awarded gifts to
each one.
Whoever was willing to receive such bounty was
richly rewarded,
and all the wedding guests returned to Castile rich
men indeed.
And so the guests departed, bidding farewell to
the Cid,
his wife, and all his noble vassals, rejoicing and
praising

the hosts, as was fitting. Joyful indeed were Diego
and Fernando,
the sons of Don Gonzalo. The Cid and his
sons-in-law
stayed in Valencia. For two years the princes lived
there,
receiving the love of the family, which greatly
pleased
the Cid and his vassals. May Holy Mary and Our
Father
grant that these marriages bring happiness to
Don Rodrigo
and King Alfonso!

Here the verses of this Song end.
May God and all of His Holy Saints protect you!

9.3 Otto of Freising, *The Two Cities*

Bishop Otto of Freising (1115–1158) is one of our best sources for the German empire from the
tenth to twelfth centuries. His book *The Two Cities* is an example of a "universal history": in eight
books it proceeds from the creation of the world and the story of Adam and Eve to Otto's own time.
The goal of "universal history" was to view contemporary events in a broader context, in the effort
to see God's hand at work in the world. In this passage from Book Six (ch. 27–33) Otto relates the
German leaders' role in spreading Latin Christianity into eastern Europe, among the Poles and
Hungarians.

[27] In the year 1001 from the Incarnation of Our
Lord, the emperor Otto [III] died without an heir,
and Duke Henry of Bavaria, the son of Hezilo, was
elected to succeed him by all the nobles. He was the
eighty-seventh ruler in line from Augustus. Henry
waged many wars—bravely, successfully—throughout
Germany, Bohemia, Italy, and Apulia until God finally
granted him his rest, and being so devout in his
Christian faith, he established the renowned bishopric
of Bamberg and endowed it with the many lands and
honors we see in our own lifetime. Moreover, he gave
his sister Gisela in marriage to Stephen, the king of
the Hungarians, in return for having Stephen and all
his people convert to the true faith. The Hungarians,

to this day a most pious Christian people, regard
Stephen as the founder of their faith and even revere
him as a saint. But the pious emperor Henry departed
from the world in his twenty-fourth year as duke (the
eleventh of his years as emperor) and was buried in
the cathedral church at Bamberg, where, as is well
known, his tomb is today renowned for the miracles
performed at it.

[28] In the year 1025 from the Incarnation of Our
Lord, Conrad, a Frank, was unanimously elected to succeed Henry, who had died without an heir and had personally recommended Conrad, even though Conrad
had not been a royal favorite during Henry's time on
the throne. Conrad thus became the eighty-eighth in

line from Augustus. On his father's side, Conrad was descended from Duke Conrad of Worms, who had died in Otto [III's] wars against the Hungarians; on his mother's side, his ancestors included the most illustrious princes of Gaul, descended from the ancient race of Trojans, and baptized in the faith by the Blessed Remigius. Conrad's wife was also named Gisela, who sprang from the ancient and glorious blood of the Carolingians. As one writer put it:

> When one adds four generations to the ten
> already shown,
> From Charlemagne's line comes Gisela, for her
> wisdom renowned.

She had previously been married to Duke Ernest of Swabia, the brother of Margrave Albert of Upper Pannonia, and have given him two children, Ernest and Herman; it was after her husband's death that she married the Conrad we are discussing.

As king, Conrad was energetic in war, wise in counsel, tactful, sagacious, utterly devoted to the Christian faith, and was filled with the humility that is so becoming in a king. Early in his reign, Duke Boleslaw, the Polish noble recently defeated in battle by Conrad's predecessor Henry, plotted to break away from the empire and establish a kingdom of his own, but he died unexpectedly and was succeeded by his son Mieszko. This Mieszko planned to follow his father's intentions, and towards that end he drove his own brother Otto from his principality, and so King Conrad led his army into Poland in order to restore Otto to his rightful place and punish Mieszko for the harm he had caused. Mieszko proved unable to repulse the king's attack, and so, having taken a few shards of Germany, he fled to Duke Udalrich of Bohemia, who had already set himself up as an enemy of the kingdom.

Udalrich, however, hoped to get back into Conrad's good graces by handing Mieszko over to him, only to find that Conrad, being so chivalrous by nature, refused to receive an enemy from the hands of a traitor. Meanwhile Otto had taken possession of the Polish duchy and sent to Conrad the crown that his and Mieszko's father had unlawfully and disgracefully fashioned for himself. Otto made a further point of subjecting himself to Conrad in all things. Not long after this, Otto died at the hands of a treacherous

armorer, and Mieszko—now an exile instead of a king—went to Conrad to beg forgiveness. Thanks to the intercession of Queen Gisela, Conrad restored to Mieszko a one-third part of what he had previously held entire, and it is well known that that smaller province has remained subject to the German kings ever since and has paid tribute to them.

Around the same time two kinsmen of Conrad's—the duke of Worms, also named Conrad, and Ernest, the duke of Swabia and the Alemanni (who was also King Conrad's stepson)—rose up in rebellion, just when the king had departed for Italy, first naming his infant son Henry as his successor. Queen Gisela, Duke Ernest's mother, advised him quickly to travel to Italy to reconcile with the king and offer him aid. Conrad's military train celebrated the start of Easter at Vercelli, where he met with Margrave Rainier and the citizens of Lucca; once these had submitted to him, he marched on to Rome.

[29] In the year 1027 from the Incarnation of the Lord, Conrad was crowned in Rome by Pope John on the very day of the Easter Festival. He entered the coronation ceremony walking in the position of honor between King Canute of England and Duke Rudolph of Burgundy—Queen Gisela's uncle; and from the people of Rome he received the titles *emperor* and *augustus*. At some point during the week a riot broke out between the local citizens and the emperor's troops, and a terrible battle ensued, in which many Romans fell or fled and the emperor emerged victorious. He promptly made peace with the citizens, however, and withdrew his troops from the city. He also captured a notorious local bandit named Tahselgart and hanged him. But as he was returning to France by way of the Pyrenees, Conrad learned that his stepson, Duke Ernest, had once again rebelled against him, having been so advised by Count Werner [of Kiburg]. Conrad then rendered a most solemn judgment against him, and by the authority of his royal majesty he banned Ernest from land and sea, compelling him to go into exile in the forest—where he was subsequently killed by some of the king's loyal followers. Ernest's brother, Herman, succeeded to the dukedom.

[30] Around the same time King Rudolph of Burgundy (also known as Gallia Lugdunensis) died. In his will he bequeathed his crown to his nephew Henry, who was Conrad's son. . . .

[31] When Rudolph made this bequest, Count Odo of Gallia Celtica (the son of Rudolph's sister) advanced the unreasonable claim that the kingdom belonged by right to him instead of Henry, and he led his army into it just when the emperor Conrad was busy subjecting the Poles, as mentioned earlier. When the emperor heard of Odo's action, he marshaled his own army to invade Burgundy. This was around Christmas-time, however, and so it was too cold for his men to march all the way there, and so they waited until the following summer. In three weeks they had reduced all of Odo's land to dust and ashes, forcing him to plead for mercy, and only after Odo gave assurance under a solemn vow that he would not further trouble Burgundy did Conrad return home.

The next year Conrad ventured into Burgundy once more and accepted the submission of all the princes there, including the Metropolitan of Lyons; taking several of them as hostages-to-the-court he returned to Germany in peace. Not too much later he ventured into Italy to squash a rebellion by a rabble of insolent commoners who had nearly unseated their noble masters. He celebrated Christmas at Verona, then traveled by way of Brescia and Cremona to Milan, where he arrested the bishop for having joined a conspiracy against him, and handed him over to the Poppo, the Patriarch of Aquileia. The bishop eventually escaped, unnoticed, and fled, which prompted Conrad, after celebrating Easter Day at Ravenna that spring, to lay waste to the district surrounding Milan, conquering and demolishing many strongholds while receiving the submission of many others. Then he marched on to Cremona, where he met with the pope, whom he received most graciously and treated with the utmost respect. After he sent the pope on his way [back to Rome], Conrad journeyed to the mountain districts [to the north] in order to avoid the summertime heat.

But while these events were taking place in Italy, Count Odo once again broke his vow and rose up against Conrad one more time, in Gaul. He died in disgrace, however, for when he was besieging a certain stronghold called Bar-le-Duc, he was killed by Duke Gozelo of Lorraine and some other troops loyal to the king, who then sent his standard to Italy as a token

of their victory that was sure to please the emperor. Also at that time the bishops of Piacenza, Vercelli, and Cremona were convicted of treason and sent into exile, although this was and still is a controversial matter. Soon thereafter the emperor was celebrating Christmas at Parma when a riot broke out in which Conrad's chamberlain was killed. The emperor was enraged by this and attacked the city most bitterly. The citizens defended themselves bravely, but in the end too many of them fell to ward off Conrad's attack. The city was put to the torch.

Around this time the pope in Rome excommunicated the archbishop of Milan, who had also rebelled against Conrad. The emperor was then on the other side of the Apennines, having brought all of the eastern portion of Italy under his control, and was entering Apulia. (Queen Gisela, in the meantime, had gone on pilgrimage to Rome and would rejoin him later.) He passed through Capua, Benevento, and a great many other cities of that region, and planned to return home by way of the Adriatic coastline' but the district was suffering from a contagion that made the air unhealthy to breathe, and many of his leading nobles and other soldiers died, including Duke Hermann, the son of Queen Gunnhild (who was, in her turn, the bride of Conrad's son), and Duke Conrad of Franconia. These catastrophic losses inspired a poet to compose some verses on the fragility of human life; their style is simple but tragically expressive. They begin with the lines:

> Let him with a voice both clear and strong
> Gather all around him to hear this song.

Not much later, but after he had returned from Italy, the emperor took ill in the middle of the Feast of Pentecost, which he was celebrating in Frisia, in the city of Utrecht, and died. It was the seventeenth year of his reign as duke and the fourteenth of his reign as emperor. They buried his heart and other vital organs there in Utrecht and transported the rest of his body to Speyer, where it was laid to rest in the Marienkirche.

[32] In the year 1040 from the Incarnation of Our Lord, Henry III, the son of the aforesaid Queen Gisela, began his sole reign as the eighty-ninth emperor in line from Augustus—having already started to govern

while his father was still alive. With Henry the imperial title finally returned to someone born of the ancient and noble stock of Charlemagne. Henry equaled his father in all respects and even surpassed him in the best qualities. He governed with moderation, although he made a rash mistake at the very start of his reign when he launched a campaign against the Bohemians, who were opposed to his rule, and lost many men in the dense forests there. These losses fueled his righteous indignation, however, and prompted him to inflict far greater damages on the people of Bohemia until their duke finally submitted to him. He also made frequent war on the Hungarians. When, instigated by the rebel leader Obo, they treacherously drove their own king, Peter, into exile, however, Henry gave him refuge. At the urging of Margrave Albert (whose brother-in-law he was), Henry marched into Pannonia with an army that, though small in number, won a great victory against a large Hungarian force; thus did Henry restore Peter to his throne—a victory that inspired Herman the Lame to compose the poem that begins:

This voice of mine must sing a lay.

Henry married Agnes, the daughter of the most illustrious nobleman in Gaul, Duke William of Poitou and Aquitaine. At the wedding celebration, which was held, according to custom, at Ingelheim, he gave to all the poor in the region the money that would otherwise have gone to the jesters and actors (those limbs of Satan!) who attended but went away empty-handed. Sadness accompanied the celebrations, though, since young Leopold, the most illustrious son of Margrave Albert, was carried off by an early death. Mourned by all, he was buried in the city of Trèves by his uncle Poppo, who was archbishop there. This was the Leopold who, together with his father, seized the Eastern March from the Hungarians and defeated, against tremendous odds, the huge army led by the traitor Obo, who was harassing his border. It was a dangerous undertaking, even for one as brave as Leopold.

About the same time a shameful state of confusion beset the Church in Rome, for three men (one of whom was called Benedict) usurped the papal throne all at once, dividing between them the office and its revenues. One sat in St. Peter's Cathedral, the second in the church of Santa Maria Maggiore, and the third (Benedict) in the Lateran Palace. I have heard from eyewitnesses that all three lived a dissolute life. A certain priest named Gratian, a devout man filled with compassion for Mother Church on account of the wretched state She had fallen into, approached the three usurpers and by the zeal of his piety persuaded them, with money, to vacate their seats. Benedict, the most stubborn person of the group, insisted on keeping the revenues from England. The people of Rome proclaimed this priest as the great liberator of the Church and chose him to be the new pope, Gregory VI. When King Henry heard about this he summoned his army and marched into Italy. Gratian met him at Sutri and reportedly offered the king a precious crown, to assuage his anger. Henry initially received him with fitting honors but later assembled a synod of bishops, who, together with the king, persuaded him to withdraw from the papacy because he had disgraced himself with simony; in Gratian's place they appointed Bishop Suitger of Bamberg, who took the name Clement, and the whole Church consented to his appointment. According to tradition, Hildebrand had followed Gratian across the Alps and into Italy, and later, when he himself was made pope, he took the name Gregory out of love for him. Gratian's name has since been removed from the list of popes. As Lucan once wrote:

The gods upheld the victorious cause, Cato the defeated one

And this is true of Hildebrand, who was much the most zealous and unyielding supporter of the Church, and the most vigorous opponent of the opinions of the emperor and the German bishops [regarding lay investiture] that ultimately carried the day.

The Roman Church, in our opinion, has been so weakened in the canonical election of popes that Clement and the four men who succeeded him, were included in the list of popes only because the emperor decided to place their names on it. I shall describe later how the Church regained Her freedom, through the tireless exertions of Hildebrand, then Leo, and then

Alexander—all of which I learned from the testimony of men I trust.[1]

[33] In the year 1047 from the Incarnation of Our Lord, the victorious King Henry III was crowned emperor and augustus at Rome by Pope Clement on Christmas Day, the ninetieth ruler in line from Augustus. Upon leaving Rome Henry led his army through Apulia before returning home to Germany. In the same year Suitger—that is, Pope Clement—died and was succeeded by Poppo, the patriarch of Aquileia [who took the name Damasus II].[2] A short time later King Peter of Hungary lost his eyesight and his kingship at the hands of a courtier named Andrew. When Poppo/Damasus died, Bishop Bruno of Toul succeeded him as head of the Church and took the name Leo IX. He came from a noble Frankish family and was King Henry's own choice to succeed to the throne of St. Peter. According to one report Henry was traveling through Gaul shortly after becoming emperor and visited the monastery of Cluny—where the afore-mentioned Hildebrand happened to hold the office of prior. Hildebrand [accompanied Henry to Rome and] boldly rebuked Leo for having risen to the papacy with the aid of a layman, saying with pious zeal that it was an unlawful seizure by force of the government of the Church. Hildebrand then urged Leo to trust him, promising that he could manipulate things in such a way that the Church's liberty to hold a free election would be restored, and that King Henry would not be roused to anger. Leo agreed, took off his papal robe, and put on again a pilgrim's garb. Then Leo and Hildebrand set off together for Rome, where, with Hildebrand's help, Leo was elected as supreme pontiff by the clergy and people of the city. Thus did the Church regain the right to free election.

Henry, in the meantime, invaded Lorraine and forced Duke Godfrey and Duke Baldwin to capitulate. After this, a synod was held at Mainz in the presence of Pope Leo and Henry. The king once again invaded Pannonia to put down Lord Andrew, who had arrogantly deposed King Peter and usurped the Hungarian throne. The Hungarians, though, fled from the German army and either hid or destroyed the stocks of food they had; with no way to keep his soldiers fed or supplied, Henry therefore laid waste the whole countryside, and then returned home. The next year he invaded Pannonia yet again, taking Pope Leo with him.

Then the Normans—a restless people—invaded Apulia. Led by Duke Robert Guiscard, a man of common birth but uncommon energy, they inflicted every type of misery on the people there, using guile and violence in equal measure. Pope Leo, after returning to Rome with an army, wanted to bring the Normans to heel, making them subject to the Church and the German Empire. He marched against the Normans, and a great battle ensued. Many died, and Leo was forced to flee to Benevento. So many died, in fact, that to this day the people of Benevento point to a hill that they insist is made of the piled-up bones of all those killed that day. Leo died one year later and is buried in St. Peter's in Rome; his tomb is renowned for the miracles it performs. Gebhardt of Eichstätt succeeded him, taking the name Victor, and then another German succeeded him, taking the name of Stephen.

The next time Henry went to Italy he returned to Germany with his kinswoman Beatrice, the mother of Mathilda. Beatrice's husband, Margrave Boniface, had just died. Henry himself took ill not long afterwards at a place called Bodfeld, which is on the border of Saxony and Thuringia. He performed a public confession of his sins, and died. It was the seventeenth year of his reign as duke and the eleventh of his reign as emperor. He is buried next to his father. Herman the Lame has thoroughly described his deeds and virtues, as well as those of his father, in a short book.

---

[1] Otto should not have been quite so trusting of his interviewees, since the account he gives in ch. 32 is filled with errors. The priest Gratian was actually one of the three usurper-popes, under the name Gregory VI. His meeting with Henry III took place at Piacenza, not Sutri. Henry's synod did take place at Sutri (December 1046), but it ousted only Gratian/Gregory and the second pope, Sylvester III; the third pope, Benedict IX, had remained in Rome and refused to recognize the synod. His pseudo-pontificate ended only with his death in 1048.

[2] Another mistake—Damasus II was not Poppo of Aquileia, but Poppo, bishop of Brixen, another German. He died within a year.

9.4 Ibn Hawqal, *A Portrait of the World*

Muhammad Abu'l Qasim ibn Hawqal, a Spanish-born Arab, was a geographer, whose massive compendium *A Portrait of the World* (*Surat al-'Ard*) gives a detailed account, based on his own travels and observations, of the physical and cultural geography of the Mediterranean. His depiction of the island of Sicily, which like Spain had a mixed Christian, Muslim, and Jewish population, is remarkably detailed and tells us not only what the place looked like but also what the inter-religious atmosphere was like prior to the start of the Crusades. He visited the island in 973.

Among the most prosperous of places under Muslim control is the island of Sicily. It has the shape of an isosceles triangle, its acute angle being formed by the western side of the island. In area, it consists of sevens days [of travel] from west to east, and fours days from north to south. It lies to the east of al-Andalus, in the middle of the sea, opposite the lands of the Maghrib and Ifriqiya. . . . Most of the island consists of mountains, in which there are many castles and forts; most of the land is settled and used for farming. . . .

The capital city, and the only city that has any renown, is Palermo. It lies on the northern coast and consists of five districts. These districts are quite distinct and have clear boundaries between them, but they are not far from one another. All are part of the great city called Palermo. A long, high, and strong stone wall surrounds the entire city. Many merchants live there. It has a vast communal mosque that was a Byzantine church before the Muslims conquered the island; this mosque has within it a large shrine that some writers say contains a wooden coffin in which the Greek philosopher Aristotle is interred. Christians used to venerate this tomb and sought cures from it. . . . Opposite this mosque is the district known as al-Khalsa. This district has a stone wall of its own, though unlike the one that surrounds the entire city. This is where the sultan and his court reside. It has two bath-houses, but no markets or hostels. There is a small plain communal mosque. The sultan's soldiers reside in this district, so too do the naval officials and their staff. . . .

Most of the city's markets lie in the area between the mosque of Ibn Saqlab and the New Quarter. These include: the olive market, the grain and flour merchants,

money-changers, apothecaries, blacksmiths, other metal workers, embroiderers, fishmongers, spice merchants, butchers, greengrocers, companies of fruiterers, herbalists, potters, bakers, rope-makers, perfumers, cobblers, tanners, carpenters, joiners, and cabinet-makers. Outside of Palermo proper there are more markets for butchers, potters, and rope-makers. Altogether, Palermo has nearly two hundred butcher shops. Some are in the city-center, at the head of the main artery.

The main communal mosque in Palermo holds about seven thousand men—which I reckon from the fact that there are thirty-six rows for prayer and each row can hold a maximum of two hundred men. Mosques exist throughout Palermo, especially in the al-Khalsa district, and even in the outlying neighborhoods outside the walls. Most of them are built by surrounding trellises with walls and doors. According to knowledgeable people, the city has three hundred mosques. . . .

All along the Sicilian coasts one find innumerable shacks, in which the idle and godless trouble-makers live. Hypocrites and frauds, both old and young! The wretches wear rags and kneel in prayer but rise upright when you pass by, to beg for money or to hurl abuse at decent women. These men are a chastisement sent from On High, wastrels and criminals. Many of them offer women for sale, and some of them regard such doings as honorable—the hypocrites! Most of them chose their wretched way of life, displaying their ignorance of the religious obligations of hygiene and other basic Islamic traditions. Thus their poverty inclines them to idleness, and the filthiness of their hovels incline them to vagrancy and begging. They will sometimes offer to share their meager food, but the whole scene is too disgusting to mention and I will say no more of it. It would appear that creating these hovels was un-Islamic, considering the care the Sicilians put into building their mosques. In truth, many Muslims in Sicily have fallen into ruin, and many have died, on account of the rebellions and revolts against the sultan. . . .

To judge from their works, the city of Palermo does not have a single right-thinking person in it, not a single person of sophistication, not a single scholar in any discipline, not a single man of virtue, nor one renowned for piety. Most of the townspeople are ill-mannered louts, possessing neither good sense nor genuine faith. . . .

In truth, there are many schools in the city; there are also many teachers—but these vary only in the degrees of their dementia and idiocy. They are more stupid than the teachers in any other country or region I visited. They even criticize the sultan's way of life and his attitudes, describing his faults in shameful language and making no clear distinction between his good qualities and his bad. There are no fewer than three hundred of these imbeciles in the city—more than I found in any other place or territory. Their number benefits them little, though, when it comes to attacking Christians in jihad (which they detest). Sicily forms part of the border with the Christian world and is a place where jihad is constantly waged against them.

Ever since the Muslims conquered Sicily [in 831] there has been a steady summons to jihad across the island. The governors never cease in this call to arms, and never exempt anyone except those who are willing to pay for the privilege or have some other excuse for not joining their leaders. Teachers have traditionally been granted an exemption, so long as they made the compensatory payment, and as a result the teaching profession has been filled by ignoramuses—and their prominence has succeeded in drawing more ignoramuses into the ranks. . . . The worst tragedy of all, the greatest misfortune, is that the Sicilian people are themselves so simple-minded, so uneducated, and so provincial that they actually believe these "teachers" to represent an elite class! These are their jurists, administrators, religious and legal scholars who decide what is permissible and what is forbidden, who question witnesses and pass judgments! These are the leaders who deliver Friday sermons! . . .

Most of the Sicilians are not authentic Muslims. They regard it as acceptable to marry Christians, so long as the sons produced by such a union follow their father in his inauthentic Islam; the daughters become Christians like their mothers. They do not pray, perform their ablutions, pay the alms tax, and do not make the pilgrimage to Mecca. . . .

9.5 Important Dates and Vocabulary for Medieval Jewish History

The great achievements of medieval Jewish life—development and spread of the Talmud, the creation of the rabbinical academies, the proliferation of legal, biblical, and scientific scholarship—took place amid a history of complex relations with their various Christian and Muslim overlords.

70*	Destruction of the Temple in Jerusalem; start of the Diaspora
135	Bar Kochba revolt put down; Jews forbidden to enter Jerusalem
ca. 200	R. Judah ha-Nasi compiles the Mishnah

ca. 300	Compilation of the Tosefta
ca. 400	The Palestinian Talmud
ca. 550	The Babylonian Talmud
614	Persians conquer Jerusalem; Jews permitted into city for first time since 135

638	Muslims conquer Jerusalem; Dome of the Rock mosque completed in 692
740	Conversion of Khazars in southern Russia
760	Karaites reject rabbinical Judaism
825	Crisis in the exilarchate. Rise of *geonim*, sages, *yeshivot* (Yeshivot: Jerusalem, Pumbedita, Sura)
840	Carolingian emperor starts to break up; rise of the Ashkenazim
850	Caliph al-Mu'tawakkil orders destruction of all non-Muslim houses of worship
882–942	R. Saadia Gaon, in Egypt, then Iraq
890	Pumbedita yeshiva relocates to Baghdad
921	Beginning of calendar dispute between Babylonia and Palestine

960	Embassy of Ashkenazim to Jerusalem yeshiva
1034	Sura yeshiva closed. Moves to Baghdad
1040–1105	R. Shlomo Yitzhachi (RASHI) in central France
1075–1141	R. Judah ha-Levi, in Spain
1079	Jerusalem yeshiva re-opens in city of Tyre
1127	Jerusalem yeshiva re-opens (again) in Cairo
1135–1204	R. Moses b. Maimon (Maimonides, or RAMBAM), in Spain, later Egypt
1195–1270	R. Moses b. Nahman (Nahmanides, or RAMBAN), in Spain

* All dates CE.

Halakah	Rabbinical legal judgment.
Mishnah	Comprehensive collection and edition of halakah by R. Judah ha-Nasi
Gemara	Collected commentaries on the Mishnah
Talmud	Combined editions of the Mishnah and Gemara
Tosefta	Post-Talmudic collection of halakah
Exilarch	Leader of the Jewish community in exile, descended from Davidic or priestly lines
Yeshivot	Rabbinical academies
Geonim	Leaders ("presidents") of the yeshivot
Rabbi	Scholars of religious law; leaders of synagogue-life
Shtadlan	"Intercessor" with non-Jewish religious authorities
Negidim	"Intercessor" with non-Jewish secular authorities

10. THE REFORM OF THE CHURCH

10.1   The Pseudo-Isidorian Decretals

The vast collection of forgeries known as the "Pseudo-Isidorian Decretals" were produced and compiled over a period of roughly 20 years in the middle of the ninth century. No single author can be attributed to them. Rather, a group of probably Frankish bishops launched a systematic campaign to create a whole dossier of fake documents that would lay out, certify, and extend the authorities and privileges of all bishops. They attributed the bulk of the collection to a fictitious scholar named Isidore Mercator (sometimes confused with St. Isidore of Seville). Below is the prologue supposedly written by him. My translation omits the one-sentence chapter titles given to each paragraph, since their content is replicated within each paragraph.

In the name of our Lord Jesus Christ. Here begins the prologue to the book written by St. Isidore, the bishop.

I am directed by numerous bishops and other servants of God to gather together the statutes of canonical authority, to organize them into a single volume, and to harmonize them. But what particularly frustrates me is the fact that so many differing translations of those statues have been made; so while there is a single general view of canonical authority, there are nevertheless innumerable versions of the statutes—some longer, some briefer.

The church councils that have been published in Greek, I find to have been copied out and translated three or four times apiece, if not more. If truth is to be found in this multiplicity, let us follow the manner of the Greeks and imitate their commentaries and exempla. But if not, let those who have as many exempla as they have manuscripts speak and explicate. It seems to me that, when the texts in our [Latin] language disagree with one another, then unity and truth can be acquired only from those manuscripts in whose [Greek] tongue they are known to have been published. And so I have done so; and such as I learned from true masters, I have taken pains to include such learning in this book, to which this little preface is attached.

The Greek word "canon" denotes the Latin word "rule." It is called a rule because it is a true guide, one that never sends us in a false direction. Some have said that it is called a rule because it does in fact rule; it presents a standard for proper living, or corrects whatever is sordid and depraved. The Greek word "synod" denotes a "company" or "assembly," while the word "council" derives from the notion of common intent, since in a council everyone directs their minds toward a common goal. The root-word cilium refers to eyesight—and that is why people who disagree with one another do not make a council [concilium], for they do not see things the same way. When people meet together we call it a "convention" or "congregation"— meaning many coming together as one; and whence the term "convention" because all there are in agreement, just as the terms "convention," "meeting," and "council" all derive from the union of many into a single body.

Now, at the very start of this little book, I have decided to describe how we celebrate a council so that those who come after us may know how to do it, although I urge anyone who wishes to do better than this to proceed by the most just, canonical, and wise counsel. I privilege over all other councils the authority of the canons that are Apostolic, although I acknowledge that some scholars regard these as apocryphal, since so many others do accept them as authentic and since the Holy Fathers endorsed them in synods and included them among the canonical constitutions. Next I have inserted the decrees issued in certain papal letters, namely those of Clement, Anacletus, Evaristus, and the rest of the popes up to Pope Sylvester—whose letters I have not yet been able to locate. After these, I include in this book [the acts] of the various Greek and Latin councils, both those before and after [the Council of Nicaea], placing their canons in chronological order, although numbering them separately; next come the remaining decrees of the bishops of Rome down to St. Gregory, followed by a few of his own letters, for in papal letters there exists an authority that is not less than those of the councils—so great is the eminence of the Apostolic See. In this way, by observing ecclesiastical order in the collection and arrangement of the canons, our holy bishops may hence be guided by paternal rules and the obedient ministers and people of the Church may be inspired by spiritual examples and not be deceived by the depravities of evil men.

For indeed many such men, sunk in their depravity and greed, have oppressed our priests in the past with various false accusations, for which reason the Holy Fathers first composed the statutes that we now call the holy canons. Many are the evildoers who cast these false accusations, in the hope either of taking pressure off themselves or of getting rich by claiming others' goods. But so many good Christians remain silent and put up with what they know to be sinful lies, for the simple reason that they lack the written records with which they could prove their legitimate claims to ecclesiastical judges—for certain things may indeed be true, but they must still be demonstrated by incontrovertible evidence, in open investigations, and made public in judicial proceedings, or else they will not be believed by judges.

According to canonical authority, no bishop who has had his property taken from him, or has been expelled from his see by force or threat of force, can be accused, summoned, tried, and sentenced until everything that has been taken from him has been legally restored to his full possession and peaceful and lengthy use, or until he has been properly and formally restored to his see and allowed to exercise his office.

The Ecclesiastical History of Eusebius, the bishop of Caesarea, says as much in regard to a woman whose chastity had been legally challenged by her husband: "The emperor commanded and decreed by statute that the woman should be permitted to duly manage her household before being required to answer her husband's charges." All laws—ecclesiastical, secular, and public—agree on this point. If I were to cite every declaration they have made on this matter, the day would end before I ran out of examples, and I would produce an inordinately long document. Nevertheless, I will insert here a few examples from the trove, for others to consider. St. Leo, the bishop of Rome, sent a letter to the Council of Chalcedon—the letter beginning "Bishop Leo to the Synod of Chalcedon. I had desired, beloved brothers"—in which he wrote, among other things, the following: "I am not unaware of the fact that the well-being of many churches has been undermined by perverse rivalries, and that many of our brother-bishops have been unjustly driven from their sees and banished—and that many of them, still living, have been replaced. Before anything else, the medicine of justice needs to be applied to these wounds; therefore let no bishop be without his rightful property, lest he use something that belongs to another. Let every bishop, therefore, strive to avoid the error [of usurping another's property], so that no bishopric is ever endangered; and as for the banished bishops—every one of their rights and privileges should be re-established."

The ancient popes from the era before the Council of Nicaea decreed much the same. Indeed, the synod held at Lampsacus under [the emperor] Valentinian asserted the same points, as did countless other Roman synods. Pope Symmachus and the rest of the Holy Fathers also decreed in similar fashion, but I have demurred from inserting their statutes here in order to avoid prolixity. Should anyone care to learn about these statutes more fully, let him look them up in his own texts and read them there.

Let these examples suffice, in this brief preface. An infantryman makes do with just the weapons he can carry, without burdening himself unnecessarily; let it be the same way with us. Out of the vast store of statutes, one or two examples should be enough—just whatever is necessary. A soldier needs but a single spear, and perhaps a second weapon, to overcome an enemy. Let us overcome our adversaries with but one or two statutes of undoubted authority.

If rights and privileges were established for lay men and women, how much more ought they to be given to priests and [higher] ecclesiastics! Church laws and secular laws command the same things, and similarly the accusers and accusations prohibited by secular law are utterly rejected by canonical authority. The authority of synods in convocation was granted by special right to the Apostolic See, and I find no evidence anywhere that a synod not convened or recognized by the Apostolic See has any validity. Canonical authority bears witness to this, the whole history of the Church corroborates it, and the writings of the Holy Fathers confirm it.

You, the eighty bishops who commissioned me to undertake this laborious work, and all the priests who serve the Lord should know that I found among the statutes of the Council of Nicaea more than twenty canons that are still in force, but I read in the letters of Pope Julius that there ought to be seventy canons extant from that council. I have placed that letter of Julius in its proper place among the rest of the papal decrees, for anyone who wishes to know more about these matters and investigate them further. As it happens, many texts testify that there were more than twenty canons established at the Council of Nicaea. In the records of the Council of Constantinople, for example, it says: "It is clearly established that a provincial synod should regulate all matters relating solely to that particular province; it was so decreed at the Council of Nicaea." And in Pope Innocent's letter to Bishop Vitricius of Rouen it says: "In cases where a dispute has arisen between the clergy and the laity, or between the clerics of a major or lesser order, it was resolved at the Council of Nicaea that a judgment should be rendered once all the bishops of the province [in which the dispute has arisen] have convened." No less a person than Bishop Theophilus of Alexandria, of blessed memory, recounted in one of his letters that the Council of Nicaea had decreed that whenever a new moon occurs in the twenty-eight day period between eight days prior to the Ides of March and the Nones of April, the new moon marks the start of a first month [of the year]. He emphasized that the fourteenth day should

be carefully calculated—from twelve days before the Kalends of April until fourteen days before the Kalends of May, even if it happens to fall on a Saturday—in order that Easter may be celebrated on the following Lord's day (that is, on the fifteenth day of the lunar month). If the fourteenth day of that same first lunar month happens to fall on the Lord's day, then Easter should undoubtedly be celebrated, according to Theophilus, on the Lord's day of the following week.

From such examples as these, as indeed from many others, it is clear that more than twenty canons were enacted at the Council of Nicaea, and that the aforementioned letter of Pope Julius is authentic and accurate. In addition, numerous brethren of ours from the East have sworn to me that they have seen [the complete acts of] the Council of Nicaea in a volume about the size of the four Gospels, that contained all the sessions held by the bishops, the presentations and judgments of various quarrels, numerous definitions and constitutions, as well as affidavits and subscriptions to all the above. They affirmed also that [the acts of] the great Council of Chalcedon were drawn up in imitation of this Nicaean registers—as were, later, the acts of the Council of Constantinople that convened by order of the emperor Justinian to combat the enemies of God (namely, Origen, Didymus, and Evagrius), and as were, later still, the council held by Pope Agatho and the emperor Constantine against Bishop Macharius, his disciple Stephen, and the rest of those bishops who sowed tares for grain, in their churches, mixed wine with water, and gave rampant destruction to their neighbors for a drink, like wolves pretending to be lambs, presenting their lies as though they were the truth.

You should know that there are four principal councils that have passed on to the Church the fullest expression of the true faith regarding the Father, Son, and Holy Spirit, and the Incarnation of the Son, Our Savior. These four do not, however, invalidate any of the other councils.

The first of the four is the aforesaid Council of Nicaea, where 318 bishops convened under the leadership of the emperor Constantine. This council condemned as blasphemous the treachery of Arianism—the teaching, that is, of Arius about the supposed inequality of the Holy Trinity; it also established as a confessed definition that the Son of God is consubstantial with God the Father.

The second synod gathered 150 fathers at Constantinople under the emperor Theodosius the senior. This council condemned Macedonius, who denied that the Holy Spirit was God, and it asserted that the Spirit is consubstantial with both the Father and the Son. It also gave a fuller expression to the Confession that the entire Greek and Latin worlds preach in church services.

The third synod, of two hundred bishops, was the first to gather at Ephesus, under the leadership of the younger emperor Theodosius. It anathematized Nestorius, who taught that there are two persons in Christ, and established instead that the one person of Our Lord Jesus Christ remains in two natures.

The fourth council, of 630 bishops, was held by the emperor Marcian at Chalcedon. At this council the bishops spoke with a single voice to condemn in the strongest terms Eutyches, the abbot at Constantinople, who claimed that the Word of God and the flesh were of a single nature; it condemned also Eutyches' defender, Dioscorus, the former bishop of Alexandria, and Nestorius himself again, along with those who remained in his heresy. This synod also proclaimed that Christ is God, born of the Virgin Mary, in one substance containing both His divine and human natures.

As I said before, these are the four principal and venerable councils defining the Catholic faith. If other councils convened, after these first four, that the Holy Fathers, filled with the Holy Spirit, sanctioned, then let them be confirmed in all strength. And as I also said before, I inserted an order for the proper celebration of a council. Following next are the Apostolic canons, the decrees of the ancient popes (that is, from St. Clement to St. Sylvester), and the acts of the various councils.

10.2 Pope Gregory VII, *Letters*

Gregory VII (r. 1073–1085) was the most zealous and radical of the reforming popes, so much so that the Church Reform is widely named after him. While he certainly was a forceful figure, it would be a mistake to consider him only as a Machiavellian pursuer of power for its own sake. The following sampler from his collected letters shows his personality from a variety of angles.

LETTER TO THE BISHOP OF LINCOLN, REGARDING A PRIEST SENT TO ROME TO CONFESS HIS GUILT IN KILLING A MAN (1073)

Bishop Gregory, servant of the servants of God, to Bishop Remedius of Lincoln, in England, sends greetings and apostolic blessing.

The bearer of this letter—the priest whom you charged, in your letter to me, with the crime of murder—cannot ever be permitted to serve the sacred altar in future, by any sanction of the holy fathers. Neither can I consent to his restitution [to holy orders], for that (Heaven forbid!) would go against canon law.

However, if you, in your compassion, find that he displays before God sufficient penance for the crime he committed, then as an act of charity you should see to it that he is granted some means of support from the Church, lest he be crushed by poverty and led to ungodly living. While he may never, under any condition, merit a return to priestly life, he may justifiably receive some provision from the Apostolic See.

On the other matter for which you wrote—namely, your request that I absolve you of your own sins by the authority of the chief Apostles, Sts. Peter and Paul, in whose place I, however unworthy, serve—I hereby do so, so long as you do all you can to preserve the purity of your body as a temple before God.

And as for your final request, that I command your best services on my behalf, I hereby issue this particular demand—that you strengthen me with your prayers, so that we may together be worthy of eternal joy.

LETTER TO THE BISHOP OF CHALON-SUR-SAÔNE, REGARDING REPORTS OF SIMONY AND OTHER ABUSES COMMITTED BY KING PHILIP I OF FRANCE (1073)

I have learned from several trusted sources that among the rulers of our time who have brought ruin to God's Church by greedily putting it up for sale. . . . King Philip of France so greatly oppresses the French churches that he seems to have become the epitome of this hateful sin. His actions are even more offensive since they occur in a realm widely known for its good judgment, piety, strength, and its steadfast devotion to the Roman Church. I am particularly outraged (that is, not simply as a matter of fulfilling my duties as pope) by his actual destruction of churches. We need to condemn much more severely such audacious attacks on our very religion. Through his chamberlain Alberic, the king gave us every assurance that he would respect our position, reform his personal life, and set the churches of France in good order.

For these reasons I wish now to test the value of his promise in regard to the church of Mâcon, which has long lacked a bishop and has been reduced practically to rubble, and therefore it is my desire that he permit the archdeacon of Autun, unanimously elected by the clergy and people there and (I am told) approved by the king, to be installed as the new bishop of Mâcon—and that this installation take place, as of course it ought, without any payment of money. If Philip refuses, let him know without any doubt that I will not permit such ruination of the Church, but will attack his stubborn persistence in disobedience with all the canonical severity I possess, by the authority of the Blessed Apostles Sts. Peter and Paul. Either the king will abandon his evil commerce in the heresy of simony and freely allow worthy people to be installed in the leadership of the Church, or the people of France will be cut down by the sword of a general anathema. Unless they intend to reject the Christian faith altogether, the people will refuse to obey him in future.

I go to the trouble of entrusting this letter to you, my ever-watchful and loving brother [in Christ], so that you will convey it to King Philip and make every possible effort—in writing, speech, or action—to persuade him to allow the church of Mâcon, and every French church, to be provided with pastors according to canon law. I have laid this duty upon you because I know you to be of sound judgment and to be close to the king. If I have overlooked anything, please supply it by your own keen intelligence. May you carry out this purpose in such a way that you win God's favor and my good will.

AN EARLY CALL TO CRUSADE (1074)

Bishop Gregory, servant of the servants of God, to all who are willing to defend the Christian faith, sends greetings and apostolic blessing.

You should know that the person bearing this letter, returning from across the sea, came to Rome and met with me, in which meeting he repeated the news we have already heard from so many others—namely, that a pagan people have vanquished the Christians [in the East] and with unimaginable cruelty have laid waste to all the lands almost to the very walls of Constantinople; that these conquered territories they are now ruling with tyrannical violence; and that they have slain untold thousands of Christians as though they were so many sheep. Out of our love for God and our wish to be recognized as Christians, we ought to be overwhelmed with grief at the wound done to this great [Byzantine] empire and the murder of so many faithful Christians, and yet we are called to more than grief alone. The example of Our Redeemer and the bonds of brotherly love summon us to offer our lives in order to liberate them: "Because He has laid down His life for us, and we ought to lay down our lives for our brothers" [1 John 3.16].

You should therefore know that, trusting in God's mercy and the power of His might, we are now doing all that we can to prepare to bring aid to the Christian [Byzantine] Empire as soon as possible, and therefore we beseech and admonish you, by the faith in which you are united through Christ in caring for all the sons of God, and by the authority of St. Peter, the Prince of the Apostles, to feel compassion for the wounds and blood of your brethren and the threat now confronting the aforesaid empire. For the sake of Christ we beg you to join in the difficult task of bringing aid to our brothers. Send us your messengers at once, informing us of what God inspires you to do in this matter.

LETTER TO THE DIOCESE OF CONSTANCE (1075)

Gregory, bishop and servant of the servants of God, to all the clergy and laity, both great and small, in the diocese of Constance who love Christian law, greetings and an apostolic blessing.

We sent to our brother Otto, your bishop, a most earnest letter in which (as our office requires) we ordered him, by our apostolic authority, to root out the heresy of Simony from his church and to uphold by zealous preaching the requirement of chastity among the clergy, and to enforce its steadfast maintenance by episcopal visitation. The words of the Gospels and the letters of the apostles, not to mention the decrees of authoritative council and the teachings of our most honored doctors have all commended it, and so we cannot disregard the issue or neglect it without risking great injury to our soul and the souls of all the people of Christ. Your bishop, however, has been inspired neither by reverence for St. Peter's command nor by the duty of his office—for we have discovered that he has not made any efforts to carry out our fatherly instructions. Instead, we have heard that he has openly permitted his clergy to act in ways repugnant to our (indeed, St. Peter's) command—which turns his guilt of disobedience into one of rebellion. For he has not only allowed clergy who already had women to keep them, but has even permitted those who did not have women the unlawful shamelessness of taking them!

Having learned of this, we were deeply angered and sent him a second letter that made the depth of our indignation quite clear and enjoined him even more sharply to obey our command. At the same time we summoned him to appear at the Roman Synod called for the first week of the next season of Lent, to give an account of himself and to explain to the entire assembly the reasons (if there can possibly be any) for his disobedience.

Dearest sons, we bring all of this to your attention in order to help save your souls. For if he remains determined to be openly hostile and belligerent to St. Peter and the Holy and Apostolic See, then it is clearly shown that a man who does not honor his mother and father has no right to expect or ask their faithful children to give obedience to him. It is unseemly for a man who submits to no master to lord it over disciples of his own. Therefore by our apostolic authority, as already stated, we charge all of you, both great and small, who stand on the side of God and St. Peter to show [Bishop Otto] neither respect nor obedience while he continues in his determined obstinacy; you need not fear endangering your souls on this account. For if he remains determined to resist our commands, as we have already stated, then by the authority of St. Peter we absolve all of you from every necessity to obey him; even if you are bound to him by a sacred oath, as long as he is a rebel against God and the Apostolic See you shall owe him no loyalty at all—for a man should obey no one before his Creator, Who has pride of place over all others. We are obliged to resist anyone who is self-proud against God, so that he may, in the face of this resistance, learn to turn back to the path of righteousness.

What a dangerous thing it is, and how far removed from Christian law, to refuse to be obedient, especially to the Holy See—as you can learn from the words of the blessed prophet Samuel (the very words that Pope Gregory [I] took care to expound in the last book of his Moralia). We set them in writing now, so that we may keep them before us; in this way you will know beyond doubt that this is no new teaching we are speaking of. We are merely rehearsing the ancient teaching of the holy fathers: "But Samuel said, 'Obedience is better than sacrifice, to listen, better than the fat of rams. For a sin of divination is rebellion, and arrogance, the crime of idolatry'." [1 Sam 15.22–23] It is right that obedience be valued more than sacrifices, because in sacrifice we kill flesh that is not our own, but in obedience we kill our own will. How much more readily a man pleases God to the extent he overcomes his own willful pride and sacrifices himself before God's eyes by the sword of His command! Disobedience, though, is likened to the sin of witchcraft in order to show by contrast how great is the virtue of obedience; the contrast makes it clear how much we should praise the latter. For if rebellion is like the sin of witchcraft, and stubbornness like the crime of idolatry, then only obedience brings the reward of faith—for without obedience a man can appear to be faithful while actually being the opposite.

TO THE ALMORAVID RULER OF MAURETANIA, THANKING HIM FOR HIS RECENT GIFTS AND THE RELEASE OF SOME PRISONERS (1076)

God, Who created the universe and without Whom we can neither do nor even think anything good, has inspired you, in your heart, to this act of kindness; and as He enlightens all who come into this world, He has enlightened your mind to this end. The Almighty God, Who desires that all people be saved and none perish, mercifully urges us, above all, that apart from loving Him we love one another, desiring to do nothing to another that we would not want done to ourselves. For this reason, we—that is, you and I—are especially obliged to show to the nations an example of this loving kindness, for we believe and confess the same One God, although in different ways, and we praise and worship Him daily as the Creator of all things and the Ruler of this world. As the Apostle [Paul] says: "He is our peace, Who has made us both one." [Eph. 2.14] Many of our leading figures here in Rome, when I informed them of your gracious act in the name of God, expressed admiration and approval of your good will and virtue. . . .

The Lord knows that we extend to you our love, for His honor, and that we hope for your salvation and glory, both in this life and in the next; and we pray in our heart and with our lips that God will lead you to the Abode of Happiness, the bosom of the holy patriarch Abraham, after many years of life here on earth.

TO ABBOT PETER OF FUCECCHIO AND PRIOR RUDOLF OF CAMALDOLI (1081?)

Gregory, bishop and servant of the servants of God, to Abbot Peter of Fucecchio and Prior Rudolf of Camaldoli, greetings and an apostolic blessing.

You requested that I absolve Ughiccio the son of Bulgarelli even though he has neither confessed his sin nor repented of it. As you know, before he sinned so grievously I held him dear and loved him more than any of his fellow-princes in Tuscany, because, like his father before him, he worked diligently to defend the good and to establish true religion in his lands. That is why, if it were at all possible to agree to your request, I would gladly grant him absolution on account of his own former goodness and his wife's current prayers, along with your own request. But neither reason nor the custom of the Holy Church permits this; neither does the example of the Holy Fathers offer a precedent for absolving someone who has been properly and canonically excommunicated, refuses to admit his fault, and does not seek forgiveness with his whole heart. Unless a man repents with his whole heart and confesses his sin, any absolution offered him would be without effect and could only be regarded as a lie.

But since Count Ughiccio continues to defend his wickedness by insisting his excommunication was unjust and done in order to win political points elsewhere, he should himself investigate and ponder the writings of the Holy Fathers on such matters. He should remember that he took part in a sacrilegious conspiracy by the citizens of Lucca and not make matters worse for himself by defending his actions. On top of this, he brought down the sword of anathema on himself for a second and no less serious failing: he allowed, and even encouraged, the lawfully and canonically installed bishop of Lucca to be driven from his church.

In all honesty, I would not wish to excommunicate anyone against the dictates of justice, not even if I knew that I myself would have to suffer going into exile or risk injury on that account; for every person, even the most insignificant, is someone for whom Christ shed His blood. But in order to persuade Count Ughiccio to repent his crime in a fitting, Christian way, I would gladly risk any harm or danger that might come to me, and therefore I urge you and plead with you to remember him in your daily prayers, imploring God's mercy to visit, soften, and turn to penitence Ughiccio's heart and mind—so that through sincere penance, tears, and pleas for forgiveness for his sins Ughiccio may some day be counted again, by his performance of good works, among the members of the Holy Church.

10.3 The Ecumenical Councils of the Latin Church

The Latin Church recognizes the following 15 councils as authoritative, up to the year 1400; there have been 6 more since the Renaissance—the most recent being the Second Vatican Council of 1963–1965. The Orthodox Churches recognize only the first 7 on this list.

Council	Dates (CE)	Presided over by	Actions taken
Nicaea	325	Summoned and presided over by emperor Constantine I.	Arianism condemned. First version of Nicene Creed promulgated. Fixed dating of Easter.
Constantinople	381	Convened jointly by emperors Gratian and Theodosius I. Initially presided over by Gregory of Nazianzus, whose election as bishop of Constantinople was later declared invalid. Replaced by Nectarius as bishop and presider.	Revised/reaffirmed the Nicene Creed. Condemns Macedonianism (the doctrine that the Holy Spirit is not divine, thus a new form of anti-Trinitarianism). Declared that the bishop of Constantinople comes second in honor after the bishop of Rome.
Ephesus	431	Summoned jointly by emperors Theodosius II and Valentinian III and Pope Celestine I. Cyril of Alexandria, bishop of Constantinople, presided.	Condemnation of Nestorianism (the doctrine that Christ's divine nature and his human nature were separate and distinct) and Pelagianism (the doctrine denying the existence of original sin). Proclaimed the Virgin Mary as Theotokos ("God-bearer").
Chalcedon	451	Summoned by emperor Marcian over the objections of Pope Leo I. Nevertheless, the council was presided over by three papal legates: bishops Paschasinus and Lucentius, and priest Boniface.	Repudiated Monophysitism (the doctrine that Christ's divine and human natures were blended into a single hybrid nature; decreed "hypostatic union" instead. Elevated bishops of Constantinople and Jerusalem to status of Patriarchs.
Constantinople II	553	Called jointly by emperor Justinian and Pope Vigilius, but presided over by Eutychius, the Patriarch of Constantinople.	Condemned the "Three Chapters" (that is, writings by three figures who had challenged some of the earlier councils' decrees regarding Christology). Formerly thought to have issued condemnations of certain ideas put forth by Origen.
Constantinople III	680–681	Summoned by emperor Constantine IV, with approval by Pope Agatho, who sent legates. George, Patriarch of Constantinople, presided.	Condemned Monotheletism (the doctrine that Christ had a single will despite his divine and human natures).
Nicaea II	787	Convened by empress-regent Irene on behalf of her son Constantine VI, and by Paul, Patriarch of Constantinople, with approval by Pope Hadrian I, who sent legates.	Condemned iconoclasm and authorized the veneration of icons. Decreed that political rulers may not elect bishops; only other bishops may elect and appoint one to their number. Condemned "pragmatic" conversions by Jews; only sincere converts to be welcomed.
Constantinople IV	869–870	Called jointly by emperor Basil I and Pope Nicholas I. After Nicholas' death, Pope Hadrian II sent legates.	Deposed Photius, a layman who had been appointed Patriarch of Constantinople; reinstated Patriarch Ignatius. The Orthodox Church does not recognize this council. It recognizes instead as "Constantinople IV" a subsequent council (879–880, not recognized by Rome) that reinstated Photius as Patriarch.

Council	Dates (CE)	Presided over by	Actions taken
Lateran I	1123	Convened by Pope Calixtus II, who also presided.	Condemned simony (purchase of ecclesiastical office) and enacted compromise in the Investiture Controversy, affirming settlement made at Concordat of Worms. Demanded clerical celibacy. Institutes doctrine of the "Truce of God" (forbidding warfare on prescribed dates).
Lateran II	1139	Convened by Pope Innocent II, who also presided.	Main purpose of this council was to heal the schism that had occurred after the death of Honorius II in 1130 and the election of the anti-pope Anacletus II. Anacletus died in 1138.
Lateran III	1179	Convened by Pope Alexander III, who also presided.	Healed second schism that had resulted from conflict between Alexander and Frederick Barbarossa. Condemned Catharism and Waldensianism. Also promulgated first formal condemnation of sodomy. Excommunicated any lay ruler who attempts to tax the clergy. Condemned usury. Forbade Jews and Muslims from owning Christian slaves.
Lateran IV	1215	Convened by Pope Innocent III, who also presided.	Established the seven sacraments. Promulgated the doctrine of transubstantion. Condemned Joachim of Fiore.
Lyons I	1245	Convened by Pope Innocent IV, who also presided.	Excommunicated and deposed the emperor Frederick II. Authorized the 7th Crusade, to be led by Louis IX of France.
Lyons II	1274	Convened by Pope Gregory X, with encouragement from Byzantine emperor Michael VIII Paleologus. Gregory presided.	Sought reconciliation with Orthodox Church (filioque). This re-union was later repudiated by Michael's successor as emperor, Andronicus II. Recognized Rudolf I von Habsburg as German emperor.
Vienne	1311–1312	Convened by Pope Clement V, who also presided.	Abolished Templar order. Condemned Beguines. Ordered establishment of professorships in Arabic, Aramaic, Greek, and Hebrew at the universities of Avignon, Bologna, Oxford, Paris, and Salamanca.
Constance	1414–1418	Summoned by Pope John XXIII, with support from German emperor Sigismund. John presided until 1417; succeeded by Martin V.	Convened to settle the Great Schism (three-way papal dispute). Deposed Popes John XXIII and Benedict XIII; third pope (Gregory XII) subsequently resigned. Martin V elected as unifying pontiff. Condemnation of John Wycliffe and Jan Hus.

10.4 Usamah ibn Munqidh, *Memoirs*

A Muslim knight, diplomat, and poet, Usamah ibn Munqidh (1095–1188) provides a distinctive account of living on the receiving end of the Latin Crusades. Usamah served the Muslim leaders Zengi, Nur al-Din, and finally Saladin—to whom he dedicated his work—but had Crusader friends, too. Written in Arabic, Usamah's *Memoirs* are a string of anecdotes and morality tales that reveal how the Muslims and Christians managed to live side by side in Syria. Interspersed among the hostilities are genuine moments of entertainment and camaraderie, such as the section reprinted here in which the Templars defend Usamah at prayer; or his exaggerated disbelief that a woman would cast aside a Muslim nobleman in favor of a Frankish shoemaker.

IN THIS PASSAGE, USAMAH PROVIDES A GLIMPSE INTO ONE SIDE OF SALADIN'S CHARACTER

I myself witnessed numerous things that Saladin (may Allah forgive his excesses!) did and which corroborate what is so often said about him. . . . One day our army marched against the city of Homs. The previous night it had rained so hard that our horses could not move, on account of the deep muddy ground; our foot-soldiers were off fighting at a distance. Saladin and I stood together, watching them fight. Suddenly one of our infantry ran over to the other side and began to fight on behalf of the people of Homs. Saladin saw the whole thing, and called to one of his retinue: "Bring me the soldier who fought next to that one who has just deserted!" The officer went and fetched the soldier, and when he had been brought back, Saladin asked him: "Who was the soldier who ran from your side and joined ranks with Homs?" The man replied: "By Allah, I do not know." Saladin immediately ordered the soldier to be cut in half, crosswise.

I interrupted, saying: "Lord Saladin, imprison him instead, and investigate further into the identity of the deserter! It would be different if this man did know the deserter's identity, or was related to him; then you would be right to cut his head off. But as it is. . . ."

For a moment it appeared as though Saladin was leaning in my direction, but another attendant who stood nearby spoke up, saying: "Whenever a soldier deserts, the one who stood next to him is to be seized, and either is to be decapitated or is to be cut in half at the waist."

But this remark so roused Saladin's wrath that he ordered this other attendant to be cut in half. And accordingly several soldiers tied him up, as per custom, and cut him in half at the waist—even though his only fault was to speak out of turn without fear of being punished by Allah (exalted is He!).

I witnessed another of Saladin's notorious deeds, which occurred after we returned from battle at Baghdad. The atabek, who was eager to display his resolve and strength, had ordered Saladin to launch a surprise attack upon the emir Qafjaq, and so we set out from Mosul—which was some six miles from Qafjaq's camp—even though we were weak in numbers. When we reached Qafjaq's encampment we discovered that he had retreated into a remote part of the mountains of Quhistan, so we instead marched upon the castle at Masurra and by the following sunrise had established a siege. . . . Saladin came down from his horse and devised his plan for taking the castle. Since the castle was built entirely of clay and was manned only by peasants, he ordered some soldiers to drill mineshafts under one of the towers. . . . These soldiers were from Khurasan, and after they had undermined the tower it collapsed. Two men had been standing on it at the time, one of whom was killed when it fell and the other of whom was taken captive by our men and brought before Saladin.

"Cut him in half," ordered Saladin.

"My lord," I interrupted, "we are in the month of Ramadan! This man is a Muslim. To kill him would be an unpardonable sin."

"Cut him in half, so we can complete the taking of the castle!" Saladin replied.

"But my lord," I countered, "the castle is yours for the taking."

"Cut him in half!" repeated Saladin, adding that we should do it without any further delay. Accordingly, our soldiers cut the man in two, and we took possession of the castle.

AN UNUSUAL EPISODE

In the Christian church at Hunak there was a window at a height of forty cubits from the ground, and every day at midday a leopard came to this church and jumped up to this window and slept there until dusk. Then it would leap to the ground and disappear. Hunak was then a land held in fief by one of the satanic Franks, named Lord Adam. When Lord Adam heard about the leopard he told the people to call him the next time they saw it.

The leopard came at its usual time and leaped up to the window, and one of the peasants went to inform Lord Adam, who put on his armor, mounted his horse, grabbed his lance and shield, and rode to the church. Now this church was a ruin, and the only part of it that still stood was the wall with the window in it. As soon as the leopard saw Lord Adam (he was still on his horse) it sprang from the window, broke his back, and killed him; then it disappeared. The peasants then called the leopard "the mujahidin leopard."

It is known of leopards that if one of them wounds a man, and a mouse later urinates on the wound, the man will die. It is difficult to keep mice away from a man who has been wounded by a leopard. And this is why people wounded by leopards so often are placed on beds that are surrounded by water, and have cats tied to the corners of their beds—to scare away the mice.

ANOTHER CURIOUS CASE

One day my father (may Allah's mercy be upon him) brought home several Frankish girls who had been captured, to serve as maids. The Franks (may Allah's curse be upon them) are a vile race who marry only among themselves. My father saw a pretty girl among them, in the bloom of youth, and told one of his women-servants to take this girl to the baths, mend her clothing, and get her ready to travel, all of which she

did. He then sent the girl to one of his man-servants and instructed him to deliver the girl to the emir Shihab ad-Din Malik ibn Salim, the lord of the castle of Ja'bar, who was a dear friend of his. He also wrote him a letter that said "We have won some prizes from the Franks, which I wish to share with you."

The girl was pleasing to Shihab ad-Din, who took her. She bore him a son whom he named Badran. Shihab ad-Din appointed Badran as his heir when he came of age, and when Shihab ad-Din died, Badran became the governor of Ja'bar and its people. But his mother held all real power. She joined in a company of conspirators who lowered her from the castle by a rope. Others in the company received her and took her to the town of Saruj, which the Franks then held. There she married a Frankish shoemaker, even though her son was the governor of the castle of Ja'bar.

THE ODD CUSTOMS OF THE FRANKS

Every newcomer from the Frankish lands is more rude than those who have lived among us Muslims and become accustomed to our ways. Here is an example of their rudeness.

I always visit the al-Aqsa mosque when I travel to Jerusalem. Now the Franks have taken a small mosque next to al-Aqsa and converted it into a Christian church, and whenever I visited al-Aqsa (which was administered by the Templar knights, who are our friends) some of the Templars would empty the small mosque next door so that I could pray in it. One day I entered this small mosque and chanted "Allah is great." After I stood and was still in my prayers one of the [newcomer] Franks ran to me, grabbed me, and turned me until I faced eastward. "This is how you pray!" he shouted. Some Templars hurried over, grabbed the man, and led him away while I continued my prayers. But as soon as the Templars were busy with something else, the man rushed again at me and turned me eastward. "This is how you should pray!" he repeated.

The Templars came to my aid again and led the fellow out, and then they apologized to me, saying, "He is a newcomer, just arrived from France. He has only seen people pray to the east."

"I've finished my prayers," I said to myself. I left the mosque. To this day I wonder at this devilish man's conduct, the color that rose in his face, his shaking in fury, and his reaction to seeing someone pray toward Mecca.

In Nablus I once witnessed a duel fought by two Franks. This was the cause of their conflict: some Muslim raiders had taken a nearby village unexpectedly. One of the peasants in the village was rumored to have aided the raiders in their attack, and so he fled. The Frankish king ordered all the villagers to be brought before him.

The peasant who had fled then returned and said, "I challenge to a duel anyone who says I aided the raiders in our village!"

The king turned to the knight who held Nablus as a fief and said, "Bring someone to fight a duel with him." The knight therefore went to the village and brought back a blacksmith, ordering him to fight. (This way the knight was assured not to lose one of his peasants, to the detriment of his estate.)

I saw the blacksmith, who was a strong young man but who had a weak heart; he could walk only a short distance at a time, then he would have to stop and ask for a drink. The villager who had called for the duel was an old man but strong in spirit. . . . Then the governor of the town gave each fighter a club and a shield, and ordered the people to form a circle around them.

The two men fought. The old man drove the blacksmith backward until they reached the circle, then he would return to the middle of the circle. They traded blows with one another until they both looked like pillars stained with blood. The fight was taking a long time, and so the governor called out, "Hurry up!" Because the blacksmith was accustomed to hammering, he had an advantage, and the old man grew tired. The blacksmith hit him again and made him fall. The old man's club lay underneath him. The blacksmith crouched down to stick his fingers into the old man's eyes but could not do so because of all the blood,

and so he stood again and smashed the old man's head with his club, and killed him.

Several men then tied a rope around the old man's head and dragged him away and hanged him. The knight who had brought the blacksmith to the duel gave him his mantle and had him mount his own horse behind him. They rode off together.

This is how the Franks perform justice and maintain the law. May Allah's curse be upon them all!

REFLECTIONS ON OLD AGE

I did not know, in my younger years, that weakness of the mind affects everyone whom Death has overlooked. I have reached my ninetieth year and am worn out. . . . Weakness of body makes me crouch over, so that my body looks like it has collapsed into itself. I can hardly recognize myself, and look back on my past with sorrow. Here is how I describe myself now:

> Now that I have lived the long life
> for which I always wished, I now wish only
>   for death.
> Long years have left me weak; I have no strength
> to fight the battles that each day brings.
> My strength has become weakness, and my
>   old allies—
> Sight and Hearing—have abandoned me in my age.
> When I rise [in the morning], I feel the weight
> of a mountain on me, and when I walk it is
>   as though
> I am shackled. I move slowly with a cane in
>   the hand
> that used to carry a lance and sword. At night I lay
> on a soft bed but cannot sleep. I may as well
>   recline
> on solid rock. Old age reverses life—once
>   we reach
> maturity, we return to the infancy from which
>   we began.

10.5 Chronology of the Crusades

The Crusades were not an unending state of military conflict between the Christian and Islamic worlds, but occasional irruptions of violence—generally as seldom as once per generation—in an otherwise ongoing relationship.

Crusade	Date	Led by	Main opponent
1st Crusade	1095–1099	Godfrey, lord of Bouillon Baldwin, lord of Boulogne Raymond, count of Toulouse Stephen II, count of Blois Robert II, count of Flanders Robert II, duke of Normandy Bohemond, prince of Taranto	Kilij Arslan, sultan of Rum [T]
2nd Crusade	1147–1149	Louis VII of France	Nur ad-Din [K]
3rd Crusade	1189–1193	Richard the Lionheart of England Philip Augustus of France Frederick Barbarossa of Germany	Saladin [K]
4th Crusade	1202–1204	Boniface, marquess of Montferrat Theobald, count of Champagne Louis, count of Blois	N/A
Albigensian Crusade	1209–1229	Simon de Montfort	Count Raymond VI of Toulouse
5th Crusade	1217–1221	Andrew II of Hungary Leopold VI, duke of Austria William I, count of Holland	al-Kamil, sultan of Egypt [K]
6th Crusade	1228–1229	Frederick II of Germany	al-Kamil, sultan of Egypt [K]
7th Crusade	1248–1254	Louis IX of France	al-Mu'azzam Turanshah, sultan of Egypt [K]
8th Crusade	1270	Louis IX of France	Muhammad al-Mustansir, caliph of Tunisia [B]
9th Crusade	1271–1272	Prince Edward of England	Baybars [T], sultan of Egypt
Aragonese Crusade	1284–1285	Philip III of France	Peter III of Aragon
1291	al-Ashraf Khalil [T], the Mamluk sultan of Egypt seizes Acre, ending the history of the crusader states in the Holy Land.		

[B] = Berber.
[K] = Kurd.
[T] = Turk.

11. THE RENAISSANCES OF THE TWELFTH CENTURY

11.1   Peter Abelard, *Sic et Non*

Peter Abelard was an early proponent of the new learning of the twelfth-century Renaissance. A rascally student and later a brilliant teacher, he made a name for himself with his first important book *Sic et Non* (*Yes and No*), which was a compilation of contradictory passages from patristic sources and Church councils. Abelard's purpose was to highlight the fact that ecclesiastical tradition alone is insufficient to lead the faithful to truth. A critical intelligence and the application of logic was required—precisely the tools offered by the new learning. The preface to the book is printed below. The ellipses [. . .] consist mostly of examples he quotes to illustrate his points.

If some of the writings of the saints not only differ from one another but actually contradict each other, we ought not to rush to judgment (given the sheer multitude of their written words) about those great figures by whom the world itself is to be judged—for as the Scriptures say, "The saints shall judge the nations" [Wisdom 3.7–8], and also, "You will also sit as a judge" [Matthew 19.28]. So let us not presume to dismiss as liars, or condemn as mistaken, those men of whom the Lord Himself said, "Whoever listens to you, listens to Me; and whoever rejects you, rejects Me" [Luke 10.16]. Remembering our own weakness of mind, let us be more sure of our lack of understanding than of their inability to write, for they are the ones of whom He Who is Truth Itself once said, "For it is not you who are speaking, but the Spirit of your Father Who speaks through you" [Matthew 10.20]. Is it any wonder, then, since we lack the Spirit through Which these things were written, spoken, and revealed to the saints, that we should also lack the means to understand their teachings? Especially given the fact that each of those writers is as overflowing in wisdom as in words. As Cicero pointed out, sameness in everything destroys the appetite and causes one to feel queasy; and so it is fitting that the writings of our forefathers vary on issue after issue and that they are not cheapened by the use of low, common language. As St. Augustine observed, ideas should not be reviled simply because they are obscure; indeed, they should be more highly valued, the more difficult they are to investigate and understand. Considering the great diversity of the people we are talking about, it is to be expected that their writings are an assortment. The precise meaning of any of their words might be unknown or unfamiliar to many readers. And if we are going to use these texts for considering matters of doctrine, we ought to pay more attention to how they have been understood [down the centuries] than how their specific wording functions, as no less an expert on language than the great grammarian Priscian has taught us. . . .

Whenever we confront writings of the saints that appear to contradict truth, we ought to be especially careful not to be misled by false attributions of authorship or corruptions in the text, for there are many apocryphal works in circulation that have saints' names attached to them in order to give them greater authority, and even the texts of the Holy Scriptures are sometimes corrupted by scribal errors. This is what St. Jerome, the most trustworthy author and reliable translator of all, warned of in his letter to Laeta, concerning her daughter's education: "Let her be wary of all apocryphal writings. Even if she wants to read them not for their dogmatic truth but only to enjoy their miracle stories, she should know that they were not written by the men listed as their authors. It takes a great deal of discernment to find any gold hidden in such mud." . . . [Jerome also found scribal errors in the Holy Gospels:] "We find another instance in the gospel of Matthew, where it says 'then he gave back the thirty pieces of silver, as it is written in the book of the prophet Jeremiah' [Matthew 27.9] Only we do not find this phrase in Jeremiah; it is in Zechariah [Zechariah 11.13]. Behold—an error, just like any other." Is it any wonder, then, since scribes in their ignorance have even introduced errors into the gospels, if we see mistakes creeping into the writings of the later Church Fathers, which are far less authoritative? Therefore, when we encounter anything in the books of the saints that seems to be contradictory to truth, the pious, humble, and charitable thing to do . . . is to assume that at that specific point the text may have been corrupted or incorrectly translated, or else to acknowledge that we do not understand it.

No less important is it to consider whether such passages come from writings by the saints that they themselves later retracted or corrected once they had discovered the truth. St. Augustine did this many times. Or perhaps they were writing to cite the opinion of someone else rather to express than their own view—as Ecclesiastes often did, introducing many unsound statements into the Scriptures. He wanted to be understood, not to stir up confusion. . . .

It is an element of everyday speech to describe the existence of things according to the perceptions of our senses. For example, we know that no truly empty space exists anywhere in the world—that is, a space that utterly lacks air or any other type of matter—and yet we straightforwardly call a box or chest "empty" because that is how our sense of sight perceives it. We judge things by the evidence of our eyes: thus sometimes we speak of the starry heavens, and sometimes not; sometimes we say the sun is hot, and other times not; sometimes we say the moon is more or less bright, and sometimes not so much. Similarly, we sometimes say that things will remain the same forever, when it is clear to us that they will not. Why is it so surprising, therefore, if we occasionally find ideas

expressed by the Holy Fathers in their writings that are their own opinions rather than the actual truth? Whenever contradictory things are said about a single issue, we must be careful to distinguish statements offered with the force of a command, from those offered with a measure of indulgence, and from those offered as exhortations to perfection. Only by considering the intentions behind such passages, can we hope to find a remedy for statements that oppose one another.

If a statement is a direct command, we must decide if it is general or specific—that is, one applicable to everyone in general, or to certain individuals alone. We need to take into account when certain statements were made, or the reasons for their being made, because it often happens that what one time-period permitted, another one forbade, and what is often commanded with great insistence is sometimes tempered with flexibility. It is especially necessary to make these distinctions when dealing with the Church's decrees and canons. It will be easy to resolve many controversies if we can be on our guard for different authors using the same words but for different purposes.

Any reader who cares to resolve conflicts in the writings of the saints will pay attention to all these matters. If a conflict is so great that it cannot be resolved by reasoning, then the authorities must be weighed against one another, and whichever side has stronger evidence and more likelihood [of being correct] should be retained above all. Thus did St. Isidore say to the bishop of Massio: "To close this letter of mine, let me add that whenever opposing opinions are found in the acts of Church council, more weight should be given to the view that is of greater and more ancient authority."

Indeed, it has happened that various prophets have lacked, at times, the grace of prophecy, but being in the habit of prophesying have offered false statements of their own making, believing as they made them that the spirit of prophesy was truly upon them. God allowed the errors to occur as a means of keeping the prophets humble—that they might recognize more clearly what things come from the Spirit of God, and what comes from their own spirits; and know that when they possess the spirit of prophecy they have it as a gift from the Holy Spirit, Who can neither lie nor be mistaken. For when this Spirit is upon one, just as it does not bestow all its gifts on one person, so does it not enlighten the mind of the prophet regarding everything; instead, it reveals a bit here, and a bit there, and whenever it clarifies one thing it conceals another. St. Gregory said as much in his first homily on Ezechiel, using clear examples. And even St. Peter, the prince of the apostles, shimmering with miracles and the gifts of divine grace after the extraordinary pouring out of the Holy Spirit, promised by God, and who taught his disciples nothing but the truth, was not ashamed to abandon a pernicious untruth [he had asserted] about the practice of circumcision and various other ancient rites, after he was publicly and soundly corrected (although in a friendly way) by the Apostle Paul.

When it becomes clear that even the prophets and apostles were no strangers to error, what is the surprise in finding some mistakes in the numerous writings of the holy fathers, or in their scribal transmission? Just as these saints should not be accused of lying, if at one time or another they have said something contrary to the truth, for they were acting out of simple ignorance rather than duplicity—so too, and in the same way, one ought not impute to presumption or sinfulness something that someone says out of love and in order to teach. For as all know, God distinguishes between actions on the basis of the intentions that lay behind them, as it says in Matthew, "If your eye is sound, your whole body will be full of light" [Matthew 6.22]. And in the treatise *On Ecclesiastical Discipline* by St. Augustine: "Have charity, and do what you can." . . . For it is one thing to lie, quite another to make an error when speaking—so long as one falls away from the truth by mistake rather than out of malice. If God allows this to happen even to His holy saints, as we have pointed out, in situations where no harm is done to the faith, then it does not fail to bear fruit for those very saints, who undertake all things for the sake of the good. Even the Doctors of the Church—who are so diligently attentive—believe that there exist errors in their writings that need correction; this is why they grant to posterity the license to emend those texts or simply not to follow them, if they themselves did not have the time to retract or correct their works. . . .

One ought to read literature not with the requirement of believing it but with the freedom to judge it.

And in order that the room for this freedom be not lost, and that the healthy work of treating difficult questions and translating their language and style is not denied to later authors, the excellence of the canonical authority of the Old and New Testaments has been set apart from the books of later authors. If anything <u>there</u> strikes the reader as absurd, he cannot say that the author of this or that book did not possess the truth. Either the manuscript is corrupt, or the translator made a mistake, or the reader has failed to understand. . . .

[St. Augustine] calls the canonical writings of the Old and New Testaments texts about which it is heresy to say that something in them contradicts truth. In this regard he wrote, in his fourth letter to St. Jerome: "In commenting on the Letter of Paul to the Galatians I came across something that distressed me terribly. But if something in the Holy Scriptures is, or can be shown to be, a lie (even a "white lie") then what authority will the text have thereafter? How can anyone pass judgment on the Scriptures? Who is so shameless as to crush them under the heavy weight of falsehood?" And in another letter on the same issues: "It seems to me to be an exceedingly dangerous thing to regard anything in holy books as a lie—that is, to think that the men through whom the Scriptures were written and passed on to us would have lied about anything in their books. For if a single lie, even the smallest one, is acknowledged to exist in so lofty an authority, then not a single particle of the books will remain, which someone will not explain away as the invention or imagining of the author's mind, using this incredibly dangerous excuse whenever someone comes across something difficult to practice or hard to believe." . . .

With these points now made, may it please you that I have here endeavored to gather various passages from the holy fathers that stand out in my memory on account of their apparently differing opinions on various issues. May these passages inspire young readers to strenuous exercise in seeking out the truth, and may the search make them sharper readers in the end. The first key to wisdom is defined, of course, as determined and frequent questioning. Aristotle, the most insightful philosopher of them all, urged his students to embrace the act of questioning with their whole hearts; in his preface "Ad aliquid" he wrote: "Perhaps it is difficult to declare confidently on matters of this sort, unless one does it often and in great detail; but it would not be useless to doubt a number of specific points." For indeed, by doubting we come to questioning, and by questioning we discover the truth. "Seek, and you will find," said the One Who is Truth Itself; "knock, and the door will be opened for you." He taught us with His own moral example. Sitting at age twelve amidst His teachers and inquiring into those things He wanted to discover, He showed us by His questions the way to be a student rather than the way to be a teacher by exposition, even though the full and complete wisdom of God was present in Him.

Therefore, when certain passages of Scripture are laid before us, the authority of those very Scriptures is commended the more they excite the reader and spur him to seek out their truth.

For this reason it pleased me, in this current book, to compile into a single volume numerous passages from the writings of the saints, following the decree of Pope Gelasius regarding the books that are held to be authentic. Thus it is assured that I have introduced nothing from apocryphal writings. I have appended excerpts from the *Retractations* of St. Augustine, from which it will be clear that I have quoted nothing that he himself later retracted or corrected.

11.2   Ibn Rushd, *On the Harmony of Religious Law and Philosophy*

Ibn Rushd (full name: Abu al-Walid Muhammad b. Ahmad b. Muhammad b. Rushd) was born in Cordoba, the grand capital city of Islamic Spain, in 1126. His family was a prominent one, made up of distinguished religious jurists and physicians, and he received a sound classical Islamic education. He later served as a qadi and physician, but his greatest intellectual love was for philosophy. His most important works, apart from his commentaries of Aristotle, were *On the Harmony of Religious Law and Philosophy*, *The Methods of Proof in Regard to Religious Doctrine*, and *The Incoherence of the Incoherence*. The last book was a response to *The Incoherence of the Philosophers* by al-Ghazali—hence the odd title. Translated below is an abridged version of the third chapter of *On the Harmony of Religious Law and Philosophy*; it treats the issues of fate and predestination. Ibn Rushd died in Marrakesh, Morocco, in 1198.

The question of fate and predestination is one of the most complicated questions in all religion, because the traditional teachings on this problem, when closely viewed, are seen to be contradictory. But this is also true of rational efforts to address it. The first contradictions appear in the Qur'an and the hadith. Many verses in the Qur'an proclaim as universal truth that all things are predestined, and that man is fated to do all that he does; but many other verses say, to the contrary, that man's actions are freely chosen and not fated at all.

These are some verses that say everything is determined and inevitable (many others could be cited as well):

"Say: 'Yes, those of old and those of later times, all will certainly be gathered together for the meeting appointed for a Day Well-Known." [Qur'an 56.49]

"Allah doth know what every female [womb] doth bear, but how much the wombs fall short [of their time or number] or do exceed. Every single thing is with Him in [due] proportion. He knoweth the Unseen and that which is open: He is the Great, the Most High." [Qur'an 13.8–9]

"No misfortune can happen on earth or in your souls but is recorded in a Book before We bring it into existence: That is truly easy for Allah." [Qur'an 57.22]

As for verses that state that man's actions are the result of his free will, or that proclaimed things are possibly and not necessarily going to happen:

"Whatever misfortune happens to you, is because of the things your hands have wrought, and for many [a sin] He grants forgiveness." [Qur'an 42.31]
"But those who have earned evil will have a reward of like evil." [Qur'an 10.27]
"Those who believe, and do deeds of righteousness, and establish regular prayers and give zakat, will have their reward with their Lord: on them shall be no fear, nor shall they grieve." [Qur'an 2.277]

Sometimes contrary statements even appear within a single passage:

"It is part of the Mercy of Allah that thou dost deal gently with them. Wert thou severe or harsh hearted they would have broken away from about thee: so pass over [their faults], and ask for [Allah's] forgiveness for them; and consult them in affairs [of moment]. Then, when thou hast taken a decision, put thy trust in Allah. For Allah loves those who put their trust [in Him]. If Allah helps you, none can overcome you. If He forsakes you, who is there, after that, that can help you? In Allah, then, let believers put their trust." [Qur'an 3.159–160]

or

"Whatever good, [O man!] happens to thee, is from Allah; but whatever evil happens to thee, is from thyself and We have sent thee as a Messenger to [instruct] mankind. And enough is Allah for a witness. He who obeys the Messenger, obeys Allah: but if any turn away, We have not sent thee to watch over them." [Qur'an 4.80–81]

We can see this also in the Prophet's *hadith*. On one occasion he said, "Every child is born in the true religion [Islam]. It is his parents who later turn him into a Jew or a Christian." But on another occasion he said, "Some people were created for Hell and live lives fit for it; others were created for Heaven and live lives fit for it." Clearly the first teaching states that the situation one is born into is the cause of disbelief, since true belief is natural to all, but the second teaching says that evil and disbelief are set by Allah and man is fated to follow them.

Because of this, Muslims have split into two factions. The first are the Mutazilites, who believe that one's goodness or wickedness result from one's own action—and that one will be rewarded or punished accordingly. The Jabarites hold the opposite view, asserting that one is fated to do whatever one does in life.

The Asharites are a group that has tried to follow a compromise between these two extremes. They maintain that one chooses one's actions, but the power to perform the actions is the creation of Allah—and only in this sense one can say that Allah creates the actions themselves. This, however, makes no sense, for if an action and the power to perform it are both created by Allah, then the man is logically compelled to perform it. This is only one reason for the confused split over this problem. . . .

It may be asked, therefore, how is the contradiction between tradition and reason to be reconciled—which surely is the role of religion, not to keep divided what ought to be reconciled by pursuing a middle course? It is clear, first of all, that Allah created the power we possess to perform deeds that are contradictory. But our actions are not brought to fulfillment except from outside of us, by Allah's intention for us, which removes the obstacles to our doing them; therefore our actions are only effected when our will and ability are in alignment with Allah's intent. In this way our completed actions result from our own will and from the fitness of our will with Allah's design for us, from the outside, and this alignment is what we call predestination. Allah's design therefore neither impels our actions nor hinders them, but it is the cause of our willing the actions. Our intentions are produced either by our imagination or by our desire to effect something that is not in our power but is in the power of something outside of us. For example: if we see something good, we admire it and desire to acquire it even though it is not in our power to achieve. Similarly, if we see something bad, we turn from it instinctively. Our intention, our will, depends on causes outside ourselves. . . .

To understand causes is to understand the secret knowledge of the essence of a thing before it comes into existence. But since it is the arrangement of causes that brings something into existence at a particular time, the knowledge of a thing must exist prior to the thing itself. To understand all causation, therefore, is to know what exists and what does not exist at any given moment. Praised be Allah, Who has complete understanding of all creation and all causation! This is what the words "Keys of the secret" mean in the verse "With Him are the keys of the Unseen, the treasures that none knoweth but He. He knoweth whatever there is on the earth and in the sea. Not a leaf doth fall but with His knowledge: There is not a grain in the darkness [or depths] of the earth, nor anything fresh or dry [green or withered], but is [inscribed] in a Record Clear [to those who can read]." [Qur'an 6.59]

If this argument is true, then it should now be clear how we freely choose our own actions even while they are predetermined by fate. This reconciliation is the true purpose of religion, and of those Qur'anic verses and *hadith* that appeared contradictory. In defining those passages' universal nature in this way, all contradictions disappear—and so do all doubts raised by the apparent contradictions. Everything that comes into existence by means of our will is brought to fulfillment by the combination of our will and the causes that lie outside us. Doubts arise when we take in account only one aspect of agency. . . .

[Al-Ghazali] writes that a man who asserts any cause to be co-existent with Allah is like a man who equates the role of a pen, in writing, with the work of the scribe who uses it. In other words, the pen and the man are both to be called scribes, because the word

writing can be applied to both. That word, however, is the only thing they share; apart from it, they have nothing in common. Such is the case with the word *creator*, when we apply it to Allah and to causation. But I argue back that his example is faulty, because Allah is the creator of the essences of everything that affects causation, whereas in al-Ghazali's example the scribe is not the creator of the essence of the pen, and of the act of writing, and of the words written. This is why I say that there is no creator but Allah—a statement that harmonizes our perceptions, our reason, and our religion. . . .

So praises to "the Wise, the All-Knowing!" [Qur'an 67.14] Allah has shown us the truth in His Book, "And what will explain to thee what is the Day of Sorting Out?" [Qur'an 77.14] And again, "He has made subject to you the Night and the Day; the Sun and the Moon; and the Stars are in subjection by His command: verily in this are Signs for men who are wise." [Qur'an 16.12] And again, "And He is Allah: there is no god but He. To Him be praise, at the first and at the last." [Qur'an 28.70] He also says, "This is [true] guidance: And for those who reject the Signs of their Lord is a grievous chastisement of abomination." [Qur'an 45.11] There are many other verses that I could cite on this matter. If there were no wisdom in the messages with which Allah has favored us, we would not possess the blessings that we have and for which we are ever grateful to Him.

11.3 Al-Ghazali, *The Deliverer from Error*

Abu Hamid al-Ghazali (1058–1111) is widely regarded as medieval Islam's greatest thinker, a Muslim counterpart to Christianity's St. Augustine. Born in the Khurasan province in today's Iran, he was a precocious youth who quickly showed extraordinary intellectual ability. He studied Islamic law, *kalam* (a kind of elementary theology), philosophy, and the sciences, excelling in each. At the early age of 34 he was appointed professor of Islamic sciences at the Nizamiyah *madrasa* in Baghdad, perhaps the most prestigious academic position in the caliphate. A few years later, however, he went through a spiritual crisis that resulted in his loss of belief in religious rationalism and his embrace of the mystical Sufi tradition. He spent several years in travel and meditation, then re-emerged in public life and devoted his last years to teaching Sufism. His memoir *al-Munqidh min al-dalal* (*The Deliverer from Error*) describes his spiritual journey. Below is a passage recounting his discovery of Sufism.

Having had my fill of these types of teachings, I turned my mind instead to the Way of the Sufis, which I understood as a discovery that can be made not by the intellect but by action. Sufi wisdom consists of a kind of carving away, ridding oneself of bad habits and vicious sentiments—for these are spiritual stumbling blocks—in order to empty one's heart of everything except the thought and remembrance of Allah. I soon found that the theory was easier than the practice. I began studying Sufi teachings by reading their books . . . until I had learned all that I could, of their teachings. Gradually, however, it became clear to me that the essence of their wisdom cannot be acquired through study; it can only be attained by tasting it, by ecstatic release, by transformative experience. Consider how great is the difference between knowing the definitions, causes, and symptoms of health and stability, and actually being healthy and stable. . . . In a similar way, there is a difference between knowing the definition, causes, and symptoms of mystical rapture and actually experiencing it—and consequently longing to rid oneself of the things of this world. . . .

I had already clearly learned that my only hope of achieving eternal blessedness lay in pious living and denying my heart its passions, and that the necessary way to begin was to detach my heart from the world, to withdraw utterly from this place of illusion, and to devote myself solely to Allah, the Most High, and His eternal realm. I understood that I could achieve this only by turning my back on fame and fortune, and to flee from all my activities and relationships. I focused on the reality of my existence and beheld the extent to which I was consumed on all sides. My daily actions—even the most noble of them, being engaged in public and private teaching—were devoted to sciences that mattered nothing to my journey to the realm of paradise. My public teaching was not intended, as it should have been, to glorify Allah but was geared and driven by my desire for fame and honor. I saw that I was standing on the edge of a cliff that was giving way, about to fall into the Endless Fire, unless I changed my ways.

I meditated endlessly on this, wanting to do something about my life while I still had the ability. One day I would be determined to quit Baghdad and cut myself off from all responsibilities—but then the next day I would change my mind. One step forward, then one step back. In the morning I might long only for the things of the afterlife, but by evening my baser desires would come to the fore. Earthly concerns held me in chains, while spiritual longing cried out, "Get away! Get away! A long journey awaits you, and time is running out. All the [intellectual] trappings that engulf you are nothing but trickery and nonsense. When will you prepare for the afterlife, if not now? If you will not cut yourself away from earthly concerns now, when will you ever?" Then my spirit would revive and I would be determined, absolutely determined, to take off and flee; but Satan was quick to respond. . . .

When I realized how powerless I was to make up my mind, how totally paralyzed I was, how lost I was with no idea how to proceed, I turned to Allah the Most High, and He "Who listens to the distressed when he calls on Him" [Qur'an 27.62] answered me. He guided my heart away from fame and fortune, away from family, children, and friends. I announced publically my decision to leave for Mecca, even though I secretly intended to go instead to Syria, since I feared the caliph and my colleagues learning of my plan to reside in Damascus. I was crafty and careful in my arrangement about leaving Baghdad, just as I was rock-steady in my resolve never to return. All the religious leaders in Iraq talked about me incessantly, since none of them could imagine that my departure had a spiritual motive. My position among them, after all, they regarded as the pinnacle of status. "That is their attainment of knowledge." [Qur'an 53.30] . . .

I left Baghdad after distributing whatever wealth I had accumulated, setting aside only as much as I needed to survive and to support my children. I explained to everyone that my Iraqi fortune was intended to support the people, being my pious alms [zakat]. Truly this is the best of all possible arrangements available to a scholar, to support his family. Then I went to Damascus, where I lived for two years. I devoted myself entirely to ascetic withdrawal, solitude, and spiritual disciple, in order to purify my soul, to increase in virtue, and to clean my heart and keep it focused always on Allah the Most High—all as I had been taught by the writings of the Sufi masters. I often prayed all day in the mosque, all alone, isolated high up in the minaret. I went from Damascus to Jerusalem, shutting myself daily in the Dome of the Rock. Eventually I felt called to make the hajj, to receive the blessings of Mecca and Medina, and to visit the tomb of the Prophet of Allah (May Allah's peace and blessing be upon him!), after first visiting the tomb of Ibrahim the Friend of Allah (May Allah's peace and blessing be upon him!). So I set out for the Hijaz.

Just then, however, certain problems and pleas from my children drew me back to Baghdad, even though I had been utterly resolved never to return there. But even while back in Baghdad I chose to live apart, desiring not to disturb the purification of my heart or my constant mindfulness of Allah. Local events, family issues, and the daily need for sustenance pressed in upon me, however, and marred my peaceful solitude. The state of spiritual ecstasy came to me only seldom, although I never stopped pursuing it. Obstacles always appeared in my way, but I never gave up the pursuit.

I lived this way for ten years. It is impossible to describe in detail the things that were revealed to me in those ecstasies that did come, but I can say this much—in the hope that it may be of some use: The Sufis are without a doubt the ones who most perfectly follow the ways of Allah the Most High, who live the best of all lives, the most holy, and the most pure.

Not even if one combined all the knowledge of the scholars, all the wisdom of the sages, and all the teachings of the theologians, the total still would not equal even a single aspect of Sufi conduct and belief—for everything a Sufi does and meditates upon, whether in public or in private, is inspired by the light of prophecy, and no light on earth shines brighter than the light of prophecy.

How else to describe it? The first requirement of Sufism is purity, the total purification of the heart from everything other than Allah the Most High. It is the complete absorption of the heart by mindfulness of Allah, reminiscent of the prayer *Allahu al-akhbar*. The goal is to dissolve oneself into Allah. . . .

As soon as one sets upon the Sufi path, visions reveal themselves. Even when wide awake, a Sufi may see angels or the spirits of the prophets, and may hear their voices teaching him. One's spirit can ascend beyond seeing visions of forms and likenesses, to reach a stage that is beyond words. To even attempt to describe this stage is to commit an error that one must be careful to avoid. In only a most general way, the ascent is a closeness to Allah that some call absorption, or identification, or union—all these words fail.

11.4 Maimonides, *Letter to Yemen*

R. Moshe b. Maimon (1135–1204) was the greatest Jewish scholar of the Middle Ages. Born in Cordoba, during the regime of the Almoravids, he studied Torah and Talmud with his father, who was also a rabbi, and read Greek philosophy in the Arabic translations then circulating in Spain. He became a physician, which is how he supported his family after they (along with many other Jews) went into exile after the brutal Almohad regime replaced the relatively benign Almoravids in 1148. Maimonides lived in Morocco for many years before settling in Fustat, Egypt. An extraordinarily prolific writer, Maimonides composed his *Letter to Yemen* in 1172, in response to a request for guidance from the Jewish community there, which was experiencing persecution from two sources—the local Islamic ruler and a Jewish reformer who had declared himself the Messiah and announced the approaching End of Days.

. . . Remember always that ours is the true, divine, authentic religion, as revealed to us by Moses, who is pre-eminent among all the prophets from beginning to end. It is through this faith that the Holy One has set us apart from the rest of mankind. The Holy Scripture says: "Yet it was to your fathers that the Lord was drawn in His love for them, so that He chose you, their lineal descendants, from among all peoples—as is now the case" [Deut. 10.15]. This is not owing to our merits, though. It was the will of the Holy One, because our forefathers knew Him and submitted to Him. We read: "It is not because you are the most numerous of peoples that the Lord set His heart on you and chose you—indeed, you are the smallest of peoples; but it was because the Lord favored you and kept the oath He made to your fathers that the Lord freed you with a mighty hand and rescued you from the house of bondage, from the power of Pharaoh king of Egypt" [Deut. 7.7–8]. The Holy One has set us apart with His laws and teachings, and our unique status is the consequence of those commandments and statutes. The Scripture says of His mercies to us: "Or what great nation has laws and rules as perfect as all this Teaching that I set before you this day?" [Deut. 4.8]. This is why all the nations on the earth rise up against us, out of their envy and malice. This is why all the kings of the earth persecute us, out of their hatred and injustice. All have wanted to impede the Lord, but in vain. From tyrant to slave, everyone who has ever lived since the time of the Covenant and has sought dominion on earth, if he was violent and crude, has tried from start to finish to destroy our Law and obliterate our religion. Whether by sword, murder, or riot, all have done so—Amalek, Sisera, Sennacherib, Nebuchadnezzar, Titus, Hadrian, and others. May their bones be ground into dust! And they are only the first of two types of men who have tried to impede the Lord's will.

The second type consists of the most civilized and sophisticated of peoples—the Syrians, the Persians, and the Greeks. These too have tried to destroy our Law and obliterate our religion, but they have done so with crafty arguments and the controversies their thinking has stirred up. They try to undermine the Law with their argumentative writings, to obliterate it with words just as the tyrants attempt to do with swords. Neither of them, however, will ever succeed, for we possess the Holy One's promise, through Isaiah, that He will destroy all who seek to weaken the Law or demolish it with armies. The Holy One will destroy them—but this must be understood as a metaphor only, a way of saying that any enemy's attempts will be wholly frustrated. . . .

And after [the Syrians, Persians, and Greeks] there came a new sect that combined their methods into one, both conquest and controversy, thinking thus they could wipe out the entire Jewish nation and religion. This sect claimed the power of prophecy and established a new religion, contrary to our own. They claimed an equally divine revelation, in the hope of raising doubt and creating confusion. . . . The first to do so was Jesus the Nazarene. May his bones be ground into dust! He was a Jew, having a Jewish mother, but his father was a Gentile, for our Law states that a child born of a Jewish mother and Gentile father (or, of course, of a Jewish mother and a slave) is a true Jew. Thus one can only call Jesus a non-Jew in an indirect manner of speaking, for he led his followers to believe he was a prophet sent by the Lord to explain the Law, and to believe that he was the Messiah anticipated by all. But his teaching of the Law was faulty and opened the way to its total annulment, the undoing of its commandments, and the breaking of its prohibitions. Our sages of blessed memory rendered a fitting punishment on him, after learning of his reputation and teachings. . . .

Another sect arose not long afterwards, a sect based on Jesus and taught by one whose lineage was of Esau. He [Paul] did not set out to create an entirely new religion. He was not an offense to Israel, and he stirred up no antagonism [toward the Jews] among his followers. The faults of his teachings, however, were obvious to everyone, and his activity ceased when we caught him. His fate is well known.

After [Paul] came the Madman [Muhammad], who followed the path laid out for him by his predecessor. The Madman, however, had ambition to rule others and subject them to his power, and so he invented his well-known religion [Islam].

All of these men presumed to compare their ravings with our divine religion, but only an idiot would set human inventions alongside divine revelations. Our religion differs from theirs as much as a living person differs from a statue of marble, wood, bronze, or silver, no matter how elegantly carved. . . .

Only someone who knows nothing at all about the Holy Scriptures' hidden meanings and the Law's deeper truths could possibly think our religion has anything in common with any other he compares it to. Only such an imbecile would equate the fact that our Law contains commandments and prohibitions, and that other religions also detail permitted and not-permitted actions; or that both contain systems of required rituals, positive and negative commands, and apportion rewards and punishments thereby. Only if one grasps the inner meanings of the Law, can one appreciate the fact that the essence of our true religion rests on the deep, hidden meanings of its commandments and prohibitions—every single one of which will benefit anyone straining after perfection, by removing every impediment that stands between him and his goal. . . . The teachings of those religions that outwardly resemble our own, however, have no deeper meaning. They are mere imitations of ours. Their supporters have copied our faith in order to give themselves honor by pretending to be like us. Their fakery is obvious to those who know, which makes them laughing-stocks and fools; one laughs at them just as one laughs when seeing apes imitate the actions of men.

This foolishness was prophesied by Daniel, when he predicted that arrival of someone who would proclaim a religion supposedly like ours, with its own Scriptures and oral traditions, and would be arrogant enough to proclaim a special revelation from the Lord and to have spoken with Him, among other extraordinary things. Here we see Daniel prophesying the rise of the Arabs after the destruction of Rome, with his declaration of the appearance of the Madman who would destroy Rome, Persia, and Byzantium. . . . Bear in mind that the Holy One told Daniel that He would destroy the Madman despite his successes and endurance, and destroy also the followers of his predecessors [Jesus and Paul]. All those who have persecuted us will perish in the end—those who sought to destroy us with the sword, those who used argument, and those who now mimic us. . . .

You write that there is a man in one of your cities who claims to be the Messiah. I am not surprised, neither at him nor his followers. No doubt the man is mad, and as a sick person he is not to be condemned or rebuked; an illness is not the fault of the sufferer.

As for his followers, I suspect they fell under his sway because of the wretchedness of their lives and their failure to understand the true meaning and importance of the Messiah. They probably are confusing the Messiah for the son of their anticipated Mahdi. But I am surprised that you, an enlightened man who has read the teachings of the rabbis, are tempted to believe in him. Don't you know, my brother, that the Messiah will be a prophet more luminous than any who has come in Moses' wake, and that a willfully false prophet deserves capital punishment. . . .

Remember, the Christians falsely attribute prophetic power to Jesus the Nazarene—may his bones be ground into dust!—and believe he rose from the dead and performed other miracles. Even if (just for the sake of argument) these claims were true, there still would be no reason to believe Jesus is the Messiah. I could show you a thousand proofs from the Holy Scriptures to contradict their claim.

In the end, who would ever claim Messiahship except one who wishes to make a public fool of himself? If this man you mention acts out of pride or spite, I would say he deserves death, but it appears to me instead that he has a melancholy and confused mind, and so I advise you—for your own good as well as for his—to put him in chains and detain him until the Gentiles learn that he is insane. Once you have broadcast loudly the news of this man and his illness, you can then release him without putting him at risk. If the Gentiles learn of him after you have incarcerated him, they will examine him and declare him mad, and you will be left unmolested. But if you do nothing about him until after the Gentiles have learned of him, then you will incur their wrath.

Remember, my brother: the Holy One has thrown us among the Arabs who now persecute us so severely. The Scriptures warned us of the unfair laws they would raise against us: "Our enemies themselves shall judge us" [Deut. 32.31] Never did any nation abuse, belittle, demean and hate us, the way they do. . . .

11.5   Trotula, *Handbook on the Maladies of Women*

Originally associated with a female physician named Trotula of Salerno (eleventh–twelfth centuries), this compendium of medical care for women deals with infertility, childbirth, and birth control methods, as well as cosmetics, beautification techniques, and dietary advice. These selections pinpoint a handful of concerns that medieval women had, from family planning to aesthetics.

Here begins the Book on the Maladies of Women according to Trotula.

When God, the Creator of the universe, first established the world He distinguished between the individual natures of things—each according to its kind—and He endowed human nature with a single dignity above all other things: He gave humans freedom of reason and intellect. This gift set mankind above the condition of all animals. And God, in wanting to sustain human generation in perpetuity, carefully and providentially created males and females, thus establishing the foundation for the production of offspring. And He created them in such a way, to ensure the arrival of fertile offspring, that their natures formed a pleasing interlocking mixture; for the males He constitutes a hot and dry nature, to which He opposed the cool and wet nature of the females. Thus, should a man overflow with an excess of one of his qualities, the woman could contain it. In this way the stronger qualities of heat and dryness dominate the man, who is the stronger and more worthy of the sexes, while the weaker qualities of coolness and wetness dominate the woman, who is the weaker and less worthy sex. God did this so that the male, in his strength, might pour out his essence into the woman just as seed is sown in a field, and that the female, in her weakness a natural subject to the man, might receive the seed provided by Nature.

But because women are weaker than men and frequently experience childbirth, maladies often abound in them, especially in the organs dedicated to Nature's work; and whether because of their fragile nature, shame, or embarrassment, they seldom reveal their sufferings and illnesses (which occur in such a private area) to any physician. Their general misfortune is pitiable, and this fact, together with the prompting of a certain specific woman stirring my heart, has led me to give clear explanations about their maladies and how to restore them to health. With God's help I have worked diligently to collect passages from the better parts of the works of Galen and Hippocrates, to the end that I might discuss and explain the causes, symptoms, and cures of women's diseases. . . .

[74] Some women are incapable of conception, either because they are too skinny and lean, or because they are too fat and the flesh of the womb-orifice shuts out the man's seed and does not let it enter. Other women's wombs are smooth and slick, which means that the man's seed, once received, cannot be kept inside. This also happens sometimes because the man's seed is too watery; once it enters the womb, its excessive fluidity causes it to flow outside. Some men, too, have very cold and dry testicles, and they rarely generate, if ever, because their seed is incapable of the task.

[75] Treatment. If a woman is barren either on account of her own difficulty or her man's, let the following treatment be attempted. Take two pots and place some wheat bran in each one; add some of the man's urine to one of the pots, and add some of the woman's urine to the other. Let the pots sit for nine or ten days. If the barrenness is the woman's fault, you will find many worms in her pot and the bran will stink; you will find the same thing in the man's pot if the barrenness is his fault. If you find this in neither of the pots, then neither of them is at fault and they should be able to conceive if aided by certain medicines. . . .

[83] If a woman chooses not to conceive, she should wear against her naked flesh the uterus of a goat that has never had offspring. . . .

[86] Another method would be to take a weasel and remove its testicles without killing it. The woman should then wrap them in the skin of a goose or of

some other animal, and wear them against her naked bosom. Then she will not conceive.

[87] If a woman has previously been badly torn in childbirth and fears ever getting pregnant again, she should put into her afterbirth as many grains of barley or spurge as the number of years she wishes to remain barren. If she wishes to remain barren forever, she should put in a whole handful. . . .

[126] A wet nurse should be young and have good coloring—a woman who mixes a little red with white, who is neither too close to, nor too far removed from, her last birth, who is unblemished, whose breasts are not too flabby nor too swollen but who has a healthy, ample chest, and who is moderately fat.

[127] Diet. A wet nurse should avoid eating salty, spicy, and acidic foods, and anything in which the heat is strong; also astringent foods like leeks and onions; and any of those spices that are added to give food more flavor, such as pepper, garlic, or rocket—but especially garlic. She should avoid stress and be careful not to induce her menses. If her milk runs low, she should eat porridge made of bean-flour or rice; she should also have wheat bread mixed with milk, sugar, and perhaps some fennel—for these things increase the milk supply. If her milk becomes too thick, let her nourishment be cut back, and compel her to work. One could also give her a vinegary syrup or light wine. If her milk becomes to thin, on the other hand, her foods should be thick and strong, and she should get extra sleep. If the child's bowels are loose, the wet nurse should eat whatever makes her constipated. . . .

[245] There is an ointment used by noble women that removes hairs, refines the skin, and removes blemishes. Take the juice from the moist leaves of a cucumber and mix them with almond milk in a bowl. Add quicklime and orpiment; then add some gum resin that has been beaten together with a little wine. Let the mixture rest for a day and a night. Then cook. Once it has been well cooked, remove the gum resin and add a little oil or wine, plus some quicksilver. Remove the concoction from the heat, and add a powder made of the following herbs: mastic, frankincense, cinnamon, nutmeg, and clove, all in equal amounts. The ointment thus produced has a sweet smell and gently softens the skin. Noblewomen in Salerno regularly use this as a depilatory.

[246] Once a woman has rubbed herself all over with this ointment, she should sit in very hot steam—but she should not further massage her skin or else it will become chapped. Once in the steam, she should simply pull out her pubic hairs. If they do not come out easily, she should pour hot water over herself and wash herself thoroughly, though drawing her hand gently over her skin. If she rubs too vigorously when her skin is tender, she will be quickly excoriated by the ointment. Having done all this, let her enter a lukewarm bath and be washed well. She should then exit the bath, take a paste made of bran and hot water, strained, and pour it over her body, for this cleanses and smooths the skin. Then she should wash again in warm water, and stand to let her skin dry a little. Then she should take a mixture of henna and egg whites, and rub this all over her body. This too smooths the flesh, and removes any inflammation that may have resulted from the depilatory. Let her remain thus anointed for a while, then rinse herself with warm water, wrap herself in a very white linen cloth, and go to bed. . . .

[250] If a woman desires long black hair, she should take a green lizard, remove its head and tail, and cook it in regular cooking oil. Then rub the oil into her hair. It will make the hair long and black.

[251] A method acquired from the Saracens. Take the rind of an extremely sweet pomegranate and grind it, then boil it in vinegar or water, and strain it. Add to the residue a large amount of powder made from apples or alum, until it reaches the texture of a poultice. Wrap this, like dough, around the entire head. Afterward, mix some bran with oil in a pot and heat it until the bran is burnt. Then sprinkle the bran-ash on the head. She should then wet her hair thoroughly, then wrap her head a second time in the method described. Leave it on overnight, for best results. Then wash the hair, and it will be completely black.

12. THE PAPAL MONARCHY

12.1 Lucius III, *The Medieval Inquisition*

Pope Lucius III (r. 1181–1185) initiated the reform that led directly into the creation of the medieval process of inquisition with his bull *Ad abolendam*, which he promulgated in 1184. The bull centralized authority for investigating heresy in the Church to address the problem of irregular application of the law by secular courts.

In order to abolish the evil of the various heresies that sprung up recently throughout the world, it is fitting that the authority held by the Church should be aroused, so that the Church, aided by the power of the imperial office, might crush the insolent and impertinent actions of the heretics on behalf of their false teachings, and so that the simple truth of Catholic doctrine might shine brightly in the Holy Church, and all may see that She continues on, purified and free from the wretchedness of the heretics' false teachings. For this reason, supported by the presence of our most dear son Frederick, the most illustrious emperor, ever diligent in enhancing the life of empire, and with the usual advice and counsel of our beloved brethren, plus that of the other patriarchs, archbishops, and princes who have gathered here from around the world, we hereby stand firmly against these heretics—who go by different names, according to the false doctrines they profess—and by the sanction of this general decree and Our apostolic authority we hereby condemn all their heresies, by whatever names they be known.

Specifically, we declare all Cathars, Patarines, those called the Humiliati (or the Poor of Lyons), the Passagini, Josephines, and Arnoldists to be under a permanent anathema. And since some people, under an appearance of piety but lacking the genuineness thereof (as the Apostle says), claim for themselves the authority to preach (for as the same Apostle says, "How can they preach, except they be sent?"), we bind by the same penalty of perpetual anathema all those who, whether banned or not commissioned, shall presume to preach either publicly or privately without having first received authority to do so from the Apostolic See or the bishop of the their respective dioceses. Likewise we place under anathema all those who have no fear of thinking or teaching anything other than what the Holy Roman Church preaches and observes regarding the sacrament of the Body and Blood of Our Lord Jesus Christ, or of baptism, or of the confession of sins, or of matrimony, or the other sacraments of the Church. Generally also, all those who have been judged to be heretics by the same Roman Church or by individual bishops in their dioceses with the counsel of their clergy, or by the clergy themselves, whenever a see happens to be vacant, with the counsel, if opportune, of the neighboring bishops.

We likewise declare liable to the same punishment all those who house or defend these heretics, all those who show them any favor or support, and all those who in any way affirm or strengthen them in their heresy, whether they go by the name of the Conforted, the Shouters, the Perfect, or whatever other superstitious name they give to themselves.

Despite the fact that the severity of ecclesiastical discipline, which is necessary to the correction of sin, is sometimes condemned by those who do not understand its virtue, we nevertheless decree that any member of the clergy or anyone who attempts to hide himself in a religious order, if he be convicted of any of these errors, shall be immediately stripped of all prerogatives of the Church orders, and being so divested of all offices and benefices, he shall be handed over to the secular authorities, who will punish him as they deem fit—all of this, that is, unless the accused voluntarily returns to the truth of the Catholic faith and submits to a public renunciation of his errors, and makes suitable satisfaction to the bishop of his diocese. As for any layperson who is found guilty of any of the aforesaid crimes, either publicly or privately, we establish that he is to be turned over to the secular authorities to receive appropriate punishment as they deem fit—unless, of course, he too renounces his heresy, makes satisfaction, and so returns to the orthodox faith.

As for those who are investigated by the Church on suspicion of heresy, unless they give full evidence of their innocence when commanded to do so by their bishop—evidence proportionate to the degree of suspicion they are under, and according to their status in the world—they shall be liable to the same punishment. But all those who have cleared themselves of suspicion, and all those who have fully renounced their errors, if they be found to have relapsed into heresy by their bishop, we decree that they be immediately handed over to the secular authorities and that their possessions be confiscated by the Church without any further hearing.

We further decree that this excommunication of all heretics, which we assert with all our will, be renewed and reconfirmed by all patriarchs, archbishops, and bishops on all major feast days, at all public solemnities, and at all other suitable occasions, to the glory of Our Lord and the halting of all heretical depravity. We assert also, by our apostolic authority, that if any bishop be found wanting or slow to act in this regard, he shall be suspended for three years from his episcopal dignity and administration. Moreover, upon the advice of our bishops and the suggestion of the emperor and the princes of the empire, we add that every archbishop or bishop, either in his own person or as represented by his archdeacon or some other fit and honest person, shall once or twice a year visit any parish in which it is reported that heretics dwell, and if there be cause he shall have men of good repute (two, three, or the entire parish, if need be) give sworn testimony of whether or not any heretics are known to reside there, or people who frequently attend private meetings, or who differ from the common run of men in word or manner; and these witnesses shall report to the bishop or archdeacon, who will then summon the accused to stand before them. The accused shall then be punished according to the standards applicable to their station unless they clear themselves of the charges laid against them; and if they are so cleared but later relapse into their old unbelief, they shall be punished at the bishop's discretion. And if anyone, acting out of a damnable superstition, shall refuse to testify under oath, then that fact alone shall suffice to convict him as a heretic and make him subject to the penalties described above.

Furthermore, we order that all earls, barons, governors, and city councilors, as well as leaders of other sorts of communities, recognizing the leadership of their respective bishops and archbishops, shall swear earnestly and effectively to assist the Church in all these particulars against all heretics and their accomplices, whenever so requested, and promise to faithfully execute, so far as their official positions allow, all ecclesiastical and imperial statutes concerning the matters contained in this decree. Anyone who refuses to obey this command shall be stripped of their honors and authorities, forbidden to receive any new honors and authorities, placed under sentence of excommunication, and have all their goods confiscated by the Church. If any city refuses to obey this decree, or neglects to punish anyone who refuses to obey it, we forbid that city to engage in commerce with any other city and we shall strip it of its episcopal dignity.

Lastly, we ordain that anyone who speaks well of heretics shall be stigmatized forever as a person of infamy, unqualified to serve as a lawyer, give testimony, or hold any public office.

All individuals who are exempt from diocesan jurisdiction will hereby come directly under the jurisdiction of the Apostolic See. In regard to these specific statutes on heresy, it is our desire that all such persons, regardless of their current exempt status, shall be subject to the judgment of our archbishops and bishops and shall obey them as delegates of the Apostolic See.

12.2   The Inquisition at Work

The medieval inquisition was a legal process rather than a standing institution, a tool in the Church's toolkit. Throughout much of the thirteenth century, that tool was utilized to pry out the remnants of the Cathar heresy in southern France, along with newer suspect groups like the Fraticelli and the Spiritual Franciscans. For nine years, from 1273 to 1282, the Church investigated suspected heretics in the city of Toulouse. Translated below is the registered transcript from the interrogation of one local woman, Guillelma, who testified about another local woman, her neighbor Fabrissa, whose family were heretics.

On the Wednesday after the Feast of St. Agatha, in the same year as above [February 7, 1274], Guillelma, the wife of Thomas de St.-Fleur, a carpenter, being a resident of Toulouse who lives on the island of Tounis, was sworn in as a witness and was questioned.

She testified that she never saw anyone whom she knew to be a heretic, and that she places no hope or faith in heretics.

She said, however, that she personally witnessed (and several of her neighbors also suspect) that Fabrissa, the wife of Pierre Vital, carpenter, and their daughter Philippa (who is the wife of Raymond Maurel, also a carpenter) are heretics, as judging by their words and deeds.

She said, in fact, that on one occasion she heard Fabrissa say that it was Lucifer who created man, and that God had told Lucifer to give man speech; but when Lucifer replied that he couldn't, God then breathed into man's mouth, and man spoke.

Asked where she heard Fabrissa say these words, Guillelma replied "at Tounis." Their houses were next to each other but not connected.

Asked when this happened, she answered that it was a year before last Christmas. She also said that she had asked Fabrissa how it was that God sent His spirit into a work of the devil, and Fabrissa replied that He placed His will there.

Asked whether anyone saw them [in this conversation], she said that no one else was about.

She added, though, that she heard Fabrissa speak ill of the clergy around the same time, saying they neither had a good faith nor taught the truth in declaring that the bread [of the Mass] was the body of God.

She said too that she heard Fabrissa say, three or four times, that she and her daughter had a plan to leave the country in order to do penance, but wanted to keep the matter secret. She testified further that she asked Fabrissa not to leave without telling her first—to which Fabrissa replied that if they were going to reveal their plans to anyone, it would be to Guillelma.

She testified that on several occasions she heard Fabrissa praising a woman from Lombardy named Piacenza, saying that she was a good woman, faithful, and a friend of the good Lord. Some time later this Piacenza arrived with her husband and a small donkey, and they stayed with Fabrissa in her house for three days or more. Guillelma did not recognize the woman at first, but upon hearing her being called Piacenza, she recalled Fabrissa's earlier praise of her; assuming that this was here, Guillelma approached her and said, "Are you from Lombardy, friend?" She said that she was. Guillelma then asked, "Do you know Bartholomew Fogassier?" Piacenza replied, "Yes, I do. He is doing well." From this response Guillelma concluded that Piacenza was a messenger for the heretics.

Asked when this conversation occurred, Guillelma said it was a year before the last grape harvest.

Guillelma said that one day Fabrissa said to her that she should ask God to deliver her from the demon that was in her belly. Guillelma was pregnant at the time.

She testified too that she saw Bernard Fogassier visit Fabrissa and her daughter Philippa several times, converse with them, and hide out in their home.

Philippa guarded the door when her mother was ill for a time. Sometimes the pair saw Bernard going about in public, and then Fabrissa would say to Philippa, "Don't look at him!"

She said next that Fabrissa cried out, "Holy Father! Holy Father!" in sadness when Guillaume Aribaud (who had been imprisoned and branded with the mark of heresy) died; he used to live on the street of the Jews. And when Philippa admonished her against crying aloud for someone who was not a relative, Fabrissa said that her grief was on account of the fact that Guillaume had never been able to act as he wanted. On the preceding night he had sent his wife and son to the Carmelite church in order to keep vigil for him, and when "the worthies" had approached him, he could no longer speak. Guillelma believes that these "worthies" were heretics who wanted to draw him into their heresy.

She believes that this happened about a year ago, last August.

She said too that when the mother of the Fogassier family died, around that same time, and she [Guillelma] mentioned the fact to Fabrissa and Philippa, Fabrissa replied that no lady ever had "better sons in spirit" than she had; Philippa was a witness to this.

She said too that she saw Pons de Gomeville, who is now a fugitive suspected of heresy, talk with Fabrissa and Philippa on several occasions before he fled.

She said that when Fabrissa's mother, Raymonda, was sick with the illness that killed her, she refused to see Guillelma or any other neighbors for about eleven weeks, maybe more; no one ever saw the Body of Christ being brought to her. When Raymonda finally died, she says, Fabrissa cried out, "Holy Father! Receive the spirit of my soul!" Guillelma then approached Fabrissa and said that Raymonda had been wrong to keep her illness a secret, for Guillelma and the others in the neighborhood, both men and women, would gladly have visited her. Fabrissa answered that she had turned no one away from the door and prevented no one from seeing her mother.

Guillelma also said that Raymonda had once told her, before she became ill, that she loved her especially because she knew that if she happened to become sick the so-called "worthies"—that is, her heretic friends—could come to her [Guillelma], whom she trusted to

bring them to her, for she [Raymonda] did not trust her grandson-in law, Raymond, whom she called a "dirty peasant."

All these things Guillelma attested in the presence of Friar Ranulf, inquisitor. The witnesses were Friar Pierre Rey, Friar Daide Faure of Montpellier, Friar Bernard Bonet, and myself, Atho de St. Victor, public notary of the inquisition, who wrote these things.

* * * * *

On the Thursday after the Feast of St. Gregory, in the same year as above [March 15, 1274], the same Guillema added to her confession, declaring that one day when she, Navarra (the wife of Arnaud Lescure), Aladaicis (Navarra and Arnaud's daughter), Fabrissa (the wife of Pierre Vital), Philippa (Fabrissa and Pierre's daughter), and Raymonda (Fabrissa's mother) were all talking together, on the island of Tounis in Toulouse, about a certain cleric who had been burned [at the stake] in town for heresy, when the king was present, Guillelma heard Fabrissa say that no one had ever handled an interrogation by the Dominican and Franciscan inquisitors better than that cleric had done—at least up until the time of the king's arrival. Guillelma and the others then asked Fabrissa, "Then why was he burnt?" To which Fabrissa answered that the cleric used to teach that whoever received the Body of the Lord consecrated it. Raymonda then spoke out, "Why was he burned for saying that? Isn't that the truth?" Guillelma then responded, "The devil is making you say that!" All this happened in the summer of last year.

She testified also that she once heard Philippa once say, in her vineyard beyond the river Garonne, that her grandmother Raymonda's first husband had been burned at the stake. When Guillelma asked why, Philippa replied that he had been judged a heretic by the inquisitors because he refused to kill a cock when ordered to do so, arguing that the cock had done nothing wrong and hence there was no reason to kill it. This happened last year, sometime before the harvest.

She said also that she had once heard Philippa say that she would be willing to have an ear cut from her head, if only her husband, Raymond Maurel, had the faith that Pons de Gomeville had; and that she never would have agreed to marry Raymond if she had known he did not share her faith. This occurred in August of last year.

All these things Guillelma attested at Toulouse in the presence of the Dominican Friars Ranulf de Plassac and Pons de Parnac, inquisitors. The witnesses were Guillaume Capellier and Guillaume Rotond, in the church of Dalbade, Sicrad Lunel, and myself, Atho de St. Victor, public notary of the inquisition, who wrote these things.

* * * * *

Two days before the Nones of April, in the year of Our Lord 1273 [sic], Guillelma added to her confession, saying that she once heard Fabrissa, the wife of Pierre Vital, assert that God did not create new souls in babies, and that He would have quite a lot to do if He created new souls every day.

She also heard Fabrissa say that the soul of the late Guillaume Aribaud would pass from body to body until it landed in the hands of the "worthies." She said that she heard her say this about a year and a half ago.

She said, too, that she once heard Fabrissa say that those who handed people over [to the inquisitors] were not people but devils. And that she [Fabrissa] knew such things that she would never reveal to anyone, not even if her whole body was pierced with nails. This was at the same time as the above.

12.3 *Gospel According to the Marks of Silver*

What follows is a rare piece of medieval satire, written before Geoffrey Chaucer. This twelfth-century poem lampoons the financial corruption of papal officials.

**HERE BEGINS THE GOSPEL
OF THE MARK OF SILVER**

And then the Pope announced to the officials
    of Rome,
"When the Son of Man comes to the seat of Our
    Majesty,
The first thing you say is, 'Friend, why have
    you come?'
If He keeps knocking without greasing your
    palms, it's a travesty;
    Throw Him out into the night."

It happened soon after that a poor humble priest
Came to the Pope's court and loudly cried,
"None show me mercy, but I know *you* will, at least;
For the hand of poverty has me hog-tied.
    I am poor and in need. I beg you! Ease my
    plight!"

After hearing him out, the aides shook with fury
Saying, "You and your poverty, friend, can go
    straight to Hell.

You're penniless: get behind us, Satan, and hurry!
You shall not enter—amen and farewell—
    The presence of your Lord until you've paid
    your last nickel."

So the poor wretch left and sold the clothes off
    his back
And everything he owned, and gave the pope's
    men all the money—
cardinals, aides, and chamberlains; but they threw
    him out with a smack,
"What's this pittance? Where's the rest? Are you
    trying to be funny?"
    He left, wretched and hopeless, weeping not
    in a trickle.

Later a rich cleric came, coarse, fat, and bloated;
He had even committed a murder or two. But he
    paid off
The aides, the chamberlains, and the cardinals,
    who toted
Up the sums they'd received and then asked for
    more, in a trade-off.

The pope heard of the lavish gifts his courtiers
had been handed

And felt so sickened he nearly died. The rich man
then quickly
Sent medicine in the form of silver and gold.

The pope felt better at once and admonished his
men, prickly:
"Don't fall victim to the empty promises you're told.
Do as I do, Brothers, and you'll make out like
a bandit."

12.4   Innocent III, *Decree Regarding Treatment of the Jews*

Innocent III (r. 1198–1216) remains a mysterious and divisive character. Usually depicted as a determined and crafty political manipulator (which he was), he was also a soulful and sincere Christian who wanted to spread the Gospel. He was an ardent champion of harsh measures like crusades and inquisitions, but he also was an equally ardent supporter of the mendicant orders created by Sts. Francis and Dominic. Quoted below are two of his decrees that call for all Christians to respect the autonomy and safety of the Jews.

Although the disbelief of the Jews is in many ways to be condemned, it is nevertheless the case that the truth of our own faith is proved by their example, and therefore we the faithful may not oppress them—for as the psalmist says, "Do not slay them, or my people will forget." [Ps 59.11] It is as though he were saying directly to us, "Do not wipe out the Jews, or else the Christians might forget Your Law. The Jews, even though they do not understand it, nevertheless pass it on in their writings to the Christians, who do."

Just as the Jews should not presume to transgress the bounds of what the law permits them in their synagogues, so should they suffer no prejudice in those things that the law has in fact granted to them. Since these men would rather continue in their inflexibility than know the revelations of the prophets and the mysteries of the Law, and come thereby to know the Christian faith, still, since they seek the help of our aid, we, acting in a properly meek spirit of Christian piety and in the footsteps of Our predecessors of happy memory (the Roman pontiffs Calixtus, Eugene, Alexander, Clement, and Celestine), admit their petition and grant them the shield of our protection.

We therefore solemnly decree that no Christian may use force to compel any Jew to receive baptism. If a Jew, because of a spiritual conversion has freely taken refuge with Christians and made his intention to convert known to them, then he may be brought to baptism without any opposition; but anyone who has not sought Christian baptism of his own free will cannot have genuine Christian faith. Neither shall any Christian do any Jew a personal injury, deprive him of his property, or refuse to recognize his customary rights and privileges, except in the execution of a formal judgment by a magistrate. No Christian may disturb the Jews during the celebration of their festivals, neither by clubs nor stones. No Christian may compel them to perform any service except what they customarily perform. And since especially we wish to stop the avarice and viciousness of wicked men, we forbid any Christian to deface or vandalize their cemeteries, or to extort money from them by threatening to exhume the bodies of their dead.

After the content of this decree is made known, if anyone proceeds in violation of it (may it never happen!), then let him be punished with the penalty of excommunication unless he makes satisfaction equal to his presumption.

We wish, however, that the only people granted this protection be those who have not dared to conspire in the subversion of Christian faith.

Given at the Lateran by the hand of Archbishop Raynaldus of Acerenza, on behalf of the chancellor, in the year of the Incarnation of Our Lord 1199, in the second year of the pontificate of Pope Innocent III.

[CANON 68 FROM THE FOURTH LATERAN COUNCIL, 1215]

In many lands Jews, Muslims, and Christians are distinguished by differences in dress, but in certain others such confusion reigns that they cannot be told apart, and thus it happens that Christians accidentally have relations with Jewish or Muslim women, and that Jews and Muslims have relations with Christian women. In order to deny anyone the pretext of an honest error as an excuse for their violation of prohibitions on intercourse, we decree that Jews and Saracens of both sexes in every Christian land and at all times be clearly identified and made distinguishable to the rest of the public by their dress. This is particularly necessary since it is written in the books of Moses [Numbers 15.37–41] that this exact law has already been enjoined upon them.

In addition, we order that the Jews may not appear in public at all during the last three days before Easter and especially not on Good Friday—for we hear that some of them choose those very days to go out in their finer clothing as a way to mock the Christians who observe the memory of the Most Holy Passion by wearing mourning-clothes.

Most severely of all, we forbid anyone to publicly insult Our Redeemer, and since we cannot ignore any insult to Him Who redeemed our sins, we command that anyone guilty of such impudence should be handed over to the secular princes, who may impose on them a fitting punishment, so that no one will dare to blaspheme Him Who was crucified for us.

[FROM A LETTER TO KING PHILIP II OF FRANCE ON THE KEEPING OF SLAVES BY JEWS, 1204]

Moreover, it was recently decreed by the Lateran Council that Jews should not be permitted to have Christian slaves in their homes—not as servants, nor on the pretext of being wet-nurses, nor for any other reason. It was decreed too that any Christian slaves who live with Jews should be excommunicated. Nevertheless, some Jews continue to have Christian servants and wet-nurses, whom they treat abominably. It is incumbent on me to point this out; it is more incumbent on you to mete out a suitable punishment.

12.5   Innocent III, *A Christmas Sermon*

Innocent III had a strong pastoral aspect to his personality that scholars usually overlook in favor of the clever and ruthless politician. The following sermon appears in his collected *Sermones de sanctis* (*Sermons for Holy Days*).

For a child is born to us, a son is given to us; upon his shoulder dominion rests. They name him Wonder-Counselor, God-Hero, Father-Forever, Prince of Peace. [Isaiah 9.5]

Just as our Catholic faith confesses three substances in Christ—divinity, humanity, and spirit—so also do the Sacred Scriptures bear witness to three births in Him: the divine is born from the Father, the human comes from the Mother, and the spiritual is born of the Mind. In other words, from the Father proceeds divinity, from the Mother humanity, and from the Mind proceeds the spirit. Or this: from the Father is the way, from the Mother is the truth, and in the mind is the life. He says, *I am the way and the truth and the life.* [John 14.6] He proceeds eternally from the Father; He was born once from the Mother; and He proceeds often in the Mind. Behold, an original and ever-new miracle: that He proceeds both forever, once, and repeatedly, all at once! . . . The Church represents all three of these births of Christ in today's three Masses—in the Mass sung at night, the Mass sung at dawn, and the Mass sung during the day. . . . For Christ is conceived through love, born through effort, and nourished through progress, which is why this third Mass we are celebrating takes place in the daytime hours. . . .

A son is given to us. He was given to us by God so that He might repay for us what we owe to God. For grave and hostile discord had arisen between God and mankind, since man in his sin had withdrawn from service to God and had distanced himself from Him, thus becoming a traitor and a servant of the devil. There was thus no way, reasonably, to make peace between them unless man were to put right the harm he had done, but man had no way to make a worthy compensation to God. . . . That is why God, recognizing the man could not by himself escape the yoke of damnation, won man's heart through mercy alone, so that afterwards He might free him through justice. God atoned for man's sin by freely giving him the one thing that could repay man's debt, and therefore He gave a Man to man, One Who would restore man to God. But in order for the redemption to be worthy, the Man God gave was not only a man but was something greater. That is why we say *the Word was made flesh,* in that God-Man was given to man, as Isaiah had predicted when he said *A child is born to us, a son is given to us;* a spiritual son, as the Apostle says, *God did not spare his own Son but handed Him over for us all.* [Romans 8.32] . . . Therefore a child is born to us, so that we are born again and a son is given to us, so that we are saved. Born again in grace, we are redeemed in glory; born again from water, we are redeemed in His blood. . . .

And his name is called Wonderful. God is truly glorious in His saints and wonderful in His majesty, and He performed wonders even in His human state—for the Gospel teaches us that *the people were astonished at His teaching* [Mark 1.22], and *all who heard Him were astounded at His understanding and His answers.* [Luke 2.47] And his name will be called Counselor, because he knows the counsels of peace, as He Himself bore witness, saying, *I think thoughts of peace and not of affliction* [Jeremiah 29.11], and as the Apostle says, *Oh,*

the depth of the riches and wisdom and knowledge of God! How inscrutable are His judgments and how unsearchable His ways! For who has known the mind of the Lord, or who has been His counselor? [Romans 11.33–34]

And his name will be called God. Therefore this child is God and is called Mighty. The name of the Divine One is explained in various ways throughout the Scriptures: in essence, according to nature; by adoption, according to grace; by authority, according to office; and by usurpation, according to vice. According to nature, as in the verse *Hear, O Israel! The Lord is our God, the Lord alone!* [Deuteronomy 6.4]; according to grace, as in *I declare: Gods though you be, offspring of the Most High all of you* [Psalms 82.6]; according to office, as in *You shall not despise God, nor curse a leader of your people* [Exodus 22.27]; and according to vice, as in *For the gods of the nations are idols.* [Psalms 96.5] This Child, however, is called God in essence, according to His nature. What is more—and this is in order that heretics may be confounded and the Jews may be ashamed—the proofs are multiplied everywhere through both the Old and New Testaments, the way a wheel is contained within a wheel, and a base is contained in a column. But since, as Scripture says, *A charge shall stand only on the testimony of two or three witnesses,* we cite the Apostle John (*In the beginning was the Word and the Word was with God and the Word was God* [John 1.1]), the Apostle Thomas (*My Lord and my God* [John 20.28]), and the Apostle Paul (*Who, although He was in the form of God, did not regard equality with God something to be grasped* [Philippians 2.6]). Moreover, David says, *Therefore God, your God, has anointed you with the oil of gladness above your fellow kings* [Psalms 45.8]; Jeremiah says, *Such is our God; no other is to be compared to Him* [Baruch 3.36]; and Habbakuk says, *Yet I will rejoice in the Lord and exult in my saving God* [Habbakuk 3.18]. For man had wanted to be like God, and so it was necessary for God to become man; as great as man's sin of pride was, so great was the virtue of God's humility.

And his name will be called Mighty. Who is this king of glory? It is the Lord Himself, mighty and strong, invincible in battle—for God is wisdom, which always defeats malice, and God's wisdom *spans the world from end to end, mightily, and governs all things well* [Wisdom 8.1]. Christ is God's wisdom, about which the Apostle Paul says, *Christ is the power of God and the wisdom of God* [1 Corinthians 1.24]. Christ's power reaches from end to end—that is, from highest heaven to the depths of hell—and it reaches mightily, casting down the proud angels from heaven and leading the souls of the just out of hell. He governs all things well—that is, He redeems the lost and brings sinners to righteousness. He is the true David who, with a mighty hand, defeated the bear, conquered the lion, and brought down the Philistines. He is the true Samson, who slew the lion's cub and struck down a thousand men with the jawbone of an ass, who carried away the gates of Gaza. Coming so unexpectedly, the Almighty One defeated the strength of arms.

And his name will be called Father-Forever. As a father, He is one who gives—for as the Gospel bears witness, *the Father in heaven [will] give the Holy Spirit to those who ask Him* [Luke 11.13]. God comes to the faithful not in order to give them the present world but the future one; not earthly goods but heavenly blessings; not passing pleasure but eternal joys; not the sun but the entire universe; not the Earth but Heaven Itself. That is what is meant by the words *Father-Forever!* He gives, and gives in abundance, the inheritance of life yet to come! That is why He taught us the words *Your kingdom come,* and *My kingdom is not of this world* [John 18.36]. In Christ's kingdom is life without death, day without night, certainty without doubt. In Christ's kingdom there will be safety without fear, joy without sorrow, rest without labor. There will be beauty without ugliness, health without weakness, decency without sin, love without malice, truth without falsehood, happiness without misery. Above all, there will be the bliss *that the eye has not seen, and the ear has not heard, and that has not entered the human heart* [1 Corinthians 2.9].

And his name will be called Prince of Peace. For He is the peace of God that surpasses all understanding. [Philippians 4.7] *He is our peace, he who made both one and broke down the dividing wall of enmity.* [Ephesians 2.14] *He came and preached peace to you who were far off and peace to those who were near.* [Ephesians 2.17]. He is the One Whose birth caused the heavenly host to sing *Glory to God in the highest, and on earth peace to those on whom His favor rests.* [Luke 2.14]. He is the One Who, at His passion, said to the Apostles, *Peace I leave with you, My peace I give to you. Not as the world gives do I give to you.* [John 14.27] And He is the One Who, after the resurrection, said to them again, *Peace be with you, and saying to them again, Peace be with you.* [John 20.19] Peace to all sinners—the peace of eternity, to which He Himself leads us, He Who is above all things. May God be blessed forever and ever. Amen.

12.6   Caesarius of Heisterbach, *Dialogue on Miracles*

Caesarius (1180–1240) was the Master of Novices at the Cistercian monastery of Heisterbach, responsible for the religious education of young monks. He held the post for many years and composed a lengthy textbook called the *Dialogue on Miracles*, in which he relates a series of conversations between an unnamed Master (presumably Caesarius himself) and a young Novice. The Master leads his pupil through a discussion, in 12 books, of conversion, contrition, confession, temptation, demons, purity of heart, the Virgin Mary, visions, the Eucharist, miracles, death, and Judgment Day. Below is a passage from the fifth book, which describes the Waldensian and Cathar heresies, and one from the seventh book, on the Virgin Mary.

MASTER: Several years ago, when the learned Bertram was the bishop, the Waldensian heresy broke out in the city of Metz. Here is how it happened. It was a feast day—I do not know which one—and Bertram was preaching to the crowd inside the cathedral, when all of a sudden he saw two demons (servants of Satan) standing amid the crowd. He cried out, pointing his finger, "Look!

Two messengers from the devil are among you! They were condemned at Montpellier as heretics and were evicted from the city. I witnessed it with my own eyes!"

The two men hurled abuse at the bishop. They were accompanied by a friend, a scholar, who also barked at him like an attacking dog, spewing insults at him. When the three left the cathedral, they began to preach their heretical lies to a large crowd that gathered around them.

Several priests were present, who asked, "Gentlemen, does not the Apostle Paul say, 'How can people preach unless they are sent?' So we ask you: Who sent you here to preach to us?"

The men replied, "the Holy Spirit."

The bishop could not use force against them because a number of very powerful citizens had befriended the heretics (this was because he hated Bertram for having once excommunicated one of their relatives, for usury). The heretics had actually been sent, of course, by the spirit of error instead of the Holy Spirit. But that is how the Waldensian heresy came to Metz, and to this very day it has not been extinguished.

NOVICE: How sad it is that even today there are so many heresies in the Church!

MASTER: They are the fruits of Satan's fury and malice.

Now in the time of Innocent [III], the predecessor of our current pope Honorius [IV], when the bitter rivalry between Philip and Otto for the title of 'King of the Romans' was brewing, Satan's envy caused the Albigensian heresy to spread, or rather, to develop and ripen. Its popularity was so great that the faith of the entire kingdom seemed to fall into error, like wholesome grain into worthless chaff. Several of our Cistercian abbots were dispatched with a handful of bishops to root out the bitter stalks with the harrow of true Catholic teaching. But the resistance of the enemy was so great that they had hardly any success at all.

NOVICE: What were the heretics' errors?

MASTER: The leaders of the Cathars had cobbled together some ideas from Manichean teaching, joined them with a few of the mistakes Origen had produced when writing his tract against Periarchon, and mixed all of these with a great number of errors of their own making. They follow Manicheanism in believing that there are two sources of Creation—two Gods, in other words, one good and the other evil (i.e. Satan). They maintain that the evil God created human bodies, whereas the good God created human souls.

NOVICE: But Moses made it plain that God created both our bodies and our souls, when he wrote, *Then the Lord God formed man out of the dust of the ground and blew into his nostrils the breath of life.* [Genesis 2.2]

MASTER: But the Cathars do not accept Moses and the prophets; if they did, their heresy wouldn't exist. Instead, they deny the resurrection of the body; they mock the idea of any benefit accruing to the dead by the actions of the living; they insist there is no point in going into any church to pray. They are really worse than Jews or pagans, who at least believe in these things. Cathars repudiate baptism and blaspheme against the sacrament of Christ's Body and Blood.

NOVICE: Then why are they willing to endure the severe persecution meted out to them by the faithful, if they expect no reward in the future?

MASTER: They claim to look forward to a glorification of the spirit. One of the abbots I just referred to, who was a monk of course, once saw a knight sitting on a horse and talking with a peasant who was plowing the field. Suspecting the fellow was a Cathar, which he in fact was, the monk approached him and asked, "My lord, whose field is this?" When the knight replied that the field belonged to him, the monk went on, "And what do you do with the crops it produces?"

"I and my family live upon them," he answered, "and I give some to the poor."

The monk said, "And what do you hope to gain by your charity?"

"That my soul may walk in glory after my death."

"Where will your soul go, if I may ask?"

The knight replied, "Wherever it deserves to go. If I have lived a good life and earned the blessing of God's reward, then my soul will leave my body and enter the body of some future nobleman, perhaps even a prince or a king, where it will find happiness. But if I have lived an evil life, my soul will enter the body of someone poor and wretched, where it will find nothing but suffering."

You see, this fool believed—as all Cathars do—that human souls are reincarnated through different bodily lives, even those of beasts and reptiles, all according to what they deserve.

NOVICE: What a foul heresy!

MASTER: The Cathars' errors spread so far and fast that it quickly infected more than a thousand towns. It may well have corrupted the whole of Europe, if the faithful had not taken arms against it. In the year of Our Lord 1210 there was a crusade preached against all the Cathars in Germany and France; one year later Duke Leopold of Austria, Provost Engelbert (who afterwards became the archbishop of Cologne), his brother Count Adolphus of Altenberg, Count Wilhelm of Julich, and a host of others, of all ranks and stations in life, rose against the heretics in Germany. The same thing happened in France, Normandy, and Poitou. Abbot Arnold of Citeaux, later the archbishop of Narbonne, was the cleric who led them all.

When they came to Béziers—a great city, reputed to have more than a hundred thousand residents—they besieged it. The heretics there made a show of desecrating the Holy Gospels most unspeakably right in front of them, before throwing the book from the city walls and shooting arrows at it. As they did so, they called out to the Christian army, "Here is your gospel, you miserable wretches!" But Christ, the True Author of the Gospels, did not let such an insult go unavenged. Some of His faithful soldiers, burning with zeal, set ladders against the city walls and pounced up them like the lions we read about in the book of the Maccabees. The heretics panicked and fled—and as they did so the Christian soldiers opened the city gates to the rest of the army. Thus they took possession of the city.

But once they learned, from the confessions made by some of the heretics, that a number of good Catholics were still living there, they approached Abbot Arnold and asked, "My lord,

what should we do? We cannot tell the faithful apart from the heretics." Now the abbot was afraid, like many others, that the frightened heretics would pretend to be Catholics in order to escape, only to return to their heretical ways afterward, and so he said, "Kill them all. *The Lord knows those who are His.*" [2 Timothy 2.19] And so countless numbers were killed there.

By God's grace, the army took possession of another town, near Toulouse, Minerve—called "the Beautiful Valley town" on account of its location. Arnold and his men examined everyone in the town, and won the promise to return to the Catholic faith from almost all of them. Four hundred and fifty heretics, though, refused to do so, having been made obstinate by the devil. Four hundred of them were burned at the stake, and the rest were hung.

Similar things took place in other towns and other castles, with the wretches handing themselves over to death, as often as not. When the people of Toulouse itself were under attack, they promised profusely to return to Catholic orthodoxy—but they lied, as subsequent events made clear. The fact of the matter is that the count of St. Egidius—a treacherous prince and the leader of all the Cathars—formally surrendered his entire domain (lands, castles, farms, and towns) at the [4th] Lateran Council; but once that good Catholic lord, Simon de Montfort took possession of them by right of conquest, the wicked Count dashed off to Toulouse, from which he still assaults and attacks the true faithful even to this day.

This was the year when Lord Conrad, the cardinal-bishop of Porto who had been appointed as legate to the Cathars, wrote to the monks at Citeaux in order to relate that one of the nobles at Toulouse committed a crime, out of his hatred for Christ and in order to sow discord among His faithful, a crime so horrible that it would rightly outrage even the very enemies of Christ. What was this nobleman's abomination? His outrageous and disgusting act? At the very altar of the Toulouse cathedral he and several of his henchmen, heaping madness upon madness, villainously vandalized the Crucifix! They pulled the sacred image from its place and cut off Christ's arms! Truly, they showed themselves to be even worse men than the soldiers of King Herod, who had at least spared our dead Savior of the indignity of breaking His legs.

NOVICE: Who can hear this and not be astonished at the long-suffering patience of God!

MASTER: *The Lord is slow to anger* [Sirach 5.4], but *His wrath comes to rest on the wicked.* [Sirach 5.6] Indeed, He Who so grievously punished the wicked people at Damietta when, after their victory, they celebrated by tying a rope around the neck of a crucifix and dragged it through the streets, will never look past what those blasphemers did in Toulouse.

Before God's army rode against the Cathars, those heretics had gone so far as to invite the king of Morocco [Muhammad al-Nasir ibn al-Mansur (r. 1199–1213)] to become their ally! He crossed over from Africa, into Spain, with so enormous an army that he hoped to overrun all of Europe. He even sent a letter to Pope Innocent [III], announcing his intention to stable his horses in the portico of St. Peter's and raise his standard over the cathedral. His prediction came true, though not in the way he had planned. Since God always brings down the haughty, on 16 July in the year of grace 1212, forty thousand of the Moroccan king's soldiers were killed [at the Battle of Muret]. Muhammad himself fled to Seville, where he soon died of grief. But his personal standard was captured in the battle, and was sent to Innocent— who promptly set it up in the church of St. Peter to the glory of Christ!

But now, let us talk no more of the Cathars.

* * * * *

MASTER: A young knight once was living with his master, a wealthy older knight, by whom he was kindly treated. The young knight was in the full bloom of youth but was even more appealing on account of his virginity. But the devil soon worked his wiles upon him, and soon the youth was aflame with desire for his master's wife. Laboring upon this temptation for a full year,

he finally found the burden of it unbearable— and so, casting off his natural modesty, he confessed to his mistress how he ached with longing for her. He soon felt even more afflicted, however, for she was an honorable lady, a faithful wife, and she rebuffed him straight away. The knight then visited a holy hermit whose advice he trusted and tearfully confessed his passion for the lady.

"Is that all that bothers you?" asked the holy man. "Let me give you some advice that will satisfy you. Go to church every day for the next year and recite the Angelus one hundred times, and say one hundred prayers to Our Lady the Blessed Virgin Mary, the Mother of God, begging for forgiveness. Through Her intercession you will receive all that you most desire."

The holy man spoke thus, because he knew full well that the Queen of Chastity would never turn Her back on a chaste youth, even though he had fallen into error.

The young knight followed this advice with the purest and most simple reverence for Our Lady, and one day, as he was sitting at his lord's table, he realized that was the very anniversary of the year. He rose immediately, mounted his horse, and rode to the nearby church, where he made his now-customary prayers. As he was leaving, afterwards, he saw a most beautiful maiden, one whose loveliness surpassed all human beauty, who was holding his horse's bridle. As he marveled at her, wondering who she might be, the maiden spoke.

"Does my appearance please you?"

The knight replied, "Truly, I have never seen anyone even half as lovely as you."

"Would you be satisfied, if I were your bride?"

"Your perfect beauty would satisfy any king! Happy indeed would be the man who was married to you."

Then the maiden answered, "I will be your wife. Come, kiss me." The knight did so; then the maiden gently pushed him back. "Our bond has begun. And it will one day be made complete in the presence of My Son."

When she spoke these words the knight realized who she was—the Mother of Our Lord, whose chastity delights in human purity! Our Lady held the horse's stirrup and ordered the knight to mount. The knight obeyed, being wholly under Her command. And from that moment on he was utterly freed from his passion for his lord's wife, so much so that even the noble lady was astonished.

Some time later the knight reported all of this to the holy hermit, who, marveling at the goodness and humility of the Mother of God, replied to him, "I wish to be present on the day your holy marriage is made complete. For now, though, set all your worldly affairs in order."

The knight did as he was told. On a certain day, some time later, the hermit came to the young knight and asked, "Are you in any pain?" When the knight answered that he was not, the hermit went away briefly; one hour later he came back and asked again.

"Yes," said the knight. "I do begin to feel unwell."

Having said these words, the knight straightaway fell into agony, breathed out his soul, and entered the heavenly mansions—to celebrate his promised nuptials.

MASTER: Another time, a young nun was approached by a priest who uttered licentious words to her. And Behemoth—*whose breath kindles coals* [Job 41.21]—blew so violently that her lust was inflamed. In her heart she consented instantly to the priest's desires and said that she would meet him at an appointed time and place. She was the caretaker of the church. When the nuns had all sung Compline and had returned to their dormitory, the young sister tried to leave the church [to meet with the lustful priest], but at the door she suddenly beheld Christ hanging with outstretched arms upon the Cross. Her way barred, she turned and ran for the opposite door. She was so burning with desire for the priest that she had half-lost her mind and could not see that divine powers were blocking her way. She tried every door, but encountered the Crucified One each time.

The nun finally came to her senses and said in her terrified heart, "It is God's will that I not leave this place." She has always devotedly said a special prayer, each day, concerning the Passion of Our Lord—and this is presumably why the Lord rewarded her with so priceless a vision at the moment of her most perilous crisis. Trembling uncontrollably, she threw herself before a statue of the Blessed Mother of God and begged forgiveness for her weakness, but the statue turned away from her. The nun approached nearer and repeated her prayer—when suddenly the statue turned back toward her and with a raised hand struck her hard on the jaw.

"Foolish girl!" cried Our Lady. "Where do you want to go now? Return at once to your dormitory!"

So violent was the blow that the nun fell to the floor and lay there unconscious until morning. At Matins, when the bells were rung in the dormitory, no answering bell came from the church. The other nuns thought the young sister must either be at prayer or be sound asleep. They rushed to the church and found her lying there, still unconscious. They were able to awaken her at last, and she promptly told them of everything that had happened to her, to the honor of God.

Our Lady's blow had indeed been a heavy one, but it enabled the nun to free herself from lustful desire. Grievous illness requires strong medicine.

NOVICE: Indeed! All men should be kindled with love for Our Lady, seeing that she relieved the knight of lustfulness with a single kiss, and the nun with a single blow to the face, in spite of the fierceness of their evil and perverse desires.

12.7   Hildegard of Bingen, *The Book of Divine Works*

Hildegard (1098–1179) is among the most renowned medieval mystics. The daughter (and tenth child) of a Rhineland noble family, she was sent to a Benedictine convent at the age of eight. She took her vows as a cloistered nun several years later. In 1151 she moved to a new convent at Rupertsberg, along the Rhine River, near the town of Bingen, where she was installed as the Abbess. She had begun writing her mystical literature a dozen years before the move to Bingen. *The Book of Divine Works* is actually one of the last books she wrote. Translated below are the prologue and part of the opening chapter. As she herself admitted, Hildegard was not a gifted writer; her Latin is often clumsy and difficult to parse. Of particular interest, though, is the variability of her perspective: it often appears that she slides back and forth between speaking for herself, presenting God speaking, and occasionally writing in the first person though in the character of God. The effect of this grammatical hash is to heighten the sense of her union with God while experiencing her visions.

It happened in the sixth year of my troubles, after I had already spent five years being disturbed by the most marvelous and true visions, visions in which the Everlasting Light had shown me—me, an utterly ignorant person!—the astonishing diversity of life.

It was the beginning of the first year of my present series of visions when this took place. I was fifty-six years old. I had a vision so profound, so overwhelming, that my whole body trembled and I took ill—so weakened was I. I then spent seven years writing about this vision, but was never able to put it all into words. It was therefore in the year of the Incarnation of Our Lord 1163 (the emperor Henry was still in the midst of his oppressive campaign against the Holy See), when a voice from Heaven called out to me.[1]

O most wretched creature! Daughter of toil! Even though you have been utterly consumed by bodily sufferings, yet the vast depth of God's mysteries has permeated you. Therefore, for the benefit of all mankind, you are to pass on an accurate account of what you have seen in your mind and have heard in the inner ear of your soul. In this way people will learn how to know their Creator and will no longer refuse to adore Him with fitting reverence. So write these things down, but not according to the inclinations of your own heart! Write as I tell you to write, for I am without any beginning or end. This vision is not your invention, nor has it been conceived by any other human person. Instead, I established it, entire, before the creation of the world. Just as I knew humanity before its creation, so too I saw in advance everything that mankind would need.

Despite my wretchedness and weakness, and despite the fact that I was beset by countless illnesses, I started to write with a trembling hand. I was confident in what had been told me by the man I wrote about in my earlier visions, and whom I had sought out and visited privately; I had confidence, too, in the girl I also named in earlier visions.[2]

Setting myself to begin the process of writing, I lifted my eyes once more to the True and Living Light, wondering what He wanted me to write. In all my earlier visions, everything I wrote I later came to understand had been the work of divine mysteries working through my body, even though I was awake and in my right mind the whole time. The inner eye of my soul

---

[1]   The emperor she is referring to was actually Frederick Barbarossa (r. 1152–1190), who was contending with Pope Alexander III (r. 1159–1181).

[2]   These were Hildegard's secretary, Volmar, and her assistant, Richardis of Stade.

saw it, my inner ear heard it. In all these experiences I was never asleep, nor in any state like it, nor was I in spiritual rapture, as I have emphasized repeatedly in my earlier writings. Moreover, I offered no interpretations of anything; I only testified to the truth I received from the heavenly mysteries. Not a word was the work of human endeavor.

Once again I heard the voice calling to me from Heaven: "Write down what I tell you!"

* * * * *

Within the manifold mysteries of the Lord I beheld a wondrously beautiful image in the midst of the southern breezes: a human form, with so beautiful and bright-radiant a face that I could more easily have looked directly into the sun. A wide ring of gold encircled its head, and within this ring there appeared a second face, like that of an elderly man; his chin and beard rested on the crown of the first man's head. Two wings grew out from the man's shoulders, and rising upwards above the golden ring they were joined together. Hovering over the curve of the right-hand wing was the head of an eagle. It had fiery eyes, in which the brilliance of the angels were reflected as though in a mirror. Above the curve of the left-hand wing was a human head that shone like the gleaming stars. Both of the faces—the eagle's and the man's—were turned to looking eastward. Also from the shoulder of the central figure came a third wing, reaching down to his knees. The figure was wrapped in a garment that was as brilliant-bright as the sun. In its hands it carried a lamb, which also glowed like sunshine. The figure's feet stood upon a dreadful-looking monster, poisonous, black; a serpent had sunk its teeth into the monster's right ear, and coiled its body around its head. The serpent's tail reached down the monster's left-hand side, stretching all the way to its feet.

And then a heavenly voice called out:

I, the supreme and fiery power, have kindled every spark of life. I emanate nothing deadly; I choose all reality. I fly with majestic wings over the Earth. In My wisdom I have put all of Creation in order. I am the fiery life of the Divine Essence, burning with a beauty beyond that of meadows. I gleam upon the waters, and my light shines in the sun, moon, and stars. I stir everything to life with every breeze that blows, invisibly, life that touches everything. The air lives and turns things green and makes them blossom. The waters flow as though they were alive. The sun shines in its brilliance, the moon is kindled by the light of the sun and is revived after darkness. The beaming stars emit clear light. I have erected the pillars that hold up the Earth and provide a base for the might of the winds which, once again, subordinate wings—weaker winds, in other words—which resist with gentle power the great and mighty winds, lest they become dangerously strong. In the same way, the body encapsulates the soul and maintains it; if it did not, the soul would blow away. As the breath of the soul nourishes and fortifies the body, so that it does not disappear, the mighty winds revive the smaller winds around them, so they can fulfill their purpose.

Thus I remain hidden—a fiery power existing in everything. Because of Me everything burns with life, just as our breath animates us, like a flickering flame within a larger blaze. All that lives, lives in its true essence. There is no death in it. I am Life, but I am also Reason and bear within Myself the breath of the resounding Word, through Which all of creation was made. I breathe life into everything, such that nothing is mortal in its species. For I am Life Itself.

Yes, I am Life—perfect and whole. Not cut from any stone, not blooming forth from a stem, not rooted in human fertility. Rather, all that lives has its roots in Me. Reason is the root, and the resounding Word springs from it.

God is Reason. Therefore how is it possible that He Who causes of all divine actions to come to pass through human beings is inactive? God created man and woman in the divine image and likeness, and He shaped all creatures in proportion to man and woman. God had it in His Mind from all eternity to create man and woman, His handiwork, and when He had finished creating them He began to interact with them, as the work of His own hands.

There I serve by helping mankind, for all of life springs forth from Me. I am Life, and I remain ever the same throughout time, with no beginning and no end. Life is God, always in motion, always in action, always manifest in a three-fold power. Eternity is called "Father," the Word is called "Son," and the breath that binds them together is called "Holy Spirit."

God has shaped all of mankind, giving them body, soul, and reason. I glow brilliantly above the beautiful Earth, because the Earth is the material from which God shapes mankind. I shine in the waters that signify the soul—and the soul permeates the body just as the waters flow through the whole Earth. I am ablaze in the sun and the moon, and their light represents Reason. The shining stars are the innumerable words of Reason. I awaken the universe with a puff of air—the invisible stuff of life—because everything that grows and matures is brought to life and is sustained through air and wind, everything springing from its inner essence.

God, Who created everything, shaped man and woman according to the divine image and likeness, and proportioned all creatures, great and small, in relation to them. God loved man and woman so greatly that He awarded them the place from which the fallen angel [Satan] was expelled, and He intended to give them all the glory and honor that [Satan] lost when he fell from joy.

The image you are now seeing, [Hildegard,] is the proof of this love. The image that appears to you as a surpassingly beautiful figure in God's mystery and in the midst of the southern breezes, an image like that of a human being, signifies the Heavenly Father's love. In fact, it is Love. It lives in the majesty of the eternal Godhead, complete in perfect beauty, marvelous in the gifts of divine mystery. Love appears in human form, just as the Son of God redeemed humanity when He became human flesh in the service of Love. This is the reason why the image glows with such splendor and beauty that to look at the sun is easier than to look directly at it. The fullness of Love glows and shines in the divine lightning-flash of Its gifts, so brilliantly that It surpasses every insight of human thought, the means by which we come to understand everything that exists in our minds. For this reason, no human mind can grasp this fullness.

13. POLITICS IN THE THIRTEENTH CENTURY

13.1 John of Salisbury, *Policraticus*

John of Salisbury (1120–1180) learned philosophy from Peter Abelard in Paris. Summoned to serve as chancellor in Henry II's court in 1154, he left shortly thereafter and composed his two major works, the *Metalogicon* (a study of university education and a program for its reform) and the *Policraticus* (an examination of political and moral standards). He published both works in 1159, after which he joined the court of Theobald, the archbishop of Canterbury, and his successor, Thomas Becket. He was appointed bishop of Chartres in 1176 and remained there until his death. As the following passage (from Bk. 4, ch. 1–2) from the *Policraticus* shows, John is less concerned with forms of government than with the ethical qualities of those in positions of power.

[1] On the whole, the main difference between a ruler and a tyrant is the fact that the first obeys the law, governs his people in a spirit of service to them, and appoints rewards and responsibilities within the state according to the law; in this way he ennobles his prominent position in such a way that he elevates himself in the process—for while common people look after their own common matters, a ruler concerns himself with the well-being of the whole community. This is why it is fitting that power over his subjects be conferred upon him. Only if he is self-sufficient in the ability to discover and implement the effective use of everyone in society, can he possibly arrange the affairs of the state in such a way that everyone interacts with everyone else properly. It is necessary to follow the dictates of nature—our best guide for living—and nature has made the head the depository of all the senses; the head is thus a microcosm of the whole man, the small center of the entire being, to which the rest of the body is subjected. In this way, provided that the head is sound, the parts of the whole operate and interact properly. A ruler achieves greatness and fame, therefore, by virtue of the number and extent of the privileges accorded to him in order to fulfill his necessary functions. This is rightly so, since nothing is useful to society except what is needed by the ruler—whose will ought never to be the enemy of justice.

Therefore, to offer a general definition, a ruler is the public expression and certain image of divine majesty. There can be no doubt that the essence of divine virtue assuredly resides in a just ruler, since at his command people bow their heads, or offer their necks in sacrifice to the axe. The influence of the divine causes everyone to fear him—he who is fear itself. I believe this can only have happened by divine command, since all power comes from the Lord, is with Him always, and belongs to Him forever. All that a ruler achieves, therefore, comes from God—for there is no power apart from God; a ruler's authority is but a representation of God's power and causes all things to know His justice and mercy. "Therefore whoever resists authority resists what God has appointed" [Romans 13.2]. Only God can confer authority, and it is only by His will that authority can be withdrawn from, or mitigated in, a ruler. If a ruler governs his subjects harshly, he does so not by his own will but by a divine dispensation from the Lord. Who wishes either to punish or to discipline His people. We saw in the persecutions committed by the Huns, that Attila, when asked who he was, by a holy bishop of some city, responded, "I am Attila, the Scourge of God!" It is reported that the bishop then venerated him as an emblem of divine majesty, saying "God's minister is worthy of honor," and "Blessed is he who comes in the name of the Lord." Moreover, the doors of the bishop's church were ordered unlocked—even though, sadly, they admitted the persecutor by whose hand the bishop's martyrdom was attained. The bishop had not dared to deny the Scourge of God, because he knew very well that the Lord's cherished Son had been scourged, and that no power could have scourged Him without the Lord willing it.

Therefore, if power is honored by those who are good, even to the extent that it is a scourge to the elect, who would dare not to venerate what God has established for the punishment of evildoers, for the benefit of the good, and for the strengthening of loyal observance of the law? As the emperor [Justinian] put it, "It is indeed a saying worthy of the majesty of kings, that a just ruler is ruled by his own laws, for the authority of a ruler is determined by the authority of right. Truly, submission to the laws made by rulers is a greater honor than an imperial title." This is why a ruler should think of himself as permitted to do nothing inconsistent with the demands of justice.

[2] In pointing out that God's justice, being eternal and being fairness itself, is superior to the justice meted out by an earthly ruler's statutes, one is not denigrating that ruler. As all legal scholars assert, fairness is a matter of what is appropriate. The role of reason, in this regard, is to level—that is, to restore equality to situations of inequality. But equity consists of granting to each person that which is his own. Law interprets how to do this, since it is through laws that the spirit of equity and justice are expressed. This much did Chrysippus show, when he stated that law has power over all divine and human affairs; law presides over all things, both good and evil, and is the sure ruler and guide of things as well as of mankind. Papinian too, a man of great experience in legal matters, along with the great orator Demosthenes, agreed on the need for all men to submit to the authority of the law; law is a form of divine revelation, a gift from God, the teaching of the wise, an antidote to willful excess. It restores harmony to society by banishing crime, and everyone who lives in a political community needs to live according to it. For this reason, everyone [in a community] is understood to be bound by the need to obey the laws. Only the person who mistakenly imagines that he somehow has a license to break the law, does so.

A ruler, though, should be understood as a binding law-unto-himself—not because he has a right to break the laws, but because it is proper for him not to fear the penalties of the law since he loves justice and fairness, secures the good of the public, and always privileges the common good over his personal gain. But who, in any community, can speak of the will of the ruler, since rulers are inspired not by their own will but by the desire for justice and fairness? What are their judgments except judgments for the common good? In matters of state, in fact, his will has the force of judgment. No matter the circumstance, whatever truly pleases a ruler has the force of law, and his judgment cannot be other than the expression of the desire for fairness. "From you let my vindication come; let your eyes see the right" [Psalms 17.2]. An honest judge is one whose judgments result from careful contemplation of the idea of equity. The ruler is the minister of the public good and the servant of the good; in him the public persona is made manifest. He punishes injuries, wrongs, and crimes with level-headed justice. Moreover, his rod and staff, implemented always with the restraining power of wisdom, guide all who deviate and err back to the path of fairness. This is why the Holy Spirit can deservedly sing the praise of a just ruler, "Your rod and your staff, they comfort me" [Psalms 23.4]. His shield is strong, but it protects the weak and defends the innocent from the blow of the wicked. Those who benefit the most from his official acts are those who can help themselves the least; and those who draw the greatest hostility from him are those who most desire to harm society.

The ruler's sword may shed innocent blood, but even this is not without its purpose; one may kill many and still not be a man of blood, or deserve to be called a murderer and criminal. The great St. Augustine pointed out—and we believe him—that King David is called a man of blood because of the affair of Uriah, not because of the wars he fought. The prophet Samuel killed Agag, the fat king of Amalek, yet he is nowhere called a man of blood. These are instances of a "sword belonging to a dove," one that quarrels, but without rancor; slaughters, but without wrath; fights, but without resentment. For the law prosecutes the culpable, but not out of animosity; and the ruler is right to punish transgressors, so long as he does so motivated not by wrath but by the peaceful will of the law. A ruler may in fact have several executioners at his command, but we ought to think of the ruler as his own executioner—but one who is allowed to have a proxy take his place. And we can certainly agree with the Stoic philosophers who examined carefully the names of things, when they assert that the title of "executioner" (*lictor*) is derived from "the stick of the law" (*legis ictor*), since his public duty to strike down whomever the law judges should be struck down. This is why, in ancient times, those officials whose duty it was to carry out the judgments against the guilty were told "Obey the will of the law" or "Carry out the law" when they lifted their swords over the necks of the condemned. Thus the gloominess of the situation was mitigated by merciful words.

13.2   Giano della Bella,
Speech in Praise of Republican Government

Giano della Bella (d. 1313) was a popular urban reformer from a middle-class merchant family in Florence. The city was famously a hot spot in the Guelf-Ghibelline struggles of northern Italy. Giano was a charismatic leader of one of the Guelf parties and was instrumental in passing the anti-aristocratic and anti-Ghibelline laws known as the Ordinances of Justice (1293). Because of Giano's work, Florence remained staunchly republican and mercantile. Giano himself left no written records that have survived. (Dante praises him as a true champion of the Florentine common people, in *Paradiso* 16.127–132.) What follows is a recreation of the speech he gave, rallying the city's populace against the aristocratic faction, in the *History of Florence* written by Leonardo Bruni (1370–1444), the Renaissance humanist. Although a later text, it highlights the medieval origins of Renaissance republicanism.

Good and wise citizens, I have always believed and am now more convinced than ever that the well-being of our republic demands that we must curb the ambitions of our magnate families—or else lose our very freedom. Simply put, we have reached a point where tolerance and liberty are no longer compatible, and I am sure that no sensible person can doubt which of those two principles is to be preferred. It is dangerous to talk this way, I know, but I am not afraid. And I know this to be true: No good citizen places his own comfort first, when his republic needs his advice; neither does he edit his public positions for private gain. I will speak my true mind, and freely.

It seems to me that a people's freedom depends on two things above all: laws and magistrates. When these two things prevail over the power of any individual citizen, then liberty is saved. But when some people can abuse the laws and ignore the magistrates, and get away with it, then liberty is dead. How can anyone be free, when some people can inflict whatever violence they wish upon you or your family, without fear of judgment? I want all of you to think honestly about what your lives here in Florence are like, and then think about the crimes committed by our nobles. Tell me, anyone, do you think our city is free, or do you recognize that we have been long under the magnates' thumbs? Anyone here who has an aristocrat for a neighbor, whether here in the city itself or in the surrounding countryside, will be able to answer quite quickly. There is not a single thing we possess that they do not want for themselves! Can anyone name a single thing that the magnates have desired but not tried to steal and did not feel perfectly justified in doing so? It does not matter to them whether they use legal or illegal means. If we really are honest, we are not even free in our own bodies! Think of how many common citizens have been beaten and driven from their homes in recent years! How many victims of arson, rape, assault, and murder there have been!

Everyone knows who is behind these crimes. It's public knowledge. And the evildoers stay in plain sight, either unable to conceal their crimes or simply not bothering to try to cover them up. These men, who deserve to be whipped and imprisoned, instead strut around Florence surrounded by armed guards, terrorizing the people and intimidating the magistrates. Can anyone call this liberty? What distinguishes these criminals from tyrants? For they both kill, confiscate, and steal to their hearts' content, without fear of the law. Why condemn a man who destroys liberty in another state, yet put up with a whole crowd of them who do so in our own city? We have been enslaved for a long time, believe me, and it is shameful that we still call ourselves a free republic.

But perhaps you object. Maybe you say: *You are right, obviously—but what can be done about it? There is no point in complaining.* I can only reply that if we set our minds to it we can shake off this slavery rather easily! If disregard for the law and our magistrates is the cause of our enslavement, then let us restore our liberty by simply getting rid of the criminals! If it is freedom that you want—and freedom is as important as life itself—then bring back the rule of law and magistrates, and protect them with all the strength and energy you have. We have written many laws against extortion, murder, theft, assault, and what-have-you; the time has come to enforce them against these noblemen. What is more, we should taken even further measures since the perversity of these fellows gets worse every day.

The first thing to do is to sentence nobles more harshly than anyone else who breaks the law. When you are tying people up you use a stronger rope for a powerful man than you do for a puny one. A cord suffices for little beasts; for a lion you need a chain. Punishments are the bonds of the law, and must be greater for powerful men. The ones we use now simply don't work.

Second, we must stipulate that punishment of the nobles extends to their families and households. Their kinsmen are complicit in their crimes and enable them; let them share in the punishment too!

Two obstacles now confront our magistrates: inability to bring the criminals to justice, and the difficulty of proving cases. The nobles terrify witnesses from testifying against them, which destroys the entire system of justice at a stroke. And even if evidence and testimony are presented, the magistrates are too afraid to convict.

If we do not change these things, the republic is dead. . . . All this was foreseen, when the Ministry of Justice was first created, and I'm amazed at how the Ministry's power and reputation has disintegrated. But it is stupid to be amazed, I suppose, since the common people stopped caring. No wonder our beaten officials have lost their nerve. . . . The Ministry needs more than the thousand men-at-arms allocated to it by the constitution; it ought to have four thousand—all of whom should be drawn from the common people. The Minister of Justice himself should reside in the same building as his officers, so he will personally hear citizens' complaints and provide for the needs of the republic. . . . And a new law needs to be instated, one that forbids any nobleman to become an officer of the Ministry, even if he becomes a member of a guild, because then he would be in a position to help out his fellow criminals and make a mockery of the idea of justice. The power of the nobles is already unbearable enough; we should not make them even stronger by allowing them access to positions of public authority. . . .

These reforms are easy to effect. You can do it. Who here is so downtrodden that he would rather keep living in pain and humiliation than live equal to everyone else in right and honor? Our ancestors refused to obey even the Roman emperors. The dignity of their homeland and their fellow citizens made the idea of servitude [to Rome] unacceptable. Are you really willing to continue giving in to these vile aristocrats? Our ancestors endured pains, the loss of their goods, and even death, and they carried on, against unimaginable difficulties, for the sake of their dignity and autonomy. But you, out of fear and laziness, submit yourselves to tyrants who ought to be obeying you! A community made up of a multitude of strong men—men who have conquered all their neighboring rivals and defeated a thousand enemy battalions—ought to be ashamed of letting a few noble families domineer them and make them into slaves.

I'll stop now, lest my enthusiasm make me go too far. I revere our community too much to insult it; but when I think of your degenerate passivity, it is hard for me to keep quiet. All I ask is that you think hard about your own liberty and welfare.

13.3   Ordinances of the Merchants' Guild of Southampton

Guilds were among the most prominent and influential elements in urban life. Southampton, on England's southern coast, was a vital port city through which goods entered and left England for many centuries. Heavily damaged in the Norman Conquest (1066), the city gradually recovered, and by the end of the twelfth century it was among the most active harbors in northern Europe. The merchants of Southampton had been organized into a guild long before the Conquest but came to particular prominence with the development of the textile trade with the Low Countries.

[1] The merchants' guild shall elect and empower from its members: an alderman, a steward, a chaplain, four assistants, and an usher. Let it be known that the alderman shall receive four pence from every member of the guild; the steward, two pence; the chaplain, two pence; and the usher, one pence. The guild will convene twice a year, on the Sunday following the Feast of St. John the Baptist [24 June], and on the Sunday following the Feast of the Blessed Virgin Mary [8 December—Feast of the Conception].

[2] Whenever the guild is in session, no member shall be accompanied by a non-member except when either the alderman or the steward requests a particular non-member's presence. The alderman and the steward may each have a sergeant [i.e. secretary] to serve him; the chaplain may have his clerk; and there may be two secretaries to serve the four assistants.

[3] Whenever the guild is in session, and for as long as it is in session, the alderman is to receive two gallons of wine and two candles every night, and the steward is to receive the same. The four assistants and the chaplain are to receive one gallon of wine and one candle apiece, while the usher shall receive one gallon of wine [but no candle].

[4] Whenever the guild is in session it shall give, as alms, eight gallons of ale to the leper hospital of La Madeleine, and eight gallons of ale to the patients at the hospital of St. Julian (also known as God's House); the local Franciscan friars shall receive eight gallons of ale and four gallons of wine. Sixteen gallons of ale shall be given, as alms, to the poor of Southampton every time the guild meets.

[5] Whenever the guild is in session, no member shall leave the city for any reason without the permission of the steward. If a member does so, he shall be fined two shillings.

[6] Whenever the guild is in session, if it happens that a member is not in Southampton and does not know that the guild is meeting, he shall receive a gallon of wine, provided that his servants come to get it. If a member is in the city but is ill and cannot attend, provisions will be sent to him: two loaves of bread, a gallon of wine, and one cooked dish from the guild's kitchen. Moreover, two men chosen by the guild will visit him and take care of him.

[7] Whenever a member of the guild dies, all the other members who are present in the city shall attend the church-service for the deceased, and selected guildmen shall carry the body from the church to the burial site. Any member who refuses to do this will pay, on oath, two pence, which will be given to the poor. Members who live in the neighborhood of the deceased shall be responsible to appoint a man to keep vigil over the deceased's body while it remains at home [prior to the funeral service]. Throughout the vigil and the service for the dead, the guild will keep four candles lit—each candle weighing at least two pounds, in order that it might last until the body is buried. These candles shall remain in the keeping of the guild's steward.

[8] The steward shall keep the records and treasure of the guild, under the seal of the alderman.

[9] Whenever a guild-member dies, his eldest son or nearest heir shall receive his father's seat. If a man's

father was not a member of the guild but his uncle was, he may receive his uncle's seat [if he is the uncle's heir]; but he may not receive the seat of any other relative. Moreover, he need not pay anything to assume his membership in the guild. No man, however, may acquire a seat in the guild by right of his wife or of her ancestors.

[10] No member may sell or give his seat in the guild to anyone. The son of a guild-member who is not the eldest son may receive the member's seat upon payment to the guild of ten shillings, after which payment he may take the oath of membership.

[11] If any member of the guild is imprisoned anywhere in England during peacetime, the alderman, the steward, and one of the assistants will travel, at the guild's expense, to ransom the member who is in prison.

[12] If any guild-member strikes another member with his fist and is convicted for the assault, he shall lose his membership; if he wishes to rejoin the guild he must pay ten shillings and take the oath again, as though he were a new member. But if a member strikes another with a stick, knife, or any other weapon, he shall lose his membership in the guild and his citizenship, and be regarded as a stranger until he is reconciled to the good members of the guild, compensated the man he has injured, and paid a non-refundable fine of twenty shillings to the guild.

[13] If a non-member injures anyone who is a citizen [of Southampton] but not a member of the guild, and is convicted, he shall lose his own citizenship and be imprisoned for a day and a night.

[14] If a stranger—that is, someone who is neither a guild-member nor a citizen of Southamption—strikes a guildsman, and is convicted, he shall be imprisoned for two days and two nights, unless the injury he has caused is severe enough to merit a harsher penalty.

[15] If a guildsman libels or slanders a fellow member, and the complaint is brought before the alderman, and if the guildsman is convicted, he shall pay a fine of two shillings to the guild. If he cannot pay, he shall forfeit his membership.

[16] If a non-member who is a citizen of Southampton slanders a guildsman, and is convicted, he shall pay a fine of five shillings [to the guild] or forfeit his citizenship.

[17] No one who is not a member of the guild may appear before the guild's council.

[18] Anyone who forfeits his membership in the guild by any act or injury, and who is expelled by the alderman, steward, assistants, and the twelve syndics of the city, but who wishes to join the guild again, must start anew just as one who has never been a guildsman. He must first make amends for the harm he has done, as judged by the alderman and the syndics. If a guild-member and citizen brings a lawsuit against another guild-member and citizen in another city, with or without a writ, he will forfeit his membership in the guild, if convicted.

[19] No person who lives in Southampton shall purchase any commodity with the intent to sell it again in the same city unless he is a member of the merchants' guild and a citizen. Anyone who violates this ordinance, and is convicted of it, shall forfeit his property to the king. No one who is not a member of the guild and a citizen shall be exempt from taxation every year.

[20] No one may trade in honey, fat, salt herrings, any kind of oil, millstones, furs, or any kind of animals skins, in the city of Southampton, unless he is a member of the merchants' guild. Nor may anyone operate a tavern or wine-shop, sell textiles at retail (except on market-days and fair days), nor store grain in a warehouse beyond fifteen months, to sell at retail, if he is not a member of the guild. Anyone convicted of these things shall forfeit all his property to the king.

[21] No member of the guild may enter a partnership or dealership with anyone engaged in these businesses who is not a guild-member, by any trick of covering up, fraud, deceit, or conspiracy whatsoever. Anyone who does so, and is convicted, shall forfeit all his goods to the king and lose his membership in the guild.

[22] Any member of the guild who falls into poverty and cannot support himself, is unable to work and care for his family, shall receive one mark of silver from the guild at each of its meetings, to relieve his suffering. No guild-member may claim [a poor member's] goods for himself, for fear of doing harm to the city's commerce; but if he does so, and is convicted, he shall forfeit his guild-membership and his citizenship, and the goods claimed will be forfeited to the king.

[23] No private individual [of Southampton] or stranger may bargain for, or purchase, any merchandise coming into the city before an agent of a guild-member has the opportunity to bargain for it or purchase it. Anyone who does so, and is convicted, shall forfeit his goods to the king.

[24] Any member of the merchants' guild may share in the merchandise purchased by another member, if he wishes to do so and is present when the merchandise is purchased, provided he gives due payment to the seller and a surety for his portion. But no one who is not a member of the guild may share in the merchandise purchased by a guild-member, without that member's permission.

[25] If any guild-member refuses to share merchandise with another guildsman, he shall relinquish the right to buy or sell anything in the city for that year, except for his food.

13.4   Ibn Battuta, *Journeys*

Ibn Battuta (1304–1368) was born in the city of Tangiers, in Morocco. Of mixed Arab and Berber descent, he received a sound if unremarkable education. He was permanently restless and dedicated his life to traveling as far as possible throughout the entire Islamic world. His travels consisted of three main journeys. Between 1325 and 1332 he traveled across North Africa, through the Holy Land and the Hijaz, across Iraq and the central Arabian peninsula, and down the eastern cost of Africa, as far south as today's country of Tanzania. From 1332 to 1346 he visited Anatolia, southern Russia, Uzbekistan, Afghanistan, Pakistan, India, southeast Asia, and the Chinese coast as far as Beijing. Finally, from 1349 to 1354 he traveled southward from Tangiers through northwestern Africa—today's nations of Morocco, Algeria, Mauretania, Mali, and Niger. Altogether, Ibn Battuta logged roughly 80,000 miles, and his travel account, the *Risala* (*Journeys*), provides an extraordinary look at Muslim life. Translated below is a portion of his report on life among the Turks in Anatolia.

Turks arrange their trips through the deserts [of the region] in much the same way as pilgrims undertake the *hajj* [to Mecca] along the main thoroughfare of the Hijaz: setting out right after morning prayers, halting at midday, then traveling again after the midday meal, and continuing on until dusk. Whenever they stop they loosen their horses, camels, and oxen from the wagons and set them to pasture, to graze at will. No one, not even the sultan, bothers to transport forage for the animals, since the nature of their land is such that its grasses are as beneficial to their beasts as barley. No other area enjoys such a natural benefit, which explains the unusually high number of animals it can support. Because the Turks' laws against theft are so severe, no one ever needs to stand guard over their flocks and herds. For example, their law states that anyone found in possession of another man's horse must return it immediately, along with nine additional horses as compensation; if he lacks the horses to hand over, he must surrender his sons; and if he has no sons, then he is slaughtered like a sheep.

The Turks do not eat bread, and hardly any solid food. Instead, they eat something they call *dughi*. which is made from a grain similar to millet. After heating some water until it boils, they pour in a certain amount of this *dughi*, along with some bits of meat. After this is cooked, each man takes a portion in a bowl and spoons some yogurt on top. They also use mares' milk sometimes, which they call *qumizz*. The Turks are strong, hardy, and hearty. . . . They also use *dughi* in order to make a fermented drink. Candied foods, however, they find repulsive. I once attended an audience with the sultan Uzbak during Ramadan. Lamb was served, along with horse-flesh (which is, in fact, the meat they eat most frequently) and a kind of cooked pasta that is eaten with mares' milk. That night I laid before him a dish of sweetmeats that one of my companions had prepared. The sultan touched one of the pieces with his finger and tasted it, but otherwise would not eat it. Tuluk-tumur, the *emir*, later told me that the sultan (who had as many as forty sons and grandsons) said to one of his highest ranking *mamluks* the next day, "If you can eat those sweets, I will free all of you." But the *mamluk* refused and said "I wouldn't eat them if you threatened to kill me!" . . .

The number of their horses is unbelievable, with the result that they cost next to nothing. One can buy a fine horse for fifty or sixty *dirhams*, which in our money is about one *dinar*. These are mixed-breed horses, the kind the Egyptians call *akadish*, and most Turks earn their living by raising them—similar to the way that our people raise sheep, only on a much larger scale. It is common for a single Turk to have thousands of horses. They keep track of their herds by tying a strip of cloth (about the width of a hand) to a long stick; each piece of cloth represents one thousand horses. They place these sticks on the corners of the wagons, in which their women ride. I myself have seen sticks that had as many as ten strips of cloth on them, although most have fewer than that. . . .

I remained in Azaq for three more days after the *emir* Tuluk-tumur had departed, until the governor Muhammad Khwaja could prepare all the supplies I needed for my journey. Once everything was ready I set out quickly for al-Machar, a fair-sized city that is among the loveliest the Turks inhabit. It is located on a great river and has many gardens filled with fruit-trees. We lodged at the hostel of Muhammad al-Bata'ihi, a very old and pious *shaikh* who came originally from the marshlands of southern Iraq. He was an agent for the *shaikh* Ahmad al-Rifa'i—may Allah be pleased with him. In this hostel there were about seventy indigent men—a mix of Arabs, Persians, Turks, and Greeks, some of them with families—who survived solely off alms. The Turks of that area believe in the virtue of caring for the poor, and bring a number of horses, cattle, and sheep to the hostel every night. The sultan and his wives also visit the *shaikh* regularly and receive his blessing for their great generosity. They give large amounts of money to the hostel, especially the wives, who give alms profusely and perform many pious deeds.

Once when we were in the city of al-Machar we attended Friday prayers, and we waited as 'Izz al-Din climbed up the steps of the pulpit. He was a jurist, one of the greatest scholars in Bukhara. He had a coterie of students and readers who would practice reciting in front of him. He preached a sermon before the governor and some of the leading citizens of the city. When he was finished, the *shaikh* Muhammad al-Bata'ihi stood up and announced, "Our learned preacher is setting out on a journey, and we wish to present him with gifts." Then he took off a goat-hair cloak and gave it to him, saying "This is from me." Others who were present also presented him with cloaks and robes, horses, and money. Altogether they presented him with a bounty.

In the market square of this city there was a Jew who addressed me in Arabic. When I asked him where he came from, he said that he was from al-Andalus. He had left Spain four months earlier, traveling entirely by land, not be sea, and had come by way of Constantinople, the lands of Rum and of the Jarkas. Others I spoke with assured me of the truth of what he said.

Among the many remarkable things I saw in this country was the way in which the Turks treat their women. Women, in fact, are held in higher esteem even than men. When I left al-Qiram I saw the wife of the *emir* Saltiya in her wagon; this was the first time I beheld any of their noblewomen. Her wagon was covered in an expensive blue wool cloth. Her tent was open, and I could see that she had four girls, each of surpassing beauty and richly dressed, attending to her. A train of wagons followed hers, each filled with other, similar attending girls. As her wagon approached the *emir*'s camp, his wife stepped to the ground with about thirty girls following her. Her cloaks had small circlets attached above the hemline, and as she walked his servant-girls carefully held these in order to lift her skirts so they did not trail on the ground. She walked in a most noble manner. When she reached her husband, the *emir* stood, saluted her, and sat her down at his side. Her attending-girls stood at a distance. Several goat-skins of *qumizz* were brought out, and then the *emir*'s wife filled a bowl with it and presented it, kneeling, to her husband. After the *emir* had drunk, she performed the same service for his brother—and then the *emir* himself performed the service for her. When food was brought out she ate with the men. When the meal was ended the *emir* presented his wife with a fine robe, and she departed.

That is how the wives of *emirs* are treated. I will describe how the wives of the Turkish kings are treated later, but as for the wives of merchants and commoners, this is what I saw: When riding in a wagon, a Turkish wife will have three or four girls attending to her. She will wear a cone-shaped headpiece called a *bughtaq*, that will be decorated with precious stones and peacock feathers. Her tent will be open and her face visible, for Turkish women do not veil themselves. A woman will come like this to the market, with a handful of male slaves who will be carrying milk and sheep, which she will sell in return for spices. Sometimes she will be accompanied by her husband, who, from appearances, could just as easily be one of her servants, since he will wear only a sheepskin cloak and a hat that they call a *kula*.

13.5 Giovanni da Pian del Carpine, *History of the Mongols*

Fr. Giovanni (1182–1252) was an early member of the new Franciscan order, one who knew St. Francis personally. In 1245 he set off on a mission, assigned to him by Pope Innocent IV (r. 1243–1254), to convert the Mongols. He lived among the Mongols, learned their language and customs, and wrote the *Historia Mongolorum* (*History of the Mongols*), which is less of a history than an ethnography. The passages translated below describe the Mongols' appearance, manners, and customs.

CHAPTER 4: THE APPEARANCE, CLOTHING, AND FOOD OF THE MONGOLS

In appearance, the Mongols—or Tartars—are unlike all other peoples. Their eyes and cheekbones are more widely set than in other races, and their cheekbones are prominent. They have smallish, flat noses, small eyes, and their eyelids stand straight up, and on the crown of their heads they are clean-shaven, like our clergy. They wear their hair longer on the sides than in front, but in the back they grow it quite long, like our women do. They make two braids in back and bind one behind each ear. Their feet are small.

Men's clothing and women's clothing are alike. They do not use cloaks, hats, or caps. They do, however, wear buckram, scarlet, and baldacchino tunics of remarkable shape; these have hair or fur on the outside, are open in back, with tails that hang as low as their knees. They never wash their clothing, nor will they allow them to be washed, especially not when it is thundering. Their homes are round and are cleverly built of reeds and sticks, rather like a tent. In the middle of the roof they make an opening that lets light in and smoke out; a fire burns constantly in their homes. The walls of these homes are of cloth, the doors too. These structures can be taken down, and put up, quite quickly; they are carried by their pack animals. The few that cannot be disassembled are stowed upon carts. Wherever the Mongols go, whether it be to war or anyplace else, they bring these shelters with them.

They are rich in cattle, camels, oxen, sheep, and goats. I believe they have more horses and pack animals than all the rest of the world combined—although they do not have any swine or other beasts. Their ruler, princes, and other nobles abound with gold, silver, silk, and precious stones.

As for food: they eat anything that can be eaten. I have even seen them eat lice. They drink the milk of animals, especially mare's milk, in tremendous quantities. They steep millet in water, making it thin enough to be able to drink it; they all drink a cup or two of this in the morning, and sometimes they do not bother to eat anything else all day. In the evenings, however, a portion of meat is given to each one to eat, and they drink the broth they make out of it. In summertime, when they have ample supplies of mare's milk, they seldom eat meat—usually only when some is given to them as a gift, or when they have taken some beast or bird in the hunt.

CHAPTER 5: OF THEIR MANNERS—BOTH THE GOOD AND THE BAD

Many of their manners are quite commendable; some others are simply detestable. They are far more obedient to their noble lords than to anyone else in the whole world, whether clerical or lay; in fact, they revere their princes and will never deceive them in either word or deed. It is a rare thing for them to fall out among themselves—wars, brawls, assaults, and murders simply never happen among them. Theft and robbery, of any great scale, is hardly to be found, and therefore they never bother to secure their homes or carts with locks or bars even if they contain things of value. When an animal goes astray, whoever finds it either lets it go or brings it to an official whose job it is to restore strays; the owner of the animal simply requests it from this official and receives it without any trouble.

Every Mongol honors every other one, and they share their food generously with all their friends, even when their supplies are low. Their endurance-levels are high; even after going a day or two without any food whatsoever, they sing and are as good-natured as if they had just come from a feast. When riding, they endure extremes of hot and cold with patience. They never grumble, and even when they drink heavily they never quarrel in their drunkenness. No one scorns another; rather, they all help and support one another as much as possible. Mongol women are chaste, and one never hears a word of scandal raised about any of them, even though Mongol men do occasionally use rough and obscene language.

Toward other peoples, however, the Mongols are extremely haughty and insolent, regarding all non-Mongols as insignificant, whether noble or not. I myself have seen, in the great khan's court, the prince of Russia, the son of the king of Georgia, and countless great sultans receive none of the honor due to them. Even those Mongol men assigned to attend to the visitors would

walk in front of them, seat themselves in more honorable positions, and sometimes even make the princes sit behind them, even though the attendants might be among the lowest of the base-born. Toward all non-Mongols they are angry, disdainful, and deceitful in the extreme. They speak politely enough at the start, but in the end they sting like scorpions. They are sneaky and dishonest, willing to use any trick in order to get the advantage of someone. When they want to treat someone ill, they hide the fact amazingly, so that their victim can hardly prepare himself or repair matters after the fact. They eat and drink (and do certain other things too) in a most messy manner. Drunkenness is positively honorable to them, and if any one of them drinks so much that his stomach cannot handle it, he simply vomits it all up and then sets to drinking again. They are the most demanding and possessive of peoples, and also the least generous. And to kill a non-Mongol is nothing at all to them.

CHAPTER 6: CONCERNING THEIR LAWS AND CUSTOMS

Among their laws and customs is this: anyone, man or woman, caught in the act of adultery is put to death. Similarly, if any maiden has sexual relations with a man outside of marriage, they are both put to death. If someone is caught in robbery or theft, he is killed mercilessly. If a man fails to keep to himself things told him in confidence, especially in times of war, he receives a hundred blows or more on his back with a rod, given by a stout rustic. If any commoner offends against a superior, he receives no mercy but is punished with heavy blows.

In marriage, a Mongol can marry anyone, even a close relative, so long as it is not his mother, daughter, or sister. It has long been their custom to marry their half-sisters or even their stepmothers, after the death of their father. When a married elder brother dies, a younger brother, or some other close relation, will marry the widow.

Once, while I was living among them, a Russian prince named Andrei was accused before Batu Khan of stealing horses from the Mongols and selling them abroad; despite the fact that the charges could not be proved, they killed him. Hearing of this, Andrei's wife and younger brother came to the court and begged that Prince Andrei's land not be taken from them.

Batu Khan ordered the young prince and the widowed sister-in-law to marry, according to Mongol custom. She replied that she would rather die than transgress the [Russian] law. Regardless, Batu Khan married them. They both resisted as much as they could, but in the end they were carried into bed and, the younger brother shouting and weeping the whole time, they were forced to commit incest. Mongol women, after their husbands' deaths, hardly ever marry again unless it is to their dead husbands' brother or to one of his sons by another woman. They do not distinguish between their legitimate and illegitimate sons, and each man bequeaths whatever he wants to each.

It happened recently that the king of Georgia had two sons—one legitimate, named Melich, the other illegitimate, named David—and when he died he left a good portion of his realm to his bastard. Melich, to whom the realm passed by right of his mother (since it used to be governed by women), journeyed to the Mongol khan since David had already set out for the court. They both entered the court and offered extraordinary gifts to Batu Khan. David, the illegitimate one, asked for justice according to Mongol custom. Batu decided against Melich, stating that David, as the elder of the brothers, took precedence and ought to hold peaceably and unmolested, the portion of the land awarded him by their father.

When a Mongol has a number of wives, each one has her own home and family to herself. The husband eats, drinks, and sleeps with one wife one day, another day with another wife. One wife is regarded as chief among them, and he spends more time with her than with the others. While there may be many wives to a husband, it must be said, they seldom argue among themselves.

14. ART AND INTELLECT IN THE THIRTEENTH CENTURY

14.1   St. Thomas Aquinas, *Summa contra Gentiles*

St. Thomas Aquinas (1225–1274) is the greatest of the scholastic theologians. Born into a prominent southern Italian family, he resisted their efforts to place him in the Benedictine monastery at Monte Cassino and instead joined the Dominican order. He studied and taught in Paris, Cologne, and Naples. His *Summa theologica* is one of the monumental works of the scholastic age. His *Summa contra Gentiles* is an abridged version of the longer work, one intended, as its title indicates, for intellectual debate with non-Christians. Below is the text of Book 3, ch. 27.

[III, 27] HUMAN HAPPINESS IS NOT TO BE FOUND IN CARNAL PLEASURES

From what is shown above, it is obviously impossible that human happiness can be found in carnal pleasures—the chief of these being the pleasures of the table and of sex.

We have already shown that Nature is so designed that pleasure exists to advance Nature's cause, not to impede it. So if any of Nature's cause is not the goal of any action, the pleasure entailed in that action cannot either result in Nature's goal nor be a goal in itself. Now it is obvious that actions that are accompanied by pleasures of the table and of sex cannot be goals in and of themselves, for they are guided solely to achieve specific ends: eating, that is, for the sustenance of the body, and sexual intercourse for the begetting of children. By this reasoning, these activities are not ultimate goals, and neither are they constitutive of the ultimate goals—and therefore human happiness cannot be found in them.

A second point: Human will is superior to sensual appetite—for as we saw earlier, it controls the appetite. But we already know that happiness is not willed. How much less, therefore, can happiness be the result of pleasures associated with mere appetite.

A third point: Happiness is a quality unique to mankind, for it is an abuse of language to speak of happiness in brute animals. The pleasures of food and sex, though, are found in both mankind and brute animals—and therefore happiness cannot be attributed to them.

A fourth point: Happiness is the most noble quality to be found in reality, because it is in accord with what is best for Nature. But the pleasures of food and sex are not in accord with what is best and most noble in mankind, which is the intellect, not the base senses. Therefore happiness cannot reside in those pleasures.

A fifth point: The supreme goal of mankind cannot consist in his being united with things beneath his dignity, and can only consist in his being united with things above and beyond his dignity. A [noble] goal is superior to anything that contributes to attaining it. Sex and food tie man to his senses, which is to say, they tie him to things beneath his dignity, and therefore we cannot attribute happiness to them.

A sixth point: Anything that must exist in moderation in order to be good cannot be intrinsically good; rather, it attains whatever goodness it has from its moderation. Sex and food can only be good to us if we partake of them moderately. If left unchecked, they would conflict with one another, and therefore cannot be considered intrinsically good for mankind. The supreme good is good in and of itself; anything whose goodness depends on something else cannot be a supreme good. By this reasoning, the pleasures of sex and food cannot be considered mankind's supreme good—which, of course, is happiness.

A seventh point: In all statements of the *per se* type, if A is absolutely constitutive of B, then any increase in A will result in an increase of B. For example, an object that is hot radiates heat, a hotter object radiates more heat, and the hottest object radiates the most heat. Accordingly, if sex and food were intrinsically good, then the more one engaged in them, the better. But this is clearly untrue because overindulging in them is sinful: it is harmful to the body and hinders other types of bodily pleasures. For this reason, sex and food cannot *per se* be regarded as mankind's good, and human happiness cannot be found in them.

An eighth point: Virtuous actions are worthy of respect because by definition they contribute to human happiness. So therefore, if happiness consisted in sex and food, all virtuous acts would be praiseworthy to the extent that they contribute to the pleasures of sex and food rather than to the abstention from them. But this is clearly false. The virtue of temperance lies in its abstinence from pleasure, as its name implies. Therefore happiness cannot be found in those pleasures.

A ninth point: The ultimate goal of life is God, and therefore we maintain that man's ultimate happiness lies in the approach to God. Sex and food cannot help us to approach God, since they impede contemplative prayer (our surest route to God), and actually hinder our approach to Him, since they pull us into a world of sense-pleasure that distracts us from the contemplative world. And therefore, once more, human happiness cannot be found in the pleasures of sex and food.

By these arguments we have utterly refuted the error of the Epicureans—those philosophers who attribute human happiness to carnal pleasures. Solomon spoke for them when he said: "Besides, all their days they eat in darkness, in much vexation and sickness and resentment. This is what I have seen to be good: it is fitting to eat and drink and find enjoyment in all the toil with which one toils under the sun the few days of the life God gives us; for this is our lot." [Ecclesiastes 5.17–18] And again: "Let none of us fail to share in our revelry; everywhere let us leave signs of enjoyment, because this is our portion; this is our lot." [Wisdom 2.9]

We have also hereby refuted the error of the Cerinthians, who taught that human happiness will be gained "in the one thousand years after Christ's resurrection, when people will indulge in the carnal pleasures of the table." [Quoting from St. Augustine, *De haeresis*, ch. 8] These Cerinthians are also known as Chiliasts, or believers in the Millenium.

Thus too are refuted the myths of the Jews and Muslims, who pretend that such pleasures will be the reward for human righteousness. No. Happiness is the reward for virtue.

14.2   Roger Bacon, *Opus Maius*

Roger Bacon, O.F.M. (1214–1294), was the boldest and most ambitious of the scholars of the thirteenth century. His knowledge of languages and history, mathematics, the sciences, theology, and patristic literature was without equal in his time. His life's goal was to compose a vast interpretive summary of all natural philosophy, which he felt was an urgency confronting Christendom, given the imminent approach of Armageddon. Written around 1268, his *Opus Maius* could be regarded as an interim report, or even as a grant proposal; it provides a summary of his ideas in order to secure papal approval for more extended and extensive study. The following passage comes from the fourth book, which is dedicated to "mathematics in the service of divine matters."

And now, having shown how important mathematics is for philosophy, theology, and God's Holy Church, I turn to showing its significance for the secular governance of Christendom. The power of mathematics is manifested in two ways especially—first, in its contribution to our understanding of temporal matters (past, present, and future), and second, in its practical value for everyday concerns. Inevitably, human beings are subjected to endless dangers, and therefore the attempt to understand what the future holds is an urgency. And considering that God has given us gifts of surpassing importance—namely, our bodies and souls—and has promised us eternal life, then surely He will not have denied us blessings of lesser value. The sun rises even upon the wicked. The sea welcomes all, even pirates. How much more, therefore, He must have granted the knowledge and understanding of nature to good men! . . .

In the second book of *De generatione et corruptione*, Aristotle writes that the materials on which a craftsman works matter less than the tools and instruments he uses. But we usually credit only the craftsman for what he produces, not his tools; the carpenter, not his axe. It follows, therefore, that the chief determinant of all earthly things must be found in the heavens, since the active agents are the heavens themselves and the elements that they use as the tools of their craft. Inductive reasoning proves the point. No one doubts that the heavens are the cause of every inanimate thing, for inanimate objects cannot create anything, not even further objects of their own species. A stone, for instance, cannot create another stone in the way that a donkey can produce another donkey or a human produce another human. Therefore it is clear that creative power residing in the heavens and embodied in the material elements is what creates all things, animate and inanimate. . . .

Thus the first axiom of our investigation is that every point on Earth is the apex of a pyramid through which the creative power of the heavens is transmitted. To advance my argument in simpler and clearer terms, I must direct our attention to the great diversity that exists in the various regions of the earth, how those regions change over time, and how the various things in any one region are subject to multiple influences at the same time. All of this depends on having a clear image of the size and shape of the earth on which we live, and its regions and zones. To that end, we begin with the assumption (which I have proven earlier) that the earth is a sphere. Now imagine three lines going through the earth and intersecting at right angles at the center—one extending to the heavens from right to left, that is from east to west; the second going vertically

from the north pole to the south pole; and the third passing forward and backward. . . . Next, picture a circle encompassing the earth from east to west [that is, along the y-axis] and passing through the third line [that is, the z-axis]. This circle will divide the heavens into two equal parts, half on the side of the north pole, half on the side of the south pole, and we shall call it the Equinoctial [i.e. the Equator] because those who live along it will always have days and nights of equal length, and also because everyone on Earth experiences an equinox when the Sun passes over it in the course of a whole day—which happens twice a year, at the beginning of spring and autumn when the Sun enters the constellations of Aries and Libra. Lastly, imagine a second great circle encompassing the earth, that passes through the north and south poles and intersects the Equinoctial at right angles. This circle is called the Colure. . . .

Thus we have the heavens divided into four parts—two above the part of the earth in which we live [i.e. the northern hemisphere], and two above the lower part of the earth [i.e. the southern hemisphere]. . . .

Similarly, we should picture the three straight lines with which we began, passing through the earth and intersecting at right angles at its center; these lines are perpendicular to the surface of the earth. The point of intersection of these lines is both the center of the earth and the center of the entire universe. . . . Thus the earth itself must lie at the center of the universe. . . .

[The Colure and the Equinoctial] divide the earth into four parts, two of which appear in the half of the earth's surface that can sustain life (the other two appearing in the other half). . . . Now, Ptolemy writes in *De dispositione spherae* that only about one-sixth of the earth is habitable because the rest is covered by the sea. . . . Aristotle, however, states at the end of his *De caelo* that more than a quarter of earth is inhabited, and this opinion has been confirmed by Averroës. . . . And this conclusion is further supported by the words of someone with a quite different perspective. Esdras writes in his fourth book that six parts of the world are inhabited, while only a seventh is covered with water. Everyone knows that our ancient saints used this book [II Esdras] constantly in order to teach the sacred truths, and that passages from it were once even used in the divine office—so no one should dismiss the authority of the passage simply because the book itself is apocryphal; its authority should be accepted here, even if Esdras himself was not its author.

I insist, therefore, despite the fact that Ptolemy and his camp squeeze the inhabited world into a quarter of the whole earth, that far more than a quarter of it is in fact fit for human habitation. Aristotle must have had a clearer understanding of the matter [than Ptolemy did]; after all, with support from Alexander [the Great] Aristotle dispatched two thousand scholars throughout the world, to report back on what they found. Pliny relates this in his *Natural History*. As for Alexander, he witnessed everything at first-hand all the way to the East, as we know from the *History of Alexander* [of Arrian] and his own letters back home to Aristotle, in which he described the surprising wonders he kept encountering on his campaigns. Aristotle, therefore, should be

regarded as a greater authority than Ptolemy. The same might be said of Seneca, whose pupil, the emperor Nero, sent out many men to investigate the poorly understood issues about the nature of the world—as Seneca relates in his *Naturalia*. Following Aristotle and Seneca, therefore, we must conclude that the inhabitable land [in our hemisphere] that is covered by the sea must be quite small. . . .

More than one-half of the quarter [of the earth] in which we live is still unknown to us; its cities and towns are mysteries even to philosophers, as I will show presently. As for the remaining two quarters [of our inhabited quarter], we must conclude, following the same lines of reasoning, that they too are not covered by water, despite what our mathematicians have stated. . . .

14.3   Marie de France, *Lanval*

Lanval was one of the most popular of chivalric romances in the Middle Ages, although it is less well known today.

The brave and courteous king Arthur established
his court at Carduel because the Picts and Scots
were laying waste to the realm. They had already
    invaded
Logres and left it in ruins. At Pentecost,
Arthur held his summer court and gave rich gifts
to his counts and barons, all members of his
    Round Table.
So great a company had never been brought
    together before.
He bestowed lands and wives to all who served him
—all except one: Lanval, whom Arthur forgot.
None of the other knights gave him a thought
    either.
They envied Lanval his valor and generosity,
His handsome looks and his bravery.
    A few of them
Feigned to love him, too, but if anything ill
Were to befall him none of them would care.

Lanval was a king's son, of a proud line, but
He was far from the land of his birth. Now he
Belonged to Arthur's household, for he had spent
What money he had had. Arthur offered
    him none
And Lanval was too proud to ask. Now, in straits,
He was heavy with sorrow and troubled.
Do not be surprised, my lords—for one who is
Alone and friendless in a foreign land, is sad indeed,
and knows not where to turn for help.

This Lanval, of whom I am singing, who had
    served
The king for so long, one day mounted his horse
and rode off in search of amusement. He left
    Carduel
behind him and came, all alone, to a meadow
where he dismounted by a flowing stream.
    His horse

was trembling, and so he undid the saddle
    and set him free
to wander through the field; then he folded
    his cloak
and laid his head to rest on it as he
    lay down.

Oppressed by his troubles, he could think of
    nothing
To brighten his mood. But then, gazing along
    the riverbank
He saw two young maidens approaching, more
    beautiful
Than any he had ever seen before.
    They were dressed
In robes of deep purple, tightly laced,
    and their faces
Were beyond beautiful. The elder of the two
    carried
A golden bowl of marvelous workmanship
    (it is the truth
I'm telling you!) and the younger held
    a towel.
They came straight to where the knight
    was lying;
Lanval, being well bred, rose to greet them,
    but they
Spoke first and gave him this message:

"Our most excellent lady, who is wise and
    beautiful, has sent
us to you, Sir Lanval. Come with us, and we will
    guide you
to her pavilion. See, it is not far!"

The knight went with them, without a thought
    for his horse
Who he left behind, feeding in the meadow.
    The maidens led him
Up to the pavilion, which was beautiful and
    handsomely situated.
Neither wise Queen Semiramis, with all her
    wealth and power,
Nor the emperor Octavian himself could have
    afforded
A single flap of its draped walls. Atop the tent
    was a golden

Eagle whose value was beyond counting. Neither
    could anyone
Reckon the cost even of the ropes and poles
    that held
The tent up. No king under heaven could
    purchase
Its equal, at any price.

A lady awaited inside, one more beautiful than a
    lily or rose
When they are in full bloom in mid-summer.
    She lay on a bed
(the bedclothes alone were worth a castle!)
    dressed only
in a simple shift. Her body was shapely and
    elegant.
Because of the heat, she had cast off a mantle of
    white ermine,
Trimmed with Alexandrian purple, which left
    her side
Uncovered. Her face, neck, and bosom were
    whiter than
A hawthorn flower. Lanval moved forward when
    the lady
Addressed him, and sat beside the bed.

"Lanval," she said, "O my sweet love! You are the
    reason
I have traveled so far from home. If you are brave
    and courtly,
Then no one—emperor, king, or count—will
    ever know
Such good joy as shall be yours; for I love you
    beyond all else."
He was quick to answer, and most suitably:
    "Fair lady,
If it pleased you, there is nothing in the world
You might command of me that I would not do!
    I would do
To my utmost ability anything, wise or foolish,
    if only
You might love me! I will obey your every
    command.
For you I will renounce everyone I know. More
    than anything,
I wish never to leave your side."

And when this lady heard him speak words of
    love, she granted
Him all she had—her heart and her body.

Now Lanval was feeling better! After their
    lovemaking
She gave him another gift, a promise that he
    would never again
Be wanting. Whatever he desired he would
    receive, and
No matter how much he spent or gave away,
    she would
Forever make it up to him. Lanval was well cared
    for now.
The more he spends, the more gold and silver
    he will have.

"My love!" she said, "But I must warn you
    (and this warning
is both a command and a plea): You may never
    let anyone
know of our love. Here is why: If anyone finds
    out, you will lose
me forever. Forever! Never again beholding or
    enjoying
my body." He swore to obey her exactly as she said,
and lay by her side in perfect contentment. All
    afternoon
and into the evening he stayed by her side; he
    would
have stayed even longer, if she had consented—
    but she said,
"Get up, my love! You can stay no longer, and
    must go.
I will remain here, but I make you this promise:
Whenever you want to be with me, you have only
    to wish it
And I will be there to satisfy all your desires.
    Any place
You can think of, where a man might enjoy his lover
Without reproach or embarrassment. And only you
Will be able to see and hear me!"

It made Lanval very happy to hear this. He kissed
    his lady-love
And got up. The two maidens who had brought
    him to the tent

Dressed him in such fine clothes that there
    was no more handsome
A man in the world, but he was no ill-bred fool.
    They brought
Him water and a towel, so he could wash his
    hands, and then
He ate dinner with his lady-love—he would not
    be refused.
The maidens served him with every courtesy,
    and he enjoyed
Every course. The meal pleased the knight fully, and
He held his lady close and kissed her often.
    After dinner
His horse was brought to him, saddled and ready.
Lanval bid farewell, mounted, and rode back
    to Carduel.

But as he rode he kept looking back, and he
    grew worried.
Marveling at his adventure, he began to doubt
    himself
And was not sure what to think. Would he
    ever see her again?
Returning to his rooms he found his men
    all dressed fine;
He entertained them all lavishly, but no one
    knew where
His money came from. There was not a single
    knight
In Carduel who needed a place to stay whom
    he did not invite
To join him and enjoy such splendid hospitality.
Lanval bestowed gifts on all; he ransomed prisoners;
He provided for minstrels; he treated everyone
    lavishly.
No one, friend or stranger, was overlooked.

Great now was Lanval's delight. He summoned
    his lady-love
At any hour of day or night, and enjoyed her
    to the full.
She was utterly at his command.

Sometime in that same year, I believe it was
    after the feast
Of St. John, about thirty knights were at leisure
    in an orchard

Beneath the tower where the queen lived. Sir
    Gawain was there,
And so was his cousin, the handsome Yvain.
    Gawain, the noble and brave
So loved by all, spoke: "My lords! I swear to
    God that we wronged
Our fellow Lanval by not bringing him here to
    join us. After all,
He has been so generous and courteous, and his
    father is a king."
So they all went back to Lanval's lodging and
    prevailed on him
To join in their revelry.

Queen Guinevere happened to be at her window,
    looking out,
Joined by three ladies-in-waiting. She was
    watching the royal retinue
Pass by, and happened to rest her eyes on Lanval.
    Straight away
She ordered one of her companions to assemble
    all the ladies-in-waiting,
All of whom were beautiful and refined, so that
    they all might
Set out for the orchard where the knights were going.
Numbering over thirty, the ladies came down the
    steps and were met
By the knights who were delighted to see them.
    Each knight
Took a lady by the hand and began to converse
    pleasantly.

Lanval, however, went off to the side, away from
    the rest. Yearning
for his love—to embrace her, kiss her, possess
    her—he cared little
for others' pleasures if he could not have his own.
    When Guinevere saw him
by himself, she crossed directly to him, sat by his
    side, and revealed her heart.

"I have treated you with much honor, Lanval, for
    I do love and adore you.
I offer myself to you in love! Tell me whatever you
    desire, and I

Will satisfy you with my love. I promise—you will
    be pleased!"

"My lady!" cried Lanval, "no more of this! I have
    no designs on you!
I have served our king a long time, and have no
    desire to betray him.
I will not harm my lord king—not for you or
    your love."

At this the queen grew angry and hurled an
    insult: "Lanval!
I'm not surprised you have no interest in pleasure.
    Many have told me
That you do not care for women, and that you
    have no shortage
Of beautiful boys in whom you delight. You are a
    foul coward,
A louse and a cripple! My lord king made a
    grave error
When he agreed to have you join the court. For
    all I know,
God may even punish him for it!"

Hearing all of this, Lanval's spirit darkened, and
    in his wrath
He spat out words he would later regret. "I know
    nothing
Of the kind of love you mentioned. But I do
    love, and am loved by,
One who excels in beauty every woman
    I have known.
And there's one thing more—I may as well
    tell you all:
Any one of her ladies-in-waiting, even the
    plainest of them,
Far surpasses you, my queen, in beauty of face
    and form,
In graciousness and in goodness!"
The queen stormed away to her chamber and
    wept. Angry
And hurt by his insult, she collapsed sick into
    bed and vowed
Never to rise until King Arthur had given her
    satisfaction

For Lanval's grave offense. Now Arthur returned
   from the forest,
Having enjoyed a pleasant day, and entered the
   queen's chamber.
When Guinevere saw him she fell at his feet,
   begging for mercy
And complaining that Lanval had dishonored her
   by seeking her love;
And that when she denied him, he insulted and
   abused her
By boasting that he had a lover who was of such
   refinement
And beauty and bearing that even her plainest
   chambermaid
Was lovelier by far than the queen.

Arthur was enraged and vowed that if Lanval
   could not defend
Himself in court, he would be hanged or burned.
   He left the queen
And commanded three of his barons to seize him.
   Now Lanval
Sat alone in his room, vexed and saddened. He
   called for his
Lady-love again and again, but to no avail. He
   complained and moaned;
He fainted; a hundred times he cried out for
   mercy and the chance
To speak to his love. He cursed himself in his
   heart and with
His mouth. It is a wonder he did not kill himself.

At this point, roughly halfway through the tale, King Arthur summons his court to place Lanval on trial for treachery. Lanval proclaims his innocence, but since he cannot produce his lady-love to prove it, the king is prepared to announce a verdict of guilty. Suddenly (as if you weren't expecting it), she rides into Carduel on a white horse, and all who see her are dazzled.

She wore a white linen shift that revealed her
   sides, where the lacings were.
Her body was magnificent: slender hips, a neck
   whiter than snow
On a tree-branch, bright eyes, a white face,
   beautiful mouth, finely-shaped nose,
Dark eyebrows and a noble forehead. Her hair
   was curled and blond.
Golden wires do not shine so much as her hair in
   the sunlight. She had
A dark purple cloak wrapped tightly around her,
   and on her wrist
She carried a sparrow hawk. A greyhound
   followed her.

There was not a single person in Carduel—man
   or boy, old or young—
Who failed to watch her, and as she passed they
   all knew there had been
No lying about her beauty. She road on slowly.
   The judges marveled
At the sight of her, all of them warmed with
   delight. Friends of Lanval

Rushed to tell him of the woman's approach.
   May it please God to rescue him!

"Dear fellow," they cried, "a woman approaches!
   She is neither sun-tinged nor dark;
undoubtedly she is the most beautiful woman in
   the world!"

When Lanval heard this, he raised his head.
   Recognizing his lady-love,
He let out a sigh as the blood rose to his face.
   "By my faith,"
He quickly announced, "that is my love! Now
   I don't care if I'm killed;
All I want is her forgiveness. Just in seeing her,
   I am restored!"

The lady entered the palace, and indeed no one
   so beautiful
Had ever been there before. She dismounted
   before King Arthur
And stood there to be seen by all—she even let
   her cloak drop

So they could get a better view. The king, ever
    courteous, rose and
Stepped forward, and everyone in the court
    honored her and
Offered their service. After everyone had had a
    chance to behold
Her loveliness and speak in praise of it, she spoke:

"I have loved one of your knights. You see him
    there before you—
Lanval, the defendant in this trial. I do not want
    him to suffer
For what he said. You should know, king, that
    your queen was in the wrong.
Lanval made no advances upon her. As for the
    boast he made—
If your seeing me acquits him, then let your
    barons set him free."

The king had promised to abide by whatever
    judgment the barons made,

And to the last man they all agreed that Lanval
    had defended himself
Against the charge. They granted him freedom,
    and the lady departed.
The king tried to persuade her to stay, for there
    were servants enough
To offer her hospitality. Outside the palace stood
    a great and dark
Marble stone, used by heavy men when mounting
    to ride from court.
Lanval climbed on this, and when his love rode
    through the gate, he leapt
Onto her horse, directly behind her. He rode with
    her to Avalon,
Which the Bretons assure us is a most lovely
    island. There they rode,
And Lanval was never heard from again.
    My tale is finished.

14.4 Two Fabliaux

Fabliaux were bawdy comic tales told in verse. Enormously popular in their own time, they were largely ignored in the Renaissance and Reformation eras, which found their humor crude and their blunt language distasteful, and eventually were forgotten. Scholars in the nineteenth century, keen to explore their national literary traditions, unearthed them, and since then they have been a favorite object of study by medievalists. Few of them have been published in English translation, however. Below are two of the shorter (and less obscene) fabliaux that poke fun at some of the privileged figures in medieval life and celebrate the cleverness often found among the common people.

THE RING THAT PRODUCED ERECTIONS

I, Haiseau, have one more thing
To tell: a man once owned a magic ring;
Whoever wore it on his finger
Soon had a hard-on that grew ever bigger.

It happened one day as he was going
Across a field where a stream was flowing,
when he saw it he climbed down from his horse
and went to help himself, of course.

He washed his hands and then his face
After first placing the ring in a safe place.
But when he was finished, he rode away
Forgetting that his ring on the grass still lay.

A bishop then came riding by,
And as soon as the river appeared to
    his eye
He dismounted and found the ring.
Because he found it so appealing

He put it on—and it befell
That his private member began to swell.
Since he was more than a little distressed
He got back on his horse and rode away as best

He could, but found that soon, and with
          great vigor,
His penis just kept getting bigger.
Nothing, it seemed, could make it stop:
It stretched and swelled, until, with a POP,

It burst the stitches of his pants
And stood erect. In a kind of trance
Of shame the bishop asked his retinue
If they had any idea what he should do.

His men replied, though, they were stumped;
None knew it was the ring that had pumped
His pecker so. It kept growing until it fell to
          the ground.
The bishop ordered his men to ask around

And find someone who understood
How he could deflate his plank of wood.
The man who had lost the ring soon heard
Of the strange marvel that had occurred.

He rushed over to the bishop's side, then he
Offered to cure him—for a fee.
The suffering bishop promised him twice,
"Anything! Anything! Name your price!"

The man replied, "Then I will ask,
Before I undertake this task,
For all the rings you're wearing, plus a hundred quid."
"Done!" cried the bishop. The man then did

as he promised. And without the ring,
the bishop's boner began shrinking.
It slowly returned to its normal size
Before the bishop gave the man his prize.

An honest deal it was—most highly vaunted—
In which each man got what he most wanted!

THE MAN WHO SAVED ANOTHER
FROM DROWNING

There once was a fisherman, they say,
Who took his boat out one fine day,

And casting his nets he looked around
And saw a man who was about to drown.

The fisherman was strong and in his prime,
And so, without wasting any time,
He threw his hook and line straight to the guy
But in the process he poked out his eye.

He hauled the poor man in, and what's more
He steered his boat back to the shore.
He left his nets in the ocean foam,
So concerned he was to get the man home.

The wound was tended to most carefully,
But the victim responded most unprayerfully.
He thought a long time about his eye—now
          just one—
And felt his rescuer should pay for what he
          had done.

"That villain gouged out my eye!" he thought,
"There's nothing I ever did to him—so ought
I not to take the fellow to court?
A suit for damages! A profitable tort!"

He went to see a magistrate
Who heard his story, then set a date;
Both men appeared, to begin the hearing.
The victim spoke first, his one eye tearing.

"My lord," said he, "I have a right
to sue this man, who out of spite
struck me with a hook and plucked
my eye out of my head. I'm fucked!

I ask only for what's coming to me,
An innocent victim—as you surely can see."
The fisherman responded without delay,
"My lord," cried he, "what can I say?

I did in fact pluck out his eye,
But let me tell you the reason why.
Once you've heard, no doubt you'll consent
To judge that I am innocent.

This fellow was on the verge of dying,
Drowning at sea—and while there's no denying
The fact that my hook was the cause of
          his wound,
Still, I saved his live! Please be attuned

To that simple fact. His case is a fraud.
Grant me justice, for the love of God!"
The men who were deciding the case
Were flummoxed, but then, by God's sure grace

One fellow stood up and began to shout,
"My lords, how can there be any doubt
About what to do? It's clear to me
That the plaintiff should be thrown back
    into the sea!

If he's able to escape by himself
The defendant should have to cough up some pelf!
This is the right choice, it seems to me."
And the other judges were quick to agree.

"Well done," they cried, "This case is through!"
And then they turned as one, and withdrew.

When the one-eyed fellow heard that he
Was going to be thrown back in the sea

To struggle with the waves and chill,
He all of a sudden lost the will
To pursue the suit, and so be caved—
And the crowd then saw how he'd misbehaved.

Through this tale you can see, without doubt,
That you never should help an evil person out.
Whoever befriends a criminal, bear in mind,
Will never receive a reward of any kind.

Charity shown to the wicked, it should be
    averred,
Is instantly forgotten—as though it never occurred.
In fact, they're more willing to repay
Right with wrong, if the chance comes their way.

14.5 *The Arabian Nights*

The vast collection of tales known as *The Arabian Nights* is one of the masterpieces of medieval literature. Its author or compiler is unknown. Like the *Shahnameh* of Hakim Ferdowsi (940–1020), *The Decameron* of Giovanni Boccaccio (1313–1375), and *The Canterbury Tales* of Geoffrey Chaucer (1343–1400), it is a compendium of separate stories linked by a narrative device. In the case of *The Arabian Nights*, a fictional king of the Sasanid dynasty, Shahryar, finding himself cuckolded by his wife, kills her, then proceeds to take a new wife every day, executing each one the following morning, hoping in this way to avoid being embarrassed again. One bride, Shahrazad, avoids death by telling the king, each night after their lovemaking, a story that either concludes with a "cliff-hanging" ending—or with the promise of a follow-up story even more entertaining than the one just finished. Finally, by the compendium's end, Shahryar regrets his "love them and behead them" attitude and lives happily with Shahrazad. The following tale relies for its humor on common prejudices of the era. Shahrazad narrates throughout.

But even this tale, O king, cannot top that of the tailor, the hunchback, the Jew, the magistrate, and the Christian. "Tell that tale!" begged Shahryar.

Well then, I heard once that a long time ago, in ancient China, a tailor lived in a certain city. He was a generous man, who enjoyed his pleasures and pastimes and liked to take his wife with him sometimes for an evening's entertainment. One day, the pair of them went out in the afternoon and came home in the evening, and they came upon a funny-looking boy, a hunchback. . . . The tailor and his wife stopped to look at him, then invited him home to spend the evening with them. The hunchback agreed, and followed. When night fell, the tailor went to the market and bought some cooked fish, bread, lemons, and yogurt, and when he got back home he laid the food out for all of them to enjoy. His wife took a large piece of fish and stuffed it into the hunchback's mouth. "You have to swallow it without chewing!" she said, as she held her hand over his closed mouth. The hunchback did so—but the piece of fish had a bone in it which stuck in the hunchback's throat and killed him. . . .

"What shall we do now?" asked the tailor.

"Get up," said his wife. "We must act right away. Carry him, and follow me. If anyone asks, tell him that this is our son and we are taking him to the doctor." . . .

They arrived at the home of a Jewish doctor and knocked on the door. A black slave girl answered, and when she saw the tailor with a child in his arms she asked his wife, "What's the matter?"

The tailor's wife answered, "We would like the doctor to look at our son here. Here is a coin; give it to your master and tell him to come right away."

The slave girl left. The tailor's wife stepped through the doorway and said to her husband, "Leave the hunchback here, then let's go!" The tailor, agreeing, propped the hunchbacked boy up against the wall, and they departed.

The slave girl went upstairs to the Jew and said, "A man is at the door with a sick child. His wife gave me this coin and asked if you will come downstairs and take care of the boy."

The Jew was thrilled at the sight of money and stood up quickly. He rushed down the stairs in the dark, but when he reached the bottom he stumbled over the corpse. "O Ezra! O Moses! O Holy Ten Commandments! O Aaron and Joshua, the son of Nun!" he cried. "I've tripped over this sick fellow, and now he has fallen down the stairs and died! Whatever shall I do with the corpse?" . . .

[The doctor's wife tells him to leave the body in the courtyard of their neighbor, who is an inspector of the royal kitchens.]

Then the Jew and his wife climbed onto the rooftop, carrying the hunchbacked boy. They lowered him into the courtyard, leaning against the wall. Then they disappeared. The inspector came home just then. . . . "What's this?" he shouted. "Someone is trying to steal from me!" . . . He picked up a hammer, held it high, and smashed it against the dead body's chest. But when he saw that the hunchback was dead, he was filled with sorrow and feared for his life. . . . He picked up the body and carried it to the market square, where he leaned it up against a shop's wall, then disappeared.

A Christian who worked for the king was the next to come by. He was drunk. He had intended to go to the bath-house, but realized that it was nearly time for matins; he staggered down the street as he drew near the corpse. He stopped to piss, and saw something out of the corner of his eye. Now earlier that very night, the drunken Christian's turban had been stolen, and when he saw the hunchbacked boy he thought that his new turban was going to be snatched also, and so he clenched his fist and struck the hunchback on the neck and knocked him down. He shouted for the night watchman, and in his drunkenness he fell upon the hunchback, pummeling him and choking him. . . .

"By God, what a scene this is!" shouted the watchman. "A Christian, killing a Muslim!"

[The chief of police, informed of the situation, was about to execute the Christian for murder when the kitchen inspector showed up and said that he, not the Christian, had killed the hunchback. When the noose was placed around the inspector's neck, the Jew appeared and said that he, not the inspector, was the true guilty party. Then the tailor arrived and confessed. Just when the chief of police was about to hang the tailor, the king's chamberlain arrived. The hunchback, it turns out, had been the king's favorite court jester.]

When the chamberlain arrived, he found the chief of police about to hang the tailor. "Stop!" he shouted. He then had everyone—the police chief, the tailor, the Jew, and Christian, and the kitchen inspector, and the dead hunchbacked boy—brought before the king. The police chief kissed the ground in front of the king and told the whole story of what had happened to all of them. The king was amazed and delighted, and ordered that the entire story be recorded for posterity.

"Has any of you ever heard a more amazing story?" asked the king.

Then the Christian stepped forward, kissed the ground, and said, "O great King! With your permission, I will tell you an even more remarkable tale—one that happened to me personally. This story could make even a stone weep!" . . .

[*And so Shahrazad survived another day.*]

15. DAILY LIFE AT THE MEDIEVAL ZENITH

15.1 William Fitz Stephen, *Daily Life in London*

William Fitz Stephen (d. 1191) was a cleric who served in the retinue of St. Thomas Becket during the eight years of his archiepiscopacy (1162–1170) and afterward wrote a renowned *Life* of the murdered saint. He attached as a curious preface to the *Life* an essay entitled "A Description of the Most Noble City of London." Fitz Stephen shows intimate knowledge of the city, giving us a uniquely valuable guide to its customs.

London, the capital of the kingdom of England, is one of the most noble and renowned cities in the world; its glory extends farther, and its goods and commerce spread wider, than those of any other city in the realm. London lifts high its proud head; it rejoices in its healthy air, its Christian observance, its strong fortifications, the beauty of its location, the prestige of its men, and the modesty of its women. It delights in sports, too, which contribute to the city's production of upright men. Let us examine each of these matters.

The climate of London is mild, and while this fact does soften the character of its inhabitants a bit, it nevertheless does not incline them to sexual indulgence. The climate in fact prevents Londoners from being aggressive and beastly, and makes them instead rather liberal and good-hearted.

The Church of St. Paul holds an episcopal seat. It used to be the metropolitan see, and might be again if enough people return to the island; right now, though, the metropolitan see is at Canterbury, on account of the dignity of the archiepiscopal title of the blessed martyr, St. Thomas, whose body is buried there. Thomas had brought fame to both cities—London, in his rise; Canterbury, in his settling—and both cities can therefore stake a claim to distinction on his account. As for the rites of Christian worship, London and its environs have thirteen large conventual churches and one hundred and twenty-six parish churches.

To the east stands the very large and strong Palatine Castle [the Tower of London], whose keep and walls are set on extremely deep foundations and are cemented with a mortar that is cut with animal blood. There are two other castles to the west, both strongly fortified, and from them stretches out a high, massive wall with seven double gates and towers, all placed at regular intervals along the northern line. At one time London also had a turreted wall along the southern line, but over time the broad Thames river, choking with fish, has lapped against it, with the rise and ebb of the tide, until the wall was weakened and ultimately brought down. To the west, upstream, stand the royal palace [Westminster] high above the river. Few buildings can match it in its ramparts and bulwarks. It stands about two miles from London proper, but is connected to it by a heavily settled area. . . .

The three main churches—of St. Paul, Holy Trinity, and St. Martin—have schools attached to them that are famous for their special privileges and ancient reputation, but many other schools also exist in the city, thanks to the patronage of some great nobles or the gathering of teachers with high standing as philosophers. These teachers meet with their students, on feast days, in the church of whichever saint is being celebrated that day. Some of the teachers stage disputations, while others instruct [their students] by demonstrations, dialectics, and lectures. . . . Students from different schools compete with one another at composing verses and arguing over the principles of Latin grammar and the sequence of tenses. . . .

In various parts of the city there are open fields where one finds all the signs of animal husbandry: tools, large swine, milk-cows, immense oxen, woolly sheep, draught horses, mares, and young colts darting about. . . .

No people I can think of can compare with Londoners in their faith, honoring God's commands, observing feast-days, celebrating weddings and marriages, and staging feasts for guests. They put the same care into funerals and the burial of the dead, too. The only blights on Londoners' lives, really, are the frequent fires that break out, and the foolish recklessness with which many of them drink. . . .

Every morning one sees tradesmen, merchants, and laborers in their places, setting to their tasks. Along the riverbank, amid wineshops and barges, are public houses where one finds all sorts of food available: roasts, fried and boiled dishes, a variety of fish, fine cookery for the affluent (venison and fowl, for example) and offal for the poor. . . .

In the settled area just outside one of the gates there lies "Smithfield"—a smooth field, in fact as well as in name. Here, on every sixth day of the week (unless it be a major feast day, for which solemn rites are prescribed), is a well-attended fair at which horses are sold. Every earl, baron, and knight in the city seems to come, as do countless commoners, some to purchase, but most merely to watch. . . . In another part of the field are rustic wares: farming tools, swine, milk-cows, and so on. . . .

Instead of stage-plays and theatrical shows, London abounds in miracle-plays and mystery-plays, which tell of the miraculous things done by the Holy Confessors or of the sufferings of the great martyrs. On the day they call "Carnival," schoolboys bring fighting cocks to their schoolmasters, and they devote the whole morning to cock fighting. (The schools proclaim a holiday

from teaching on this day, so everyone can enjoy the fun. Remember, that we were all once boys ourselves.) After the mid-day meal all the youths rush to the field to play a popular game of ball. . . .

In the spring, after Easter, they play a game of mock naval battle. First, a shield is mounted onto a stout pole in the middle of the river, then a river-craft with many oarsmen rushes at it. A young boy stands at the prow, holding a lance with which he is to strike the shield. If he breaks his lance on the shield without losing his balance, he has succeeded. But if he strikes it without breaking his lance, he is then thrown into the river and his boatsmen rush right past him. Two rescue vessels, though, are moored on each side of the river, to fish out the boy caught in the stream. . . .

In summer, boys celebrate feast days with contests in leaping, archery, wrestling, shot-putting, and javelin-throwing, as well as with fighting with swords and bucklers. . . .

In winter, feast days are celebrated with animal contests: wild boars and hogs (soon to become bacon!) are set upon one another with their lightning-fast tusks; fat bulls butt one another with their horns; and massive bears fight to the death against packs of hounds. When the great marsh along the north side of the city freezes over, crowds of boys and girls rush onto the ice to play. Some run full-speed over the ice, then glide along with their legs spread wide. Others sit on a large chunk of ice shaped rather like a millstone and are dragged along by a number of others who run ahead, hands together, pulling on a rope. Sometimes, because of their speed, they slip—and everyone falls on their faces. Still others fashion shoes with the shinbones of animals fixed underneath them, and glide across the ice this way; it requires a great deal of skill. . . .

15.2 Giovanni Villani, *Life in Florence*

After participating in the great Jubilee of 1300 in Rome, Giovanni Villani (1276–1348), a Florentine banker, sometime soldier, and prominent political figure, decided to compose a history of his beloved hometown. His *New Chronicle*, as he entitled it, becomes more detailed and useful, the closer it comes to Villani's own lifetime. Most of his history exudes confidence and optimism, as he traces

Florence's rise under Rome, its rejuvenation in the age of Charlemagne, and its economic and culture glory in the thirteenth and early fourteenth centuries. But with the crises of the fourteenth century, a tone of gloom and despair becomes dominant. At the end, when he is describing the horrors of the Black Death, Villani has become convinced that the end of the world is at hand. He himself died of the plague; his *New Chronicle* was then carried on by his brother and nephew. Here he describes the city at its medieval zenith.

By diligent effort, I have learned that in Florence at that time [1336] there were roughly 25,000 citizens of fighting age, that is from 15 to 70, and approximately 1500 of these were nobles and our urban elites, all of whom posted bonds with the city. Around 75 knights-at-arms were enrolled—and I have learned that earlier, before our popular regime came into power, the number of such knights was at least 250. It is clear, therefore, that our magnates, since losing control of the city, have taken up knighthood in far lesser numbers.

Judging from the records we have of bread-consumption (a good indicator to use), Florence then had some 90,000 mouths to feed, including men, women, and children. In addition to these, it is estimated that the city had a more or less continuous population of 1500 foreign merchants, pilgrims, and soldiers present at any one time. These figures do not include the many monks, friars, and nuns who resided here, and whom I will discuss presently. Moreover, the rural district outside of Florence proper holds up to 80,000 people. I have learned from the priests in charge of baptizing the babies born in the outer district that they baptize between 5500 and 6000 babies a year, with boys outnumbering girls by about 500 per year. (Each priest sets aside a black bean for every boy, and a white bean for each girl, which is how we know the numbers. The beans are kept at the church at San Giovanni.) Each year, between 8000 and 10,000 children study how to read and write. Roughly 1000 to 1200 boys learn arithmetic and the use of the abacus, spread over six schools; and in four other schools, large ones, 550 to 600 boys study Latin and logic.

Of churches, the whole of Florence—that is, the city and its environs—has 110 churches, including [monastic] abbeys and mendicant houses. These are scattered through 57 parishes. Five abbeys are large enough to have two priors and upwards to 80 monks. There are 24 convents in all, housing approximately 500 nuns; and 10 mendicant houses. Florence also has 30 hospitals with more than 1000 beds in all, which serve the poor and the sick, and between 250 and 300 ordained chaplains.

Weavers and drapers number 200 or more, and together they produce 70,000 to 80,000 [bolts of cloth] per year, valued at close to 1,200,000 gold florins. About one-third of this revenue remains in Florence, representing the pay for labor (not counting the profits the cloth merchants made from that labor), and this revenue supports some 30,000 workers. I have determined, with some effort, that thirty years ago there were 300 weavers and drapers, and they produced more than 100,000 [bolts of cloth] annually; but the cloths they produced were less refined than those of today, and had only half the value. English wool was not then generally imported [into Italy], so our craftsmen did not know how to work with it as well as they do today. . . .

The number of money-changing counters now approaches eighty. The amount of coin minted each year is between 350,000 and 400,000 gold florins. . . . The number of judges is 80; of notaries, more than 600. There are just over 60 pharmacists, physicians, and surgeons, and over 100 pharmacies. General merchants and grocers seem innumerable. It is impossible even to estimate the number of shops that produce shoes, boots, and slippers; just the number of them who engaged in trade outside of Florence was over 300. Comparable numbers of stonemasons and skilled carpenters do the same.

[In 1336] there were 146 furnaces in the city. By some hard calculation, using data from the taxes levied on milling and the use of the furnaces, I have determined that the city needed [40 bushels] of grain every day, just for local consumption; one can therefore estimate what was needed every year. . . . I have learned that in the year 1280, when the city was thriving, it needed as much as 230 bushels every week. . . . It also consumed about 400 cows and calves, 60,000 sheep, 20,000 goats, and 30,000 pigs per year. In the month of July alone, 4000 cartloads of melons entered the city just through the gate of San Frediano. . . .

At that time a number of urban magistracies were held by foreign professionals, each of whom held court and had authority to inflict torture: the podestà, the captain, the "defender of the public and the guilds," the "executor of the ordinances of justice," the captain of the guard (also known as the "defender of the people," this figure had greater authority than all the others). The following magistrates could also impose corporal punishment: the judge of audits and appeals, the tax judge, the supervisor of women's dress, the commercial overseer, the magistrate of the wool merchants' guild, the ecclesiastical officials, the court of the Bishop of Florence, the court of the Bishop of Fiesole, and the inquisitor of heretical depravity. . . .

The city of Florence was well-planned and is filled with many beautiful houses. New construction is constantly going on, and existing buildings are constantly undergoing improvement to become more comfortable and elegant. Inspirations for these improvements are actively sought outside the city. There are cathedral churches, friaries, and magnificent abbeys. Moreover, there is hardly a single Florentine, commoner or noble, who has not built (or who has not dreamed of building) a great country home on a superb estate, richly appointed and beautifully designed, much lovelier than anything in the city. In this, all Florentines are sinners given to extreme expenditure.

15.3 Benjamin of Tudela, *Itinerary*

Little is known of Benjamin's life apart from what he tells us in his book *Massa'ot shel R. Binyamin* (*The Travels of Rabbi Benjamin*), which he published in 1173 after eight years of traveling through Europe, North Africa, and much of Asia. His account of China predates that of Marco Polo by a century. He recounts visits to some 300 cities and records details about the Jewish communities he encountered as well as details about local industries, markets, and schools. Throughout he faithfully records the number of Jewish families present (he identifies them patriarchically: thus a reference to "twenty Jews" means 20 Jewish households) and the conditions in which they live. Translated below is the section describing his travels through Italy.[1]

The trip from Marseilles to Genoa, another coastal city, takes four days. Only two Jews live in Genoa—R. Samuel b. Salim and his brother. Both are good men who come originally from Ceuta. Genoa is an enclosed, fortified city whose citizens, rather than serving a king, elect their own magistrates. Every townsman has a tower attached to his home, and in times of civil unrest they take to these towers and shoot at one another from their heights. The Genoese dominate the local seas in ships called galleys, which they use to attack everyone everywhere, as far away as Sicily and Greece, and bring their spoil back to the city. With the people of Pisa, who are only two days' travel [by foot] down the coastline, they are especially forever in conflict.

---

[1]   Since I do not know Hebrew, I translate here the Latin version published in Holland in the seventeenth century.

Pisa is a large city of roughly ten thousand homes, each with its tower in case of trouble. The men are strong, and like the Genoese they do not obey any king but elect their own officials. About twenty Jews live in Pisa, their congregation being led by R. Moses, R. Chaim, and R. Joseph. Pisa is not walled. Resting some six miles from the coast, it lays along a river that connects it to the sea—easy travel for most shipping.

Roughly twelve miles from Pisa lies the city of Lucca, along the border of the region of Lombardy. Lucca has forty Jews in residence—a large community headed by R. David, R. Samuel, and R. Jacob.

It takes six days to travel from Lucca to the great metropolis of Rome, the capital of all of Christendom. Some two hundred Jews live here, many of whom hold positions of high honor in society and pay no tribute; some, in fact, are officials in service to Pope Alexander [III, r. 1159–1181], who is the leader of the Christians. A number of great scholars reside here, especially the chief rabbi, R. Daniel, and R. Jehiel, who works in the papal court. Jehiel is an exceptionally good-looking man, young, intelligent, and wise beyond his years; not only does he have admission to the papal palace, but he is in fact the steward of the pope's household and possessions. His grandfather was R. Nathan, who wrote the *Aruk* [NB. a celebrated lexicographical work, tracing the etymologies of words in biblical Hebrew] and various commentaries. Other local scholars include R. Joab (the son of the former chief rabbi R. Solomon), R. Menachem, who heads the local yeshiva, R. Jehiel (who lives in the district called Trastevere), and R. Benjamin, the son of R. Sabbetai of blessed memory. The Tiber River divides Rome into two sections. One section contains the great church called St. Peter's and the palace that used to belong to Julius Caesar. Many beautiful and unique buildings decorate the city. Taking together both the inhabited and the empty quarters of the city, Rome has a circumference of roughly twenty-four miles, and within these limits there are no fewer than eighty palaces, each held by the line of eighty kings called "emperors" that stretches from King Tarquin through Tiberius and Nero (who ruled Rome at the time of Jesus of Nazareth) and down to the time of Pepin, the father of Charlemagne, who freed the Jews of northern Spain from Muslim control.

Just outside Rome is another palace that is said to have belonged to the ruler Titus, whom the consuls and senators—all three hundred of them—reviled because he needed three full years to retake Jerusalem, when they had instructed him to do so in only two. The massive palace of Vespasian is also in Rome, and so is the Colosseum. The Colosseum is a vast structure divided into 365 sections, one for each day of the solar year. Its circumference, like that of Vespasian's palace, is fully three miles. In ancient times both were the sites of many battles, and the bones of as many as one hundred thousand people lay beneath them. Rulers ordered that scenes of some of these battles be sculpted on opposing marble walls of these structures, depicting horses and warriors amid scenes of violence, to show the world their achievements.

Underground caves abound in Rome, and in them one can see the catacomb of King Tarmal Galsin and his queen, depicted seated on thrones and surrounded by a royal retinue of over a hundred. All the bodies in these catacombs have been embalmed and preserved right down to today. The Lateran Church of St. John has two bronze columns in it that were taken from the Temple [in Jerusalem]; they were fashioned in the time of King Solomon—which one knows because they bear the inscription "Solomon, the son of David." The Jews in the city inform me that on the 9th of Ab, every year, one can see these columns emitting a water-like fluid. There is another cave in which [the emperor] Titus, Vespasian's son, stashed the sacred vessels he took from the Temple in Jerusalem. Another cave, on a hillside along the Tiber, contains the graves of ten [Jewish] martyrs. In front of the Lateran Church of St. John there are two marble statues—one depicting Samson with a spear in his hand, another representing Absalom, the son of David; a third statue bears a likeness of [the emperor] Constantine the Great, who named the city of Constantinople after himself. Constantine's statue, though, is cast in bronze, with the horse he is riding overlaid in gold. Countless other sights are there in Rome, more than can be numbered.

Four days' journey from Rome lay the city of Capua, a large settlement first established by King Capys. Capua is a lovely place, although its water is foul and the surrounding countryside vulnerable to fevers.

Some three hundred Jews live there, and there are quite a few noteworthy scholars among them: R. Conso, his brother R. Israel, R. Zaken, and the late chief rabbi R. David. The district surrounding the city is called Principato.

From Capua one moves on to Pozzuoli, which is near to Sorrento, the great city built by Zur, the son of Habadezer, when he fled in fear from King David. The sea has risen since then, and now two whole sides of the original site are under water; one can still see, though, the markets and towers built in the city center. A natural spring rises from the ground here that contains the fluid called petroleum. The local people skim this oil from the water's surface and use it in several medicines. There are also about twenty natural hot springs, located near the shore. People with all sorts of ailments bathe in these waters, seeking cures. In summer it seems as those every afflicted person in Lombardy is present, to visit the hot springs.

From Pozzuoli and Sorrento a road stretches some fifteen miles underneath the mountains; this was the handiwork of King Romulus, the founder of Rome, who built it out of fear of King David and his general Joab. He also constructed two networks of fortifications, one along and within the mountains, the other along the road beneath them. These fortifications too reach as far as the city of Naples.

Naples is a particularly well-fortified city. A coastal town, it was founded by the Greeks. Five hundred Jews live here, among them are R. Hezekiah, R. Shalom, R. Elijah ha-Kohen, and R. Isaac b. Har Napus, the chief rabbi of blessed memory.

The next city down the coast is Salerno, where the Christians have a school of medicine. Some six hundred Jews live there, including several noteworthy scholars: R. Judah, the son of R. Isaac (himself the son of R. Melchizidek, the great rabbi who came there from the city of Siponto), R. Solomon, R. Elijah the Greek, R. Abraham of Narbonne, and R. Hamon. A stout wall protects Salerno on the landed side, with a sturdy castle atop the hillside just behind; the other side of

the city faces the sea. Only a half-day's journey away is the town of Amalfi, where twenty Jews live—among these are R. Hananel (a physician), R. Elisha, and a secular prince named Abu al-Gir. The Amalfitans are all merchants. No one there works the land, for the city is lodged on craggy hills and mountains. Nevertheless, if one has money one can buy anything there: fruits of every sort, wines and olive oil, and everything found in any garden or farm field. Best of all, they are protected against warfare, given their unique position.

From Amalfi it is a day's journey to Benevento, a city recessed from the coast, in the mountains. Two hundred Jews live in Benevento, and their leaders are R. Kalonymos, R. Zarach, and R. Abraham. Two days' journey further on is Melfi, in the district of Apulia, where two hundred Jews live under the guidance of R. Achimaaz, R. Nathan, and R. Isaac. Another day's trip and one reaches Ascoli, a town with about forty Jews, led by R. Consoli, his son-in-law R. Zemach, and R. Joseph. Two days of further travel brings one to Trani, another coastal town. Trani is a convenient gathering point for pilgrims on the route to Jerusalem. It is a large, lovely city, home to two hundred Jews under the care of R. Nathan the Expounder and R. Jacob.

One further day-trip brings one to Colo di Bari, which was a great city until it was destroyed by King William of Sicily. Now no one lives there, neither Jew nor Gentile, and all is in ruins.

From Colo di Bari it is a day and a half to Taranto, which is part of the duchy of Calabria. All the inhabitants of Taranto are Greek. It is a large place with three hundred Jews in residence. Among the scholars there are R. Meir, R. Nathan, and R. Israel. From Taranto it is another day's trip to Brindisi, another coastal town. Only about ten Jews live there, all of them dyers. Otranto lies two days' journey further on; it faces the Greek sea. Here are about five hundred Jews, led by R. Menachem, R. Caleb, R. Meir, and R. Mali. From Otranto it takes another two days, by sail this time, to reach the island of Corfu, where only a single Jew lives—R. Joseph. This marks the limit of the kingdom of Sicily.

15.4   Prominent Rabbis of the Middle Ages

Medievalists are familiar with the great Churchmen of the Middle Ages, but too few can name or are even aware of the great rabbis. Here is a selective list. Most of the following distinguished themselves as biblical and/or Talmudic scholars, and most were prominent in other fields as well (most frequently in medicine) since their rabbinical work was performed gratis—the teaching of Torah being considered an honor for which no compensation was necessary.

Name	Dates	City	Most Notable Work
Amram Gaon	d. 875	Sura (Babylon)	*Siddur Rab Amram* (prayerbook)
Saadia Gaon	882–942	Fayum (Egypt)	*Emunoth ve-Deoth* (Beliefs and Opinions)
Dunash ben Labrat	920–990	Fez (Morocco)	poet and grammarian
Rabbeinu Gershom	960–1040	Metz; Mainz	Tal.
Hananel ben Hushiel	990–1050	Tunis	*Sefer ha-Miktzo'ot* (Book of Duties)
Nissim ben Jabob	990–1062	Kairouam (Tunisia)	*Sefer Mafteach* (Key to the Talmud)
Isaac Alfasi	1013–1103	Fez (Morocco)	*Sefer ha-Halakhot* (Book of Laws)
Bahya ibn Paquda	d. 1050	Zaragoza	*Hovot ha-Levavot* (Duties of the Heart)
Rashi	1040–1105	Troyes	Tor./Tal.
Joseph ibn Migash	1077–1141	Seville; Lucena	Tal.
Abraham ibn Ezra	1089–1164	Tudela; Cordoba	Tor./Tal.
Abraham ben Isaac	1110–1179	Narbonne	Tor./Tal.
Abraham ibn Daud	1110–1180	Cordoba; Toledo	*Sefer ha-Kabbalah* (Book of Tradition)
Zerachiah ha-Levi	1125–1186	Girona	*Sefer ha-Maor* (Book of Light)
Abraham ben David	1125–1198	Vauvert; Nîmes	*Sefer Ba'alei ha-Nefesh* (Book of the Conscientious)
Maimonides	1135–1204	Cordoba, Fustat (Egypt)	*Mishneh Torah*
Samuel ben Judah	1140–1217	Regensburg	*Sefer Hasidim* (Book of the Pious)
Samuel Ibn Tibbon	1150–1230	Marseilles	translator from Arabic to Hebrew
David Kimhi	1160–1235	Narbonne	grammarian
Meir Abulafia	1170–1244	Burgos	Tal.
Eleazar Rokeach	1176–1238	Worms	*Sefer ha-Rokeach* (Book of the Perfumer)
Isaiah di Trani	1180–1250	Trani; Venice	Tor./Tal.
Nahmanides	1194–1270	Girona	Tor./Tal.
Jacob of London	fl. 1199–1217	London	first chief rabbi of England
Isaac ben Moses	1200–1270	Vienna	Tal.
Meir ben Baruch	1215–1293	Rothenburg	
Josce of London	fl. 1217–1237	London	chief rabbi of England
Aaron of York	fl. 1237	York	chief rabbi of England
Hillel ben Samuel	1220–1295	Barcelona; Rome	Tor./Tal.

Name	Dates	City	Most Notable Work
Aharon ha-Levi	1235–1290	Girona	Tor./Tal.
Solomon ben Aderet	1235–1310	Barcelona	Tor./Tal.
Menachem Meiri	1249–1310	Perpignan	*Beit ha-Bechirah* (The Chosen House)
Mordechai ben Hillel	1250–1298	Nuremburg	Tal.
Menahem Recanati	1250–1310	Bologna	Tor./Tal.
Yom Tov Asevilli	1250–1330	Seville; Zaragoza	Tor./Tal.
Asher ben Jehiel	1259–1327	Worms; Toledo	Tor./Tal.
Jacob ben Asher	1269–1343	Cologne; Toledo	Tal.
Judah ben Asher	1270–1349	Cologne; Toledo	Tal.
Elias of London	fl. 1237–1257	London	chief rabbi of England
Gersonides	1288–1344	Bagnols	*Sefer Milhamot ha-Shem* (Book of the Wars of the Lord)
Nissim of Gerona	1320–1376	Girona	
Isaac ben Sheshet	1326–1408	Barcelona	Tal.
Hasdai Crescas	1340–1411	Barcelona	*Or Adonai* (Light of the Lord)
Israel Isserlein	1390–1460	Maribor; Vienna	Tal.
Israel Bruna	1400–1480	Brno; Ratisbon	Tor./Tal.
Joseph Colon Trabutto	1420–1480	Chambéry	Tor./Tal.
Don Isaac Abravanel	1437–1508	Lisbon; Toledo	
Obadiah ben Abraham	1445–1515	Bertinoro	Tor./Tal.

City = Place of birth, or place associated with.
Tor. = Torah commentary.
Tal. = Talmud commentary.

16. CHANGES IN RELIGIOUS LIFE

16.1 Pope Gregory IX, *Canonization of St. Francis*

Pope Innocent III recognized the two most significant mendicant orders of the Middle Ages, the Franciscans (Order of Friars Minor, or O.F.M.) and the Dominicans (Order of Preachers, or O.P.). The founders of those orders, St. Francis and St. Dominic, were both canonized by Pope Gregory IX. Below is the bull *Mira circa nos*, issued on July 16, 1228, which formally canonized St. Francis of Assisi (1182–1226).

[1] Behold how wonderfully merciful God is to us! How precious is the grace of His love—a love that offered His own Son as a sacrifice to redeem slaves! God has neither withheld the gift of His mercy nor ever failed in the constant protection of the vineyard He planted with His own hand. And now, at the eleventh hour, He has provided workers armed with hoes and plowshares to cultivate the vineyard, uprooting thorns and thistles as they go—just like [the Biblical figure] Samgar, when he killed six hundred Philistines [Judges 3.31]. This vineyard, once pruned of its overgrown branches and stripped of its irksome nettles, will assuredly produce luscious and ripe fruit that will ferment in the wine cellar of eternity, after being purified in the wine-press of fortitude. The wall protecting this vineyard had been under attack by the blazing fire of wickedness; human hearts had grown cold and like the Philistines had succumbed to the poison of worldly pleasures.

[2] But bear in mind that when the Lord decided to destroy the earth by a flood, He saved the only just man, by means of a humble bit of wood [Wisdom 10.4]; in the same way, He stopped the sword of the ungodly from falling upon the necks of the just [Psalms 124.3]. Now, at this eleventh hour, He has brought forth Blessed Francis, His servant and a man after His own heart [1 Samuel 13.14]. Francis was a beacon sent [to us] in a fateful hour, directed by God into His vineyard to uproot the thorns and thistles in it. The Lord set him as a beacon against the attack of the Philistines and by him He illuminated His land; and like an urging sentry, Francis called us to be reconciled to God.

[3] Francis rose without hesitation the moment he heard the voice of his Divine Friend in his soul, and with God's grace giving him the strength of a new Samson, he shattered the fetters of this vain world. Spurred on by the zeal of the Holy Spirit, he seized the jawbone of an ass and subdued not a thousand but many thousands of Philistines [Judges 15.15–16] with the simple purity of his preaching; his words were direct and unadorned—he eschewed eloquent wisdom [1 Corinthians 1.17]—and were made powerful by the grace of God, Who always chooses the weak to prevail over the mighty [1 Corinthians 1.17]. He accomplished all he did with the help of the Lord, Who merely touches mountains and they smoke [Psalms 103.32]. He brought to renewed spiritual life countless people who had become slaves to the pleasures of the flesh. For all of these fallen, downtrodden, and thirsty individuals, whose worst and most sinful qualities died away, freeing them to live not for themselves but for God, Francis was a flowing source of pure water—refreshing them, cleansing them, making them fruitful. But this rushing river—reaching unto eternal life [John 7.38]—could not be purchased with silver; it came at no cost [Isaiah 55.1]; its streams spread far and wide, watering the vineyard whose branches reached to the sea and whose boughs extended to the river [Psalms 79.12].

[4] Like our patriarch Abraham, Francis bid farewell to his country, his countrymen, and even his own father's house, to go to a land that the Lord showed him in spirit [Genesis 12]. He cast aside every obstacle until he reached the goal to which his heavenly call directed him [Philemon 3.14]. Following the path of Him Who, though rich, became poor for our sake [2 Corinthians 8.9], he cast off the burden of material wealth in order to pass more easily through the narrow gate [Matthew 7.13]; he gave his riches to the poor, so that the Lord's justice might endure forever [Psalms 111.9].

Like Abraham, Francis approached the land he had seen in spirit and offered his own flesh as a sacrifice to the Lord on the mountain indicated to him [Genesis 22.2], the mountain that is the excellence of faith. He sacrificed his flesh, which had previously troubled and confounded him, just as Jephthe had done with his own daughter [Judges 11.34], igniting it with the fire of love, punishing it with hunger, thirst, cold, nakedness, and countless fasts and vigils. And after he had crucified it, purging it of vice and sinful desire [Galatians 5.24], he could say along with the Apostle: "I live, but it is Christ, not I, who lives in me" [Galatians 2.20]. For it is true that he no longer lived for himself, but for Christ, Who died for our sins and rose from death to justify our lives [Romans 4.25], that we might no longer be slaves to sin [Romans 6.6].

Purged of his vices, he rose, like Jacob, upon hearing the Lord's call [Genesis 35.1–11], renounced marriage, his farm, and his cattle—anything that might be a distraction to one called to the great feast [Luke 14.15–20]—and did battle with the world, the flesh, and all the spiritual forces of wickedness. With the help of the sevenfold grace of the Holy Spirit and the eight Beatitudes of the gospel, he traveled to God's house at Bethel—a path that marked out the fifteen virtues represented mystically in the Psalter. Truly, he made of his heart an altar for the Lord and offered upon it the incense of devout prayers, prayers that were lifted to the Lord in the hands of the angels, whose company he would soon join.

[5] But he desired not to be the only person to enjoy the blessings of the mountain [of faith], not to be alone, as it were, to know the embrace of Rachel (that is, a life of beautiful but fruitless contemplation), and so he descended to the forbidden house of Leah. From there he led into the desert a whole flock fertile with twins [Canticles 4.2] in search of life-giving pastures [Genesis 29]. There, where the manna of divine sweetness restores all who have been cast off by the busy world, he would sit with the princes of his people and receive the crown of justice. Having sown his seed in tears, he would return with his arms filled with sheaves to bring into the storehouse of eternity [Psalms 125.5–6]. He never sought his own interests, only Christ's, Whom he served energetically like the proverbial bee. Like the morning star on a cloud-filled dawn, or like a full moon in a pitch-black night, he held in his hands a lamp, to guide the humble by the example of his marvelous deeds, and a trumpet, with which he warned the proud, with loud and stern signals, to abandon their wickedness.

Together with the aid of Him Who encompassed the whole world with His authority even while living in the cloister of the Virgin's womb, the strength of Francis' charity gave him the courage to seize the camp of the Midianites [Judges 7.16–22]—that is, those people who regard with contempt the teachings of the Church; and he stripped away the weapons which the well-armed man trusted to keep guard over his house, parceling out the spoils [Luke 11.21–22], and he led Captivity Itself into submission to Christ Jesus [Ephesians 4.8].

[6] Having defeated the threefold earthly enemy, he then stormed the kingdom of heaven and seized it by force [Matthew 11.12]. He won many great battles in the course of his victory of the world, until, in the end, he who was knowingly unschooled and wisely foolish was able to return to the Lord and take a place of honor above many others who were more learned.

[7] It is clear that Francis' life was so holy, passionate, and life-affirming as to earn him a place in the Church Triumphant. But since the Church Militant, which can see only external appearances, does not presume to judge on its own authority those not sharing its essence, it therefore proposes for veneration as saints only those whose earthly lives abundantly merited such recognition—for remember: an angel of Satan may sometimes transform himself into an angel

of light [2 Corinthians 11.14]. The All Powerful and Merciful Lord generously provided that Francis, the servant of Christ, might come to the earth and serve Him worthily and duly. Not wanting so great a light to remain hidden under a bushel, but instead wanting to place it upon a lampstand for the consolation of those dwelling in the house of light [Matthew 5.15], God made clear through an abundance of miracles that Francis' life was acceptable to God, and that his memory should be forever honored by the Church Militant.

[8] Therefore, since the glorious events of his devout life are so well known to those of us who enjoyed his familiarity even while in positions of less honor, and since we are assured by the testimony of many witnesses to his magnificent miracles, we and the entire flock of the faithful, entrusted to us by God, have every confidence in the aid of his intercession, and we delight in having a patron in heaven whose friendship we enjoyed here on earth. Having consulted with our brothers, and with their approval, we have therefore decreed that Francis' name be inscribed in the catalog of saints worthy of veneration.

[9] We decree that his birth shall be celebrated, duly and solemnly, by the universal Church on the fourth of October—that being the day on which, freed from the prison of human flesh, he entered the kingdom of heaven.

[10] We beg, admonish, and urge all of you, in the name of the Lord, and we do hereby command you by this Apostolic Letter, that on the day appointed to honor his memory you dedicate yourselves zealously to divine praises and implore Francis' patronage, so that through his intercession and merits you may be found worthy of joining his company, with the help of Him Who is blessed forever. Amen.

Given at Perugia, on the fourteenth kalends of August, in the second year of our pontificate.

16.2   Pope Gregory IX, *Canonization of St. Dominic*

On July 13, 1234, Gregory IX formally canonized St. Dominic (1170–1221), almost exactly six years after he had canonized St. Francis.

[1] Our Lord Jesus Christ—the Font of Wisdom, the Word of the Father [Ecclesiastes 1.5]—Whose nature is goodness and Whose work is mercy, redeems and restores those whom He created. He does not abandon the vine that he brought out of Egypt [Psalms 79.9], nor shall do even until the end of the world [Matthew 28.20]. In His wisdom He produces new signs and portents for confused minds and works miracles against the diffidence of the unbelievers. Thus at the very beginning of the newborn Church—that is, upon the death of Moses (meaning the end of the Old Law)—He was prepared to mount the four-horse chariot of the Gospels (those true fonts of salvation) and tramp under foot the presumption of Jericho (that is, the vainglory of the world), when, to the amazement of the people, He accomplished this goal with the strength of His preaching. He took hold of the ark of the sacred word, which He held tight in His hands until He reduced the Jew to powerlessness [Psalms 57.8]. Then, renewing to us the oaths He had made to our forefathers, He laid out a path in the sea for His horses and portended the salvation of all nations with Raab's scarlet cord [Joshua 2.18–21].

[2] In the first of the four chariots that emerged, according to the prophet Zacharias, from between two mountains of brass, the Lord harnessed red horses—that is, the princes and powerful men of the earth. These men, adhering obediently to the faith of the God of Abraham, the father of all believers, followed their leader's example: in order to strengthen the bonds between them, they dyed their clothes in Bosra [Isaiah 63.1] (signaling the anguish of tribulation)

and reddened the insignia of their alliance. They did not fear the swords of this world, but with their eyes set upon the joy of future glory they became martyrs—that is, witnesses; and by their confessions of faith they inscribed the Book of the new land, just as by the public witnessing of their miracles they expedited the work on which they were so intent. With the blood of thinking men, not of brute animals, they dyed the Book and the Tabernacle created by God, together with the vessels of the Gospel's ministry. They built up the Church by casting wide over the vast sea the net of preaching, thus greatly increasing in number the faithful from all nations under heaven.

[3] But presumption quickly took hold of the multitude, and malice followed upon freedom, and so the Lord sent forth the second chariot under the color befitting those who repent and weep [Zachariah 6.12]. In this chariot rode a whole company of soldiers into the desert of the cloister, guided by the Holy Spirit under the leadership of a new Israel—namely, the holy St. Benedict. These sons of the prophets, as though they were being led by a new Elisha, re-created the vision of a blessed community of shared life that had been lost among the vast crowds, and in so doing they stitched back together the torn net of human unity. Their pious works penetrated northward—whence every evil arises [Jeremiah 1.14]—and inspired the One Who refuses to reside in a sinful body [Wisdom 1.4] to dwell in those who have entered the storehouses of the snow [Job 38.22] and have contrite hearts.

[4] Our Lord next wanted to refresh His weary army and replace its sorrows with joys, and so He harnessed to the third chariot a team of white horses—that is, the brethren of the Order of Citeaux, a tonsured flock with a rich store of charity, whom He brought forth from the bathing pool of penitence along with St. Bernard. Bernard, the ram of this flock, was clothed from on high with the power of the Holy Spirit. He led the brethren into the abundant grain fields in the valleys below, and those brothers, having been led to freedom by him, were able to call out powerfully to the Lord, sing hymns of praise, and establish camps for the Lord of hosts upon the sea [Genesis 32.2].

With these three armies the new Israel was able to match, man for man, the troops arrayed by the Philistines [1 Kings 13.17].

[5] At the eleventh hour, however, as day gave way to night and people's loving kindness grew cold because the abundance of their sins; as the sunbeams of justice turned toward the west; and when the thorns and nettles of vice invaded the vineyard that He had planted with His own right hand—and foxes too—spoiling the land and turning the vines bitter and foul (even though the father sometimes sent workmen into the field at a wage of a denarius apiece [Matthew 20.2]), He organized a new and more mobile force against the hostile crowd.

And thus have we seen, following upon the first three symbolic chariots, the appearance of a fourth—the legions of the Friars Preachers and the Friars Minor—pulled by grizzled and mighty horses, the generals He selected to lead them into battle. The Lord stirred the spirit of St. Dominic and saddled him with great strength of faith and passion for preaching, as though fitting out the horse of His glory and garlanding its neck with mane [Job 39.19]

[6] Dominic possessed from earliest childhood the heart of a mature man and subsequently chose a life of the mortification of the flesh, the better to seek the Author of Life. Given to the Lord as a Nazaraean and consecrated under the Rule of the Blessed Augustine, he took the prophet Samuel as his model in dedicated service to the sanctuary, and followed the path of Daniel in the castigation of earthly desires. A fearless athlete, he painstakingly followed the paths of justice and of the saints, and never for a moment left the tabernacle of the Lord by abandoning his role as teacher and minister in the Church Militant. Always subjecting his flesh to his soul and his passion to his reason, he became one in spirit with the Lord and turned all his attention constantly to seeking out God even in the recesses of his mind. Yet he never lost his love for his neighbors and always delighted in their company. When he vanquished the pleasures of the flesh and warmed with light the stone-cold minds of the impious, the entire sect of the heretics quaked and the whole Church of the faithful rejoiced.

[7] Grace increased with age, and buoyed with the ineffable joy drawn from his intense love for others, Dominic dedicated himself to spreading God's word in a new way by becoming, through Christ's Gospel, the father of many [spiritual] children by converting a

vast and disorderly multitude of souls who now understand the obligations of their Christian status. How well he deserves to attain here on earth the glory and renown of the great patriarchs of our past! As pastor and illustrious leader of the people of God, he founded the new Order of Preachers, a holy labor that he further adorned by his exemplary life and his unceasing support for it with numerous genuine miracles. Among the holy acts and proofs of virtue he showed in his lifetime: he cured myriad infirmities, made the mute to speak, the blind to see, the deaf to hear. He gave the power of movement to paralytics and restored to health countless people suffering from a variety of ailments. By all of which things, it is clear that the Holy Spirit Itself dwelled in the members of his own most holy body.

[8] We ourselves, thanks to the deep friendship we shared with him when in minor orders, saw proof of his sanctity in witnessing the pure testimony of his life; and now many other competent witnesses have come forth to give evidence of the truth of the miracles so many people have spoken of. Together with the whole of God's flock which has been given to our care, we have confidence that, by God's mercy, we all can be aided by his intercession, and that we who were fortunate to enjoy the pleasure of his gracious friendship here on earth may now have the blessing of his powerful patronage in heaven.

[9] And so, upon the advice and with the consent of our brethren [the cardinals of the Church], as well as of all prelates around us at the Holy See, we have decided to inscribe Dominic's name in the catalog of the saints, and we hereby firmly establish and command all of you, by virtue of this Apostolic Letter, solemnly to celebrate his birth into heaven on the Nones of April—the vigil of the day on which, casting aside the burden of the flesh, Dominic, being so rich in merits, entered heaven and joined in the glory of the saints. May God, Whom he honored all his life, be moved by Dominic's prayers to grant us grace in this world and glory in the world to come.

[10] Finally, we desire that the venerable tomb of this great confessor, who illuminates the whole Church by working his extraordinary miracles, be solemnly visited and honored in keeping with Christian piety. Trusting in the mercy of Omnipotent God, as well as in the authority of the Blessed Apostles Peter and Paul, we mercifully grant the remission of one year of penance, annually, to all the Christian faithful who, being confessed and in a true state of penance, visit Dominic's tomb on his feast day and give it all the devotion and respect it deserves.

Given at Rieti on the fifth of the Nones of July, in the eighth year of our pontificate.

16.3   Mechthild of Magdeburg, *The Flowing Light of Divinity*

Mechthild (1212–1282) was born into the Saxon nobility, experienced her first mystical visions at the age of 12, and six years later joined the beguinage in the city of Magdeburg, where she spent the next four decades. Under the influence of her confessor, she joined the Dominican Order as a tertiary and began work on the ecstatic poetry that eventually appeared under the collective title *The Flowing Light of Divinity* (*Das fliessende Licht der Gottheit*), one of the few works of mystical writing to be composed in the vernacular. A Latin translation was prepared afterward, possibly in connection with an investigation into her orthodoxy. In 1272, amid calls for her prosecution for heresy, she entered a Cistercian abbey at Helfta, where she was granted refuge until her death—traditionally ascribed to 1282. Her book is divided into seven books; below is Book 2, ch. 25.

CH. 25. THE LAMENT OF THE LOVING SOUL, AFTER GOD SEEMED TO AVOID HER AND TO WITHDRAW HIS BLESSING FROM HER; HOW SHE PLEADED WITH GOD TO EXPLAIN WHO AND WHAT SHE IS; AND THE DESCRIPTION OF A VISION OF A GARDEN FILLED WITH FLOWERS AND SINGING MAIDENS

O Lord! Infinite treasure of blessings! Endless and ineffable marvel! Eternally honored in the majesty of Your glory! How bitter it is, when You avoid me!

> Not even if every person alive cried out on my
>   behalf
> It would not be enough to describe for You
> The inexpressible pain I suffer. Death
> Would be a blessing, in comparison.
> My soul searches for You
> Like a bride seeking out her bride-groom;
> So completely bound to You, I am in agony,
> For my bonds are stronger than I am,
> And I can never free myself from my love.

> With deep desire but a pitiful voice
> I cry out for You; with a heart of heaviness
> I wait for You restlessly.
> I burn constantly in the fire of Your love;
> I search for You with all my strength, but
> Even if I had magnificent strength
> I could not keep up with You
> Or follow Your footprints. Oh, my Love!
> Do not run ahead of me. Out of Your love
> For me, rest a while! Let me catch up!

Lord, since You have taken away from me all that I once had of You, grant me at least what every creature has by right—the grace of remaining true to You, O Master, in my time of need, desolate as I am. For I truly desire this more than I long for Your Heavenly Kingdom.

[The Lord responds:]

> Sweet dove, listen to My words.
> So far beyond you does My Divine Wisdom
>   extend
> That I portion out My blessings to you,
> Lest your mortal body be overwhelmed.

> Your private searching always finds Me;
> Your heart's agony always finds Me;
> But the passion of your pursuit wearies Me
> And I long for a restful moment, in your heart's
>   hot prison.

> The throbbing cries of your pained heart
> Have driven My Justice away from you for a time.
> It benefits us both—for we can never be fully
>   parted
> Nor cut off from one another. But no matter

> How gently I touch you, it pains you.
> If I were to give Myself to you
> As much as you long for Me to do; then
>   I would lose
> [by your death] the dear refuge from the world
>   I have in you.

> Not even a thousand hearts
> Could equal the passion of the love in your soul,
> But beware—the greater your love,
> The greater, but more blessed, your pain!

O dear Lord! Do not spare the dark prison of my heart, in which I drink the sorrows of this world and eat, amid sorrow, the bread of ashes that is my sinfulness. The burning rays of Your love all but kill me. For the moment, go! Leave me here, in torment, bereft of Your blessing!

[The Lord responds:]

> Dear sweet heart, My queen! Why so vexed?
> If I cause you such great hurt,
> Do I not also heal you in My love
> At the same time?

> The glory of My Kingdom awaits you,
> And there you shall rule even over Me!
> I draw ever closer to you in love.
> The gold of My love balances the scale

> Against the weight of your sins.
> All that you have sacrificed, lost, and suffered
> For love of Me, I will repay
> With eternal forgiveness, as you desire.

O Lord! I beg two things of You especially. In Your mercy explain to me. Pay no attention, if my eyes pour with wretched tears, if my lips fall dumb with amazement, if my voice resounds with lamentation, or if my senses cry out "What is wrong with me?" minute by minute—for all these sufferings I have from You, dear Lord. But tell me, Lord, tell me: When the flesh falls from my body, my blood runs dry, my limbs shrivel, and pain wracks every vein in my body—will my heart still dissolve in Your love and my soul still thunder like the roar of a hungry lion? And where will You be then, O my beloved?

[The Lord responds:]

You are like a new-married bride
Clinging in sleep to her husband, to whom
She has faithfully given herself and cannot bear
That he should leave her side even for an hour.

When such a bride awakens
And finds herself alone in the bed
She is filled with a sorrow that is
More than her heart can bear.

But even though her husband is not
At her side, she is ever in his heart.
He says: "I will return to you for our pleasure,
But you must remain patient and quiet!

By silencing your sadness
You will increase the strength of your love!"
And now I the Lord say to you:
I Myself am in all things, everywhere.

From the beginning of time I have
Always been so. I will be there to await you
In the garden of love, and I will pluck for you
The flower of blessed union.

I will prepare for you a resting place
In the beautiful meadow of Divine Knowledge.
The bright sun of My Divinity will shine on you
With the secret wonder of My love.

For you have inspired this love in Me, and so
I will bend down toward you the bough
Of My Holy Trinity, and from it you will pick
The green, white, and red fruits of My loving
    kindness.

The power of the Holy Spirit will then
Fall upon you and protect you
From all earthly sorrows, so that
You will never again give them a thought.

Once you have embraced that tree
I will teach you a song of the holy virgins—the
    melody
And words of which are not understood
By those still troubled by earthly desires.

But they will receive their reward in due course.
My love, come! Sing and let Me hear
You sing this song, for I know
That you understand it well.

Beloved, I cannot sing, for my throat is parched and dry with virginal innocence. Yet wait! The sweetness of Your loving kindness restores sound to my voice, and so I can sing:

"O Lord, Your blood and mine are now one,
    without stain;
Your love and mine are one, forever united;
Your robe and mine are one, without blemish;
And Your lips and mine, unkissed, are one!"

17. THE CRISES OF THE FOURTEENTH CENTURY

17.1 St. Catherine of Siena, *Letters*

Catherine (1347–1380) was one of the great mystics of the late Middle Ages. She was born to a modest family (her father ran a dye-works), received mystical visions of Christ from an early age, and pledged herself to lifelong chastity at 15. She became an affiliate (tertiary) of the Dominican order a few years later, and in 1368 she experienced a "mystical marriage" to Christ that inspired her to cease living as a recluse and to engage in society. She traveled throughout northern Italy, urging clerical reform, penance, and an end to the Guelf-Ghibelline wars that engulfed the region. She also wrote letters to notables across Europe, including the papal court in Avignon, urging the pope to return to Rome. In this letter from September 1276, she complains about her treatment by a Florentine embassy. In 1375 a man named Buonaccorso di Lapo, the ambassador from Florence, visited Siena and asked Catherine to represent the city in negotiations at the papal court. Catherine then ventured to Avignon and arranged an agreement between Florence and the papacy, but another diplomatic corps arrived from Florence and insisted that Catherine had no authority to represent their city. This is her angry reply to Buonaccurso about the way she was treated.

In the name of Christ Jesus, the Crucified, and of gentle Mary. Dearest brother in Christ, the gentle Jesus.

I Catherine, the servant and slave of all the servants of Jesus Christ, write to you [Buonaccurso] in His precious blood. How I long to see you and your councilors with your hearts and souls at peace in His dear blood, in which all hatreds and wars are quenched and all human pride is brought low. In His blood we bear witness to how God came down to us and took on human form, and how the human-God was nailed upon the cross and was torn open so wide that from His wounds the blood of the Crucified Christ pours out—the blood that is administered to all of us by the ministers of the Holy Church. For love of Christ I beg you to accept the treasure that I, the bride of Christ, give to you. Be reconciled to her, O be reconciled to her in His blood! Acknowledge how you have sinned against her and offended her—bearing in mind that all people who acknowledge their guilt, and act to prove themselves humble in that acknowledgement, always receive mercy, whereas those who speak the words of repentance, but fail in penitential action, never receive

it. I say these things not so much for your sake but for the sake of whoever might be the guilty party in this regard.

Oh! Oh! I am heartbroken, dearest brother, over the way you chose to plead with the Holy Father for peace, for I have seen more evidence of words than of action. I say this because when I first came to Florence and met with you and your fellow councilors, you all spoke words of repentance and declared yourselves willing to humble yourselves by asking for the Holy Father's mercy. I said at the time, "Listen, gentlemen! If you are truly willing to speak and act with all humility, and are willing to have me offer you to the Holy Father as lost children, then I will do all that I can to promote your cause. But I will not go under any other condition." And your councilors all expressed their assent.

But Oh! Dearest brothers, this is the only way forward, the only door by which you may enter. There is no other. If you had indeed produced actions equal to your words, you would have had the most glorious peace anyone ever had. I am not just saying this lightly, for I know what the Holy Father was willing to offer you! But once you left the straight path and began to scheme and plot in the ways of the world—taking actions absolutely contrary to what you had earlier promised—the Holy Father had good cause to reject a possible peace, and to remain in conflict. Your ambassadors acted shamefully when they were here, not at all the way they had been instructed by one of the servants of God. You yourself kept your distance, and I was never even able to meet with the others despite all that you had told me when I first asked for a letter of credentials. You had promised before that you would tell the councilors that we would all be in contact with one another about every issue. Your very words were "We are convinced there will never be a resolution [of the conflict], except through the intervention of one of the servants of God." And yet your actions were exactly the opposite.

All of this happened because of sinfulness, the true extent of which we will never know. I can see now that your humble speech was the product of fear and necessity rather than of love and virtue. If you had any understanding of your sinfulness, you would have matched your actions to your words and truly trusted me, the servant of God, to gain the things you want and need from the Holy Father. I could have worked things out to satisfy the needs of both Florence and the Holy Father, and resolve your conflict. But you failed. And the offence you have caused to God, and our collective regret at the lost chance for peace, both cause me great anguish. You have no idea how much evil and trouble will result from your stubborn insistence to chart your own path.

Ah me! Free yourself from the bondage of pride! Bind yourself instead to the humble Lamb [of God]! Give up your scornful defiance of the Vicar of Christ, and let there be no more strife, for the love of Christ Crucified! Do not hold His blood so cheap. Do now the things you ought to have done before, and do not be bitter or complain when the Holy Father places harder and harder demands on you now. He will not demand the impossible from you. He is, truly, simply acting like a real father who punishes his son when he has done wrong; if he scolds, it is in order to promote a spirit of humility that will inspire the son to recognize his sin. No good son ever holds this against his father, for he knows that the father acts out of love. The more such a father scolds, the more the son returns to him and asks for mercy.

I tell you this in the name of Christ Crucified: though you may be scolded by your father, who is Christ here on earth, do not turn away from him. Let him scold. He has good reason to do so.

And look! He is returning to his bride—the abode of St. Peter and St. Paul! Rush to him now, with true humility in your heart, and repent of your sins, following the holy principle with which you began. Both spiritual and bodily peace will be yours, if you do. But if not, then all of us will suffer worse than any of our ancestors did, for we will be calling down God's wrath upon ourselves and will never more share in the blood of the Lamb.

I will say no more.

Be as diligent as you can—especially now that the Holy Father is returning to Rome. As for me, I will do what I have always done, even to the point of death, to exalt the honor of God, to win peace [for Italy], and to pave the way for a new, sweet, and holy crusade. If this failure of ours were the only evil to beset Italy, it would still be enough to merit us a thousand hells.

Give your heart to our gentle Christ Jesus. I trust in His goodness always, and if you act as you should you will achieve a lasting peace. Live in God's holy and tender love. Gentle Jesus! Jesus Love!

17.2 Boccaccio, "The Great Plague"

The Decameron is Giovanni Boccaccio's (1313–1375) literary masterpiece, a tapestry of 100 short stories told by a group of friends who fled Florence at the outbreak of the Black Death; in order to amuse themselves, each tells a story—one each day for 10 days. Boccaccio prefaced the collection with a famous prologue that sets the scene; it is one of the most powerful surviving contemporary descriptions of the plague that hit Europe at the very end of 1347. Boccaccio lost his father to the plague, a fact that probably inspired the somber description he offers below.

tell you, then, that in the 1348th year from the Blessed Incarnation of the Son of God there appeared in Florence, the fairest of all Italian cities, the deadly plague. Whether it was spread by the influence of the celestial bodies, or came upon us men through the just wrath of the Lord as punishment for our sins, it had originated many years earlier in the East, where it annihilated innumerable people, propagating itself relentlessly from place to place until it came at last, calamitously, to the West.

In Florence, in the early spring of the aforesaid year, the wretched effects of the disease appeared for the first time, with symptoms that were beyond belief—and despite all that human ingenuity and care could think of to avert it: the whole city cleansed of pollutants by officials appointed especially for the purpose, the refusal to admit entry into the town by anyone appearing ill, and the adoption of countless other precautions to maintain good health. Despite too all the humble prayers addressed to God, and chanted repeatedly in public processions, by the devout.

The symptoms of the sick differed from those in the East, where a nosebleed was the first visible hint of the inevitable approach of death. Among the men and women in Florence alike, the first sign of the pestilence was the appearance of certain tumors in the groin or the armpits. These swellings usually grew to the size of an apple or of an egg; sometimes, larger, sometimes smaller. The common folk called these tumors *gavoccioli*. From the groins and armpits these *gavoccioli* spread quickly and randomly in every direction. Once the spreading had begun, a second symptom appeared: livid black spots along the arms and thighs. Sometimes these spots were few in number but large in size; sometimes they were just the opposite—many but small. The spots were as certain a sign of the victim's approaching death as were the *gavoccioli*. Every effort by physicians, whether in technique or medicine, proved no match for either the symptoms or the sickness itself. Whether because the plague was fundamentally untreatable or because our physicians were simply not up to the challenge, hardly anyone contracted the disease and recovered; instead, most victims were dead within three days of the first visible symptom and usually without showing a fever or any other accompanying symptom. Apart from the actual physicians, a horde of men and women without the least bit of medical knowledge tried to care for the sick, but in their ignorance they applied all the wrong remedies.

The viciousness of the plague was made even worse by every type of human contact, which passed the disease from one person to another just as a raging fire devours every flammable thing brought in contact with it. But this proved even worse, for a person did not need to touch or converse with an inflicted sufferer in order to place himself in immediate and deadly peril; anyone who even touched the clothes of the sick, or anything else that the sufferer had used or touched, was apt to contract the disease.

What I am about to say seems unbelievable, and if many so people—myself included—had not witnessed it directly, I would hardly dare to write it down; a single witness would never suffice.

So virulent and unstoppable was the pestilence that it was propagated not only from person to person but, even more startling, it was observed many times to spread from objects belonging to one of the sick or newly dead to some animal (that is, not a human being at all) and to cause not merely the animal's sickening but its almost instantaneous death. Let me describe for you something I once saw with my own eyes. The rags of a poor beggar who had succumbed to the plague were left lying it a street; two hogs approached and rooted their snouts around in them and then, taking them in their teeth, slapped the rags back and forth with shakes of their heads, and then all of a sudden they convulsed once or twice and dropped to the ground dead, as though poisoned. They fell on the very rags they had been unlucky enough to disturb.

These happenings, plus countless others that were similar in nature or even worse, caused a host of fears and wild beliefs to take root among those who survived, with the result that they settled on a single and cruel precaution—namely, they all sought to preserve their own health by avoiding or running away from anyone who was sick and from anything that belonged to them. . . .

In the face of so much suffering and misery, all respect for law—whether divine or human—broke down and virtually disappeared, because the administrators and executors of the laws were, like everyone else, either dead or ill, and they had too few subordinate officials available to carry out any of their duties. The result? Everyone was free to do whatever they wanted. Most people steered a middle course between the extremes of either fasting obsessively (like some did) or indulging themselves in drinking and wantonness (as many others did). Instead, they simply took care to meet their needs and satisfy their appetites. Instead of locking themselves away, they walked about freely—although usually with a posy of flowers in their hands, or a bundle of fragrant herbs or a packet of different spices, which they continually pressed to their noses, thinking to comfort their brains against the stench of corpses, sick bodies, and medicine that filled the air. Others pursued the more selfish but probably safer alternative of simply running away, believing that the best and most effective measure against the disease was distance. Convinced of this, and caring for no one but themselves, vast numbers of men and women abandoned the city, their homes, their relatives, their estates and belongings altogether and fled to the countryside or even further, as if God in His wrath would use this plague to punish mankind for its sins on the basis of where they happened to be, and attack only those who happened to be within city walls. Perhaps they thought that the entire urban population would be annihilated, that the city's last hour had finally arrived.

Not all the people in any particular group died; nor did all the people in any particular group survive. To the contrary, many fell ill in each and every camp. But having established themselves as examples to the healthy, those who survived languished away with virtually no one to care for them, abandoned by everyone. Not only did one town-dweller avoid another, neighbor avoid neighbor, or relative avoid relative, everyone communicating only at great distance, but the plague had so struck people's hearts that brothers abandoned brothers, uncles their nephews, sisters their brothers, and even wives their husbands. Worst of all, and almost beyond belief, mothers and fathers deserted their own children and refused to care for them, abandoning them like strangers. . . .

Many people died, therefore, who might have survived if they had received any help. That is why, apart from the natural virulence of the plague itself, the number of deaths reported day and night was so enormous that it dumbfounded everyone who heard it, to say nothing of the people who witnessed it directly. And that is why a number of new customs arose among those who survived, customs altogether contrary to established ways of doing things. . . .

Among the city's common folk, the burghers for the most part, a pathetic spectacle appeared. Whether immobilized by hopelessness or unable to leave because of concern for their property, they remained in the city and so fell ill by the thousands every day, and lacking anyone to care for them or help them, they almost inevitably died without exception. Many dropped dead right in the streets, day and night; others, who died in their homes, were only discovered when the stench of their rotting corpses caught their neighbors' attention. As a result, dead bodies lay everywhere. People soon fell into a regular routine, more out of fear of contamination by the corpses than out of respect or affection for the dead: acting alone or with the help of others, they would take the bodies of the newly deceased out of their homes and leave them lying outside their front doors. Anyone who came down the street, especially early in the morning, thus saw countless corpses every day. Funeral biers were then sent for, and if there were none of these available, workers carrying mere planks of wood would cart the bodies away. It was not uncommon to see a single bier that had two or even three corpses on it—a husband and wife, perhaps, or a group of siblings, or a father and his son, or some other clutch of relatives. It would be impossible to count the number of times when two priests, carrying a cross in front of a bier on the way to a burial, would suddenly have three or four other biers fall in line behind them; thinking themselves on their way to conduct a single burial, they would find by the time they reached the churchyard that they were six, seven, or eight more to perform. Even so, no tears or candles or mourners were involved, to honor the dead. Conditions were so bad that most people showed no more care for the human dead than nowadays they show for a dead goat, for it was quite clear that death—the one thing that, in normal times, no wise man ever accepted with patience (even though it happened relatively rarely and unobtrusively)—had been brought home to even the most feeble-minded; the problem was that the catastrophe was so unimaginably great that no one was really able to care. There were so many corpses arriving at all the churches every day, and almost by the hour, that in no time at all they ran out of consecrated ground, especially if, as by ancient custom, they were to grant a separate burial plot for each person. So when all the graves were filled up, they dug huge pits in the churchyard, into which they placed newly arrived corpses by the hundreds, piling then atop each other like ship's cargo with only a thin layer of dirt over each, until each pit was filled.

In addition to all the calamities we suffered in the city, I ought to make clear for you that the dreadful things happening in the city were suffered in the countryside as well. In all the fortified towns the situation was just as in Florence, although on a smaller scale, but in the rural villages and the countryside proper the poor miserable peasants and their families, having no physicians or servants to help them in any way, collapsed in the dirt lanes, in their fields and cottages at all hours of day and night, dying more like animals than human beings. Like the townspeople, they paid no attention to their duties or possessions, believing each day might be their last, and so they did not bother to till the fields or tend to their animals or do anything to prepare for a future. Instead they just abandoned what they had, with the result that their oxen, asses, sheep, goats, pigs, chickens—even their faithful dogs—were driven away and allowed to roam at will through the fields, where the unreaped and ungathered crops were simply neglected. . . .

What more can be said, except that the cruelty of heaven (and possibly, to some degree, the cruelty of mankind) was so terrible that between March and June of that year, by the fierceness of the plague and the fact that so many of the sick were poorly cared for or flat-out abandoned at their neediest moment because the healthy were too frightened to approach them, more than one hundred thousand people died within the walls of Florence.

17.3   The Battle of Poitiers (September 19–22, 1356)

Two views are offered here, one by the contemporary English writer Geoffrey le Baker (d. 1360) and another by the later French writer Jean Froissart (d. 1405). Geoffrey le Baker's chronicle is direct, terse, and sounds as though it was written by an eyewitness. Froissart's chronicle is a vast, sprawling, narrative in overwrought flowery language that emphasizes the chivalric grandeur of both the English and French nobility; spectacle, not factual accuracy, is his main interest. Long lists of noblemen's name and titles, loving descriptions of their colorful banners, shining weaponry, and proud coats of arms, and impossibly idealized speech characterize Froissart's writing style. (In the passage below, I have stripped away those elements in an attempt to clarify his description of the action.)

GEOFFREY'S VERSION

[Prince Edward] positioned the earls of Warwick and of Oxford in the vanguard and placed the earls of Shaftesbury and of Suffolk in the rear, while he himself commanded the central part of the army. Altogether the [English] army numbered no more than four thousand knights, one thousand infantry, and two thousand archers. When the French nobles approached, they loudly belittled the English forces, because their own army was comprised of eight thousand knights and innumerable foot soldiers, all organized under eighty-seven standards. Many of our men grumbled at the size of the French force, for a large part of our own army had earlier been sent to defend Gascony. . . .

When dawn came, very fair, early on Sunday morning, both armies stood at the ready. The cardinal of Périgord rode over to Prince Edward and begged him—in the name of Christ Crucified, for love of His Virgin Mother, out of reverence for the Truce of God, and in order to spare the shedding of Christian blood—to postpone the battle so that a peaceful settlement might be negotiated. The cardinal promised that the negotiations would be honorable, and he himself would serve as mediator for the talks, if both sides were willing.

Edward was no stubborn tyrant, and feared neither to make war nor to make peace, and so he calmly agreed to the holy cleric's request. Negotiations thus began, and while talks were underway all that day another one thousand knights and a huge contingent of infantry reinforced the French army, such that when, the following Monday morning, the cardinal rode forward again on behalf of the French king and offered a one-year truce, Edward refused, although at the cardinal's insistence he did agree to a truce that would last until Christmas. The cardinal then rode back to the French side and asked for pledges of peace, as requested by Edward. The Marquis de Clermont advised the king to agree, but was opposed by Geoffroi de Charny and Sir Douglas the Scot, both of whom had great influence over the king and who argued that the English forces did not have a chance, being so few and in a strange land and so worn out by their long campaign. The French army, they urged, were not only greatly superior in numbers but were zealous to defend their homeland. . . .

The cardinal's messengers informed Edward that the French king wanted no peace-settlement except the one he would win by force of arms, and so the prince called his soldiers together and spoke. . . . Turning next to the companies of archers, he proclaimed:

> Your courage and loyalty are well-known to me. Amid countless grave dangers, you have shown yourselves to be worthy sons and kinsmen of those brave men who, under my father's dukedom and my ancestors who served as kings of England, found no task impossible and no place impassable; there was no hill, howsoever steep, that they could not climb, no tower they could not scale, no army they could not break. By their courage they brought down many foes—the French, the Cyprians, the Syracusans, the Calabrians, the Palestinians! They defeated the stiff-necked Scots and the Irish, even the long-suffering Welsh!
>
> Circumstance, time, and danger can make frightened men brave, and beleaguered men keen. May your sense of honor, your love of England, and the promise of French booty inspire you, more than my words, to follow in your forefather's footsteps. Follow your standards, obey your commanding officers in thought and deed. If we survive this day and are victorious, we may continue forever in good friendship, of one mind and will. But if, God forbid, we are fated to go the way of all flesh, then the hangman's noose will not profane your names, for my nobles and I will share the same bitter cup with you! To defeat the knights of France will bring us glory; but if, God forbid, we are beaten, there will be no shame in so brave a defeat.

The prince noticed, while speaking, a nearby hill that was marked by many ditches and hedges. Pasture and thick brush lay to one side of it, and on the other side lay vineyards and grainfields. The French army, he was convinced, was positioned atop the hill. Between that hill and our men was a wide low valley through which a stream ran, with marshy land on either side if it. The prince sent one company of soldiers with supply-wagons down a path that led to the stream; having crossed the stream, this forward company entered the other side of the valley, hiding themselves among the hedges and ditches on the side of the hill.

The open field, where our vanguard companies stood, was divided from the plain occupied by the French by a long hedge and ditch that ran down into the marsh. The earl of Warwick held the slope leading down to the marsh, while the field along the upper region of the hedge, only a stone's throw from the hill itself, was held by the earl of Salisbury. . . .

The battle began frightfully, with knights on either side attacking with lances, spears, and battle-axes, but then our archers seized their chance. Rising from their hiding places, they shot cascades of arrows over the ditches and hedges and onto the French. Their arrows, flying swiftly and profusely, did far more damage than the French did with their swords and lances.

Our rear guard, advancing swiftly, and our vanguard, led by the earl of Warwick and driving hard from the slope of the hill, crushed the French soldiers caught in their midst. Our vanguard archers held a safe position in the marsh, where the French cavalry, whose particular mission was to overrun them, could not reach them. The French knights instead tried to save their men from harm by turning to face the archers, using their strong plate-armor and heavy leathered shields to ward off or deflect the archers' arrows. . . . The earl of Oxford, seeing this, left Prince Edward's side and led the archers to a new position, where he ordered them to shoot the flanks of the French horses. The archers did so, causing the wounded horses to kick and rear, throw their riders, and turn in wild flight, trampling their surprised masters. Having stopped the advance of the French cavalry, the archers then took up their old position in the marsh and hounded the fleeing French with wave after wave of arrows.

The battle continued in dreadful fury. The earls of Warwick and Salisbury fought like lions, their limbs dripping with hot blood, contending with each other to see which of them could spill more French blood upon the soil of Poitiers. . . .

Almost immediately, the next French army advanced, this one led by the French king's first-born son, the dauphin of Vienne. Larger by far than the army that had just been driven back, the dauphin's forces were fierce and fearsome, but it could not frighten our men, so keen were they to win honor for themselves and to revenge their comrades who had fallen in the first sortie. . . .

Prince Edward drove ahead, straight into the middle of the French forces, striking on every side until he had broken the enemy line . . . and made a direct assault on the French king's personal guard, which stood around him in a wedge formation. Then their standards wobbled and fell, as their bearers collapsed, some of them so eviscerated that they stood on their own entrails, others vomiting out teeth, and still others standing tall but with both their arms cut off. . . . The English commander is young but fights with the strength of two. He splits skulls and chops heads off, he eviscerates some, he cuts others entirely into two, showing in every action that he does not belong to the degenerate royal line of France. Prince Edward presses ever forward, striking down the proud, until at length Lady Fortune completes the turning of her wheel and Edward, with the savage generosity of a lion, spares the defeated and receives the surrender of the French king.

FROISSART'S VERSION

Prince Edward's forces were fewer than eight thousand, counting knights, archers, and foot-soldiers, whereas the French numbered sixty thousand, more than three thousand of whom were knights. . . .

Then the battle began on all sides. The forces led by the marshals of France, having been given the task of taking out the English archers, advanced upon the hedges where these were stationed. As soon as the French knights were within range, the English archers began to shoot; they shot horses and men alike, wounding many and killing many. Feeling the sharp sting of the arrows, the horses refused to advance but instead reared up, bucked, and tossed so wildly that many of them fell on their own riders and could not rise again. Because of this, the marshals' attack on Prince Edward failed. A handful of [French] mounted knights and squires did make it past the archers and tried to advance on the prince, but they too failed. . . .

Attempting to pull back, the French saw a large company of Englishmen coming at them down the hillside; some of these were mounted knights and there were many archers alongside them. These archers served their army well that day, for they shot so many arrows that the French had no idea which way to run, and so the English gained ground on them piece by piece. . . .

Then the [French] king's company attacked the English. The battle was intense, with many a blow given, and many received. King Jean and his youngest son met the forces of the English marshals—the earl of Warwick and the earl of Suffolk. . . . Alongside the king was the earl Douglas of Scotland, who fought valiantly but briefly, for when he saw the French advances stall he turned and fled. . . .

The knights on both sides suffered many pains. King Jean himself performed many marvels in arms that day. He defended himself with his battleaxe and struggled to break through the line. Captured alongside the king were the earl of Tancarville, Lord Jacques de Bourbon, the earl of Ponthieu, and the Lord Jean d'Artois, the earl of Eu; not far from the king, under the banner of the captal de Buch, Lord Charles d'Artois and numerous other knights and squires were captured too. The fighting continued right up to the gates of Poitiers, but the city's inhabitants refused to open the gates to anyone, out of fear, which caused countless men and horses to be slain and beaten down. It was a scene of horrible murder. Frenchmen who happened upon an Englishman whom they knew, immediately handed themselves over as hostages. Many of the English archers ended up holding four, five, or even six hostages apiece. . . .

Thus the battle ended. As you have heard, it took place in the fields of Maupertuis, two leagues distant from Poitiers, on the 22nd day of September in the year of Our Lord 1356. It began at dawn and ended at midday. . . . It is reported that all the flower of France was killed that day, while the captured included King Jean, his son Lord Philippe, seventeen earls, and numerous barons, knights, and squires. Between five and six thousand noble knights were killed.

17.4   Jean Froissart, *Chronicles*

Jean Froissart's (1337–1405) immense *Chronicles* is one of the chief narrative sources for the history of the Hundred Years' War. Froissart also wrote a great deal of poetry and a long Arthurian romance in verse. He is a passionate believer in chivalry who delights in the spectacle of nobleman soldiers, banners flapping in the wind, gleaming armor, and the heavy stamping of their horses' hooves. Few people read his poetry, and his fame today rests on his *Chronicles*. Froissart traveled widely throughout France and England, Italy and Spain, and was well connected. His *Chronicles* makes good reading in small batches. Here he describes one of the aftereffects of the Black Death—parades of pentitents crying out for God's forgiveness.

ON THE FLAGELLANTS

In the year of grace 1349 of Our Lord a group of penitents appeared, coming initially from Germany—wild people who performed their penance in public by scourging their backs with whips studded with small iron points. With these whips they lashed themselves mercilessly between their shoulders. Some few of them were women who dressed in bloodstained rags; they feared for their souls and despaired of what the world might come to in the absence of a miracle. In doing their penance they chanted the most pitiable dirges about the birth and holy suffering of Our Lord, and implored God to end the plague. For it was a time of death, suffering, and plague, with people dropping dead all of a sudden throughout the whole world—at least a third of the human population.

The penitents I just mentioned travelled in companies from village to village, city to city, wearing hoods made of felt. Each company had its own color. By custom, law, and ordinance they could stay in each village only a single night and were pledged to proceed on their pilgrimage for thirty-three and a half days—one day for each year of Jesus Christ's earthly life, as the Holy Scriptures testify. Each company, therefore, processed for the prescribed thirty-three and a half days, after which it returned again to whatever village, city, or castle from which it had originally set out. They lacked for nothing throughout their pilgrimages, for the good people of each village and town they passed through provided them with food and refreshment. They never lodged in these places, though, out of fear that doing so might spread the malady even faster. Instead, whenever they entered anyone's home for food or refreshment they first kneeled as a group, out of humility, and recited three Our Fathers and three Hail Marys, and they always repeated the gesture when they took their leave.

They resolved countless conflicts and established fair peace continuously, these penitents and the good people who supported them; wherever there were people of differing opinions who could come to no agreement, they found compromise after the penitents intervened.

Included in their ordinances were many intelligent and useful things, and it was either these sound ideas or simple human nature that inclined these companies' members to go on these penitential processions. Whatever the case, they did not enter the kingdom of France, for Pope Innocent, who was then in office and living in Avignon, and his cardinals had given these companies some thought and had come to a firm decision about the penitents. They declared that public penance, and public support for it, was neither permissible nor acceptable; in fact, they declared that it was forbidden. Henceforth any clergy who was among them or was a member of their company or who served them as a curate, canon, or chaplain, or who shared their opinions was to be deprived of his benefice—and if he desired absolution, he would have to request it directly from Avignon. If one contrasts this decree with all that is generally known, one can see that the popes and the kings of France regarded them as enemies and rebels, and would not suffer another Hainault. For if the penitents were to make it to Cambrai or Saint-Quentin they would be able to reach the coast. If it should happen that the penitents got that far, and if any new people joined them, the Jews [in those cities] might fear for their lives and flee, being gone for more than two hundred years. For they have a saying:

> And there will come knights carrying iron mallets who will be terribly cruel, but lacking a leader they will not be able to exert their might or perform deeds outside the German empire. Nevertheless, when they come, we will all be killed.

So they'll flee, and truly at that time countless Jews will be slaughtered in land after land until at last the popes and the kings of Spain, Aragon, and Navarre, with great effort, will re-establish peace for them.

17.5 Jakob Twinger, *Chronicle*

Jakob Twinger (1346–1420) was born at Königshofen, a small village near the city of Strasbourg. Ordained a priest in 1382, he began to write his *Chronicle* in the same year of his ordination and continued to add to it until his death, by which time he had brought the narrative forward to 1415. In 1395 he was appointed a canon of the church of St. Thomas in Strasbourg and placed in charge of maintaining its archives—a source from which he regularly drew for his history. The passage below recounts the massacres visited upon the Jews of Strasbourg in the wake of the Black Death.

In the year of Our Lord 1349 the most terrible pestilence in history occurred, spreading death from one end of the Earth to the other. Rampaging both on this side and the far side of the sea—it was in fact even deadlier among the Muslims than among the Christians—it killed so many people that in some places hardly a single person was left alive. Ships floated adrift on the sea, their holds bulging with goods, but with the entire crew dead and no one left to steer the ship. In Marseilles, the bishop and all the priests and monks died, taking more than half the city's population with them. In other cities and districts so many people perished that the desolation can hardly be described. The pope in Avignon cancelled the entire court's activities and locked himself in his chamber; no one was granted admission to him at all, and he kept a fire roaring in his room day and night. What had caused the epidemic? Even the wisest scholars and physicians could say only that it had to be the will of God. The effect of the plague here in Strasbourg was the same as elsewhere, and it lasted more than an entire year. Arriving in the summer of 1349, it killed approximately sixteen thousand people.

Everywhere throughout the world blame for the plague fell upon the Jews, who were loathed for supposedly causing the pestilence by poisoning the water-wells, and so they were thrown to the flames everywhere from the Mediterranean to Germany (except for in the city of Avignon, where the pope protected them). In the Swiss towns of Berne and Zofingen a number of Jews admitted, after being tortured, to poisoning the wells—and the poison was even found, so the townsmen burned the Jews throughout the region and wrote of their actions to the people in Strasbourg, Freiburg, and Basel, so that they might do the same.

Officials in the first two cities refused to take similar action—although in Basel the populace marched on the city hall and forced the town council to swear that they would in fact burn the Jews living there and never allow another Jew into the city for two hundred years; all the Jews of Basel were therefore arrested, and a hearing was scheduled to meet at Benfeld. The bishop of Strasbourg, all the nobility of Alsace, and representatives of the townsmen of Strasbourg, Freiburg, and Basel were in attendance, and they asked the Strasbourg officials what they intended to do with the arrested Jews. The officials replied that they had no cause to take action against the Jews, and demanded to know why the citizens of the city had closed up the wells and put away all the buckets. A huge, indignant roar rose from the crowd, and in the end it was the bishop and nobles of Strasbourg, and the people of the imperial cities, who decided to do away with the Jews—and as a result of their resolve, Jews throughout the region were fed to the flames. Jews who were merely expelled from their towns were invariably captured by the nearby peasant and were either cut down or drowned. . . .

In Strasbourg, the officials who had refused to punish the Jews were deposed and replaced by a new council that gave in to the demands of the mob.

On St. Valentine's Day, a Saturday, the new council had the Jews burned to death atop a wooden platform that they had ordered built in the Jews' cemetery; there were about two thousand of them, and they were all put to death, except for the few who declared themselves willing to receive baptism. Some children were pulled from the flames at the last moment and were forcibly baptized, against the will of their fathers and mothers who looked on. All debts to the Jews were cancelled, first, so the Jews were forced to surrender all pledges and bonds that they had taken as collateral. The town council seized all the Jews' cash, and divided it among the commoners. The money, of course, was the Jews' downfall. If they had been poor, and if the nobles had not been in debt to them, they would never have been killed. Once

their money was distributed to the citizens, some of them gave a share of it to the local cathedral or some other church, on the advice of their confessors.

That is how the Jews of Strasbourg came to be burned. Much the same thing happened to the Jews in all the Rhineland cities, whether Free or Imperial or belonging to the nobles. Some places gave the Jews a trial, first; others, not. And in some places the Jews set fire to their own homes and cremated themselves. Afterwards, officials in Strasbourg decided that no Jew should be allowed to enter the city for a hundred years, but less than twenty years later a new council voted to permit Jews back. Thus did Jews return to Strasbourg in the year 1368 after the Incarnation of Our Lord.

17.6 The Hundred Years' War: 1337–1453

This dynastic family tree shows the position of the individuals who led England and France during this extremely long dispute. The war, which began between Edward III of England and Philip VI of Valois, was carried on by their successors. It ended in 1453, the same year in which the Ottoman Turks captured Constantinople and put an end to the Byzantine Empire.

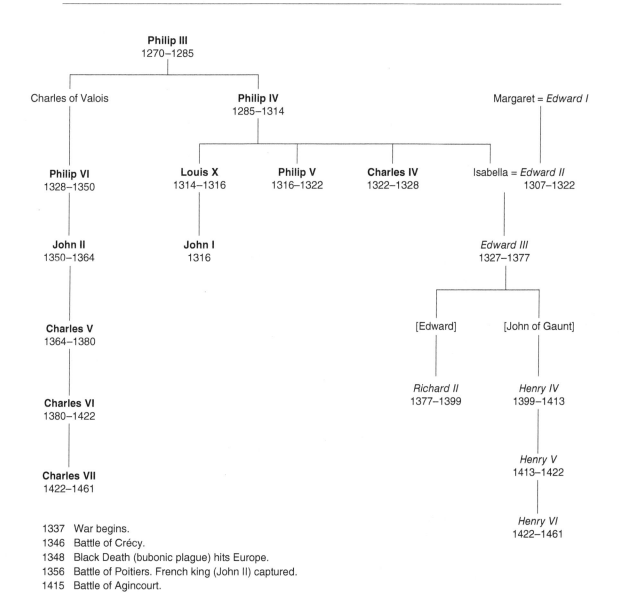

Philip III
1270–1285

Charles of Valois

Philip IV
1285–1314

Margaret = *Edward I*

Philip VI
1328–1350

Louis X
1314–1316

Philip V
1316–1322

Charles IV
1322–1328

Isabella = *Edward II*
1307–1322

John II
1350–1364

John I
1316

Edward III
1327–1377

Charles V
1364–1380

[Edward]

[John of Gaunt]

Charles VI
1380–1422

Richard II
1377–1399

Henry IV
1399–1413

Charles VII
1422–1461

Henry V
1413–1422

Henry VI
1422–1461

1337 War begins.
1346 Battle of Crécy.
1348 Black Death (bubonic plague) hits Europe.
1356 Battle of Poitiers. French king (John II) captured.
1415 Battle of Agincourt.

18. SIGNS OF A NEW ERA

18.1 Marsilius of Padua, *The Defender of the Peace*

Marsilius (d. 1342) conveniently concludes his long work *Defensor pacis* (*The Defender of the Peace*) with a summary of his principal arguments, and in so doing he mimics the form of canonical decrees emerging from an ecclesiastical council—one last dig. He lists 41 points that he believes he has proven. The Legislator he refers to is his term for the citizens of a community, acting as a community.

1. The holy and canonical Scriptures, the logical conclusions that of necessity are drawn from them, and the interpretations made of them by the general agreement of all Christians, are true—and belief in these truths is necessary to the salvation of all to whom they are known.

2. Only a general council of Christians, whether acting in unanimity or by majority-vote, has the authority to interpret doubtful passages of the divine law; and only such a council may determine what are to be regarded as articles of faith, belief in which is essential to salvation. No partial council, and no single person of any position, has sufficient authority to resolve such questions.

3. The Gospels clearly teach that no temporal punishments or penalties should ever be used, in order to force anyone into obeying God's commandments.

4. It is necessary to salvation to obey the commandments of the New Testament, the conclusions that follow logically from it, and the dictates of reason, but it is not necessary to salvation to obey all the commandments of the Old Testament.

5. No one has the right to dispense with the commandments and prohibitions of the New Testament, but a general council and an authorized Christian Legislator have the right to prohibit certain things that are permitted by the New Testament, under penalties imposed in this world or the next; no partial council or any single person of any position, however, has this right.

6. The whole body of citizens-in-community, or a majority thereof, is the human Legislator.

7. The decretals and decrees of the bishop of Rome, or of any other bishop or group of bishops, have no power to coerce anyone by any secular punishments or penalties unless they have the authorization of the human Legislator.

8. The Legislator alone—or one who governs by the authorization of the Legislator—has the power to void any human laws.

9. Any elected official or body derives its authority from the election of the group that rightfully elected it—not from the confirmation or approval of that election by some other power.

10. The election of any prince or official—especially any figure who has coercive power—derives solely from the expressed will of the Legislator.

11. There can be only one single supreme ruling power in any state or realm.

12. The number of persons holding public offices, the qualifications of those persons, and all civil matters, are to be determined solely by the Christian ruler and according to the law or established custom of the realm.

13. No prince, no partial council, and no single person in any position possesses full authority and control over other persons, whether lay or clerical, without the expressed authorization of the Legislator.

14. No bishop or priest has coercive authority or jurisdiction over any person, whether lay or clerical, even if he is a heretic.

15. A ruler who governs by the authority of the Legislator has jurisdiction over the persons and possessions of every single human who lives in the realm—regardless of their station, whether they are lay or clerical, and also every organized body of laymen or clergy.
16. Without the authorization of the Legislator, no bishop or priest, and no body of bishops or priests, has the authority to excommunicate anyone or to interdict the performance of holy services.
17. All bishops derive their authority in equal measure from Christ; it cannot be shown from Holy Scriptures that any one bishop should be over or under another, neither in temporal nor spiritual matters.
18. When acting by the consent of the Legislator, all bishops, either individually or in a body, have the same right by divine authority to excommunicate the bishop of Rome, or to exercise authority over him, as the bishop of Rome has toward them.
19. No one has the authority to permit marriages that are clearly prohibited by divine law as expressed in the New Testament; and only the Legislator (or one acting in his name and by his authority) may grant exemption for marriages that are otherwise prohibited by human law.
20. The authority to legitimize children born out of wedlock, so that they might receive inheritances or other civil or ecclesiastical offices and benefits, belongs solely to the Legislator.
21. The Legislator alone has the authority to judge the qualifications of individuals for ecclesiastical orders and to promote them therein, and no priest or bishop has such authority unless he has been awarded it by the Legislator.
22. A prince or ruler who governs by the authority of the Legislator has the right to determine the number of churches and chapels in the state, and the number of priests, deacons, and other clergy needed to serve in them.
23. Only by the authority of the Legislator may non-essential ecclesiastical offices be conferred or taken away, and ecclesiastical benefices or other property awarded or revoked.
24. No bishop or body of bishops has the right to appoint notaries or other civic officials.
25. No bishop or body of bishops has the right to license anyone to practice or to teach any profession or craft, for this right belongs solely to the Legislator (or one to whom the Legislator has awarded it).
26. Those who have been consecrated as deacons or priests, or who have been irrevocably dedicated to God in some other fashion, are to be preferred over those who have not been thus consecrated, in awarding ecclesiastical office and benefices.
27. If needed for the public good and common defense, the Legislator has authority to confiscate ecclesiastical properties once the needs of the priests and clergy, the expenses of divine worship, and the care of the poor have been satisfied.
28. Any property bequeathed for pious purposes and charitable efforts—such as bequests made for the funding of a crusade, the redeeming of captives, the support of the poor, and such like—may be disposed of by the prince, if such is the decision of the Legislator and the decision does not run explicitly contrary to the purpose laid out by the testator.
29. The Legislator alone has the authority to approve or to forbid the creation of new religious orders and houses.
30. The prince alone, supported by the Legislator, is empowered to condemn heretics, criminals, and all others who deserve temporal punishment, to inflict corporal punishment, and to exact fines.
31. No bishop or priest has the authority to release one who is bound to another by a legal oath; only the Legislator may do so, for just cause.
32. Only a general council of all Christians has the authority to create a metropolitan bishop or church, or to demote such.
33. Only a Christian Legislator (or one governing by its authority over Christian states) is empowered to convene a general or local council of priest, bishops, and other Christians; and no one can be compelled by threats of temporal or spiritual punishment to obey the decrees of a council convened in any other way.

34. Only a general council of Christians or the Christian Legislator, but no one else, may impose fasts or other restrictions on the use of food; only such a council or Legislator may prohibit the use of any mechanical arts or teachings that divine law permits to be utilized on any day; and only such a council or Legislator may compel anyone to obey the prohibition of temporal punishments.

35. A general council of Christians alone has the power to canonize and to demand that a particular person be recognized as a saint.

36. A general council of Christians alone has the power to forbid the marriage of priests, bishops, or other clergy; it alone has the authority to issue decrees on ecclesiastical discipline; and it alone (or one to whom it delegates its authority) may dissolve such decrees.

37. Any formal judgment made by a bishop or priest may be appealed to the Legislator.

38. All who have taken a sacred vow of complete poverty are forbidden to have in their possession any immovable property, unless they have the fixed intention of selling it as soon as possible and in order to give the money thus produced to the poor; moreover, they are forbidden all rights that would enable them to recover any movable or immovable property from any person who takes it away from them.

39. The people of a community, acting as a community and as individuals, are obliged by divine law to support the bishop and other clergy authorized for them by the Gospel, so that they may have food, clothing, and other necessities of life; but the people are not obliged to pay tithes or other taxes beyond what is needed for the necessities of the clergy's life.

40. The Legislator (or one who governs in its authority) has the right to compel bishops and other clergy to live in the province they serve and which provides them with the necessities of life, and to perform divine services and administer the sacraments.

41. Only the Christian Legislator (or one acting in his authority) or a general council of Christians may promote the bishop of Rome or any other ecclesiastical or spiritual minister to a non-essential ecclesiastical office, and the same reserve the sole right of removing such from any non-essential ecclesiastical office.

18.2 William of Ockham, *Letter to the Friars Minor*

In 1334, after six years of self-imposed exile in Germany following his flight from the papal court in Avignon, William wrote an open letter to all the members of his Franciscan order, explaining the nature of his conflict with the Holy See. William firmly supports the doctrine of "evangelical poverty" of the Spiritual Franciscans and rejects Pope John XXII's "heretical" arguments against it. Here he asserts that he no longer recognizes John as the legitimate pontiff.

To all consecrated members of the Order of Friars Minor gathered together at Assisi on the Feast of Pentecost in the year of Our Lord 1334, I, brother William of Ockham write in order to defend loyally the true orthodox faith.

The Divine Scriptures urge, the examples of the saints teach, right reason dictates, human laws require, and fraternal charity persuades me that I owe you a full account of my actions. And so, in the hope of following faithfully the footsteps of the glorious Apostle, the blessed Paul, I want to give the best reckoning I possibly can to everyone—both Catholic Christians and heretical ones—of what I have done, am doing, and intend to do.

Therefore let the whole Christian world know that I remained in Avignon for almost four years, until I realized that the one who presided there [Pope John XXII (r. 1316–1334)] had sunk into heretical perversity. Out of the conviction that such a person, in so great an office, should not be the one who defines what is or is not heresy, I resolved not to read, nor even to possess a copy, of his heretical writings. Eventually, however, one of my superiors found an occasion when he determined that I ought to read some of [Pope John's] writings—and so I obediently took up and studied three of them: the painfully heretical *Ad conditorem*, *Cum inter nonnullos*, and *Quia quorundam*. In these decretals I found a plethora of statements that were heretical, false, silly, ridiculous, unbelievable, insane, defamatory, and contrary to (if not directly threatening to) true orthodox faith, morality, natural reason, lived experience and fraternal charity. I summarize some of these below.

In *Ad conditorem*:

1. that our brothers' renunciation of property (that is, when they make their formal profession, they take a vow of poverty and renounce all property) "contributes nothing to their [spiritual] perfection if the same attitude existed in them beforehand." . . .
2. that "by not having the lordship" of their property transferred to the Holy Roman Church, the brothers are not "poorer than if they still possessed their property together with the lordship they claim they no longer have." . . .
3. that "the lordship reserved to the Holy Roman Church" is "simple"—that is, secret, bare, obscure, and consequently useless—because "no temporal gain has accrued from it to the Church, and it is doubted that any ever will ." . . .
4. that in regard to consumable items, the fact that they are used (i.e. consumed) cannot be distinguished from ownership or lordship. This would seem to imply that the use of something proves ownership of it—an assertion plainly at odds with the Holy Scriptures, natural reason, and common sense. After all, the fact that thieves and robbers consume certain goods does not prove their legal ownership of them. . . .

In *Cum inter nonnullos*:

1. his self-declared intent was to put an end to the scholastic dispute in which some scholars asserted that Christ and His apostles possessed and held title to nothing, individually or in common, while others maintained the contrary; and so he sided with the contrarians. But this Pope Nicholas III had already decided in favor of the former position, basing his arguments on the Holy Scriptures.
2. he declared "definitively" that Christ and His apostles must have had the right to use, sell, and give away possessions . . . or else their actions, in doing so, would have been unjust—which strikes me as a manifestly heretical position. . . .

In *Quia quorundam*:

1. he asserts that "gospel truth and apostolic teachings repeatedly bear witness" that after their return from their preaching missions the Apostles carried money—which is an error that imposes a false reading on the Scriptures., for while we do read that Judas carried a purse, nowhere in the Scriptures does it say that the apostles carried money when they returned from preaching.
2. he insists that Christ's instruction to His apostles not to carry money "was not a commandment but a granting of permission to accept the necessities of life from those to whom they preached the Gospel. . . .
3. he asserts that Christ had a purse of His own. . . .
4. he writes that "to hold some things in common does not diminish anyone's individual vow of poverty." . . .
5. he argues that Christ Himself never practiced renunciation of property, and did not require it of His apostles. . . .

It is because of all the above-delineated errors and heresies (and countless others as well) that I withdraw from obedience to the pseudo-pope John and all those who support him to the prejudice of the true orthodox faith.

Several men of outstanding learning have made it evident to me that this heretical pseudo-pope, on account of his errors and lies, must be regarded as having voided his pontificate; he should, in fact, be formally excommunicated. . . . Against this pseudo-pope "I have set my face like the hardest rock" [Isaiah 50.7]. No lies, slurs, or harassment of any sort (anything, that is, short of physical harm to me) will ever stop me from attacking and refuting his errors so long as I have a hand, paper, ink, and a pen; neither will any crowd, however great, of people who believe, defend, and support him. Before I would accept any of John's errors as compatible with true faith, I would think that the entirety of Christianity, all of Christ's promises regarding the faith to the end of time, and the whole Church of God could be preserved in a few souls, indeed in a single one; and I would judge that every single other Christian erred against the true faith—following the example of the prophet Elias, who, although he believed that he was the only true worshipper left on Earth, nevertheless never abandoned the true faith. . . .

Therefore, if anyone wishes me to retract my withdrawal from obedience to this pseudo-pope and his supporters, let him first provide an argument in support of his formal constitutions and sermons, and show how they are in accord with the Holy Scriptures; let him prove, on the basis of the sacred writings and a compelling argument, that it is impossible for a pope to fall into heretical depravity, and that anyone who knows a pope to have fallen into heresy should nevertheless continue to obey him. Let him not argue on the basis of the number of that pope's supporters, and let

him not rely on insults. . . . I have more faith in the authority of the Sacred Scriptures than in that of an idiot. I accept the teachings of the holy fathers now reigning with Christ, before the utterances of anyone still living here on Earth. . . .

If someone can show me plainly that the words of this pseudo-pope do not deviate from Catholic truth, or that one ought to obey a heretical pope whom one knows to be guilty of heresy, then I will not be slow to return to my brethren who support him. But if no one can prove either of these two points by argument or authority, then no one should regard me with hostility, nor to anyone who refuses to obey John.

I have given you the reasons for my absence from my fellow Franciscans, and I am not afraid to give an account of my actions and statements before any fair and impartial judge. I am not altogether ignorant of human wickedness. I learned more in those four years [in Avignon] about the characters of my peers, than if I had had non-stop interaction with them for forty years without the present quarrel. I understand better, now, what the Scriptures say about human nature; I see it proved every day. In times of difficulty, the truth of people's hearts and minds are revealed. But do not turn up your noses. He who now holds reign [over the Church] is mortal, but no one knows what will come after him.

May the Omnipotent Lord turn evil portents to good! Amen.

18.3 Dante Alighieri, Three Speeches from *The Divine Comedy*

Translated below are three famous speeches from *The Divine Comedy*, one each from the *Inferno*, the *Purgatorio*, and the *Paradiso*. In the first, Dante encounters Odysseus, who suffers in the eighth circle of Hell and relates how he arrived there. In the second passage, Dante's guide, the Roman poet Virgil, bids Dante goodbye after leading him through Hell and Purgatory; as a non-Christian, he can ascend no higher. The third speech consists of the hymn to the Virgin Mary that Dante here places in St. Bernard of Clairvaux's mouth, as he begs her assistance in leading Dante to the great climax of the epic: the vision of God. All of the music of Dante's language is lost in translation, of course, but here are my best efforts.

INFERNO 26.90–142

When I finally left Circe, who had held me,
   beguiled,
for more than a year near Gaeta (before it was
   styled
as such by Aeneas), neither love for my child,

nor pity for my father—then bent with age—
nor my love for Penelope—the source of
   her joy—
could overcome my longing for another stage

where I could experience the richness of life
and learn all I could of a world that was rife
with the vices and virtues of men.

That is why I set out for the open sea
with only one ship and a small company
of those by whom I never deserted would be.

From one shore to the next, I went as far as
   España,
and the land of Morocco, and the isle of Sardinia,
and all the other islands that are bathed by
   the sea.

I and my comrades had already grown
old and slow when we finally reached the place
where Hercules set up his guard of stone

to block anyone from venturing beyond.
On our right was Seville, on our left was Ceuta,
but I sailed on. 'O brothers!' I shouted,

'You have seen already many dangers,
a hundred thousand of them, so you're no
   strangers
to risk as you've come here, the far west.

You must not now deny yourselves the
   challenge
of going yet further west, and range
beyond the sun, and explore the unpeopled
   world.

Remember your lineage, the seed that gave you
   birth!
You were not made to live here on Earth
like brutes. You must pursue knowledge and
   true worth!'

I so inspired my comrades with this little speech
to continue our journey, they pushed forward
   with a screech
and it took all my strength to hold them back,
   within reach.

So turning our ship, with the stern toward morning,
we pulled on our oars; it was as though they
   were wings
and we flew, always somewhat to the left
   inclining.

In the sky at night I beheld the strange stars
of the South Pole. The familiar stars, the ones that
   were ours,
had fallen from the sky and lay below the
   horizon.

Five times did the light from the moon
   come down,
and brighten, and fail, after we had left familiar
   ground
and to that hard passage we ourselves had bound,

when suddenly a mountain, distant and dark,
rose before us, high over our barque—
the highest mountain I'd ever seen, grim and
   stark.

We were glad at first, but our joy turned to sorrow
when from that place a fierce whirlwind did blow
that hammered at our ship and crushed the prow.

Three times the whirlwind whipped us around,
and then a fourth time the cyclone wound
and flipped us, stern skyward, our prow
   pointing down.

And as though Someone desired it: the ship sank,
   and we drowned.

PURGATORIO 27.115–142

"Today your hungering will be put
to peaceful rest through the sweet fruit
that all mortals seek among life's branches."

Thus did Virgil speak, and to his solemn words
nothing ever spoken to me before
could compare, for the delight they offered.

Urge upon urge to climb ever higher
came upon me, and with every new step
I felt the strength of wings lifting me up.

When the whole staircase lay beneath us
and we stood at last on the highest step,
Virgil fixed his eyes on me, and said:

"My son, you have now seen the passing
and the eternal fires, and have reached the place
beyond which I cannot go.

I have brought you to this point through wit
    and art;
but now let joyfulness be your guide.
You have passed steeps and narrows. Now, the
    other side!

Behold the sun that shines upon your brow!
See there! Grasses and flowers and shrubs
that the Earth produces, all on its own.

You can rest here now, or stroll a while
until you behold the glad and lovely eyes
that once, full of tears, sent me to your side.

Expect no other word or signal from me.
Your will is now strong and healthy and free;
to act against it would be a mistake.

I crown and miter you, lord of yourself."

PARADISO 33.1–21

Oh Virgin Mother, daughter of your own son,
most humble and exalted of all creatures,
fixed goal of all in God's eternal plan,

it was you who so ennobled human nature
so greatly that He Who created us did not disdain,
to make Himself man, one with His creation.

Within your womb was rekindled the love
that provided the warmth needed for this flower
to come to bloom within this everlasting peace.

For all here in Paradise you are the noon-time
    torch
of charity—and down on earth, for mortal men,
you are the living spring of hope.

Lady, you are so great and so powerful,
that anyone who seeks grace without turning
    to you
is like one wishing to fly without wings.

Not only does your loving kindness race
to anyone who asks for it, but it often times
flows freely even before the asking.

In you is compassion, in you is pity,
in you generosity—in you is brought together
everything that is good in creation.

Here is a man, who from the lowest depth
of the universe up to this high place
has witnessed, one by one, the lives of souls;

he begs you to grant him through your grace
the power to lift his vision higher still,
to witness the goal of salvation.

And I, who never burned for my own vision
more than I burn for his, offer you all my
    prayers—
and I pray they are enough—

that you, through your own prayers, may
    disperse
the cloud of his mortality, that he might have
the Sum of All Joy revealed to his eyes.

I pray you also, O Queen who can achieve
whatever you wish, keep his affections sound
once he has had his vision, and returns.

May you protect him from the stirrings of
    the flesh.
Behold!—Beatrice, with all the saints,
clasp their hands in prayer, to win your assent!"

18.4   Chaucer, Prologue to *"The Pardoner's Tale"*

Geoffrey Chaucer's masterpiece is the vast but unfinished collection of *The Canterbury Tales*. Twenty-seven pilgrims set out from London to Canterbury, agreeing to help pass the time by each telling a tale. Below is the opening of the Prologue to "The Pardoner's Tale." A pardoner was a cleric who had been licensed to sell papal indulgences. In his Prologue, the corrupt Pardoner describes how he delights in making money off tricking gullible sinners. (The tale that he tells, after this prologue, is a narrative of trickery. Three travelers come across a treasure one evening; two agree to stand guard with it while the third runs to buy food and wine. After a good night's sleep, they intend to divide the treasure. The two guards decide to murder the third when he returns and keep his portion. They do so. But the third traveler had plotted against the other two and had poisoned the wine he gave them. All three subsequently perish.) The Latin line *Radix malorum est cupiditas* translates as "Greed is the root of all evil."

"My lords," he said, "in churches where I preach
I take pains to use a haughty kind of speech
And ring it out as loud and round as a bell;
I know them all by heart, the tales I tell.
My one theme is, and ever was:
Radix malorum est cupiditas.
But first I always proclaim whence I come,
And show them my bulls, each and every one.
Then the papal seal I submit for their inspection—
It's the best thing I have, for my own protection,
That no one, not even a priest or clerk,
Will stop me from doing Christ's holy work.
Then I tell my stories, as occasion calls,
Holding out my bulls from popes and cardinals,
From patriarchs and bishops; and as I do,
I speak some fancy words in Latin—just a few—
To add a hint of saffron to my preaching
And rouse their devotion with impressive teaching.
Then I bring all my long crystal bottles out,
They're crammed full of bones and bits of clout,
Relics they are, or so they are known,
Then, cased in metal, I have a shoulder-bone,
That belonged to a sheep, a holy Jew's.
    "'Good men,' I say, 'listen up! Here's some
        good news.
Take this bone and dip it in a well;
If cow or calf, if sheep or ox should swell
From eating a snake, or that a snake has stung,

Take water from that well and wash its tongue,
And it will heal immediately. Furthermore,
Whereever there is a pox or scab or other sore,
All the sheep that water at that well
Will be cured at once. Take note of what I tell.
If the good man—the owner of the stock—
Goes once a week, before the crow of the cock,
Fasting, and drinks a draught of this water too,
Why then, according to that holy Jew,
He'll find his cattle multiply extremely well.
And it's a cure for jealousy as well;
For if your husband is given to jealous wrath,
Just use this water when you make his broth,
And never again will he mistrust you, his wife,
Even if he finds out about your sinful life
With the two or three priests you bring into
        your bed.'

* * * * *

    "Believe me, my lords, many a sermon
is delivered from an evil intention.
Some aim to give pleasure by their flattery
Or gain advancement through hypocrisy,
Some out of vanity, some out of hate.
Whenever I dare not enter a debate
I'll sting my victim with words that I shape

In a sermon such that he'll never escape
My slanderous lies, if it happens that he
Has hurt my brethren or, even worse, me.
For though I never mention him by name
The congregation guesses who it is, just the same,
From certain hints that everybody knows,
And so I take revenge upon my foes
And spit my venom forth, while I profess
Holy and true—or at least plausible—holiness.
　　"But let me briefly make my purpose plain;
I preach for nothing else but gain
And use my theme (the best that ever was):
Radix malorum est cupiditas.
And thus I preach against the very vice
I make my living out of: avarice.
And despite the fact that I'm guilty of that sin
I find I have power to win
Others from it. I can bring them to repent;
But that is not my principal intent.
Covetousness for money, food, and stuff

Is why I preach. And that is enough.
　　"Then I give examples, thick and fast,
From old-time stories from the past.
Ignorant people love stories from of old,
Being the only kind their minds can hold.
What! Do you think, as long as I can preach
And get gold and silver for the things I teach,
That I will live in poverty, from choice?
You'll never hear those words from this voice!
No! Let me preach and beg throughout the lands
And never stoop to working with my hands!
Why make baskets to provide a livelihood,
When I can beg and preach?—I'm pretty good!
There's no apostle I would counterfeit;
I mean to have money, wool, cheese, and wheat
Though it were given me by the poorest lad
Or the poorest village widow, even though she had
Starving children all about her.
No! I simply need good liquor
And a jolly wench in every town!

18.5   Christine de Pizan, *The Book of the City of Ladies*

Among Christine's most popular works today is the narrative called *The Book of the City of Ladies*, which purports to describe a dream-vision she had after falling asleep over a text by a contemporary writer that criticized women for the supposed inferiority of their powers of reason, their fickleness, their concern for meaningless show. In her dream, Christine encounters three heavenly spirits—Lady Reason, Lady Rectitude, and Lady Justice—with whose help she sets to the project of building a vast, beautiful, and secure city solely for women. In her own time, Christine's book was regarded as an opportunistic imitation of Boccaccio's *Legend of Good Women.*

Here begins the Book of the City of Ladies, *whose first chapter explains why and to what purpose the Book was written.*

Here is how I pass the time and spend my life—by studying literature, and one day I was doing precisely that, sitting in my study, surrounded by numerous books on any number of subjects, my mind busy with the ideas of the various authors I had been studying for so long, when I looked up from the book I was then reading, wondering whether to take a break from ponderous thoughts and enjoy instead some cheerful poetry, and began looking around for a small volume of that sort, when my eyes settled on a book I did not know. It did not belong to me, and in fact had been given to me for safekeeping. I opened it to the title page and saw that it was written by Matheolus. I smiled at that, even though I had never seen it before, because I had heard that, like other of his books, it spoke in a complimentary and respectful way of women. I decided to indulge myself and so began to read, but no sooner had I begun than my dear mother called me to supper—it being then the time to eat—and so I put the book down, resolved to start it anew the next morning.

Taking my usual seat in the study the next morning, I did not forget that I wanted to read Matheolus' book, and so I took it up and started to read. I made little progress, however, since the contents proved to be disagreeable to anyone who does not enjoy slander. It contributed nothing to the development of virtue or proper behavior and was in fact dishonest in both its theme and approach. I read a bit here, a bit there, and took a look at the end, but then put it away and turned instead to works that were filled with superior and more ennobling contents. Matheolus' book, even though it was worthless, did nevertheless start me to thinking and wondering why so many men, both the learned and unlearned, have always been so ready to say so many evil and disrespectful things about women's character and behavior—and are still so ready to do so, not just this fellow Matheolus, a writer of no particular significance who engages in mere mockery, but real philosophers, poets, orators. All of them, it seems, whose names are too many to mention, all speak as one and come to the same conclusion—namely, that women's character always inclines to, and is full of, every possible vice.

Lost in the deepest of thought, I set to examine myself, my own behavior as a woman, as well as the countless women I see every day—princesses, noble ladies, women of the urban classes, even women of the lowest orders—who are gracious enough to share their private, intimate thoughts with me. In so doing, I hoped that I could come to a conscientious, unprejudiced judgment whether the opinions of so many noteworthy men could possibly be true. Everything I knew about the question, no matter how I looked at it or peeled away its various layers, led me to the conclusion that such opinions simply did not fit with my experience of women's natural character and behavior. I tested the critical view of women, thinking it hardly possible that so many eminent men, all of them scholars of such immense erudition and such apparent brilliance, could be so mistaken as to speak falsely. But no matter where I turned I could not find a single book on moral questions—no matter who wrote it—that did not contain somewhere in it a number of chapters or passages that spoke disrespectfully of women. This fact alone urged me to conclude that it was my own ignorance and simplicity of mind that made me fail to see the enormous defects that I and all women must possess. But I know now that I was too persuaded by the opinions of others, rather than accepting what I myself felt and knew. . . .

Here Christine describes how three noble ladies appeared to her, and how the one who stood forward of the others was the first to speak and offer her comfort in her sorrow.

Lost in these painful thoughts, with my head bowed in shame, eyes full of tears, with my chin in my hand and my elbow on the pommel of the armrest, I suddenly saw something like a ray of sunlight fall into my lap. This startled me because I was sitting in a dark corner where the sun could not reach at that hour; I jumped like one suddenly awakened from sleep. As I lifted my head, looking to see where this light was coming from, I saw three noble ladies standing in front of me, each of them wearing a crown. The brightness shining forth from their faces lit up the whole room and fell upon me. No one should doubt

how surprised I was, given that the doors to my study were securely shut. How had these ladies come here? Perhaps some spirit was casting a spell over me, I thought, and so I quickly made the sign of the Cross on my forehead.

The first lady said to me, "O dear daughter! Don't be afraid. We're here to comfort you, not to distress or frighten you. The sadness of your confusion moves us, and we want only to save you from the ignorance that blinds you. Accepting the ideas of others, you have persuaded yourself to reject what you know for certain is the truth, and to believe instead what you know for certain is false. You are like the fool in the tale, who fell asleep in a mill, and while asleep was put into women's clothing by others. When he awoke, they all laughed at him and persuaded him that he had somehow turned into a woman while sleeping. And despite his own self-knowledge he began to believe them! So tell us, dear daughter, what has happened to your common sense? Don't forget: gold does not alter or weaken when it is placed in the furnace; it becomes more pure the more it is hammered and worked. And the best ideas emerge from argument and debate. Ideas and celestial matters are the supreme concerns for humans. Judge whether the great philosophers—the very ones you are using to argue against your own sex: haven't they sometimes erred and propounded something that was wrong? Haven't they sometimes contradicted one another? Attacked one another? You have already seen this with your own eyes in Aristotle's Metaphysics, in which he argues against, and complains about, Plato and others. Think too of St. Augustine and other Fathers of the Church. Don't they sometimes criticize Aristotle, whom people call the Prince of Philosophers, the supreme master of all philosophy? You seem to think that what the great philosophers have thought are articles of faith that cannot be doubted! As for the poets you speak of, don't they speak in fables, and often mean the opposite of their literal words? You encounter them through the rhetorical figure of antiphrasis—which means, as you know, that when the text says that something is bad, it actually is good, and vice versa. My advice to you is to learn from these examples. Interpret the passages that speak ill of women as examples of antiphrasis (even if that was not the writers' intention!). It may be that the fellow called Matheolus was intended precisely this; much of what he says, after all, if we were to take it literally, is pure heresy. . . . Come to your senses! Don't bother yourself with these absurd thoughts. You know in your heart that the evil things said about all women only hurt the ones who say them."

The bulk of the Book consists of the three Ladies reminding Christine of the lives of eminent women from the past—saints, queens, writers, mothers, scholars, women who risked their lives for others or for their faith. The stories they relate form the "City" that they are building, a tradition of service, virtue, knowledge, fortitude, and generosity of which all women can be proud. At the end, having completed the construction, Christine bids farewell to Reason, Rectitude, and Justice, and now addresses her readers.

May God be praised, my most revered ladies! Our City is finished, complete! Here now is a place where all those who love virtue, glory, and praise may find lodging. It is for all women equally—past, present, and future—founded as it has been, and built by, all women of honor. It is natural for our hearts to be joyful, dear ladies, when we find that we gained the victory in our contest, and have confounded our enemies. . . . Dear ladies, let us not abuse this new possession, nor become like those arrogant people who grow proud when they become prosperous and rich. Let us live, instead, in a manner like our Queen, the Blessed Virgin, Who, after receiving the extraordinary honor of becoming the Mother of the Son of God, humbled herself by calling herself merely "the handmaid of the Lord." The more strongly the virtues are present in people, the more humble and generous those people are. And so, dear ladies, may this City occasion us to be ever more humble, virtuous, and moral.

Married ladies! Do not resent being subject to your husbands' authority, for freedom is not always good for people. The angel of the Lord said as much to Esdras. . . . Women who have gentle, kind, and modest husbands who love them, should give thanks to God for such a blessing (which is no small thing, and indeed there is hardly a greater good they could receive in this life). You should diligently serve, love, and cherish your husbands with all your heart. . . . You who have husbands somewhere between good and bad should thank God you do not have worse ones. . . . You who have husbands who are evil, cruel, violent should strive to tolerate them and give them the opportunity to overcome their evil ways and return to a sensible and good life. If a husband is so stubborn that you cannot help, you will at least acquire spiritual merit through the virtue of patience, and everyone will bless you and praise you. . . .

And you, virgin ladies! Protect your purity and live simply and quietly, avoiding the snares of evil men. Keep your gaze lowered, keep your mouths closed, and act with propriety at all times. Arm yourselves with virtue against the tricks of deceiving men, and avoid their company at all times.

Widowed ladies! Remain modest in your dress, your behavior, and your speech. Remain pious in your actions and way of life. Be prudent in your conduct, and be ever patient. Remain strong and self-protective in all your affairs, and humble in your hearts, bearing, and speech. And let all your works be in the spirit of charity.

In brief, ladies all—whether of the upper, middle, or lower orders—be aware of the world around you and protect yourselves against the challenges to your honor and chastity. Men will always accuse you of every vice. Make liars of them all, by letting your virtues shine forth; let your good deeds prove that your critics are lying. Thus you will be able to say, along with the Psalmist: "The wickedness of the evil will fall on their own heads." Chase away all lying flatterers, who use every trick and stratagem they can think of to get that which you should preserve above all— your honor and unsullied reputation. Oh ladies! Run away from their foolish declarations of love! Run, for Heaven's sake! Run! Nothing good can come of their tricks. . . . Bear always in mind, dear ladies, that men will call you weak, flighty, and fickle. And they will spare no effort and leave untried any possible trick to catch you—as though they are hunting an animal. Flee, ladies! Shun those people whose smiles mask lethal poisons. May it please you all, honored ladies, to increase and multiply our City by rejecting all vices and embracing all virtues. Rejoice and be well! And may I, your humble servant, earn your love by praying to God, Who by His grace has allowed me to live and remain in His holy service. And may He, at the end of time, be merciful toward all my sins and grant me eternal joy—and may He grant the same to you all. Amen.

19. CLOSINGS IN, CLOSINGS OUT

19.1 Francesco Guicciardini, Florence under Lorenzo de' Medici

Francesco Guicciardini (1483–1540) was a wealthy lawyer with good political connections. Like many such figures in the Renaissance, he also had cultural and intellectual ambitions. In his later years he wrote a brilliant *History of Italy* that was one of the first works of history to combine the use of extensive archival records and a critical attitude toward political motivations and intentions. His *History of Florence*, however, is the work of a young man trying to feel his way in an unfamiliar discipline. Its most incisive passage is translated below and provides a closely observed portrait of Lorenzo de' Medici (1449–1492), who ruled Florence from 1469 until his death. (Guicciardini, of course, did not know Lorenzo personally, being only nine years old when the ruler died.)

Lorenzo de' Medici was only forty-three years old when he died, after having ruled Florence for twenty-three years. He was only twenty when his father Piero died in 1469 and was still being advised by Messer Tommasso Soderini and some other elder politicians, but it took only a short time for him to come into his full strength and stature, such that he was able to govern the city just as he saw fit. . . .

Until he died in 1492 Lorenzo controlled and ran Florence as completely as if he were a Greek *tyrannos*. His renown was as widespread before his death as it has become after it. His greatness was so remarkable, and indeed without parallel in all of Florence's history, in fact, that I think it is not a mistake—and in fact may prove quite useful—if I describe his manner and character is some detail. I do not speak from my own experience, for I was still a mere boy when he died, but my information comes from reliable and trustworthy sources. Unless I have been lied to, what I am about to say is completely true.

Lorenzo had many extraordinary virtues and a fair share of vices; some of the latter came to him naturally, while some others arose from necessity. His authority in the city was so complete that it is fair to say that Florence was not free in his time, but it enjoyed as many blessings and as much happiness as there could be in any other city that we call "free" but which is in fact under a *tyrannos*. Although not everything he did was admirable, most of his actions were so tremendous and noble that the more one studies them the more impressive they appear. Glory in arms and feats of military achievement do not figure among his successes, as they do among the great figures of antiquity, but that was more the circumstance of the times in which he lived than of his own failure. You will not read here of any brave defense of the city, a celebrated capture of a fortress, a brilliant strategy on the field of battle, or a glorious upset over enemies; Lorenzo's claim to fame includes no such military splendor. What one does find in his record is every possible sign of the virtues of civic life—no one, not even his enemies and rivals, would deny his brilliance in that regard. Who could? The simple fact that he ruled Florence for twenty-three years, always increasing its power and glory, proves the point. Bear in mind that Florence is an opinionated place, full of calculating and ambitious people, and since the city is small and cannot provide for everyone, to benefit some means to skip over others. Finally, the roster of great Italian and foreign princes who counted themselves as his friend attests to his reputation. . . .

He was generally of sound judgment and wise, but his intellect transcended politics. He committed a number of ill-considered actions, such as his war against Volterra in 1473, when he conspired to get the people of that town to rebel against him so that he could have an excuse to seize their alum mines; in so doing he ignited a fire that could have engulfed all of Italy, although things turned out well in the end. And he could have avoided the civil war of 1478 if he had handled relations with the pope [Sixtus IV, r. 1471–1484] and the king [Ferrante of Naples, r. 1458–1494] more skillfully, instead of playing the role of the aggrieved innocent for all it was worth and thereby causing the war and nearly costing himself and the city their lives. His subsequent trip to Naples, also, was too rash and hurried a decision, one that placed him directly in the hands of his enemy, an untrustworthy and traitorous king. The desperate need for peace partially excuses him, but many still live who think he could have achieved it much more safely and no less effectively had he negotiated from Florence.

He dreamed of glory and renown, and indeed he desired these more than anyone else of his time. His desire for them influenced his actions even in the most minor matters—for which he may justly be criticized. Whether he was penning verses, playing a game, or doing any little thing at all, he became enraged if someone else matched or bettered him. Even in matters of real importance his lust for glory influenced him excessively. He conspired and struggled against every prince in Italy, to the great displeasure of Duke Ludovico [Sforza of Milan, r. 1489–1500]. On the whole, his ambitions were admirable and in the end they did bring him fame and renown, both within Italy and elsewhere. He worked diligently to make Florence pre-eminent in all the arts. He founded the University of Pisa as a center for the humanities. When his advisors argued that the university would never have as many students as the universities in Padua or Pavia, he replied that he would be satisfied to have more professors than they, and indeed all the most famous and brilliant scholars in Italy taught there for a time. Lorenzo spared no expense or effort to hire them, and consequently they received extraordinarily high salaries. The humanities flourished in Florence under the tutelage of Messer Agnolo Poliziano; the

study of Greek advanced under Messer Demetrios [Chalcondylas] and [Konstantinos] Lascaris; philosophy and art were the domain of Marsilio Ficino, Giorgio Benigno, Count [Giovanni] Pico della Mirandola, and other notable men. He was equally generous to the fields of vernacular poetry, music, architecture, painting, sculpture, and all other arts and disciplines. The city overflowed with superior talent, and all because Lorenzo, a universal man, was such an excellent judge of skilled men—all of whom competed with one another for his favor. In his infinite generosity, he lavished them with salaries and everything they needed for their work. For example, when he decided to establish a Greek library, he sent the learned Lascaris back to Greece to search for books of antiquity.

He employed the same liberality with princes everywhere in order to further his reputation; no expense, however great, was too much to pay if it helped him to keep the friendship of powerful people. Consequently, in places like Lyons, Milan, and Bruges, where he had business interests, his habit of spreading money everywhere made his expenses rise and his profits fall; the real fault, though, lay with some of his underlings, who did not have his talent. . . .

Lorenzo had a haughty personality. He disliked it when anyone contradicted him, and he spoke in few words, even in matters of importance, because he expected people to understand him intuitively. In casual conversation, though, he could be quite pleasant if somewhat facetious. His private home life was simple, not luxurious at all except for the banquets he threw, in which he lavished hospitality on his noble guests who visited Florence. He was lusty in his carnal appetites, and engaged in love affairs with real abandon. Some of these relationships lasted for years. So persistent was he in his conquests that many people think his extreme carnality weakened his body and brought on his early death. . . .

Many people thought him cruel and vindictive by nature, citing especially the case of the Pazzi Rebellion [of 1478], in which, after the shedding of so much blood he threw many innocents into prison and forbade the girls [of the Pazzi family] ever to marry, but one must remember how bitterly he resented the family's attempt to overthrow him, and so such harshness can hardly be surprising. Besides, he did eventually allow the Pazzi girls to marry, and freed the Pazzi boys on condition they left Florence forever. In other instances too we can see that he was not truly cruel or bloodthirsty, but simply had the flaw of excessive suspicion of others. This troublesome suspiciousness arose not from his intrinsic nature but from the fact that he had a city-state to keep under control and had to do it by means of magistrates and laws in order to maintain the appearance that Florence was a free republic. . . .

His constant distrust of others forced him not to allow powerful families to form marriage alliances. He aimed always at pairing people off in a way that did not pose any threat to his power. Sometimes he did this by forcing some young man of standing to marry a woman who was not really acceptable. In fact, the truth is that soon enough hardly any marriages took place among the important classes without his direct permission. The same suspiciousness inspired him to appoint permanent chancellors at the courts in Rome, Naples, and Milan, in order to keep an eye on the ambassadors he sent to those places. These well-paid chancellors were present to lend assistance to the various ambassadors but their real purpose was to keep Lorenzo informed of their actions.

It is true that he kept himself constantly surrounded by a large number of armed guards, who were well rewarded for their service (in fact, he even bestowed a number of hospitals and holy shrines upon some of them). He did this not out of intrinsic distrust of people, however; the truth is that the Pazzi conspiracy was to blame. Even so, it was hardly the sort of thing proper to a republic and to a private citizen; it smacked more of a tyrant ruling his subjects. In the end, one has to conclude that although Florence under Lorenzo was not a free city, it was a city that could hardly have wished for a better and more pleasing tyrant. His good qualities and virtues produced an infinity of blessings, and while the nature of his tyranny occasioned some ill-doings, these were relatively minor and never worse than they needed to be. . . .

20. THE RENAISSANCE IN MEDIEVAL CONTEXT

20.1 Petrarca, "Letter to Posterity"

This letter, which Petrarca (1304–1374) never finished, represents something of an autobiographical obituary. In it he offers a summary of his life and achievements, which, interestingly, does not include the vernacular love poetry. He wanted above all to be remembered as a scholar, a lover of classical antiquity, and a Latin poet—above all, as the author of the (paralyzingly dull) epic poem *Africa*, about the Roman general Scipio Africanus. Petrarca carries his life story as far forward as 1341; he left no notes about what he intended to include in the presumed second half of the letter.

It is possible that you may have heard of me, but I doubt it; a name as obscure and insignificant as mine cannot have travelled far in either time or space. But if you have heard of me, it may interest you to know the kind of man I was, or the results of my long labors—especially those you may have heard of them, or, at any rate, whose titles may have reached you.

To begin with myself, then, I should warn you that the things men say about me will differ considerably, since men are usually more influenced by whim than by truth whenever they are passing judgment on another; there is no limit to either praise or blame. The truth is that I was one of you, a poor mortal, of no exalted origin but neither of terribly lowly birth. I simply belonged, as Augustus Caesar once said of himself, to an ancient family. In disposition, I was not naturally perverse, nor was I wanting in modesty except as the contagion of custom may have corrupted me. My youth was gone before I realized it, and young manhood carried me away. Maturity eventually brought me to my senses and taught me, through experience, the truth I had long before read in books—namely, that youth and pleasure are vain. . . . In my prime I was blessed with an agile and active, though not particularly strong, body, and although I cannot boast of having been terribly handsome, I was good-looking enough in those days. I had a clear complexion, somewhere between light and dark, and I had lively eyes. For many years I enjoyed keen vision, but it deserted me all of a sudden around my sixtieth birthday and forced me, reluctantly, to wear glasses. I had always been perfectly healthy, but old age brought its usual array of complaints.

My parents were good people, Florentines both, and not very well off. I may as well admit it: they were in fact on the verge of poverty. They had been expelled from their native city, which is why I was born in exile at Arezzo, in 1304. . . . I have always been contemptuous of wealth; but it is not that I would not have liked to be rich—I simply hate the work and worry that seems always to accompany wealth. I never cared to give great banquets, and have led a much happier life with a plain diet and ordinary foods. . . . On the other hand, the pleasure of dining with friends is great, and nothing gives me more delight than the unexpected arrival of a friend. Nothing irks me more than ostentation, for not only is it bad in itself, being opposed to humility, but it is distracting and annoying.

In my younger years I struggled constantly with an all-consuming but pure love affair, my only one, and I would have struggled with it even longer had not my love's premature death (bitter, but in the end, salutary for me) extinguished the last flames. I wish I could say that I have been free of the lusts of the flesh, but I would be lying if I did. I can at least say this, though: even while I was occasionally swept away by the ardor of my youth and temperament, I always detested such sins from the very depths of my soul. . . .

I have taken pride in others, though never in myself, and even as insignificant as I have been, I have also thought myself even more so. In anger I have often injured myself but never another. I have always had the greatest desire for honorable friendships, and have cherished them faithfully. I can make the following boast without fear, for I know I am speaking sincerely: while I am prone to taking offense, I am quick to forget—and I never fail to remember acts of generosity. I have has the good fortune to associate with kings and princes, and to enjoy the friendship of nobles, to such a point as to excite envy. But it is the cruel fate of aging that eventually we weep for friends who have passed away. Some of the greatest kings of this age have courted and cherished my friendship. They may know why. I certainly do not. With some of them I was on such terms that they seemed, in some way, to be my guests, rather than I theirs. Their eminence in no way discomforted me; in fact, it brought me many advantages. I kept well away from many others of whom I was quite fond, for my innate longing for freedom was so strong that I carefully avoided those whose eminence seemed to threaten the liberty I loved so much.

I had more of a well-balanced mind than a keen one, one suited to many kinds of good and wholesome study but especially inclined to moral philosophy and poetry. Over time I paid less and less attention to the latter and found delight in sacred literature, discovering in it a hidden sweetness that I had earlier failed to appreciate. I came to regard works of poetry as mere amenities. I found many subjects interesting, yet focused especially on the study of antiquity, for I have always disliked our own age so much that, were it not for the love of those dearest to me, I would have preferred to live in any other period than our own. To forget the world in which we live, I have always striven to place my mind in other ages—and thus I came to love history. The conflicting opinions of people about the past has never offended me. When in doubt, I have made it a point to accept what seems to me the most probable explanation, or simply to yield to the authority of the historian I was reading. . . .

Along the breezy banks of the Rhône river I spent my boyhood, under the care of my parents, and then I spent my adolescence under the guidance of my own vanities. There were some long intervals spent abroad, though. I spent four years in the little town of Carpentras, which lies a little to the east of Avignon. In these two places I learned all that I could, considering my age, of grammar, logic, and rhetoric; or rather, I learned as much as is usually taught in school—and you, dear reader, will know how little that is. I then moved on to Montpellier for four years, to study law, and then to Bologna for three years more. . . . I was twenty-two when I finally returned home. Since habit has nearly the force of nature to it, I call Avignon—my place of exile—home. I was already beginning to make a name for myself there, and my friendship was sought by a number of prominent people. Why? I do not really know. I confess that it is now a source of surprise to me, although it seemed a natural enough thing then, when I was at the age when we are used to thinking ourselves deserving of the highest respect. I was courted first and foremost by the eminent and noble Colonna family, which then adorned the Roman Curia with their presence. . . . I spent many years in the house of Cardinal Giovanni Colonna, the brother of Giacomo, living not like a servant to Giovanni's lord but as if he were my father, or even better, my loving brother. It felt like living in my very own home. In time, though, youthful curiosity drove me to visit France and Germany. I invented a number of reasons to justify the journey to my elders, but the real impulse was simply my burning desire to see new sights. I went first to Paris, since I wanted to learn what was true in what I had heard about the city, and what was nonsense. Returning from this journey I went straightaway to Rome, which I had wanted to see ever since I was a child. There I soon came to revere Stefano Colonna, the great family's noble patriarch, an ancient hero who welcomed me in every possible way, as though I were his own son. The love and good will with which this marvelous man treated me lasted until the end of his life, and it lives on in my heart, where it will never fade until I myself cease to be.

Upon returning, I instantly felt the revulsion I have always had for city life, especially for the disgusting city of Avignon, which I truly abhorred. Seeking some means of escape, I was lucky enough to discover, about fifteen miles away, a delightful valley, narrow and secluded, called Vaucluse, where the Sorgue river (that prince of streams!) has its source. The charm of the site captivated me, and so I moved there together with all my books. If I were to tell you all that I did during my many years there, it would be a long story indeed. Almost every bit of writing I produced [in those years] was either done or begun there, or was at least conceived there; and those writings have been so numerous that even today they keep me busy and weary. My mind is like my body—more agile than strong; and while it was quite easy for me to think up new projects, I dropped many when they proved too difficult to carry out.

Inspired by the beauty of my surroundings, I undertook to write a pastoral or bucolic song: my *Bucolicum Carmen*. I also wrote *The Life of Solitude* (*De vita solitaria*), in two books, which I dedicated to the great man who is now Cardinal-Bishop Philip of Sabina, although at that time he was still the humble bishop of Cavaillon. He is the only one of my old friends who is still alive, and he has always loved me and treated me not as a bishop (as Ambrose did to Augustine) but as a brother. One Friday during Holy Week as I was hiking through those mountains I developed a powerful urge to write an epic poem, one based on Scipio Africanus the Great, who had been a favorite of mine since childhood. I began the project in a rush of enthusiasm, but because of a number of distractions I was forced to put it aside. The poem was called Africa, after its hero, and by some fate—my own or the poem's?—it did not fail to rouse the interest of many readers even before I published it. . . .

In a long passage, omitted here, he describes how he was summoned to Rome by the members of the Senate, to receive the laurel crown—the highest honor for a poet in Roman tradition.

I was very much pre-occupied with the honor I had just received, worried and fretful that I was unworthy of it, and as a result, when I was hiking through the hills again one day, I happened to cross the river Enza, in the area of Reggio Selvapiana and all of a sudden the beauty of the spot inspired me to finish writing my incomplete Africa. My enthusiasm for the project revived as from the dead and I wrote a number of lines that very day. More lines followed every day until I made it all the way to Parma, where I found a quiet, secluded house—which I later bought, and still own—and devoted myself to the poem with such energy that I completed it in no time at all, a fact that still amazes me to this day.

I was thirty-four years old. I returned to my home at the source of the Sorgue, to my beloved trans-Alpine solitude, after that long stay in Parma and Verona, where everyone I met, I am thankful to say, welcomed me with much greater honor that I deserved. Not long afterward, however, my reputation attracted the attention of Giacomo the Younger, of Carrara, an extraordinary man whose equal I doubt could be found even among the rulers of the age. He sent a constant stream of messengers and letters to me for years, no matter if I was in Italy or on the other side of the Alps, begging me to accept his friendship until at last, expecting little good to come of it, I decided to visit him and see what this persistence on the part of so eminent a man, a stranger to me, was all about. So I made my way to Parma, where I was received by him, who is now so dear to my memory, not as a mere mortal might be received but as the saints are received in Heaven—with so much joy and astonishing affection and respect that I cannot put it into words. Therefore, let me be silent. Among the many honors he gave me, he made me a canon of the cathedral of Padua (after he learned that I had been a cleric from boyhood) in order to strengthen my connection to him and his city. To put it bluntly, if he had not died so soon he would have put an end to all my wanderings. But alas, nothing mortal last forever, and everything that is sweet eventually turns bitter. Giacomo had scarcely given two years to me, to his city, and to the entire world when God, Who had given him to us, took him away. It is not out of blind love for him that I believe neither I, the city, nor the world were worthy of him. Giacomo's son and successor, a man of genuine sensibility and distinction, was likewise very friendly and respectful to me, but I could not remain with him after the death of one to whom I was so intimately connected. (We were even of the same age.) I returned to France, not because I was wanting to see again the old familiar place but because I wanted to get free of my misery, like a sick man wants, by a change of scene.

The text ends here.

APPENDIX: THE MEDIEVAL POPES

This table lists the popes in chronological order, gives the dates of their pontificates, indicates their lay names and ethnicity, and records the ecclesiastical position held by each individual prior to assuming the Holy See. The dates of pontificates are subject to much scholarly revision; I have adhered to the dates published by the Vatican's own *Anuario pontificio*.

Pope	Papacy	Birth Name	Nationality	Previous Ecclesiastical Vocation
St. Peter	d. 64	Simon	Galilean	
St. Linus	67–76		Tuscan	
St. Anacletus	76–88		Greek	
St. Clement I	88–97		Roman	presbyter
St. Evaristus	97–105		Greek	
St. Alexander I	105–115		Roman	
St. Sixtus	115–125		prob. Roman	presbyter
St. Telesphorus	125–136		Greek	
St. Hyginus	136–140		Greek	
St. Pius I	140–155		Friulian	
St. Anicetus	155–166		Syrian	
St. Soter	166–175		Latin	
St. Eleutherius	175–189		Greek	deacon
St. Victor I	189–198		North African	
St. Zephrynus	199–217		Roman	
St. Calixtus I	217–222		prob. Roman (a former slave)	archdeacon
St. Urban I	222–230		Roman	
St. Pontian	230–235 (abdicated)		Roman	

Pope	Papacy	Birth Name	Nationality	Previous Ecclesiastical Vocation
St. Anterus	235–236		Greek	
St. Fabian	236–250		Roman	
St. Cornelius	251–253		Roman	presbyter
St. Lucius I	253–254		Roman	
St. Stephen I	254–257		Roman	
St. Sixtus II	257–258		Greek	presbyter
St. Dionysius	260–268		Roman	presbyter
St. Felix I	269–274		Roman	
St. Eutychian	275–283		prob. Greek	
St. Gaius	283–296		poss. Greek	
St. Marcellinus	296–304 (poss. deposed)			
St. Marcellus I	308–309		Roman	presbyter
St. Eusebius	309–310		Greek	
St. Melchiades	311–314		North African	
St. Sylvester I	314–335			
St. Mark	336		Roman	
St. Julius I	337–352		Roman	
Liberius[a]	352–366			
St. Damasus	366–384		Roman	deacon
St. Siricius[b]	384–399			
St. Anastasius	399–401		Roman	
St. Innocent I	401–417		Roman	
St. Zosimus	417–418		Greek	presbyter
St. Boniface I	418–422		Roman	presbyter
St. Celestine I	422–432		Roman	archdeacon
St. Sixtus III	432–440			
St. Leo I the Great	440–461		Roman	deacon
St. Hilarius	461–468		Roman	archdeacon
St. Simplicius	468–483			
St. Felix III (II)	483–492		Roman	
St. Gelasian	492–496		North African	archdeacon
Anastasius II	496–498		Roman	
St. Symmachus	498–514		Sardinian	deacon
St. Hormisdas	514–523		Roman	
St. John I	523–526		Tuscan	
St. Felix IV (III)	526–530		Roman	presbyter

(Continued)

Pope	Papacy	Birth Name	Nationality	Previous Ecclesiastical Vocation
Boniface II	530–532		German (Ostrogoth)	archdeacon
John II[c]	533–535	Mercurius	Roman	presbyter
St. Agapitus I	535–536			deacon
St. Silverius	536–537 (abdicated)		Roman	subdeacon
Vigilius	537–555		Roman	deacon
Pelagius I	556–561		Roman	deacon
John III	561–574	Catilinus	Roman	deacon
Benedict I	575–579		Roman	deacon
Pelagius II	579–590		German (Ostrogoth)	deacon
St. Gregory I the Great[d]	590–604		Roman	monk (O.S.B.)
Sabinian	604–606		Roman	deacon
Boniface III	607		Roman	deacon
St. Boniface IV	608–615		Roman	monk (O.S.B.)
St. Adeodatus I	615–618			priest
Boniface V	619–625		Neapolitan	priest
Honorius I	625–638			
Severinus	640		Roman	
John IV	640–642		Croatian	archdeacon
Theodore I	642–649		Greek	
St. Martin I	649–655		Roman	monk (Basilian)
St. Eugenius I	654–657		Roman	priest
St. Vitalian	657–672		Tuscan	
Adeodatus II	672–676			monk (O.S.B.)
Donus	676–678		Roman	
St. Agatho	678–681		Sicilian	monk (O.S.B.)
St. Leo II	682–683		Sicilian	
St. Benedict II	684–685		Roman	priest
John V	685–686		Syrian	archdeacon
Conon	686–687		Sicilian	priest
St. Sergius I	687–701		Syrian-Sicilian	priest
John VI	701–705		Greek	
John VII	705–707		Greek	
Sisinnius	708		Syrian	
Constantine	708–715		Syrian	
St. Gregory II	715–731		Roman	deacon
St. Gregory III	731–741		Syrian	

Pope	Papacy	Birth Name	Nationality	Previous Ecclesiastical Vocation	
St. Zacharias	741–752		Greek	deacon	
Stephen II (III)ᵉ	752–757		Roman	priest	
St. Paul I	757–767		Roman	priest	
Stephen III (IV)	768–772		Sicilian	priest	
Hadrian I	772–795		Roman	deacon	
St. Leo III	795–816		Roman	priest	
Stephen IV (V)	816–817		Roman	deacon	
St. Paschal	817–824		Roman	monk/abbot (O.S.B.)	
Eugenius II	824–827		Roman	archpriest	
Valentine	827		Roman	archdeacon	
Gregory IV	827–844		Roman	priest	
Sergius II	844–847		Roman	priest	
St. Leo IV	847–855		Roman	priest	
Benedict III	855–858		Roman	priest	
St. Nicholas I	858–867		Roman	deacon	
Hadrian II	867–872		Roman	priest	
John VIII	872–882		Roman	archdeacon	
Marinus Iᶠ	882–884		Roman	priest/bishop of Caere	
St. Hadrian III	884–885		Roman		
Stephen V (VI)	885–891		Roman	priest	
Formosus	891–896		Roman	priest/bishop of Porto	
Boniface VI	896		Roman	priest	
Stephen VI (VII)	896–897		Roman	priest/bishop of Anagni	
Romanus (deposed)	897		Roman		
Theodore II	897		Roman		
John IX	898–900		Roman	monk/abbot (O.S.B)	
Benedict IV	900–903		Roman	priest	
Leo V	903		Roman	priest	
Sergius III	904–911		Roman	priest/bishop of Caere	Period of papal history often referred to as the "Pornocracy"
Anastasius III	911–913		Roman		
Lando	913–914		Roman		
John X	914–928			priest/archbishop of Ravenna	
Leo VI	928		Roman	priest	
Stephen VII (VIII)	928–931		Roman		

(Continued)

Pope	Papacy	Birth Name	Nationality	Previous Ecclesiastical Vocation
John XI	931–935		Roman	
Leo VII	936–939		Roman	monk (O.S.B)
Stephen VIII (IX)	939–942		Roman	priest
Marinus II	942–946		Roman	
Agapitus II	946–955		Roman	
John XII[g]	955–964	Octavianus	Roman	layman
Leo VIII	963–965		Roman	layman
Benedict V	964		Roman	deacon
John XIII	965–972		Umbrian	bishop of Narni
Benedict VI	973–974		Roman	deacon
Benedict VII	974–983		Roman	bishop of Sutri
John XIV	983–984	Pietro Campanova	Lombard	bishop of Pavia
John XV	985–996		Roman	priest
Gregory V	996–999	Bruno of Carinthia	German	priest
Sylvester II	999–1003	Gerbert d'Aurillac	French	priest/archbishop of Ravenna
John XVII	1003	Giovanni Siccone	Roman	layman
John XVIII	1004–1009	Giovanni Fasano	Roman	priest
Sergius IV	1009–1012	Pietro Boccapecora	Roman	priest/bishop of Albano
Benedict VIII	1012–1024	Theophylact	Roman	layman
John XIX	1024–1032	Romanus	Roman	layman
Benedict IX[h]	1032–1048	Theophylact	Roman	layman
Sylvester III	1045	Giovanni Crescenzi	Roman	priest/bishop of Sabina
Gregory VI	1045–1046	Giovanni Graziano	Roman	archpriest
Clement II	1046–1047	Suitger von Morsleben	German	bishop of Bamberg
Damasus II	1048	Poppo	Austrian	bishop of Brixen
St. Leo IX	1049–1054	Bruno von Egisheim	Alsatian	bishop of Toul
Victor II	1055–1057	Gebhart	Swabian	bishop of Eichstätt
Stephen IX (X)	1057–1058	Frédéric de Lorraine	French	abbot of Monte Cassino (O.S.B.)
Nicholas II	1059–1061	Gérard de Bourgogne	French	bishop of Florence
Alexander II	1061–1073	Anselmo da Baggio	Milanese	bishop of Lucca
St. Gregory VII	1073–1085	Hildebrand di Soana	Tuscan	monk (O.S.B.)
Bl. Victor III	1086–1087	Dauferio [Desiderius]	Beneventan	abbot of Monte Cassino (O.S.B.)
Bl. Urban II	1088–1099	Eude de Châtillon	French	monk/card.-bishop of Ostia (O.S.B.)
Paschal II	1099–1118	Raniero	Roman	monk/abbot of S. Paolo (O.S.B.)
Gelasius II	1118–1119	Giovanni Coniulo	Amalfitan	monk/card.-archdeacon (O.S.B.)

Pope	Papacy	Birth Name	Nationality	Previous Ecclesiastical Vocation
Calixtus III	1119–1124	Guy de Bourgogne	Burgundian	archbishop of Vienne
Honorius II	1124–1130	Lamberto Scannabecchi	Roman	archdeacon/card.-bishop of Ostia
Innocent II	1130–1143	Gregorio Papareschi	Roman	card.-deacon
Celestine II	1143–1144	Guido del Castello	Tuscan	card.-priest
Lucius II	1144–1145	Gerardo Caccianemici	Bolognese	card.-priest
Bl. Eugenius III	1145–1153	Bernardo Pignatelli	Pisan	abbot (O.S.B. Cist.)
Anastasius IV	1153–1154	Corrado della Suburra	Roman	card.-bishop of S. Sabina
Hadrian IV	1154–1159	Nicholas Breakspear	English	abbot/card.-bishop of Albano (O.S.A.)
Alexander III	1159–1181	Orlando Bandinelli	Sienese	card.-priest
Lucius III	1181–1185	Umbaldo Allucingoli	Tuscan	monk/card.-bishop of Ostia (O.S.B. Cist.)
Urban III	1185–1187	Umberto Crivelli	Milanese	archbishop of Milan
Gregory VIII	1187	Alberto de Morra	Beneventan	monk/card.-deacon (O.S.B.)
Clement III	1187–1191	Paolo Scolari	Roman	priest/card.-bishop of Palestrina
Celestine III	1191–1198	Giacinto Bobone	Roman	card.-deacon
Innocent III	1198–1216	Lothario dei Segni	Roman	card.-deacon
Honorius III	1216–1227	Cencio Savelli	Roman	card.-priest
Gregory IX	1227–1241	Ugolino dei Segni	Roman	priest/card.-bishop of Ostia
Celestine IV	1241	Goffredo Castiglione	Milanese	monk/card.-bishop of Sabina (O.S.B. Cist.)
Innocent IV	1243–1254	Sinibaldo Fieschi	Genoese	priest/bishop of Alenga
Alexander IV	1254–1261	Rinaldo dei Conti	Roman	card.-bishop of Ostia
Urban IV	1261–1264	Jacques Pantaléon	French	patriarch of Jerusalem
Clement IV	1265–1268	Gui Faucoi	French	archbishop of Narbonne
Bl. Gregory X[i]	1271–1276	Teobaldo Visconti	Milanese	card.-archdeacon
Bl. Innocent V	1276	Pierre Tarantaise	French	archbishop of Lyons (O.P.)
Hadrian V	1276	Ottobuono Fieschi	Genoese	card.-deacon
John XXI	1276–1277	Pedro Julião	Portuguese	archbishop of Braga
Nicholas III	1277–1280	Giovanni Orsini	Roman	card.-deacon
Martin IV	1281–1285	Simon de Brie	French	card.-priest
Honorius IV	1285–1287	Giacomo Savelli	Roman	card.-deacon
Nicholas IV	1288–1292	Girolamo Maschi	Abruzzese	bishop of Palestrina (O.F.M.)
St. Celestine V[j]	1294	Pietro Murrone	Neapolitan	monk (O.S.B.)
Boniface VIII	1295–1303	Benedetto Gaetani	Tusculan	card.-priest
Bl. Benedict XI[k]	1303–1304	Niccolò Boccasini	Venetano	card.-bishop (O.P.)

(Continued)

Pope	Papacy	Birth Name	Nationality	Previous Ecclesiastical Vocation
Clement V[i]	1305–1314	Bertrand de Got	Gascon	archbishop of Bordeaux the "Avignon Popes"
John XXII[l]	1316–1334	Jacques Duèse de Cahors	French	card.-bishop of Porto
Benedict XII	1335–1342	Jacques Fournierc	French	bishop of Palmiers (O.Cist.)
Clement VI	1342–1352	Pierre Roger	French	archbishop of Rouen (O.S.B.)
Innocent VI	1352–1362	Etienne Aubert	French	card.-bishop of Ostia
Bl. Urban V	1362–1370	Guillaume Grimoard	French	abbot (O.S.B)
Gregory XI	1370–1378	Pierre Roger de Beaufort	French	card.-deacon
Urban VI	1378–1389	Bartolomeo Prignano	Apulian	archbishop of Bari
Boniface IX	1389–1404	Pietro Tomacelli	Neapolitan	card.-priest
Innocent VII	1404–1406	Cosimo dei Migliorati	Abruzzese	archbishop of Ravenna
Gregory XII	1406–1415	Angelo Correro	Venetian	bishop of Castello
Martin V[m]	1417–1431	Odo Colonna	Roman	card.-deacon
Eugenius IV	1431–1447	Gabriele Condulmaro	Venetian	bishop of Siena (O.S.A)
Nicholas V	1447–1455	Tommaso Parentucelli	Bolognese	bishop of Bologna

[a] Liberius is the first pope not to be canonized.

[b] Siricius is the first pope to use the title *papa* ("pope").

[c] John II (533–535) was the first pope to take a new name upon election to the Holy See. He did so presumably because of the pagan connotations of his birth name. The taking of a new pontifical name did not become the norm until the turn of the first millennium CE. Prior to the year 1000, only four popes (John II, John III, John XII, and John XIV) did so.

[d] Gregory I (590–604) was the first monk to become pope. Innocent V (1276) was the first Dominican pope, and Nicholas IV (1288–1292) was the first Franciscan.

[e] On March 23, 752 a man named Stephen was elected pope, which would have made him Stephen II. But he died only three days later and is sometimes omitted from papal lists. On March 26, 752 another Stephen was elected; he is usually considered Stephen II (as here)— but in some lists he is referred to as Stephen III.

[f] Marinus I (882–884) was the first bishop to become pope. Canon XV of the Council of Nicaea (325) forbade the translation of bishops from one see to another, and since the office of the papacy was inextricably linked with the episcopacy of Rome, no bishop of another city could be considered a candidate. A handful of exceptions were made in the difficult post-Carolingian period (of which Marinus was the first), but the Nicaean ban was gradually set aside during the Gregorian Reform, paving the way for the virtual monopoly on the papacy held by bishops since the eleventh century.

[g] John XII (955–964) was the first layman elected to the papacy.

[h] Benedict IX was pope three separate times: 1032–1044, April–May 1045, and 1047–1048.

[i] The papacy was vacant from November 29, 1268 (Clement IV's death) to September 1, 1271 (Gregory X's election).

[j] The papacy was vacant from April 4, 1292 to July 5, 1294.

[k] Prior to his pontificate, Benedict XI was the Minister-General of his Dominican order.

[l] The papacy was vacant from April 20, 1314 to August 7, 1316.

[m] The papacy was vacant from July 4, 1415 to November 11, 1417.